S0-AZM-270

PATHS OF EMANCIPATION

PATHS OF EMANCIPATION

JEWS, STATES, AND CITIZENSHIP

Edited by

Pierre Birnbaum and Ira Katznelson

PRINCETON UNIVERSITY PRESS

PRINCETON, NEW JERSEY

PUBLISHED BY PRINCETON UNIVERSITY PRESS, 41 WILLIAM STREET,
PRINCETON, NEW JERSEY 08540
IN THE UNITED KINGDOM: PRINCETON UNIVERSITY PRESS,
CHICHESTER, WEST SUSSEX

LIBRARY OF CONGRESS CATALOGING-IN-PUBLICATION DATA

PATHS OF EMANCIPATION : JEWS, STATES, AND CITIZENSHIP / EDITED BY
PIERRE BIRNBAUM AND IRA KATZNELSON.
P. CM.
INCLUDES BIBLIOGRAPHICAL REFERENCES AND INDEX.
ISBN 0-691-03460-5 (CLOTH). — ISBN 0-691-03461-3 (PBK.)
1. JEWS—EMANCIPATION. 2. JEWS—LEGAL STATUS, LAWS, ETC. 3. JEWS—IDENTITY. 4. JUDAISM AND STATE. I. BIRNBAUM, PIERRE. II. KATZNELSON, IRA.

DS147.P38 1995 323.1′192404′09034—DC20 94-37635 CIP

THIS BOOK HAS BEEN COMPOSED IN SABON

PRINCETON UNIVERSITY PRESS BOOKS ARE PRINTED
ON ACID-FREE PAPER AND MEET THE GUIDELINES FOR
PERMANENCE AND DURABILITY OF THE COMMITTEE ON
PRODUCTION GUIDELINES FOR BOOK LONGEVITY
OF THE COUNCIL ON LIBRARY RESOURCES
PRINTED IN THE UNITED STATES OF AMERICA

1 3 5 7 9 10 8 6 4 2

1 3 5 7 9 10 8 6 4 2
(PBK.)

For our children

CONTENTS

PREFACE

IN 1987, Pierre Birnbaum and Ira Katznelson co-taught a course, "The Modernization of the Jews," at the Graduate Faculty of the New School for Social Research. At the time, Birnbaum was deeply involved in research on French Jewry and Katznelson sought to extend his interest in institutions and political identities to Jewish subjects. They sought to systematically and comparatively explore the political and economic insertion of Western European and North American Jews into the institutional realms of nineteenth-century states by bringing together relevant considerations drawn from general literatures in the social sciences and history with work by students of the Jewish experience. The course looked mainly at France, England, Germany, and the United States, while treating the Russian case as a comparative foil; that is, as a critical instance where Jews did not secure political or economic emancipation. It focused on a distinction between state emancipation and societal emancipation of the Jews and explored the implications of these paths of emancipation for the constitution of Jews as political actors.

What quickly became apparent in the construction of the curriculum and in week-to-week teaching was that this kind of analytical and comparative effort was not a feature of the most important extant work. There was a considerable divide between relevant studies on such themes as state building, identity, and collective action, on the one side, and Jewish studies on the other. Further, within the ambit of investigations of the Jewish experience in the West, the relevant literatures treated the incorporation of Jews into western modernity either as a unitary experience in spite of considerable differences distinguishing specific settings, or as *sui generis* in single-country studies.

This book was first imagined as a response, and its structure and content is marked by the ambitions and goals Birnbaum and Katznelson identified when they taught their seminar. They proceeded by circulating a discussion paper to a small group of specialists in Jewish history, including colleagues whose work appears below. This document provided the basis both for a successful application to the Council for European Studies to provide funds for the creation of a Research Planning Group and for the drafting of preliminary papers that the authors discussed face-to-face at a meeting at the European University Institute in Fiesole, Italy, in May 1989. That session refined and focused the group's common questions and provided an opportunity for tough-minded collegial criticism. The authors met for a second time in Paris in March 1990 with draft essays in hand. This session was also supported by the University of Paris I and by the Fondation Nationale des Sciences Politiques. The papers in this book were revised thoroughly after this second round of discussion and critique.

As in most scholarly ventures, we owe a great deal to others. Ioannis Sinanoglou of the Council for European Studies facilitated our birth as a diverse group of scholars willing to proceed with a common enterprise. Steven Lukes at the European University Institute took a lively interest in our endeavor and facilitated the remarkable hospitality we experienced there. Michael Silber and Robert Wistrich participated actively in our discussions but were unable to complete papers for this book. The result is a volume close to the design of the Birnbaum-Katznelson seminar; one that concentrates primarily on Western Europe and North America, now accompanied by two non-Western cases. We also are indebted to two anonymous readers for Princeton University Press, who pointed the way toward alterations in the text, to our copyeditor, Eric D. Schramm, and to Lauren Osborne, our editor at Princeton University, who has been enthusiastic about this project from the moment it first was broached to her.

PATHS OF EMANCIPATION

ONE

EMANCIPATION AND THE LIBERAL OFFER

Pierre Birnbaum and Ira Katznelson

BEST KNOWN for *Berlin Alexanderplatz,* the mordant novel filmed on an epic scale by Fassbinder, Alfred Doblin was a writer, physician, psychiatrist, and socialist, and a quite thoroughly assimilated Jew.[1] In 1924, he published *Reise in Poland.* This travel memoir includes evocative and, in retrospect, remarkably poignant descriptions of Jewish life in Warsaw, Vilna, Lublin, Cracow, Lemberg, and Lodz. Doblin's personal history, his skills as an interested observer, and the timing of his trip make his text a revealing companion for more analytical attempts to apprehend Jewish emancipation in the West, treated not as a unity or a singular experience but as a complex variegated family of instances.

Doblin wrote at the end of what might be called the long century of emancipation, the period assayed in this book. The epoch opened with the creation of a new American Republic with a constitution that proscribed religious tests for office and with the annulment by the French National Assembly in September 1791 of all legal barriers to citizenship "affecting individuals of the Jewish persuasion." These radical departures effectively opened up the prospect that Jews in these countries and elsewhere could secure civic integration without the quid pro quo of religious conversion or the provision of specific utilitarian services to the state and its rulers, as had been the case for the several hundred Court Jews who had served various monarchs in the development of their fiscal instruments. A third revolution, that of the Bolsheviks, concluded the protracted era of emancipation by eliminating any formal distinction between Jews and other Soviet citizens.[2]

[1] Doblin's works were banned by the Nazis in 1933. He emigrated in 1940, first to France, then to the United States.

[2] While Russia's Jews almost universally had welcomed the February Revolution, far fewer favored the Bolshevik one; but they flocked to it once the White Guards and Ukrainian nationalists promoted a bout of fresh pogroms. An extended discussion about the relationship between revolutionary Marxism, including Bolshevism, and the Jews can be found in Jacob L. Talmon, *Myth of the Nation and Vision of Revolution: Ideological Polarization in the Twentieth Century* (Berkeley: University of California Press, 1981).

At the time of his journey, Doblin had lived for three decades in Berlin, a span that began only some twenty years after German Jews had achieved full legal and political emancipation. By the early 1920s, a great gap had opened with which he tried to come to terms: in the West there were many Jews whose traditional life and learning were fading, while in the East there were what appeared to be—misleadingly, from the vantage point of Berlin—fossilized Jewish communities, in which the vast majority of the world's Jews still resided, most only newly emancipated. Yet, even then, Jews as acculturated as Doblin were forced to deal with the incapacity of Jews or Gentiles to make issues of Jewish difference evanesce into a world of liberal individualism and rights.

"Emancipation" is a congested term. It is a shorthand for access by Jews to the profound shifts in ideas and conditions wrought by the Enlightenment and its liberal offspring: religious toleration, secularization, scientific thought, and the apotheosization of reason, individualism, the law of contract, and choice. It entailed a shift in legal position, both for the collectivity and its individual members. Much as for slaves unshackled from bondage, colonized subjects freed from imperial domination, or serfs liberated from neo-feudalism, emancipation conduced a double transformation: in standing, as Jews moved from the position of presociological and prepolitical persons to become sociological and political actors, and in the creation of new options, based on rights, for them.[3] Admission to citizenship, the central hallmark of legal emancipation, also implied access to state power and the control of capital, and it raised fresh questions about the status of community, culture, and minority rights. Although the precise provenance of the term "emancipation" is open to some question (its first usage has been located in the 1828 political writings of W. T. Krug in Württemberg by Jacob Katz and Reinhard Kosseleck, but others have found earlier applications of the term in the

[3] Leo Spitzer provides an attempt to compare the emancipation of blacks and Jews in the nineteenth century in *Lives in Between: Assimilation and Marginality in Austria, Brazil, and West Africa, 1780–1945* (Cambridge: Cambridge University Press, 1989). Our book and his represent different, if complementary, responses to the historiographical tendency to treat Jewish emancipation on its own terms as a unitary experience. Spitzer reminds us in a salutary way that the ending of legal-political disabilities for Jews was not unique; in so doing, however, he depicts Jewish emancipation in rather broad strokes. Our strategy, instead, is to treat Jewish emancipation comparatively, by focusing primarily on differences between countries in spite of similarities, rather than on similarities in spite of differences. Important parallels between colonialism and postcolonialism and paths to and from Jewish emancipation can be drawn from rich works by Benedict R. O'G. Anderson on Indonesia, *Language and Power: Exploring Political Cultures in Indonesia* (Ithaca: Cornell University Press, 1990), and Kwame Anthony Appiah on sub-Saharan Africa, *In My Father's House: Africa in the Philosophy of Culture* (New York: Oxford University Press, 1992).

dozen preceding years),[4] the language used from the start to discuss the process of Jewish incorporation spoke of civic status, naturalization, national equality, and the granting of equal political rights.[5]

At its core, Jewish emancipation was concerned with three sets of issues about citizenship and rights: (1) whether broadly liberal and republican doctrines and institutional arrangements grounded in Enlightenment values would come to govern transactions between the state and civil society to provide fresh potential bases for Jewish citizenship; (2) whether such innovative formulas for political participation, once in place, would prove sufficiently encompassing to include the Jews; and (3) whether the terms of admission to the polity these arrangements countenanced would permit a far-reaching or narrowly gauged pluralism for Jews seeking both to take up the offer of citizenship and remain meaningfully Jewish.

Each of these issues was pressed forward with a high degree of urgency once Jewish opportunities for social and spatial mobility and for novel definitions of identity multiplied after the American and French Revolutions, and, later, after other initiatives made it possible for increasing numbers of Jews like Doblin to participate in the discrete spheres of modernity without undergoing the entry ritual of baptism. The inventory of possibilities possessed by organized Jewish communities and by individual Jews for forging relationships with the main institutions and cultures of the Christian West altered decisively, if unevenly. Whether by virtue of movement across the Atlantic, or as a result of the removal of extant barriers to equal participation in the state, the economy, and civil society, or by virtue of the collapse of rights-less regimes, or the triumph of new, less enclosed forms of nationalism, Jews now were thrust into radically altered possibilities and predicaments.

Doblin himself was the son of Jews from Posen who had moved West, and, in so doing, had detached themselves from the tight embrace of religious-communal authority. In Berlin, the family attended synagogue only on Rosh Hashanah and Yom Kippur, where they prayed in German and Hebrew. Doblin's parents spoke Yiddish, Polish, and German, and they could read Hebrew; of these languages, he knew only German. He thought of himself neither as a member of the Jewish masses he observed

[4] Jacob Katz, "The Term 'Jewish Emancipation,' Its Origin and Historical Impact," in A. Altman, ed., *Studies in Nineteenth-Century Jewish Intellectual History* (Cambridge: Harvard University Press, 1964), 1–25; O. Brunner, W. Conze, and R. Kosselleck, *Geschichtliche Grundbegriffe: Historiches Lexicon zur politischsozialen Sprache in Deutschland,* (Stuttgart: Ernst Klett Verlag, 1975), 2:97–115.

[5] For a discussion, see Artur Eisenbach, *The Emancipation of the Jews in Poland, 1780–1870* (Oxford: Basil Blackwell, 1991), 8–9.

on his trip nor as an enlightened Jew, but as "a west European passerby." Later, after moving to the United States, he converted to Catholicism,[6] taking advantage of two options, one ancient and one recent, available to Jews who wished to get away.

Among its virtues, Doblin's travel account reminds us that the great mass of world Jewry remained unemancipated long after the French Revolution. Even in countries like the Netherlands, where emancipation came in 1796 on the heels of the creation of a unitary state the previous year, the new liberality initially had an impact exclusively for the narrow stratum of Jews situated to take advantage of the access now on offer. Thus, while Jews in Vienna were able to achieve a remarkable overrepresentation in educated classes and professions, even including parts of the military, the vast majority of Austrian Jews lived in penurious and unintegrated conditions in Bukovina and Galicia.[7] Only on the eve of their mid-twentieth century catastrophe did European Jews virtually everywhere, including Russia, lose their legal and political disabilities to become citizens of modern national states.

Doblin's Polish report shines a very bright light on the soon-to-be-extinguished plurality of Jewish life-forms at the conclusion of the era of emancipation. He recorded his impressions without knowledge of the unimaginable horrors just around the corner. Unmarked by the teleological issues and pressures that the reference point of Nazi genocide presses on us today, the quaint innocence of Doblin's travelogue enhances its value as a historical marker. He wrote when it was still possible for some Jews to believe, as Hannah Arendt once put it, that they were "people in general" who happened to be Jews,[8] and when it was still possible to celebrate this as a positive liberating value, at a time when choices for

[6] George Mosse comments: Doblin's "relationship to the Jews was idealistic, based upon the same idealism as his earlier socialist commitment. It proved no more lasting when confronted with the reality of political struggles among the Jews. His final conversion to Christianity took place within this context. Christ becomes the exemplification of justice and freedom, fighting to prevail in an evil world without recourse to force. The problem of revolution, force, and power, which was to occupy so many of his fellow intellectuals, had been solved. Moreover, Doblin's Christianity also gave him roots, a resting place in his wanderings. For he joined the Catholic Church, which provided him with a 'halt' and a 'harmonious coordinated system.' At the same time he castigated Jews who, after all their suffering, still clung to business-as-usual, while he seemed to have recaptured his old idealism within a more settled and traditional form." George Mosse, *Masses and Man: Nationalist and Fascist Perceptions of Reality* (New York: Howard Fertig, 1980), 150.

[7] Istvan Deak, "Pacesetters of Modernity: Jewish Officers in the Hapsburg Monarchy," *East European Politics and Societies* 3 (Winter 1989); Peter Pulzer, *The Rise of Political Anti-Semitism in Germany and Austria,* rev. ed. (Cambridge: Harvard University Press, 1988), 3–16.

[8] Cited in Moishe Postone, "Review," *New German Critique* 20 (Spring/Summer 1980): 189.

Jews about what it meant to be Jewish under conditions of emancipation seemed more consequential than they soon proved to be.

Well before the early 1920s the rumblings had begun. Certainly, the universalism of the American and French Revolutions and the liberating sense provided by the apparent fusion of aspirations for the general liberation of humankind in 1848, which promised to carry Jews to a bright new day, had given way by the late nineteenth and early twentieth centuries to a sober and anxious recognition of the practical limits to Enlightenment humanism at a time of demotic nationalism and global war. Emblems of disappointment dotted virtually all of Europe's landscape. In the East, the reaction to anti-Jewish riots, even to the Kishinev pogrom of 1903 or the Odessa pogrom of 1905, was muted, not just by forces of romanticism and reaction but among many socialists and liberals who feared too close an identification with Jewish causes.[9] The quickening pace of industrialization and urbanization in Poland and Russia produced a growing confrontation between Jews in the towns positioned as middlemen between the dominant and the peasant classes and Slavic newcomers who found Jews in niches they wished to occupy. In the West, Houston Stewart Chamberlain's immensely influential two-volume study, *The Foundations of the Nineteenth Century,* declared the emergence of the Jews from Europe's ghettos to be the century's defining characteristic, bringing with it dangers of contamination and contagion. In France, the Dreyfus affair was enfolded in a robust and popular anti-Semitism that sought to expunge the alien Jewish element from the state. In Austria, where anti-Semitism defined a pivotal axis of politics in the capital, the granting of full male suffrage in 1905 led to a larger parliamentary delegation for the anti-Semitic Christian Social Party and the Czech Social Party than for the Social Democrats—the "natural" party of the newly enfranchised working class. In Doblin's Germany, which was one of the latecomers to political emancipation, high Jewish visibility in the press, banking, the professions, literature, the arts, scholarship, and radical politics engendered popular petitions to reverse legal emancipation; furthermore, this visibility led to exclusions from the judiciary, the officer corps, and the higher civil service and to a growing partition of civil society into Gentile and Jewish clubs and associations by means of the widespread device of Aryan clauses. During the Great War, German nationalism was

[9] Yosef Hayim Yerushalmi suggests that a similar motivation, that of seeking to protect psychoanalysis from the charge that it was merely a Jewish science, accounts for the importance of Freud's partnership with Jung. For a consideration of the role Freud's Jewishness played in his life and work, including his "sense of otherness vis-à-vis other Jews which cannot be explained merely as a reaction to anti-Semitism," see Yosef Hayim Yerushalmi, *Freud's Moses: Judaism Terminable and Interminable* (New Haven: Yale University Press, 1991).

suffused with Christian symbolism, revealing "a deep gulf between Germans and Jews" who were reminded of their status as uncomfortable outsiders in a Germany of "the Volk community, the camaraderie . . . wrapped in a Christian analogy."[10] It was not only to an anti-Semite like Count Heinrich Coudenhove-Kalergi that emancipation seemed a fiasco.[11]

Just at this moment spanning the turn of the century, when Europe's Jews were suspended precariously between modernism and romanticism, universalism and nationalism, city and country, and assimilation and segregation, their condition engaged the literary imagination of Jews such as Franz Kafka, Joseph Roth, and Arthur Schnitzler who inhabited these borderlands.[12] Read in this context, Doblin's account of his journey to Poland appears as credulously unaware. Nonetheless, it was the juxtaposition of his own experience of German emancipation and post–World War I insecurities that motivated his trip. When he published his travelogue, he had left implicit the reasons he chose to go where and when he did. A quarter century later, after the Second World War, he explained:

> In the first half of the nineteen-twenties, pogromlike events took place in Berlin, in the eastern part of the city, on and around Gollnowstrasse. They occurred against the lansquenet backdrop of those years; Nazism let out its first shriek. At that time, representatives of Berlin Zionism invited a number of men of Jewish origin to meetings to talk about those events, their background, and also the aims of Zionism. In connection with these discussions, a man came to my apartment and tried to talk me into going to Palestine, which I had no intention of doing. His influence had a different effect on me. I did not agree to visit Palestine, but I had to get my bearing about the Jews. I realized I didn't know any Jews. I had friends who called themselves Jews, but I could not call them Jews. They were not Jewish by faith or by lan-

[10] Mosse, *Masses and Man,* 272. A superb overview of transformations to the character of anti-Semitism and the circumstances of Jews between 1879 and 1914 can be found in Pulzer, *Rise of Political Anti-Semitism;* also see Shmuel Almog, *Nationalism and Antisemitism in Modern Europe, 1815–1945* (Oxford: Pergamon Press, 1990).

[11] Count Heinrich Coudenhove-Kalergi, *Anti-Semitism through the Ages* (London: Hutchinson and Company, 1935).

[12] Perhaps more than any other leading figure of this kind at the time, Joseph Roth directly confronted the perilous interstitial situation of post-emancipation Jews, both in his fiction and journalism. Celebrating the values of ethnic diversity, his novels, such as his first, *The Spider's Web* (1923), and his published nonfiction collections, most notably *Juden auf Wanderschaft* (*Wandering Jews,* 1927), engaged pogroms and Jewish vulnerability, as well as the none-too-promising options available to them. What gave Roth a particularly penetrating vantage point was his own experience as a displaced person from Galicia who had secured the cultivation of an assimilated westernized Jew. Unlike Doblin, he knew both worlds firsthand. Like Doblin, he was later attracted to Catholicism. A useful discussion of Kafka's Jewishness is provided by Frederick R. Karl, *Franz Kafka, Representative Man* (New York: Ticknor and Fields), 1991.

guage; they were possibly remnants of an extinct nation that had long since integrated into a new milieu. So I asked myself and I asked others: "Where do Jews exist?" I was told Poland. And so I went to Poland.[13]

Doblin's travels came at a moment when Polish national liberation still was fresh. Walking the recently renamed streets of Warsaw,[14] he had a first encounter with bearded men dressed in ragged gabardine: "They are Jews. I am stunned, no, frightened." His German preconceptions proved inadequate to the discovery of incredible Jewish poverty or an anti-Semitic tabloid that fused liberal nationalism with anti-Jewish venom. Above all, he was staggered to find that these Jews "are a nation. People who know only Western Europe fail to realize this. The Jews have their own costumes, their own language, religion, manners and mores, their ancient national feeling and national consciousness." By contrast, "what you see in western Europe is disfigurement."[15]

As an astute observer, Doblin found the situation of Polish Jews to be unexpectedly complex. He did not happen on a singular ossified "traditional" Jewry.[16] Had he been able to read the region's Yiddish literature, with its preoccupations with secularization, the impact of modernity, the allure of the West, and ties between Jews and non-Jews, Doblin would have been better prepared for the diversity of Jewish existence.[17] What

[13] Alfred Doblin, *Schicksalsreise: Bericht und Bekenntnis* (Frankfurt am Main: J. Knecht, 1949), cited in the introduction to Doblin, *Journey to Poland*, ed. Heinz Graber (New York: Paragon House, 1991), xii. What Doblin left out of this account was his enthusiastic embrace for a period during the 1930s of the doctrine of territorialism: indifferent to Palestine as the location but committed to settling Jews on the land in order to become a legitimate Volk. "More important than the land is the Volk," he wrote in *Flucht und Sammlung des Judenvolkes* (Amsterdam: Querido Verlag 1935), 34. For a discussion, see Mosse, *Masses and Man*, 148–50.

[14] An excellent collection of papers that puts Doblin's Warsaw observations in perspective is Wladyslaw T. Bartoszewski and Antony Polonsky, eds., *The Jews in Warsaw: A History* (Oxford: Basil Blackwell, 1991), especially the two articles by Piotr Wrobel on Jewish Warsaw before and during the First World War and the essay by Edward Wynot Jr. on Jews in interwar Warsaw.

[15] Doblin, *Journey to Poland*, 7, 35, 50, 54.

[16] In part, of course, this diversity was the product of the distinctive circumstances of Jews in the different parts of Austrian, Russian, and Prussian (then German) Poland before the results of the First World War produced the possibility of a new Polish state. For an overview of Jewish demography, social structure, culture, and political activity in Poland in this period, see Ezra Mendelsohn, *The Jews of East Central Europe between the World Wars* (Bloomington: Indiana University Press, 1983). Polish Jewish diversity, it should be cautioned, while characterized by a not inconsiderable amount of acculturation, "remained basically Yiddish-speaking, lower middle class and proletarian, and strongly influenced both by religious Orthodoxy and modern separatist Jewish nationalism" (Mendelsohn, *Jews of East Central Europe*, 8).

[17] For a fine overview, see Ruth R. Wisse, "Two Jews Talking: A View of Modern Yiddish Literature," *Prooftexts: A Journal of Jewish Literary History* 4 (January 1984).

he discovered was that Polish nationalism and transformations to economic and political conditions threatened traditional Jewish autonomy and spawned a surprisingly heterogeneous set of responses by Jews. These included efforts to achieve more vigorous isolation, resignation, or cultural imitation without much participation in the wider society, and active engagement in debates about whether the new Poland would be enthusiastically multinational or a homogeneous entity that would tolerate cultural and religious differences only grudgingly. Doblin encountered the last moments of a massive out-migration, principally to America; a Zionist alternative that pitted Hebrew against the Yiddish vernacular; Communist and Socialist politics; splits between *hasidim* and *mitnagdim;* the Jewish Enlightenment, the *Haskalah;* and local styles of acculturation (ungainly by Berlin standards) that discarded Orthodox dress and demanding religiosity. He also discovered that even the provincial, insular masses had been affected by the wider European currents of emancipation. In spite of fierce, at times violent, anti-Semitic resistance and the hegemony of their antimodern leadership, these Jews, too, were being pulled into the ambit of the modern economy and state. In the industrializing petroleum districts, he found, "Polish, Jewish and Ukrainian workers work side by side," a harbinger of the intensifying integration of the Jewish economy and workforce with the larger, increasingly capitalist, economy. And in the realm of political activity, he noted, " 'State,' [and] 'Parliament' loom on the horizon—against the Gaon and the Baal-Shem."[18]

The multilayered process of emancipation Doblin and his family had experienced, and which he observed in Poland, reconstituted Jews as social actors by recasting the problem of group solidarity, that is, "the extent to which members of a group comply with its collective rules without compensation."[19] Michael Hechter has argued that such cohesion is most likely "when individuals face limited sources of benefit, where their opportunities for multiple group affiliations are minimal, and

---

Jewish writers in the East faced the problem of the public. Those who wrote in Yiddish obviously wrote for other Jews, but not all did so. Some Jewish authors, including the first to write in Russian (Grigori Bogrov, Lev Levanda, and Osip Rabinovich), sought to plead the Jewish cause to the general Russian public; none was considered an authentic Russian writer by their intended audience.

[18] Doblin, *Journey to Poland,* 54, 56–60, 177, 103. Doblin was particularly scathing about the nouveau-bourgeois of Jewish Warsaw: "I view those 'Enlightened' ones like Africans who flaunt the glass beads they've gotton from sailors, the dirty cuffs on their dangling arms, the brand-new dented top hats on their heads. How poor, how shabby, how unworthy and soullessly devastated the Western World is, giving them those cuffs; how are they supposed to know" (191).

[19] Charles Tilly, review of *Principles of Group Solidarity,* by Michael Hechter, *American Journal of Sociology* 94 (January 1989): 876.

where their social isolation is extreme."[20] Pre-emancipation Jewry had met these conditions, in part by imposition, in part by preference. By altering the structural location of Jewish life within the state, the economy, and civil society, emancipation undermined the conditions that previously had underpinned Jewish cohesion. Desired individual and collective goods now could be procured outside the ghetto. The networks Jews could join multiplied, as their isolation diminished. As a result, the capacity of organized Jewish communities to control deviant behavior became more tenuous. As Jews traversed paths to emancipation, their new condition as members of voluntary communities confronted them with choices that functioned as solvents to dissolve pre-emancipation patterns of Jewish solidarity. These options were concerned both with how to try to engage the wider non-Jewish world in all its dimensions, and about how to be Jewish in the circumstances of emancipation; that is, how to define the character of theological Judaism, the social organization of Jewry, and the qualities of Jewishness as a way of life.

"Paths of Emancipation," as a title, should be taken seriously. "Paths" connotes comparison and a plurality of passages; it also implies path dependency, as the resolution of options at a given moment shapes and constrains future developments. The book's main historiographical characteristic is a departure from evolutionist interpretations still present in much (but by no means all) modern Jewish scholarship. Our aim is to promote a systematic understanding of the great diversity of types of emancipation and of Jewish responses, including their attachment, in varying degrees, to their own values and community structures, their entry onto the public stage, their commitment to social struggles, their readiness to emigrate or join the Zionist movement, or, by contrast, their boundless attachment to the nations that had admitted them to citizenship.

If emancipation constituted a giant, step-wise change in the Jewish condition, and if it also produced a cascade of unprecedentedly diverse dispositions and patterns of behavior, the task remains to ask how, if at all, large-scale variations among countries—including their type of state and public institutions, political doctrines, cultural codes, rates and characteristics of urbanization, patterns of capitalist development, and the nature of accommodation between social classes—structured situations in a manner that biased the ways Jews chose to be Jews after emancipation.[21] *Paths of Emancipation* chronicles and analyzes this interjacency

[20] Michael Hechter, *Principles of Group Solidarity* (Berkeley: University of California Press, 1987), 54; cited in Tilly, review of *Group Solidarity*, 875.

[21] No useful comparative history of this process can be written if Jewish history is segmented from the histories of the many different societies to which Jews belonged, since their identities and practices were affected distinctively by the configuration of each case.

of elements from the perspective of variations both to the settings within which Jews found themselves embedded and in the selections they made as cognitive and strategic actors from the repertoire generated by their location in these circumstances.

In pursuing these subjects, we are keen to stride a passage located between two sets of alternatives, too often thought of as dichotomous. The first discriminates between emancipation as a unitary process and as a discrete series of single country experiences. Our focus is on variation within the family of instances with the intent to construct the cases by posing a common agenda of questions to make them susceptible to comparison.[22] The second distinguishes between Jews as historically constituted and constrained by large-scale processes beyond their ken and as self-created historical agents. We are keen to understand the Jewish experience in the dual sense of this junction term: how Jews experienced specific instances of emancipation; and their process of learning, adjustment, and action. The central challenge of this book is to find a fresh perspective from which to undertake this double-barreled analytical effort.

Historiographical Puzzles

A number of historiographical obstacles stand in the way.[23] We are entering a conversation long established, with whose terms and content we are

Moreover, responses to emancipation, whether in prospect or in fact, were not affected solely by internal factors. From one country to another, models of emancipation and assimilation also were imported or exported, thus influencing the way in which the character of each individual case was shaped, though often running up against constraints specific to each society, which, as we shall see in the case studies below, sometimes precluded the adoption of an external model.

[22] A useful collection of surveys, country by country, of the current status of Jewish historiography was published in *Modern Judaism* in 1990 and 1991. See, for examples, Jonathan D. Sarna, "American Jewish History," *Modern Judaism* 10 (October 1990); David Weinberg, "French Jewish History," *Modern Judaism* 10 (October 1990); Todd M. Endelman, "English Jewish History," *Modern Judaism* 11 (February 1991); and Shulamit S. Magnes, "German Jewish History," *Modern Judaism* 11 (February 1991).

[23] The most intractable is the inescapability of the Holocaust as a reference point. As Yasmine Ergas writes, "Like all traumas, the Holocaust can neither be assimilated nor expunged. It sets the stage, instead, for future projections of the self and limits the role which can be comfortably played." Thus, it is impossible to treat assimilation sympathetically as a positive value. A second consequence is the devaluation of the historical tale when what counted in the end was proximity to the organized violence of the Third Reich. Yet another implication is the enormous difficulty we now have in honoring the first working principle of good historical research and writing: historicization without teleology. Solutions to these dilemmas are inherently unavailable; we can proceed only in awareness of these conundrums. Yasmine Ergas, "Growing Up Banished: A Reading of Anne Frank's *Diary of a Young Girl* and Etty Hillesum's *An Interrupted Life*," unpublished manuscript, 1985.

appreciative but uneasy. The very notion of Jewish historiography as a particular craft itself is the product of the process of emancipation, as the Jews were thrust into modernity and were affected by historicity. The ways in which the story of emancipation has been rendered inevitably have been partisan. Down the ages, Jews had viewed time as immemorial and established a direct lineage between the course of their own lives and the era of the Bible. The repetition of its narrative had punctuated their daily lives and organized their perception of time. Suddenly, voluntarily or against their will, they were transformed into actors of a history in the making within the crucible of a multiplicity of revolutions well beyond their suzerainty. The ahistorical qualities of rabbinic thought had guided them away from any reference to immediate events; this helps explain the lack of a Jewish historiography. After a number of attempts which, to varying degrees, proved fruitless, it was only during the later decades of the nineteenth century that secular Jewish historians made their appearance and began to approach the richly varied history of the Jews from an angle which viewed that record as integral to the general history with which it is inextricably bound at the individual and collective levels. Not until the more recent past has Jewish history been institutionalized as a professional quest to join Jewish historians in a cross-national epistemic community. As Yosef Hayim Yerushalmi has pointed out, "It is only in the contemporary era that we find, for the first time, a Jewish historiography which is distinct from the collective Jewish memory and, on a number of crucial points, in total opposition to that memory."[24]

Constituted as an independent enterprise, this effort to write Jewish history has been doubly enclosed. Its rich harvest has ripened inside only some of the options available to Jews after emancipation. The craft of Jewish history, moreover, largely has been a specifically Jewish enterprise even when it has been located in the academy outside of such specifically Jewish institutional locations as YIVO in Vilna and New York or the Jewish Theological Seminaries of Breslau and New York. Jewish historiography thus has been caught up in and shaped by debates about contested values and strategies geared to guide Jewish destinies. In turn, the writing of most "general" history characteristically continues to sidestep the challenge of integrating Jews and Jewry into larger narratives. Jewish history remains a latent and unintegrated subject, thrust to the periphery of the historical profession. Serving as their own historians, Jews have

[24] Yosef Hayim Yerushalmi, *Zakhor: Jewish History and Jewish Memory* (Seattle: University of Washington Press, 1982). Spinoza, of course, was the first modern secular Jewish intellectual. For discussions, see Joel Schwartz, "Liberalism and the Jewish Connection: A Study of Spinoza and the Young Marx," *Political Theory* 13 (February 1985); and the outstanding biography by Yirmiyahu Yovel, *Spinoza and Other Heretics* (Princeton: Princeton University Press, 1989).

been tempted by notions of Jewish exceptionalism and have oriented most of their scholarship to specifically Jewish audiences.

We have no wish to break entirely either with this committed patrimony or its vocational motivation; nor could we. We do strive, however, to encourage a more robust engagement between Jewish historical studies and wider scholarly currents, especially with parts of the social sciences. In this effort, we are not alone. In the past two decades, a good many Jewish historians of the nineteenth and twentieth centuries have found direction from social science scholarship on ethnicity and nationalism.[25] Our effort is characterized by complementary emphases and informed by the anti-evolutionist treatment of large-scale social processes, especially state building (but also economic development, international migrations, urbanization, and associational life in civil society) generated in the past two decades by sociologists and political scientists working in a comparative and historical macroanalytical vein, as well as by social science scholarship on cognition and choice and by attempts from within liberal political theory to make a place for difference and incommensurable ways of life.

A first step in grappling with this agenda is the need to take care not to reify the circumstances and characteristics of pre-emancipation European Jewry. A reckoning with the plurality of configurations of modern Jewish history does not come easily, however, because portraits of pre-emancipation Jewry too often have been one-dimensional. In a useful commentary on Max Weber's *Ancient Judaism,* Shmuel Eisenstadt takes up just this issue.[26]

Weber, of course, sought to treat the great world religions in terms of their progressive rationalization, and to distinguish them from each other as a part of the project that sought to account for the elective affinity of Protestantism and capitalism. Eisenstadt points out that Weber might have interpreted Judaism's failure to develop the asceticism and economic ethic he ascribes to Protestantism by focusing on factors outside Jewish control, such as their political vulnerability and dependency. Instead, Weber's picture of European Judaism, before Napoleon's armies diffused liberal citizenship and equality before the law, portrays a unitary pariah people outside the social, political, and economic mainstream. This community, in his view, had come to be enclosed by its rituals as a consequence of a fateful decision taken after the Babylonian exile during

[25] This point is made with some force by Jonathan Frankel, "Assimilation and the Jews in Nineteenth-Century Europe: Toward a New Historiography?," in Jonathan Frankel and Steven J. Zipperstein, eds., *Assimilation and Community: The Jews in Nineteenth Century Europe* (Cambridge: Cambridge University Press, 1992), 17–23.

[26] S. N. Eisenstadt, "The Format of Jewish History–Some Reflections on Max Weber's *Ancient Judaism,*" *Modern Judaism* 1 (May 1981).

the period of the Second Commonwealth to transmute the universalistic potential of Judaism's prophetic tradition into a culture dominated by rabbinic legalism.

Eisenstadt shows persuasively that Weber's stark distinction between the prophetic and rabbinic is based on an overly flat reading of the forms and institutions of Jewish history. Viewing the two traditions as alternatives presents a false picture because the prophetic impulse never disappeared. While the Jewish community—or, rather, Jewish communities—came to be organized with a populist base of observant members following meticulously specified rules for daily life led by a rabbinic elite whose claims to authority were based on sacred learning, the prophetic tradition deepened to make its focus less the redemption of individuals than the community's possibilities within history. In this cultural and political crucible, one that necessarily varied from place to place, Jewish identities formed based on a fusion of ritualistic and prophetic elements. The precise mix, and their balance and content, varied considerably by location in the diaspora as a consequence of the requirement that Jews as a minority (indeed as a minority that viewed its exile as impermanent) come to terms with heterogeneous, often menacing, environments.

Notwithstanding this diversity, the promise and practice of emancipation did utterly transform the conditions of Jewish existence and the character of the challenge to Jews to develop a sense of who they were and how they might live in an uncertainly welcoming world. Emancipation both reflected and caused alterations to the context of communal life that overwhelmed the various formulas for living that Jews had developed and redeveloped since the Second Commonwealth. Everything changed—from communal social organization to religious practice to family life to migration patterns to employment to schooling to ideology to collective action. So, too, did the sheer range of Jewish orientations to the wider milieu.

It is the shared radical quality of this break that has impelled some of the leading historians of this process, preeminent among them Jacob Katz, in *Out of the Ghetto,* to present "as one fabric . . . a compound picture" of emancipation's shared linear qualities, rather than to focus on variations. Katz has viewed the Jewish community as having been marked more by "tradition than . . . the people among whom it dwelt. When the framework of traditional society all over Europe disintegrated, the more traditional a society had been, the deeper was its transmutation"; especially, he insisted, for the Jews.[27] Though we are critical of this position, both for its leveling of difference and its soft teleology, it is

[27] Jacob Katz, *Out of the Ghetto: The Social Background of Jewish Emancipation, 1770–1870* (Cambridge: Harvard University Press, 1973), 1, 4, 6.

important, nonetheless, not to underestimate the profound qualities of emancipation that can get lost in an appreciation of variation. After all, Jews were caught up in a multidimensional set of postfeudal transformations to the Europe in which they lived. With the (long and uneven) demise of feudalism, modern states were born on the basis of a partition of sovereignty from property that implied a new distinction between the sphere of political or public law and rights and the sphere of civil or private law.[28] The number of states fell dramatically as sovereignty came more and more to be concentrated. The state itself increasingly became an entity distinguishable both from the particular person of the ruler and from ecclesiastical authority. Under postfeudal conditions, states had to develop mutually advantageous relations with the partially autonomous macrostructures of the economy and civil society. Contests about the terms of these transactions within newly constituted national public spheres became the centerpiece of modern politics in the West, whose issues concerned the scope and limits of state activity, and the rights of economic actors as well as citizens and subjects.

To the extent that emancipation conduced a redefinition of the relationship of Jews to the state, these trends enfolded the diverse instances of emancipation within a more general story. The vast revisions to political structures, relationships, and policies in early modern Europe effectively ended the viability of the autonomous niche–status Jews had maintained within feudal conditions. Further, Jewish demography, urbanization, and encounters with mercantile economies and markets in capital, land, and labor shared many traits across national boundaries.[29] In these circumstances, Efraim Shmueli has noted, there was a high degree of resemblance to the normative and institutional responses of Jews to emancipation. Across different settings, they learned new languages and forgot old ones, sought to transcend a mentality of exile, and reduced the scope of religious authority and of Jewish autonomy in culture, politics, and community affairs. They also experienced a significant widening in the range of views held by members of the intelligentsia, who now ranged from traditional religious authorities to secular intellectuals seeking to embrace the opportunities of emancipation without a total sacrifice of Jewish identity.[30]

[28] See Morris R. Cohen, "Property and Sovereignty," *Cornell Law Quarterly* 13 (1927), for a discussion that is still suggestive.

[29] Calvin Goldscheider and Alan Zuckerman, *The Transformation of the Jews* (Chicago: University of Chicago Press, 1984).

[30] Efraim Shmueli, *Seven Jewish Cultures: A Reinterpretation of Jewish History and Thought* (Cambridge: Cambridge University Press, 1990). On the intellectuals of the *Haskalah,* or Jewish Enlightenment, see David Sorkin, "The Genesis of the Ideology of Emancipation: 1806–1840," *Leo Baeck Institute Yearbook* 32 (1967).

These features characterizing the points of articulation between Jews and their larger European environment authorized Katz to underscore the shared aspects of Jewish emancipation in western and central Europe rather than its diversity. "Emancipation," he stressed, "in its wider sense, occurred more or less simultaneously. It can also be said to have followed a similar, if not identical, course."[31] For all its value, however, this unitary and linear perspective pushes far too hard in the direction of singularity. One goal of *Paths of Emancipation* is to underscore just how wide a perspective, and just how much of a flattening of variations, is required to sustain Katz's landmark formulation. For the cases we consider, his "simultaneously" would need to mean a period lasting well over a century, and his "similar, if not identical" would have to encompass quite a diverse range of historical developments, including much variation in ways Jews came to define their Jewishness after emancipation. By focusing on differences in spite of similarities, the papers in *Paths of Emancipation* begin where works that underscore similarities stop, but they do so in a manner that is aimed at facilitating an understanding of each case as a distinctive instance of a larger set of historical processes.

Katz's approach (constructed on the basis of the German model viewed implicitly as the ultimate outcome toward which the history of other European Jews tended) is nested within, and complements, what Frankel describes as the nationalist current in Jewish historiography, one of whose characteristics is that of downgrading the significance of diverse paths of emancipation because it sees the history of emancipation, under the best, most liberal circumstances as leading to the dissolution of the Jewish people. David Vital, for example, maintains that the breakthrough to modernity with the French Revolution and the progressive application of the emancipating principles of equality and individualism that emerged in the age of Enlightenment spelled the end of the Jewish people. Treating figures like Doblin as emblematic, he argues that from emancipation to the Holocaust, Judaism was preserved only in eastern Europe, where community structures were sheltered and bore within them their own traditions and culture, protecting at the same time the use of a specific Jewish vernacular. In Vital's rendering, the center of Jewish existence did not, indeed could not, lie in the heart of a western Europe in the throes of modernization, but with the self-contained Jewish communities on the periphery to the East, as though awaiting their belated involvement in a process of development identical to that already experienced by the emancipated Jews of the West. Only the unemancipated

[31] Katz, *Out of the Ghetto,* 3. Katz does acknowledge the macroanalytic and comparative problem of variation between different paths of emancipation, as in his discussion of contrasts between France and Germany, but he does not take up this theme systematically.

who refused or preferred to disregard western modernization constituted the true center of a Judaism that looked with indifference at a history they interpreted as a mutilating factor. From this perspective, it follows that with their tragic extermination by Hitler's Reich, Israel alone was capable of preserving the unity of a Jewish people otherwise destined to disappear in the individualist West.[32]

This perspective is tenable only by a considerable leveling of the historical landscape. By no means is it self-evident that emancipation in the West has been accompanied by an unambiguous impairment of Judaism, leaving only the Jews of the East as the guardians of Jewish religion and culture. Such visions of modern Jewish history do not make sufficient allowance for the multifold qualities of the situations in evidence both in the West (including North America) and, as Doblin discovered, in the East. This dichotomous tendency overlooks the interdependence of West and East, manifested by migration patterns, the impact of modern ideas and movements such as the *Haskalah,* and the generation of choice for eastern Europe's Jews by the emancipation of those in the West. It also tends to disregard the reconstitution in the West of alternative Jewish community structures characterized by associative links that proved capable of transmitting a sense of belonging and loyalty. Relationships of partnership within society, as Tönnies held, need not be radically incompatible with links within a community. Given that the Jews nowhere exercised power as a nation state, is it reasonable to assume that they "stepped back" from history, that their own history simply became tributary to that of others? To the contrary, emancipated Jews maintained or pioneered distinctively Jewish networks of social relations as vectors of culture and tradition. In some instances, they even forged forms of power which, though not founded on the control of a state, nevertheless existed in other forms by means of the circulation of information and protective organizations, among other vehicles.[33]

The modern history of the Jews, in short, did not follow a linear path from servitude to liberation, from an integrated community to fragmentation, from the *pletzl* to professions in the tertiary sector, from tradition to assimilation, or from the ghetto to a citizenship oriented entirely toward general civism accompanied by a disregard of their specific identity and patterns of life. Contrary to customary interpretations of Franco-Judaism, or indeed of *Bildung,* there was no near-complete eradication of Jewish culture in the societies in which the Enlightenment and emancipation left their most striking marks. By contrast to the classical devel-

[32] David Vital, *The Future of the Jews: A People at the Cross-Roads* (Cambridge: Harvard University Press, 1990), chap. 1.

[33] See David Biale, *Power and Powerlessness in Jewish History* (New York: Schocken Books, 1987).

opmentalist theories of sociology implicit in a good deal of the historiography of emancipation that consider the social roles specific to modernity as being fundamentally different from traditional ones, we wish to embrace important aspects of the welcome historiographical trend that seeks to demonstrate the surviving existence, even the renewed vitality in some instances, of Jewish marriage patterns, institutions, and associational networks conducive to the survival and enhancement of values specific to Judaism.

Working in this mode, for example, Todd Endelman's rigorous analysis of individual destinies has shown how "acculturation, integration and secularization reshaped and attenuated Jewish identity but rarely did they extinguish it."[34] In countries profoundly affected by the Enlightenment and by modernity more generally, such as France and Germany, and, *a fortiori,* in those countries that continued to stand apart from this trend, as in much of the Russian Empire; or, finally, in those countries, especially the United States, where it was legitimate for widely different particularist cultures to be maintained, meaningful Jewish history certainly did not disappear with the advent of modernity. Even in those societies where socioeconomic modernization was most pronounced, ethnicity could persist, if often in new forms. Thus, Goldscheider and Zuckerman observe, "occupational, residential and educational change moved Jews to new locations and to greater exposure to non-Jews. But in the new order, Jews continued to interact with Jews. They concentrated in new occupations and built new communal institutions. Hence, modernization created new forms of Jewish cohesion as it destroyed old forms. . . . Ethnicity did not disappear."[35]

Goldscheider and Zuckerman are persuasive in insisting that the social and economic modernization of the Jews did not command the destruction of their particularity, just as political emancipation did not demand merely disembodied forms of citizenship. Their focus on economic and social change, however, much like Katz's on political transition in *Out of the Ghetto,* treats emancipation as a singular trajectory. Like states, nineteenth-century capitalism differed in many pivotal respects from place to place: in the degree of penetration of capitalist structures, the relations between social classes, rates of social and geographical mobility, urbanization and the growth of cities, the starkness of the division between workplaces and residential communities, the character of neighborhoods, and the complex interplay between economically grounded

[34] Todd M. Endelman, "The Chequered Career of 'Jew' King," in Frances Malino and David Sorkin, eds., *From East and West: Jews in a Changing Europe, 1750–1870* (Oxford: Blackwell, 1990), 175; also see Todd M. Endelman, "The Legitimization of the Diaspora Experience in Recent Jewish Historiography," *Modern Judaism* 11 (May 1991).

[35] Goldscheider and Zuckerman, *Transformation of the Jews,* 80.

and other identities. These variations, in turn, intertwined with differences between states. Thus, for example, in their entry into French capitalism, Jews were not as capable of maintaining their own particularistic ethnic bonds as easily as English or American Jews, due largely to the hubris of the French state and its assertive definition of citizenship. In turn, from a more sociological point of view, the growth of cities in the United States (and, later, the suburban phenomenon) was embedded within a decentralized polity that implied dispersion and a different kind of challenge to group and personal identities.

There exists today no systematic comparative study of such differences in the linkages between the state, the economy, and society for Jews during the long century of emancipation. Our aim in *Paths of Emancipation* is to suggest foci for such an effort and to make a start by way of a selective emphasis, primarily on state-centered factors, in a number of case studies in the direction of this ambitious project.

Toward Comparison

Happily, just this set of considerations—a concern to understand "flux, . . . a myriad of contexts, and . . . a multiplicity of responses," to transcend too stark a division between tradition and modernity or between East and West, and to lend "greater credence to the survivalist strategies of Western Jewry," while encouraging "a view of group consciousness as developing in open-ended, unpredictable and idiosyncratic ways"—has begun to characterize the work of leading, especially younger, students of modern Jewish history. Their pivotal insights have included a departure from the handling of emancipation as a unitary and linear process, and a recognition, informed by studies in the social sciences on ethnicity and nationalism, that in the case of Jews seeking to engage the various liberal offers of inclusion in the polity, "the loss of linguistic and cultural distinctiveness" did not necessarily bring "with it a loss of ethnic identity."[36]

In order to define where *Paths of Emancipation* stands with respect to this important historiographical trend, we should like to attend to the two leading attempts to reckon with and codify it, both of which are based on conferences held in the early and middle 1980s: a transitional volume, *Toward Modernity,* that tries by way of Jacob Katz's introductory essay to bridge the new emphasis on plurality and the German-centered unitary view for which he has been the most influential figure; and *Assimilation and Community,* a wholehearted embrace of the revisionist impulse.[37]

[36] Frankel, "Assimilation and the Jews," 31, 22.

[37] Jacob Katz, ed., *Toward Modernity: The European Jewish Model* (New Brunswick, N.J.: Transaction Books, 1987); Frankel and Zipperstein, *Assimilation and Community.*

The excellent essays in Katz's collection strain against the deep ambivalence of its editor. Ranging from thematic studies of the *Haskalah* in Hungary, Italy, Galicia, and Russia, city-based considerations of the Jews of Vienna and Prague, an overview of Jewish modernity in England, to relational studies of German Jewry and Jews in France, the Netherlands, and the United States, the volume tenses between the urge to credit the distinctiveness of each case and the impulse to tame the complex story of emancipation by way of holding on to the centrality of the German instance and to inquire about how "German-Jewish development . . . [influenced] what happened elsewhere." The book's subtitle, *The European Jewish Model,* provides a unitary description. At the outset, Katz avers that the volume's purpose is "to compare the process of modernization in German Jewry with its counterparts in other countries," and to assay whether the impact of the German experience on the others "is based on the assumption that the development in the said countries, if it had not a common source, at least reveals a common denominator." Conceding that this theme is not "made explicit in any of the essays," he contends nonetheless that this shared quality can be found "in the criterion by which the modern variation of Jewish communities could be differentiated from its predecessor, the traditional Jewish society." What distinguished the latter was the authoritative enclosure of the Jews, enforced by its communal organs with the sanction of the state; by contrast, "the post-traditional Jewish community was denied the right to impose its will concerning thought and action of the individual."[38]

We have three principal reservations about *Toward Modernity.* Our first source of disquiet is the book's lack of self-consciousness about the tension it fails to name or analyze between the treatment of emancipation as a drastic break with the past and the focus in the book's essays on the multifarious qualities of emancipation. This is an opportunity missed. Our own focus on variation is premised on agreement with Katz that emancipation entailed a radical fracture; but our definition of the breach differs from his. By focusing on citizenship, the state, and the extension of liberal political rights, we necessarily are inserting variation into the heart of the common element of emancipation. What Katz and his colleagues treat as their objects of analysis—variations in the cognitive and strategic choices of the Jews—we seek to locate within these determinate, also various, political circumstances.

The second hallmark of Katz's volume is its identification of Germany as the locus of the origins of Jewish modernity in Europe: "The process starting in eighteenth-century Germany gradually encompassed the whole Jewish world."[39] This orientation is not so much wrong—for

[38] Katz, introduction to *Toward Modernity,* 1.

[39] Katz, preface to *Toward Modernity,* vii.

many purposes it is right on the mark—as much as it is partial and distorting. For to the extent that emancipation at its core was a political process, the United States and France, as well as the Netherlands, rather than Germany, present themselves as the appropriate points of departure.

Third, Katz's collection is characterized by very heterogeneous units of analysis: cities, countries, regions, an intellectual movement, and the process of diffusion. Our comparative focus on the form and content of citizenship made available to Jews impels us instead to adopt a national framework for our cases. In each instance, we have tried to highlight the distinctive character of transactions between the state and civil society, the domain of citizenship. We do not wish to understate other sources of variation, such as the character of the economy or levels and forms of urbanization (indeed, we seek to take these into account), but we do insist on making the qualities of stateness the central axis of our approach.

Frankel and Zipperstein's *Assimilation and Community* differs from the Katz volume primarily in its assertive embrace of particularity. More specifically, as Frankel makes clear in his useful and provocative introduction, their book is premised on a reading of, and a break with, the developmentalist emphasis on singularity, an approach Frankel identifies with the "Russian-Jewish School" pioneered by Simon Dubnov in the last years of the nineteenth century. In his historiographical reconstruction, Dubnov and such distinguished successors as Ben-Zion Dinur, Raphael Mahler, and Gershom Scholem can be seen as having shifted their emphases from the theological and metaphysical foci of Heinrich Graetz and the "German School" to spotlight Jewish communal and civil history. The "Russian School" read modern Jewish history in

> essentially dichotomous terms. Bipolarity served as the key, the paradigmatic principle which supplied these works with their underlying structure. On the one hand, there was the Jewish nation which had tenaciously survived almost two millennia of exile and dispersion by dint of its internal solidarity, faith and inventiveness. On the other, there were combined forces of change which, unless creatively absorbed and organically integrated by the nation, could only set in motion a process of inexorable erosion and a process of self-destruction.[40]

In seeking to understand this bipolarity, Dubnov theorized a Hobson's choice: political liberalism heightened prospects for Jewish disintegration; illiberal treatments of the Jews enhanced their cohesion. His preferred solution was a synthesis of tradition and modernity under Jewish nationalist auspices.

Appreciatively, but critically, Frankel observes that Dubnov's overlap-

[40] Frankel, "Assimilation and the Jews," 4.

ping doublets of tradition and modernity, East and West, and liberalism and illiberalism, "encouraged the tendency to focus the spotlight on the extremes, thus leaving the middle ground, although certainly not out of sight, still in the shadows." Reform Judaism and the *Haskalah* were interpreted in this frame as exemplifying the costs of acceptance of the West's various liberal offers and as institutional moves away from Jewish national particularity; when Jews self-organized rather than assimilated their behavior was ascribed to "residual traditionalism."[41] *Assimilation and Community* delineates a broad-gauged response to this inheritance. Its mood, Frankel observes, "is antireductionist." Tapping a revisionist line of work, the book's authors perceive modern Jewish history "in terms not of bipolarity but of multiplicity. Instead of the one basic conflict between centrifugality and centripetality, now a great variety of autonomous processes, independent variables, are traced as they interact in constantly new permutations. . . . The focus has shifted from the extremes, from the dichotomous archetypes, to that middle ground where it is no easy task to distinguish the exceptions from the rules."[42]

The affinities we share with this orientation to research should be obvious; but so are the differences. The fragmentation and decentering of emancipation exacts a high price. There is far less parallelism, less of a common project, linking the essays in *Assimilation and Community* than in *Toward Modernity.* The papers in Frankel and Zipperstein teach us a great deal about assimilation in Alsace, Hungarian "casino" clubs, and gender, tradition, and the bourgeois Jewish family in Wilhelmine Germany, but there are few common denominators among them, except for a refreshing capacity to rethink received wisdom. The new multilayered historiography runs the risk of eliminating the search for a coherent object of explanation. Further, this program's strong reaction to such dichotomies as tradition and modernity, pre- and post-emancipation, and western and eastern Jewry, coupled with its principled rejection of alternative standpoints from which to consider variation between instances, erodes the prospect of systematic comparative analysis.

The overriding danger of the impulse chronicled in Frankel and Zipperstein lies in the sacrifice of confidence in the coherence and integrity of emancipation. Notwithstanding our unease with the German-centered model of Katz, it did possess a profound advantage we are keen not to abandon by way of an overreaction: the understanding that Jewish emancipation did represent, both overall and in specific national instances, a radical redefinition of the Jewish condition. It did so by redefining Jewish choices and predicaments, by vastly increasing the available repertoire of

[41] Ibid., 6, 15.
[42] Ibid., 16.

how to be Jewish, and by enlarging the scope of opportunity and danger for Jews. In *Paths of Emancipation,* we seek to problematize this break without reifying "before" and "after," without downplaying the complexity of both, and without underestimating the extent to which the experiences of emancipation moved to diverse rhythms of time and space.

In pursuit of these aims, the book's eight country studies construct the cases in three dimensions: paths *to,* paths *of,* and paths *from* emancipation. Each essay tells a story about the ways larger institutional settings imposed themselves on the type and timing of emancipation. They consider the following factors: Was emancipation externally imposed by occupation armies and ideologies or endogenously developed? Did it occur as a result of a protracted or expeditious process? Was it early, or late, in the history of emancipation? Did political emancipation precede (and thus facilitate) or follow economic and social incorporation? Was emancipation an integral part of new nationalist assertions, or liberal political movements, to which Jews were attached? Once granted, did emancipation prove durable, or were there episodes of the restoration of ante-emancipation circumstances?

Emancipation came first as a formal-legal process in France and the Netherlands, but within different statist contexts. In both countries, emancipation was the product of the French Revolution and its radical break with prior conceptions of thickly mediated citizenship. But in the Netherlands, the legacies of pluralist and consociational state building impressed themselves on the post-1795 unitary state, which, though the product of conquest by the French, was very different from the Jacobin model of a pretentious state. Dutch citizenship also differed from French republicanism. Throughout much of the nineteenth century, it was both more limited, allowing for political participation by just about one in ten people, and it permitted the ever more strong development of Catholic and Calvinist religious communities as legitimate pillars of civil society and the state.

In Germany, by contrast, because there was no national state until 1871, emancipation came about unevenly in the different German states; where French intervention initially imposed at least a partial emancipation, the rights of Jews either were arrested in incomplete status or withdrawn only to be secured unevenly later in a climate where liberal possibilities jostled with anti-Enlightenment, Romantic, and Christian definitions of Germanness. But even as Jews were excluded from the state, as in Prussia when previous gains were withdrawn, the degree of structural integration into German capitalism and cities, accompanied by a rapidly growing Jewish middle class, advanced quickly. Jewish life, concomitantly, was being modernized, even if most Jews still lived apart from their Gentile neighbors. When full legal and political emancipation came in the period between 1869 and 1871, the Jews most likely to be affected—those with a positive orientation toward acculturation and structural assimilation—already had left the confines of traditional Jewish communities.

In England, as in Germany, Jews achieved political emancipation quite late, securing in 1835 the right to vote, in the 1840s an end to other legal disabilities, and in 1858 the last civic right conceded, that of sitting in the House of Commons. (Oxford and Cambridge Fellowships were opened to Jews in 1871.) Here, too, economic participation antedated political rights. But unlike Germany, the framework of a (multi)national state was secure, and liberal rights once granted could be practiced with the assuranced assumption that they would not be withdrawn. This was also true in the United States, but with the massive difference that in America there was a liberalism so entrenched that no formal emancipation was necessary for its Jews. They had merely to cross the ocean. Nonetheless, emancipation there did not occur all at once, but was an iterative process marked by distinctive migration flows from different parts of Europe.

If the Jews of England were outsiders knocking on the door of the nation while in the United States they contributed to the constitution of a new nation, Italian Jews were located at the center of the effort to construct a modern national state. In Italy, there was a first emancipation under French aegis, and a second in 1848. Its geographic scope expanded southward with the movement of the Piedmontese army. Jews played a key role in the making and shaping of mid-nineteenth century Piedmont nationalism, the only Italian state where there had been no violence against Jews after the departure of the French. This location not only facilitated their access to key military as well as economic positions but tied their fate to the peninsula's most liberal, secular, and democratic forces. These emancipatory and nationalist developments followed the return to the ghettos after the French had withdrawn, a process redolent with resentment that drew Jews to the revolutionary societies for which they proved to be much-needed allies. Italian Jews thus were not alien to the new modern state but implicated integrally with its fragility and fate.

In Turkey, the situation of Jews altered considerably under the impact of modern state building on western models. As in Europe, Turkish Jews had governed themselves as autonomous communities under religious auspices. The process of the dissolution of their corporate autonomy was tied to the importation of the centralizing statist French model that had the effect of undercutting the status quo for all non-Muslims. With the Reform Decree of 1856 and the citizenship law of 1869, non-Muslims were granted equal rights and obligations in relationships with the state no longer mediated by minority-group communal institutions. For Jews, this alteration of status under Ottoman rule as well as the later European-style emancipation practiced by the Turkish Republic entailed the loss of communal resources without concurrent paths of entry into Turkish civil society, politics, or state institutions. The model of the Jacobin state here produced a state for Muslims without a concomitant liberal culture.

If Turkey had an emancipation without liberalism, Russia, the home of the world's largest Jewish community after the late eighteenth-century acquisitions of Belorussian, Lithuanian, and Ukrainian territory, experienced neither emancipation nor liberalism under the old order. Given the rights-less qualities of the tsarist regimes, legal-political emancipation was an impossibility. Jewish uncertainty was very high because of the essential incoherence and inconsistency of state policy toward the Jews, as different attempts were made under the tsars to combine Jewish communal autonomy with the complex categories utilized by the state to order its population by residence and property. The Bolsheviks, by contrast, made it hard to leave, but, at least until the latter part of Stalin's rule, they facilitated a remarkable level of integration for Jews as Soviet citizens, if at the steep price of large-scale cultural destruction.[43]

Jews as Actors: Cognition, Networks, and Strategy

The essays in *Paths of Emancipation* were written as responses to a common agenda of questions with the aim of constructing each case in a manner that makes it available for comparisons which neither overstate nor understate differences. From one angle of sight, these configurational narratives compose materials for a comparative macroanalytic treatment of how Jews came to be inserted into modernity by large-scale processes not under their control. From another, they highlight the emergence of Jews as anthropological subjects within the larger scope of Europe; that is, as social actors with identities, dispositions, and intentions who sought to find their way and to construct their fate within these radically altered contexts and possibilities. Just as there was no uniformity to political emancipation, Jews in specific settings always had alternatives about the qualities of their cultural formation and ethnic solidarity. As

[43] In effect, the Soviets reversed traditional pre-emancipation patterns of discrimination where Jews were tolerated to the extent that they stayed to themselves. "The opposite was true under the Soviet regime: here Jewish insularity, their willful separation from the rest of society, would not be tolerated. Jews could acquire Soviet citizenship with all the rights and entitlements that went with the honor, but they could not sustain their community life anymore." Jan Gross, "Jewish Community in the Soviet-Annexed Territories on the Eve of the Holocaust: A Social Scientist's View," *East European Politics and Societies* 6 (Spring 1992): 204–5. Though Gross was writing about a specific situation of particular duress, this description holds more generally for Jews in the USSR after an initial period of greater latitude under Bolshevik rule.

actors after emancipation, they had to make new kinds of strategic calculations, both as individuals and in interactive networks, based on expectations within a given set of values. For this reason, nineteenth- and twentieth-century Jews must be studied as they have not been to date: in a manner analogous to the ways social scientists and historians analyze the behavior of such other social groups as peasants or workers as calculating actors confronting different contexts with determinate values and preferences.[44] Acting within these contexts and with the resources of their own patterns of cognition and communication, Jews shaped, and reshaped, their political cultures. In so doing, they had a hand in designing and molding their political possibilities at the junction where large-scale social processes and microdecisions are linked. It is not the objective of the individual essays in *Paths of Emancipation,* or of the book overall, to construct strong causal accounts which predict that a specific type of emancipation must produce a definite pattern of Jewish group formation, whether it be that of seeking an exaggerated assimilation or of discovering new forms of articulation and reinsertion into the Jewish community.

Rather, the country essays construct plausible accounts that link the histories of state building, economic development, nationalism, and local qualities of liberalism to the timing and character of emancipation; and they suggest why in these circumstances the central tendencies of Jewish dispositions, organization, and activity represented coherent responses to new opportunities. The paths Jews traversed *from* emancipation were inscribed by the ways specific macroscopic features affected the timing and character of emancipation, which, in turn, shaped Jewish opportunities, institutions, and identities. In these settings, Jews, embedded in a lattice of social relationships, made choices about their identity. With emancipation, two sets of overlapping networks—within the Jewish community and between Jews and Gentiles—altered in scope, direction, and density. The loosening of spatial and social enclosure fractured once-compacted social relationships into more fine-grained networks of people, who, in turn, were intertwined within multifold relationships with the wider environment. Jewish identities were formed and reformed within the webs of these ties.[45] How this occurred, and with which con-

[44] For examples of work in this genre, see Samuel Popkin, *The Rational Peasant* (Berkeley: University of California Press, 1979); Douglass North, *Structure and Change in Economic History* (New York: Norton, 1981); John Roemer, *Analytical Marxism* (Cambridge: Cambridge University Press, 1986); and Hechter, *Principles of Group Solidarity.*

[45] In this discussion, we are drawing on John Padgett, "Networks and Identities in Political Party Formation: The Case of the Medici in Renaissance Florence," unpublished manuscript, University of Chicago, 1990; John F. Padgett and Christopher Ansell, "From Faction to Party in Renaissance Florence: The Emergence of the Medici Patronage Party," unpublished manuscript, University of Chicago, 1988; and John F. Padgett and Christopher K. Ansell, "Robust Action and the Rise of the Medici, 1400–1434," *American Journal of Sociology* 98 (May 1993): 1259–1319.

ditioning pressures from large-scale social processes, define the terrain of questions in this book.

The process of Jewish group formation was characterized in part by shifting institutional pressures on the networks themselves; by uncertainty about the durability of relationships; by competition between different Zionist, religious, revolutionary, and nationalist "entrepreneurs" who sought to mobilize networks for competing visions of Jewishness; and by a cultural repertoire of roles formulated by these alternatives. It is a central claim of this book that different paths to, of, and from emancipation defined distinctive sets of social relations both within and across the boundary of the group that structurally biased the choices Jews made about how to be Jewish and affected the ways these complex identities were reproduced. Jews as a bloc did not confront emancipation. Rather, specific Jews located within varied networks with different levels of loyalty, uncertainty, and discretion made choices about Albert Hirschman's famous triad of exit, voice, and loyalty.[46]

They did so within a cognitive matrix composed of memory, directly perceived experiences, interpersonal and intersubjective ties, and in possession of culture, language, and dispositions that defined the kinds of persons Jews could be and the types of group Jews composed. In various circumstances and in possession of these tools, Jews redefined their Jewishness and confronted their post-emancipation predicaments in a continuous, tension-ridden process. These issues of identity and solidarity were raised and at least provisionally resolved by the way emancipation in each instance affected Jewish intracommunal and external networks, provided Jews with new sets of selective incentives and disincentives concerning how to be Jewish in new circumstances, and altered the possibilities and content of Jewish life.

Read together, the country studies demonstrate, as Zygmunt Bauman has put it, that "there were few, if any straight roads in modern Jewish history."[47] The portraits of emancipation the essays paint facilitate our understanding of the impact the distinctive countenances of emancipation in the individual countries had on the various situations of post-emancipation Jews. These local qualities affected the circumstances and perceptions of Jews as they acted to deal with new possibilities and insecurities under conditions of highly uneven information. The papers consider how the various experiences of emancipation established competing forms of life from which Jews could make choices about how, if at all, to be Jewish in post-emancipation situations. Intracommunal divisions be-

[46] Albert Hirschman, *Exit, Voice and Loyalty* (Cambridge: Harvard University Press, 1970).

[47] Zygmunt Bauman, "Exit Visas and Entry Tickets: Paradoxes of Jewish Assimilation," *Telos* 77 (Fall 1988): 45.

came fine-grained and crosscutting: between social classes, Yiddish- and majority language–speakers, the spatially mobile and immobile, religiously Orthodox and non-Orthodox, revolutionaries and supporters of the status quo. The essays further suggest how Jewish group formation was a coherent response to the way opportunities of emancipation had come about and were structured. Though there was no simple or singular pattern to Jewish dispositions and activity in any specific country, the essays propose that there were modal national tendencies that are explicable as sensible reactions to the particular mix of incentives and uncertainties of individual cases of emancipation, which themselves were shaped most fundamentally by the type of state that produced these instances.

Even as the essays underscore the range of diverse responses to new opportunities, they also show how emancipation proved a maze with no right answers. Once civic inclusion became possible, if in some places only as a distant objective, there were no circumstances that simultaneously permitted the reproduction of a fully robust Jewish life based on tight enclosure and an engaged Jewish citizenry. Thus, in Italy, where Piedmont's Jews played an integral role in regional nationalism and took a leading position in fundamental changes in Italian life, and where they gained unusually strong access to parliament and key state positions (including Europe's first modern Jewish minister of war and Jewish prime minister) without having to pay the price of being dissolved as a politically conscious community, Jewish life was swiftly marked by the rise of mixed marriages and what Dan Segre describes below as "the decadence of Jewish culture" and "the growing lack of attachment to Jewish tradition." Opportunities to enter the wider society thus implied not just individual exits from bounded communities, but the internal transformation of the social order from which the individuals emerged. To the extent that Jews opted to maximize continuities in spite of the seductions of emancipation, their status became further marginalized. They became bumpkins by choice. Yet to the extent they seized the new possibilities, they soon had to confront highly uneven and incomplete qualities of acceptance, and they were compelled to live with new anxieties and strains as marginal actors whose old world was devalued but whose new world was not fully welcoming. In short, post-emancipation Jews faced a no-win situation. As Bauman observes,

> Those who felt confident enough to confront the tension on their own soon discovered that, contrary to the ostensible rules of the game, they were not *allowed* to do so. In the eyes of the majority which had emancipated them, they remained members of the accursed emancipated minority. They continued to carry the stigma of their membership for everyone to see. If they

> declared their disgust toward the less "individualized" members of the native community and refused to concern themselves with what the majority saw as their "humanization," they were branded as accomplices to the crime of difference. If they succumbed to majority expectations and engrossed themselves in communal self-improvement, this was immediately taken as proof of their partaking of the collective stigma. . . . There was only one thing left to do until it, too, was to be discredited: to lift one's own community to the level of the majority's standards—and to do it with such an uncompromising ardour that in some not-too-distant future the community might have dissolved (majority permitting) and disappeared altogether. In this case the meaning of the lifting was to be unilaterally determined by the majority—or at least by the way in which the minority elite interprets the will of the majority.[48]

As this process unfolded, Jews further paid the price of their strong identification with liberalism, and with the particular kind of nationalism that enfolded within its grasp, which many Jews embraced with the assiduousness of converts. Further, the more some pursued the options opened by emancipation, the less internally cohesive the Jewish community became, and boundaries within the Jewish world, and between Jews and Gentiles, became less certain, more fuzzy, and increasingly permeable. In these circumstances, Jews were vulnerable to multiple charges of inauthenticity, from within and from without. The most dangerous were the various romantic responses to the Enlightenment marked by the championing of precisely those *Gemeinschaft* folk cultures from which Jews were excluded by definition.[49]

Constrained though they were, Jews did weigh alternatives and select between them within this perplexing field of action. How did they react within the available repertoire of possibilities?

In a noted critique, Brian Barry proposed a number of alterations to Hirschman's strategic alternatives. Hirschman had posed a bimodal choice: to leave (the firm, the state, the organization, the community) or to complain, protest, and organize. Barry argued that the way Hirschman puts "the criterion for rational action makes it clear that to speak of a choice between exit and voice is in fact to collapse two separate choices into one another." One set counterposes leaving and staying (exit and non-exit), the other contrasts activity and participation to nonactivity and nonparticipation (voice and nonvoice). "In any situation," Barry argues, "one choice has to be made out of each pair of options, even if only by default." Thus, with respect to exit and voice, there are four possible combinations, not two. It is possible to silently not exit as well as

[48] Ibid., 51–52.

[49] For a discussion, see Ernest Gellner, *Culture, Identity, and Politics* (Cambridge: Cambridge University Press, 1987), 78–80.

silently exit; just as it is possible to combine voice with exit and non-exit.[50]

In each situation where Jews were presented with liberal offers of emancipation, they had to choose between this more complex set of options, both as organized Jewish communities and as individual Jews, at least at two levels: the bounded Jewish community and the larger institutional set of the wider state, economy, and civil society. That is, they selected whether to stay within ghetto enclosures but also whether to stay within a given country. These were separate choices. Likewise, they could opt for voice or silence within or outside traditional Jewish communities. Further, "voice" might denote collective action in search of collective goods or individual action in search of individual benefit.[51]

These selections were not made by rational calculation divorced from time and place. Consider "exit," a recurrent theme in Jewish history ever since the flight from Egypt.[52] When the wave of pogroms swept across eastern Europe in the late nineteenth century, Jewish emigration accelerated from the countryside to Warsaw, Budapest, Vienna, and other large cities in the region, and to Germany, France, Britain, and, above all, the United States. These massive population movements gave rise to profound upheavals both to Jewish communities that had not yet been emancipated and to those that already had, where the newcomer "brothers and strangers," some of whom professed revolutionary ideals, faced strongly negative reactions when their arrival was thought to call the fruits of emancipation into question.[53] To the East, in the Russian Empire, individual exit through mobility scarcely was conceivable. It was impossible to speak out in that structure which repressed the Jews pitilessly and where loyalty to the tsar could rarely be taken for granted. There, all that remained were strategies of individual exit through emigration, or revolutionary collective exit either in a universalist Marxist or particularist Jewish Bundist or Zionist dimensions.[54] In Germany, by

[50] Brian Barry, review of *Exit, Voice and Loyalty,* by Albert Hirschman, *British Journal of Political Science* 4 (January 1974): 90–91.

[51] This point is made by Barry, ibid., 92.

[52] Michael Walzer, *Exodus and Revolution* (New York: Basic Books, 1985).

[53] See Steven Ascheim, *Brothers and Strangers: The East European Jew in German and German-Jewish Consciousness, 1800–1923* (Madison: University of Wisconsin Press, 1982); and Paul Mendes-Flohr, "Fin-de-Siecle Orientalism: The *Ostjuden* and the Aesthetics of Jewish Self-Affirmation," *Studies in Contemporary Jewry* 1 (1984). On Jewish radicalism, see William Fishman, *East End Jewish Radicals, 1875–1914* (London: Duckworth, 1975); Michael Marrus *The Politics of Assimilation: A Study of the French Jewish Community at the Time of the Dreyfus Affair* (Oxford: Oxford University Press, 1971); and Robert Wistrich, *The Jews of Vienna in the Age of Franz Joseph* (Oxford: Oxford University Press, 1989).

[54] For discussions, see Jonathan Frankel, *Prophecy and Politics: Socialism, Nationalism and the Russian Jews, 1862–1917* (Cambridge: Cambridge University Press, 1981); and Michael Stanislawski, *Tsar Nicholas I and the Jews: The Transformation of Jewish Society in Russia, 1825–1855* (Philadelphia: Jewish Publication Society, 1983).

contrast, and in some respects also in the Habsburg Empire, the structure of the bureaucratic state and the rapid process of socioeconomic modernization made the Jewish choice even more complex: the Jews who were emancipated in Germany in 1869 often counted among the most faithful supporters of the Kaiser or Emperor and served him with devoted loyalty; they also succeeded without difficulty in becoming organized to make their voice heard through organizations such as the Centralverein deutscher Staatsbürger Jüdischen Glaubens, their representative in dealings with public authorities. Still almost always excluded from the state, however, and often treated as second-class citizens and confronted with persistent anti-Semitism that excluded them from many social circles, Germany's Jews did not hesitate to exit individually, by emigrating westward, by joining organizations that supported Zionism, or by embracing socialist and Marxist struggles.[55] Interestingly, Hannah Arendt also uses the notion of "exit" when she discusses the fate of her early nineteenth-century Jewish heroine, Rahel Varnhagen; since the bourgeoisie of the day refused to accept Jews rejected by the nobility, and since the alternative of a revolutionary exit did not yet exist, "All that remained for her was to wonder how she might find her own individual way out. . . . The only visible way out was Varnhagen," and through him conversion and marriage.[56] Much later, all the individual and collective exit options became possible for Germany's Jews.[57] Later still, when the rise of the Nazis to power closed all the other doors, the only conceivable exit option remaining was exile, an exit beyond frontiers already sealed.[58]

Jews, of course, were not alone in their practice of exit options or, more broadly, in confronting the multilayered universe of choice and uncertainty inherent in the possibilities that the Enlightenment and liberal-

[55] See Jehuda Reinharz, *Fatherland or Promised Land: The Dilemma of the German Jew, 1893–1914* (Ann Arbor: University of Michigan Press, 1975); Marjorie Lamberti, *Jewish Activism in Imperial Germany* (New Haven: Yale University Press, 1978); Yehuda Reinharz and Walter Schatzberg, eds., *The Jewish Response to German Culture: From the Enlightenment to the Second World War* (Hanover, N.H.: University Press of New England, 1985); Werner Mosse, ed., *Juden im Wilhelminischen Deutschland, 1890–1914* (Tübingen: J.C.B. Mohr, 1976); and Werner Mosse, *The German-Jewish Economic Elite, 1820–1935: A Socio-Cultural Profile* (Oxford: Clarendon Press, 1989).

[56] Hannah Arendt, *Rahel Varnhagen* (Paris: Tierce, 1986), 221.

[57] On the subject of choice, see the discussion between Walter Benjamin and Gershom Scholem in Scholem, *Walter Benjamin: The Story of a Friendship* (Philadelphia: Jewish Publication Society, 1981).

[58] Hannah Arendt, Walter Benjamin, and Albert Hirschman all tried to take the route across the Pyrenees to neighboring Spain, while Gershom Scholem followed this last desperate attempt by his friend Benjamin from Palestine, which he had long ago chosen as the destination for his personal "exit." See the admirable account by Lisa Fittko, *Le chemin des Pyrénées: Souvenirs 1940–1941* (Paris: Maren Sell, 1987).

ism proffered. At one level, Ernest Gellner shrewdly observed, the implications of these new doctrines "were the same for everyone, Gentile or Jew," posing "the very same problem for everyone: when embracing the new wisdom, is he also to disavow the old faith which, if taken literally, and with the seriousness which had previously been accorded to it, was plainly incompatible with the new secular revelation." But this encounter was especially problematic for the Jews, for whom "emancipation" signified a process of entry into this more generally applicable dilemma, but with a sharp and keen difference: "For a Gentile, the problem was only intellectual; abjuring the old faith did not also mean abjuring the old community. For a Jew, it did precisely mean that."[59] Jewish departures from a closed society to one with the promise of openness meant embracing the new shared idiom of the dominant majority, from within whose midst the doctrines of the Enlightenment had developed. Jews who traversed this path assumed implicitly that the thinning of their Jewish identification and practices would be complemented by a smooth insertion into a genuinely cosmopolitan environment. What they did not reckon with was the rapid depreciation of ghetto life and Jewish culture that tainted even those Jews who chose to leave these behind. With emancipation, older statist tyrannies were supplanted by those of predatory civil societies.

Pre-emancipation Jewry suffered much (blood libels, massacres, and so on) but never was wholly outside society. As in the Islamic world, Jews in Christian *ancien régime* Europe occupied niches in closed societies with many niches. Jews possessed a defined place in this order: their position outside Christian fellowship legitimated their performance of activities vital to the larger economy, state, and social system. Spatial segregation in towns and villages that reinforced Jewish isolation seemed natural in this context, at times even desirable for its relatively secure provision of social enclosure. Of course, Jewish residential places never were entirely self-contained. Not every Jew worked within their confines, and all had to come to terms with, and provide support for, larger structures of political authority. Yet Jewish civil society remained a world apart in mostly unwelcoming surroundings. After emancipation, however, urban and rural ghetto subcommunities lost their integral and functional status to become atavistic foils for modernity. Now, as Jews were enticed by liberal offers that promised inclusion in the wider world in exchange for a process of spatial, social, religious, and political dissolution, these bids were put on offer without the demand that Jews become Christians; but their terms reinforced the hostility latent in the Enlightenment to strong differences, parochial manners, and what were thought to be superstitious pat-

[59] Gellner, *Culture, Identity, and Politics*, 77.

terns of thought and behavior in conflict with modern cultural, national, and religious forms of identification and expression.

When Doblin asked, "Could I, or anyone else, return to this level?" he answered in the negative. The radical implications of the break between old and new in the specific situation of Jews, Gellner acutely notes, further distinguished the quality of their exit choices from those of other people who engaged with the Enlightenment. "The fact that the community to be abjured was a pariah one, endowed the decision with a moral ambiguity which it has never lost: was one choosing the truth and incidentally gaining an advantage, or pursuing an advantage and, as a means, changing a doctrinal cloak?"[60] To grasp this mix of practical and normative issues concerned with "loyalty," it is necessary to empathetically recapture the intentions of the actors. These are matters of culture, experience, and cognition outside the ken of the most lean and aseptic versions of rational choice theory.

The charged choices that confronted individual Jews after emancipation had collective results, for under the impact of their decisions the larger Jewish community and its institutions, now shorn of authority and enclosure, fragmented and diversified. If there no longer was a fixed status for the Jew, neither could there any longer be a singular fellowship within which this status was inscribed, or to which Jews might remain loyal. "Loyalty," of course, is the third of Hirschman's categories, but, as Barry rightly insists, it cannot be treated as being on the same plane of economistic strategic rationality as "exit" and "voice," because loyalty transcends utilitarian rationality; its solidarism is indivisible.[61] With respect to exit and voice, loyalty is a contextual variable. Preferences about staying and leaving, and about silence and noise, emerge only in specific political, economic, and cultural contexts that confer different weights to otherwise commensurable values. Moreover, the effects of loyalty vary with shifts in macroconditions. Thus, for example, under some conditions, loyalty to the Jewish community increased the appeal of Zionist exit, while in others it made voice, as opposed to this form of exit, more likely.

Loyalty, of course, can be directed to more than one target. In France, the birthplace of state emancipation, the Jews who had acquired citizenship with the French Revolution lost little time in making their appearance on the public stage, dedicating themselves to the country's universalist state. With an intense loyalty, they celebrated the Republic of Enlightenment. Paris replaced Jerusalem. Like the German Jews, their loyalty remained intact during the murderous conflicts that set these two countries against each other on several occasions. However, in France,

[60] Ibid., 77–78.

[61] Barry, review of *Exit, Voice and Loyalty*, 95–99.

where the state was hostile to autonomous groups and associations, the Jews did not make their voices heard as a specific group, which would have lacked all legitimacy. Moreover, French Jews as supporters of the emancipatory political order refrained from joining the country's Marxist or socialist organizations and parties. More often than not, they also paid no more than lip service to the ideals of Zionism.[62] The prevailing conception of citizenship presupposed the disappearance of any particularist dimension to public life, but it did tolerate continuing loyalties in the private sphere; thus even in the context of this strong state, integration did not imply outright assimilation.[63]

In less pretentious state settings, regardless of whether their political structures were centralized or organized on the model of a federation, confederation, or consociational democracy, as in Britain, the United States, and the Netherlands, the Jews once again displayed a profound loyalty outside the Jewish community, but more to the nation and its values than to the state that did not enjoy the same degree of preeminence. Jews also grouped together within organizations to make their voices heard in these quasi-polyarchical and relatively pluralistic democracies that were conducive to the creation of a diversity of civil society associations with a public purpose. In consequence, Jews in these countries nearly always rejected strategies of exit apart from the path toward individual social mobility in favor of voice conditioned by double-sided loyalties, which they understood as complementary; except for recent immigrants, they also turned their backs on the collective exit strategies of revolution at home or the achievement of a Zionist homeland in Palestine.[64] But nowhere can the particularities of exit or any other available strategy be understood without locating the networks of actors at the joining of Jews to the larger environment, including the institutional and

[62] See Pierre Birnbaum, *Les Fous de la République: Histoire des Juifs d'Etat, de Gambetta à Vichy* (Paris: Fayard, 1992).

[63] See Frances Malino and Bernard Wasserstein, eds., *The Jews in Modern France* (Waltham, Mass.: Brandeis University Press, 1985); Michael Graetz, *Les Juifs en France au 19è siècle: De la Révolution Française à l'Alliance Israélite universelle* (Paris: Le Seuil, 1989); Michel Abitbol, *Les deux terres promises* (Paris: Olivier Orban, 1989); and Pierre Birnbaum, ed., *Histoire politique des Juifs de France: Entre universalisme et particularisme* (Paris: Presses de la Fondation Nationale des Sciences Politiques, 1991).

[64] For Britain, see M. C. Salbstein, *The Admission of the Jews to Parliament: 1828–1860* (Rutherford, N.J.: Associated University Press, 1982); Stuart Cohen, *English Zionists and British Jews* (Princeton: Princeton University Press, 1982); Geoffrey Alderman, *The Jewish Community in British Politics* (Oxford: Clarendon Press, 1983); and Eugene Black, *The Social Politics of Anglo-Jewry, 1880–1920* (Oxford: Basil Blackwell, 1988); and David Feldman, *Englishmen and Jews: Social Relations and Political Culture, 1840–1914* (New Haven: Yale University Press, 1994). For the United States, see Daniel Elazar, *Community and Polity: The Organizational Dynamics of American Jewry* (Philadelphia: Jewish Publication Society, 1980).

normative configuration of national states, the degree of rigidity and closure of civil societies, and the qualities of the anti-Semitism Jews confronted. Some parts of the behavioral range—including Jewish self-deprecation, a return to tradition and conformism, or commitment to revolutionary ideals—were more characteristic in societies of extreme rigidity;[65] these orientations, in turn, further activated anti-Semitic reactions of hostility to the integration of the Jews, taking a variety of forms: sometimes through violent movements of mobilization and collective action, at others through individual rejection.

Indeed, alongside studies of emancipation, anti-Semitism as ideology and practice must also be considered comparatively.[66] To be sure, anti-Semitism everywhere in Europe during the long century of emancipation reflected common elements: the long-term refusal of Jews to disappear into Christendom, the problematic role Jews play in Christianity's grand narrative, and the anomalous status of Jews as a nation without a territory. Nevertheless, the particular forms of anti-Semitism proved widely disparate, in tandem with the specific qualities of the states Jews encountered as actual or potential citizens during their paths of emancipation.

We wish to be careful not to overstate our claim that Jewish strategies of exit, voice, and loyalty took on a widely varying significance and appeal in each country as a result of variations in political context, as did the mix of strategies and their relationships to each other; for how, in a focus on citizenship, liberal rights, and political incorporation could it be otherwise? Nonetheless, it is clear that as Jews managed to map and travel the pathways of emancipation, the nature of the state they confronted proved pivotal, shaping the character of anti-Semitism, the qualities of economic development, the contours of the class structure, the development of the public arena, and the constitution of civil society. As the essays below demonstrate, by casting the particular forms of emancipation, the type of state—its constitutionalism, claims to sovereignty, institutional ensemble, and normative vision of the good and the just—played a considerable role in the strategies adopted by the Jews themselves.[67]

[65] Isaac Deutscher, *The Non-Jewish Jew and Other Essays* (New York: Oxford University Press, 1968); Sander Gilman, *Jewish Self-Hatred* (Baltimore: Johns Hopkins University Press, 1986). For references to a more recent period, see also Judith Friedlander, *Vilna on the Seine: Jewish Intellectuals in France since 1968* (New Haven: Yale University Press, 1990). On these issues, see in particular Frankel and Zipperstein, *Assimilation and Community*.

[66] A vast body of literature exists on this subject. For useful aids and an overview, see Susan Cohen, ed., *Antisemitism: An Annotated Bibliography* (New York: Garland Publishing, 1987); and Shmuel Almog, ed., *Antisemitism through the Ages* (Oxford: Pergamon Press, 1988).

[67] For a similar perspective, see Peter Medding, "Toward a General Theory of Jewish Political Interest and Behavior," *Jewish Journal of Sociology* 2 (1977).

TWO

DUTCH JEWS IN A SEGMENTED SOCIETY*

Hans Daalder

THE NETHERLANDS historically represents the case of a highly pluralist society and, at least initially, consociational state building. At a time when many other European states developed as absolute monarchies, the Dutch Republic grew as a very loose confederacy, after a successful revolt on the basis of particularist interests. During a period of more than two centuries (from about 1579 to 1795), effective power continued to rest with individual provinces, and, within these provinces with the cities, and, to a lesser extent, representatives of the nobility.

There was a direct relation between regional diversity and religious pluralism. Although the Dutch Reformed Church was to attain a position of dominance at the time of the Dutch Republic, political offices at all levels being reserved to its adherents, Catholics remained at all times a very substantial minority of at least one-third of the total population. The southern provinces of Limburg and Brabant, which were conquered by the northern provinces only after the Counter-Reformation had reasserted the hold of the Roman Catholic Church there, were to remain homogeneously Catholic. But there also remained numerous Catholics in the Province of Holland (its rural areas still having a Catholic majority by 1650). In addition to the eventual majoritarian Dutch Reformed Cal-

*This chapter is very much a reworked version of an address originally given in Jerusalem, on 20 July 1975, on the occasion of the commemoration of the founding in 1275 of the city of Amsterdam and of the opening of its Portuguese Synagogue in 1675, under the auspices of the Institute for Research of Dutch Jewry of the Hebrew University, Jerusalem. Before it was published in *Acta Historiae Neerlandicae: Studies on the History of the Netherlands* (The Hague, 1978), it was subjected to extensive criticism, notably by Leo Fuks, Max H. Gans, Jozeph Michman, Dan Michman, Jan J. Woltjer, Theo van Tijn, Philip de Vries, and Val R. Lorwin. Their comments covered the entire spectrum of views on the place of Jews in Dutch society, from perspectives ranging from Orthodoxy to agnostic assimilation, from political Zionism to proletarian internationalism, and from any position in between. I tried to do as much justice to their subtle insights as the small amount of space in this chapter allows. Since this was written, a massive new volume has been published by Jozeph Michman, Hartog Beem, and Dan Michman, entitled *Pinkas: Geschiedenis van de Joodse Gemeenschap in Nederland* (Amsterdam, 1992).

vinists, there were small bodies of Lutherans, Mennonites, and later Remonstrants who split away from the Dutch Reformed Church during important theological and political conflicts in the early part of the seventeenth century. The Republic thus remained very much a society of mixed religion, characterized by an increasing degree of practical tolerance. Both institutional and social pluralism presented substantial freedoms for a variety of minorities. This was to attract a massive immigration of Huguenots and an increasing number of both Sephardi and Ashkenazi Jews.

Following the long period of the Dutch Republic, a unitary state was established in the wake of conquest by French troops in 1795.[1] This chapter will generally focus on events since then. But one should realize that pluralism was very much retained in the new unitary state, which was quite far from being a Jacobin construct. For almost a century after 1795, the Netherlands generally remained a stagnant and very oligarchical society. Although a parliamentary system of government arrived comparatively early (1848), its *pays légal* consisted of at most some 10 percent of the people until 1888. Religious pluralism persisted and possibly became even more pronounced. Conflicts within the once-dominant Dutch Reformed Church about dogma and structure intensified. Protestant dissenters assumed a greater social importance. Catholics slowly developed from a barely tolerated minority with a clear sense of inferiority toward the Calvinists into a better-organized and somewhat more self-confident "pillar" of Dutch society. Political conflicts of the nineteenth and the first part of the twentieth century centered to a considerable extent on the relation between the state and the various religious bodies, notably on the control of education. A powerful majority coalition of Calvinists and Catholics eventually broke the somewhat tenuous hold Liberals exercised on Dutch society in the latter part of the nineteenth century and ensured far-reaching subcultural autonomy. Later, the Socialists followed suit with the establishment of an integrated subculture of their own. But since until very recently they did not succeed in winning over large sections of the Calvinist and Catholic working class, the Dutch Socialists remained numerically weaker than almost any comparable European Socialist movement. The coexistence of three powerfully organized "segments" of Calvinists, Catholics, and Socialists left the Liberals and their like perforce relatively weak after 1900. Liberals had a recognized heritage and a secure place in policy making. They exercised an intellectual influence well beyond their numbers. But whenever heads were counted, Liberals were seen to be numerically weak. By 1930 Dutch

[1] For an analysis of developments in the Netherlands, see Hans Daalder, "The Netherlands: Opposition in a Segmented Society," in Robert A. Dahl, ed., *Political Oppositions in Western Democracies* (New Haven, 1966), 188–236.

society had thus developed into what is called a *verzuilde samenleving,* best translated as a "segmented society."[2]

The particular pattern of institutional and social relations in the Netherlands—a system of coexisting, recognized minorities—was to affect the manner of Jewish emancipation to a considerable degree. After a short description of the initial settlement of Jews in the Dutch Republic, the analysis will concentrate on this question: how did Dutch Jewry fare after the establishment of the unitary state in 1795, in processes of modernization, democratization, and *verzuiling,* or segmentation?

The chapter consciously leaves out events after 1940, when the overwhelming part of Dutch Jewry was deported and destroyed. But the analysis of developments until the German occupation cannot escape our knowledge of later events. The initiative for the destruction may have come at gunpoint from outside the Dutch borders, but we now know that this mass murder was made possible only through the partial, if generally reluctant, assistance—or at a minimum the passive toleration—on the part of many Dutch individuals and institutions, Jewish and non-Jewish alike.[3]

Post-1945 historiography tends to emphasize elements not found equally in pre-1940 writings. First, there is a definite nostalgic tone, found in such different writings as Mozes Gans's magnum opus, the *Memorbook,*[4] and the reminiscences of isolated survivors of the Jewish Quarter of Amsterdam, of which the many books by Meijer Sluyser provide an outstanding example.[5]

Second, there is in some writings a strong denunciatory element. These may be further divided into at least three categories: (1) there is the attack along class lines that seeks to "explain" pre-1940 Jewry, as well as its

[2] A number of general articles on "segmented societies" have conveniently been brought together in Kenneth D. McRae, ed., *Consociational Democracy: Political Accommodation in Segmented Societies,* The Carlton Library, vol. 79 (Toronto, 1974).

[3] Cf. Abel J. Herzberg, "Kroniek der Jodenvervolging," in Johan J. van Bolhuis et al., eds., *Onderdrukking en Verzet* (Amsterdam, 1949–54), 3:5–255; Jaques Presser, *Ondergang: De vervolging en verdelging van het Nederlandse Jodendom, 1940–1945,* 2 vols. (The Hague, 1965); in English, abridged, Jacob Presser, *Ashes in the Wind: The Destruction of Dutch Jewry* (London, 1968); Louis de Jong, *Het Koninkrijk der Nederlanden in de Tweede Wereldoorlog,* vols. 1–13 (The Hague, 1969–87).

[4] I am heavily indebted to the magnificent work by Mozes H. Gans, *Memorbook: Pictorial History of Dutch Jewry from the Renaissance to 1940* (Baarn, 1977); this is an English translation of the original Dutch edition, *Memorboek: Platenatlas van het leven der Joden in Nederland van de Middeleeuwen tot 1940* (Baarn, 1971).

[5] Meijer Sluyser wrote a series of reminiscences: *Als de dag van gisteren; Er groeit gras in de Weesperstraat; Hun lach klinkt van zover; Voordat ik het vergeet;* and *De wereld is rond, maar mijn zolen zijn plat* (Amsterdam, n.d.); for an anthology, drawn from these books, see Martin van Amerongen, *Meijer Sluyser, voordat hij het vergat* (Amsterdam, 1973).

destruction, in terms of the victimization of the poor and the proletariat by the egoism of an irresponsible Jewish bourgeoisie; (2) there are the strictures from a Zionist perspective that castigates the lack of realism of Dutch Jews who forgot—or tried to forget—their Jewish identity, let alone their special link to Jews elsewhere, or even worse, who denied to their eventual peril the inescapable momentum of anti-Semitism; (3) finally, there is a denunciatory attack from a religious perspective, which aims at the exposure of the presumed "empty" and "formalistic" qualities of much of Jewish life in nineteenth- and twentieth-century Holland, and which implicitly accuses Jewish authorities and followers alike of not living up to the tasks that the commandments of faith and history prescribed.

Third, there has been after 1945 a renewed debate on the character of Jewish-Gentile relations in the Netherlands. In the perspective of prewar times it was easy to visualize mutual relations in terms of the desirable emancipation of Jews, which for many could be identical with assimilation—if one might use the latter term to characterize the development of Jews who lived in Holland into Dutchmen of Jewish origin, if no longer of clear Jewish faith. There was in prewar Holland an air of conscious satisfaction about the place of Jews in Dutch society, almost to the point of self-congratulation. Such a view is no longer tenable. We now know that whatever their desires, Jews and non-Jews were not alike when facing the new Haman, notwithstanding the unprecedented strikes of February 1941 when Jews and non-Jews joined in one massive protest against the beginnings of pogromlike actions in Amsterdam.[6] In the end, even Jews who had practically forgotten their Jewishness—however defined—were to suffer a fate far different from any Gentile, however anti-Semitic, philo-Semitic, or indifferent to Jews the latter might be.

Having thus lost, I trust, any pristine sense of emotional detachment, let us try to reconstruct the developments of Dutch Jewry from the days of their initial settlement in the Netherlands around 1600 until 1940, by which time what began as an alien community living in the Netherlands had transformed itself into a disparate group of Jewish Dutchmen, with little affinity to either one another or to world Jewry.

Jews under the Dutch Republic

Sephardi Jews came to the Netherlands first, following the conquest of Portugal in 1580 and the seizure by Spanish troops of Antwerp in 1585. Many of them were *Cristaos novos,* Jews who had been forced to become

[6] Ben A. Sijes, *De Februaristaking, 24–25 februari 1941* (The Hague, 1954).

Catholics and were to return to the Jewish faith once they felt secure from the Inquisition. There were many leading international merchants among them, who contributed substantially to economic development in the Republic. Some of them attained positions of high economic and intellectual prestige, entertaining close contacts with both the Orange *stadhouders* and ruling city merchants. The construction of the large Portuguese Synagogue in Amsterdam, which was inaugurated in 1675 in the presence of the city mayor and many other dignitaries, was to symbolize the significant status of Sephardi Jews and to mark the place of Amsterdam as one of the major cities of Jewish settlement in western Europe.[7]

Ashkenazi Jews came to the Republic only a few decades after the Sephardim, first from Germany, soon also from Poland and other parts of eastern Europe. They established their own religious community in Amsterdam in 1635 and soon overwhelmed the Sephardim in numbers. But the Ashkenazim enjoyed far less social prestige than the Sephardim. Almost all Ashkenazim were very poor. But in the latter days of the Republic this was also to become increasingly true for many Sephardim.

Given the highly decentralized structure of the Dutch Republic, both the pattern of Jewish settlement and the legal and social conditions for Jews showed great diversity from one town to another. Some general rules applied. Thus, the Union of Utrecht of 1579, which ex post facto became the basic document underlying the constitution of the Dutch Republic, had banned any form of inquisition. No stigmatizing Jewish insignia were allowed. There was no *numerus clausus* on the number of Jews admitted or any restriction on their marrying within their own religious community. Moreover, a decree of the Estates-General of 1657 was to give resident Jews the status of Dutch subjects on a par with any other Dutchman in relations to foreign states or trading partners. But for the rest, everything depended on local magistrates. Some towns (like Utrecht and Deventer) excluded Jews until 1795 (although Utrecht made one exception for a rabbi teaching Hebrew at a university in the early eighteenth century). Amsterdam allowed free entry to poor and rich Jews alike but excluded them from citizenship. Other towns offered more generous rights. An attempt to establish a special statute on Jews by the Estates-General came to nought, but Amsterdam established a special statute of its own in 1616. It forbade to "those [males] of the Jewish Nation" not only marriage, but any relationship with Christian women on penalty of enforced banning. Jews were to behave modestly and to refrain from criticism or any possible calumny of the Christian faith. They should not attempt to convert Christians to Judaism. A special oath

[7] See Renate G. Fuks-Mansfeld, *De Sefardim in Amsterdam tot 1795: Aspecten van de ontwikkeling van een Joodse minderheid in een Hollandse stad* (Ph.D. diss., Leiden University, 1989).

was established that Jews were to use in contacts with authorities, but that also allowed them to enter on a par with others before law courts. Such special regulations were applied with considerable laxity, however, and in practice considerable freedom existed. Perhaps the greatest limitation was the exclusion of Jews from the guilds, which effectively barred them from a large number of occupations. The two religious communities were to acquire recognition as authoritative corporate authorities under their own formal leaders who had substantial powers in matters of finance, morality, and even public order. In practice, there was clear autonomy and effective freedom of religion.

When the Dutch Republic succumbed in 1795, a first national census was taken in preparation of the holding of elections. At the time, some thirty thousand Jews were registered as living in the Netherlands. More than twenty thousand of these lived in Amsterdam, of whom only a little more than three thousand belonged to the Sephardi community. The great disparity in numbers between the two communities was to persist and grow stronger. In 1930, in the last official census taken before the German occupation in the Netherlands, the Sephardim numbered 5,194, the Ashkenazim 106,723.[8]

1796 and After

A framework for national decisions on the place of Jews in Dutch society was established after 1795 when, following the invasion in that year by French revolutionary troops, a unitary state came about, and church and state became increasingly separated. Legal emancipation of Dutch Jews was marked by the decree of 2 September 1796 passed by the first National Assembly, which granted Jews full civic rights on a parity with any other Dutch subject. The decree was the high mark of a process of considerable controversy, among the powers of the day as well as among Jews at the time. The initiative for new legislation came after 1795 from a new revolutionary "patriotic" club, Felix Libertate. Though Jewish in origin, this club had consciously included Christians as members. It consisted largely of members of the upper bourgeoisie who lived according

[8] Cf. Emanuel Boekman, *Demografie van de Joden in Nederland* (Amsterdam, 1936), 16–17. In 1941 the German authorities imposed a self-registration of residents in the Netherlands by anyone who had at least one Jewish grandparent. This resulted in the following numbers: of Dutch nationality, somewhat over four thousand Sephardi and 114,000 Ashkenazi *Volljude;* some thirteen thousand half-Jews and somewhat over four thousand quarter-Jews; sixteen thousand German Jews (in overwhelming numbers refugees after 1933); and eight thousand Jews of another or no nationality. Figures are taken from Louis de Jong, *Het Koninkrijk der Nederlanden in de Tweede Wereldoorlog* (The Hague, 1974), 5:495–96.

to the philosophy of the Enlightenment, being affected notably by the lessons of Moses Mendelssohn. The new club did not find an easy reception: it was excluded from the National Assembly of Patriot Societies, at the specific bidding of rival Amsterdam patriot clubs, among others. In a number of Dutch communities, Jews were admitted to vote for national and provincial elections and to serve in the guards. But the municipal administration of Amsterdam counted Jewish votes on a separate list just in case they might be declared invalid. Amsterdam also banned Jews from voting in its elections for the new town council. It did not admit Jews to service in its armed guards. Jews were barred from attendance at the Patriotic quarter meetings.

Six members of Felix Libertate petitioned the newly elected National Assembly to recognize Jews as full Dutch citizens. The assembly appointed a special committee of inquiry and later held a seven-day debate on its report. The debates, in which a very large number of representatives took part, have been extensively analyzed, albeit from a different perspective, by Salvador E. Bloemgarten in an article published in *Studia Rosenthaliana,* and by Menachem E. Bolle in his 1960 doctoral dissertation.[9] A focal point of the debate was the question as to whether civil rights for Jews were a natural concomitant of the Declaration of Human Rights that had been promulgated earlier—if so, civil rights were an inherent individual right to which every Jew was as much entitled as any other individual Dutchman—or whether the issue was really that of the collective emancipation of the Jewish "nations" which for centuries had enjoyed a recognized corporate life in the Dutch Republic. If arguments in favor of emancipation on an individualistic basis sat easily with the "enlightened" members of Felix Libertate, they were resisted, often bitterly, by at least three groups: (1) those who continued to regard the Jews as an alien enclave in Dutch society; (2) the *parnassim,* the leaders of the Jewish communities (*kehillot*), and the more Orthodox segments of the Jewish "nations" who generally wished to retain their "autonomy"; and (3) a number of Dutch Federalists who unlike the Unitarian Patriots did not want the imposition of one central, national policy on once-autonomous town corporations. The decree that allotted Jews full civil rights was eventually voted unanimously, after a procedural move to stall the decision had been defeated 45–24. The majority of Amsterdam members in the National Assembly had resisted the early issue of the decree.

[9] Salvador E. Bloemgarten, "De Amsterdamse Joden gedurende de eerste jaren van de Bataafse Republiek, 1795–1798," *Studia Rosenthaliana,* 1,1 (Amsterdam, 1967), 66–96; 1,2 (1967), 45–70; 2,1 (1968), 42–65; Menachem E. Bolle, *De opheffing van de autonomie der Kehilloth (Joodse gemeenten) in Nederland, 1796* (Ph.D. diss., University of Amsterdam, 1960). For a very critical review of this work cf. Salvador E. Bloemgarten, *Studia Rosenthaliana,* 3,1 (1969):128–34.

Many Catholics, on the other hand, who had also suffered from discrimination at the time of the Republic, voted in favor.[10]

How to assess the importance of the 1796 decree? It enfranchised Dutch Jews and gave them in principle access to public office. It formally abolished the bar against Jews, which virtually all existing guilds had traditionally maintained. The guilds themselves were abolished some time afterward. Hence Jews obtained in principle, though not always in practice, easier access to more varied employment. The decree did away with a number of other discriminatory measures, such as the practice of letting Jewish couples wait at the town hall until all marriages of Gentiles had been first performed. It did away with special fees levied on Jews as Jews (although Friesland continued to levy such a tax until 1807).[11] It made Jews eligible for general poor-law relief and freed them at least in theory from the authority of their own *parnassim*: it did away with the coordinate powers that the *parnassim* had enjoyed together with the town authorities in matters of public order and that had extended deeply into worldly matters as well as in the religious sphere. It freed Jews from a number of oppressive communal monopolies, such as that of the Ashkenazi and Sephardi meat halls and public baths. It lessened somewhat the powers of the *parnassim* to lay oppressive taxes on "forced" marriages or on funerals.

Against such "emancipatory" effects, a number of less positive developments can be noted. The decree represented a fundamental attack on the existing structures of the two autonomous Jewish "nations." It has been argued, with some force, that the corporate pluralism of the Dutch Republic made the existence of independent Jewish communities relatively secure, although it presupposed and confirmed their secondary status. Would tolerance automatically increase, now that Jews had become equal citizens, although they still might remain aliens for generations?[12]

The "New Order" (and not least the members of Felix Libertate who acted as an active and influential pressure group) deliberately attempted to extinguish elements of specific Jewishness. For a time, the emancipated Jews formed a separate community (*kehillah*), entitled Adat Yeshurun. Some of the modern Jews began to speak with conviction of the blessings

[10] Ivo Schöffer has argued forcefully that the relatively tranquil existence of Jewish communities in the Netherlands was a function of the traditional pluralism of Dutch society. See Ivo Schöffer, "The Jews in the Netherlands: The Position of a Minority through Three Centuries," *Studia Rosenthaliana* 15 (1981):85–100.

[11] Raphael Mahler, *A History of Modern Jewry, 1780–1815* (London, 1971), 99.

[12] On continuing anti-Jewish discrimination after 1796, see Jozeph Michman, "Gothische torens op een Corinthisch gebouw," *Tijdschrift voor Geschiedenis* 89 (Groningen, 1976), 493–517.

the Supreme Being bestowed on mankind instead of evoking the God of Israel. They tried to be like other Dutchmen as much as possible, and they treasured signs of acceptance of Jews into what was basically a Christian world. The town authorities maintained their ban on small synagogue services (*minyanin*) and on the erection of holiday tabernacles (*sukkot*) on public streets, and they proscribed the benediction of the new moon. Dignitaries of the various synagogues, like Catholic clergy, should not wear their official clothing outside synagogue buildings. Mixed marriages between Jews and gentiles were legalized and even glorified.

Paradoxically, the presumed "privatization" of religion—henceforth regarded as an individual, and not a collective matter—was to lead not to less, but to greater interference by the public authorities with organized religion. Thus, a number of new regulations were imposed—on all religious communities—by Napoleon's brother, Louis Napoleon, by Napoleon himself after 1810, and by King William I of Orange after 1813, who represented a clear "Josephist" attitude in religious matters.

For the Jewish communities this led in 1808 to the establishment of a Supreme Consistory. After the French annexation of 1810, the Ashkenazi and Sephardi communities were brought together under one church organization. According to new regulations, a chief rabbi should now either be Dutch-born, or have at least six years' of residence in the Netherlands before appointment. The government encouraged the translation of the Bible into Dutch and insisted on religious and other instruction in the national language. In 1815 the king further appropriated a number of control powers, in such matters as the issue of Church regulations and the drawing up of the budget. He also appropriated the right to cast a decisive vote on the appointment of rabbis if there were a tie in voting. All official correspondence and minutes, and all readings of official announcements in the synagogues, should henceforth be in Dutch only. A chief rabbi, a sexton (*shammash*) and a cantor (*chazzan*) should be familiar with the Dutch language, albeit in a decreasing order: the chief rabbi should speak, read, and write Dutch, a shammash should be able to read and write, a chazzan need only be able to read the language. In 1827 an official royal decree promised awards for the best translation into Dutch of sermons and teaching material.

Such measures were symptomatic of the prevailing climate of a belated Enlightenment, rather than of actual religious practices. Until 1842, the Portuguese Synagogue held its proceedings mainly in Portuguese. Not until the 1850s did Yiddish fully disappear from Jewish schools. As late as 1886 a number of older members of the synagogue in Leeuwarden left in anger when it was decided to drop the use of Yiddish. But in the long run these reforms imposed from above provided the framework for the eventual assimilation of the Jewish communities into Dutch society—through their own religious institutions and practices, as much as through other public agencies.

The Mass of Dutch Jewry: Some Sociological Data

Before we turn to a more detailed consideration of these processes, however, greater attention should be paid to the great mass of Dutch Jewry.[13] One should not forget that the developments just described initially affected mainly the highest levels of the Dutch Jewish communities. They barely touched the life of the great mass of Dutch Jews. The most glaring characteristic of Dutch Jewry had traditionally been their extreme poverty, even when compared to that of other poor. If the "French" period from 1795 to 1813 helped to create an institutional framework for future emancipation, it also led to a further impoverishment of an already very poor community. Even the better-off (including many Portuguese Jews) lost much of their capital by the abolition of the United East India Company, by Napoleon's introduction of the Continental System, and by the reduction of the national debt. Alms statistics reveal that poverty among Jews lasted a very long time. In 1799 more than 80 percent of Ashkenazi Jews and 54 percent of Sephardi Jews in Amsterdam received support (mainly for food and fuel), and in 1859 this figure was still as high as 62 percent for the Sephardim and 53 percent for the Ashkenazim. Poorer leaders also had fewer means with which to practice traditional philanthropy.[14]

Further impoverishment of the Amsterdam Jews was probably the chief reason for a massive exodus of Jews from Amsterdam, which lost in the first decades of the nineteenth century as much as a quarter of the Ashkenazim, and 15 percent of the Sephardim.[15] They went in search of alternative employment in the provinces where they were now legally free to settle. For a while, therefore, the Mediene (the provinces) assumed an increasing importance over Mokum (Amsterdam). This process was reversed again after the 1850s when Jews increasingly migrated back to the western part of the country.

And even then, change was only very slow to come. It came mainly as a

[13] Cf. Jacob P. Kruijt, "Het Jodendom in de Nederlandse samenleving," in Hendrik J. Pos, ed., *Anti-Semitisme en Jodendom* (Arnhem, 1939), 190–227; Carolus Reijnders, *Van "Joodsche Natiën" tot Joodse Nederlanders: Een Onderzoek naar Ghettoverschijnselen tussen 1600 en 1942* (Amsterdam, 1969).

[14] Salomon Kleerekoper, "Het Joodse proletariaat in het Amsterdam van de 19e eeuw," *Studia Rosenthaliana,* 1,1 (1967):97–108; 2,2 (1968), 71–84.

[15] Cf. Reijnders, "*Joodsche Natiën.*"

result of the multiplier effects of new developments in diamond manufacturing, cigar making, and to a lesser extent in the clothing industry. If these developments eventually made for greater social mobility—what prominent Dutch Jew was not the son or grandson of a former diamond worker?—and if all this resulted in increasing diversification of employment, there was no escape from the basic fact about Dutch Jewry: the great majority remained poor. Within the Jewish community social distances between the relatively rich (who generally were not very rich themselves) and the unmistakably poor remained vast.[16]

A look at demographic figures—the subject of a detailed study by a prominent Amsterdam alderman in the 1930s, E. Boekman[17]—reveals a number of further characteristics about Dutch Jews before 1940. There was a slight temporary increase in the percentage share of Jews in Dutch society through the immigration of Polish and Russian Jews in the 1870s and 1880s. There was a very rapid urbanization of Jews who left the provinces in disproportionate numbers, largely again for Amsterdam. There was a quick fall in the Jewish birthrate so that the Jewish community was graying strongly and decreased after 1890 in relation to the fast-growing Dutch population as a whole. There was a strong loss in the earlier distinctiveness of the Sephardi and Ashkenazi communities who increasingly intermarried. There was an increase also in mixed marriages between Jews and non-Jews, notably in the provinces; there was also a growing reluctance on the part of persons of Jewish descent to identify themselves with the Jewish religion at census time.[18]

Data on the domicile of Dutch Jews further showed a large-scale trek away from the former Jewish quarter in Amsterdam to neighboring and other districts in the town: as a result the old Jodenhoek included only 18 percent of Amsterdam Jews in 1930.[19] This was the result partly of the demolition of the worst slum areas like Marken and Uilenburg. One of the districts cleared away was the Rode Leeuwengang, the alley from which the parents of Samuel Gompers had emigrated shortly before the birth in London of the future leader of the American Federation of Labor.[20] There was also a trek to the suburbs of Amsterdam, away from the

[16] Cf. Theo van Tijn, *De maatschappelijke ontwikkeling van de hoofdstad van de jaren '50 der vorige eeuw, tot 1867* (Amsterdam, 1965) 125ff.; Kleerekoper, "Joodse proletariaat 19e eeuw," 98ff.

[17] Boekman, *Demografie.*

[18] The percentage of Ashkenazi Jews of the total Dutch population rose from 1.81 percent of the population in 1849 to a high of 2.04 percent in 1889. Since then, the percentage steadily dropped to 1.34 percent in 1930 as a result of relatively low birthrate on the one hand and a turn away from church membership to agnosticism on the other. See ibid., 17.

[19] Kruijt, "Jodendom," 205ff.

[20] Cf. Gans, *Memorbook,* 668–69. Gompers was born in London in 1850.

core of the town. If slum clearance did away with some of the most unsanitary housing conditions in Dutch history, it also destroyed some of the intimacy and the face-to-face relationships that had characterized traditional Jewish life in Amsterdam. The Socialist leader of the Amsterdam diamond workers, Henri Polak, was to write unexpectedly lyrical reminiscences about life in the ghetto—ending with his famous nostalgic words: "En toch, en toch!" (And yet! And yet!)[21] And the demolition of part of the old Jewish quarter of Amsterdam was to inspire Jacob Israel de Haan to one of his most beautiful poems:

> Here, where for centuries we have dwelled,
> Humbly engaged in petty trade,
> Knowing bright moments and long hours of shade,
> The breaker's axe is hard at work.
> Many who have rarely stepped outside,
> Must wander now without a guide,
> While children, pale-faced, sad and wan,
> Revive like flowers in the sun.
> Life carries on, an ancient ward's no more.
> Does it spell freedom from old chains?
> Or will dilution bring new pains?[22]

The Declining Hold of the Religious Communities

By the middle of the nineteenth century, the religious organizations of Dutch Jewry were in some disarray. From 1838 to 1874, and again from 1911 to 1916, the Ashkenazim had no chief rabbi, and the Sephardi community had none from 1822 to 1900. In 1848, a change in the constitution brought a definite separation of Church and State. Soon afterward the government invited the Jewish communities to revise their statutes so as to bring them into line with the new constitutional situation. There followed a farcical period of twenty years' bickering and disagreement among the different kehillot, which was brought to an end only by direct government pressure in 1870. The two main divisive issues were (1) whether to retain or rescind the government-imposed unity between the Portuguese and the Ashkenazi communities—a matter finally resolved by a return to the organizational independence of each as had existed earlier; and (2) the particular place of Amsterdam Jews in the remaining religious organization. Amsterdam finally got its way: even though the

[21] Henri Polak, cited in ibid., 639ff.

[22] Jacob Israel de Haan, 1916, on the occasion of the exhibition "The Vanishing Ghetto," quoted in ibid., 637. Translated into English by Arnold J. Pomerans.

organization of the Ashkenazi Nederlands Israelitisch Kerkgenootschap (Netherlands Israelite Church Community) was to be built up from representatives of different kehillot, its Permanent Executive Committee was to consist of—and to be chosen by—Amsterdam Jews, and by them alone.[23]

In 1862 J. H. Dünner became rector of the Netherlands Jewish Seminary, and in 1874 he was also appointed chief rabbi of Amsterdam. Dünner's influence was massive and lasting. He built the seminary into a true training institute for Dutch rabbis—a group described in detail and with great love and piety by Gans in his *Memorbook*.[24] According to many observers, Dünner "saved" the religious institutions of Dutch Jewry. But in retrospect, his role has also come in for considerable criticism, in at least three directions. He has been accused of turning the seminary too much into a semi-university, by demanding a severe training in classics on a par with Jewish training, leading one biased former pupil to remark that it was turning out "synthetic rabbis: 50 percent Talmud, 50 percent classics."[25] It is alleged, second, that Dünner severed Dutch Jewry from the great international centers of Jewish learning, by not recognizing religious training obtained elsewhere and by being particularly severe on the use of Yiddish. And third, his influence is thought to have made effective communion between most members of the intellectual rabbinate and the mass of poor Jews more difficult, so that the religious organizations and institutions were unable to stem the large drift away of many of the ordinary one-time believers. Neighborhood and synagogues of small associations (*chevra shuls*) did something to stem this tide. Most Jews, notably those in Amsterdam, retained some minimal emotional ties with religious institutions, but then of the kind of the man who said: "I am a Dutchman of the Jewish faith, who does not care about the Jewish faith." If circumcision and religious marriages and funerals were kept up, the observance of the sabbath or dietary laws declined rapidly.

There were other clear signs of loosening bonds. Counts of seats and of actual attendance of services revealed in both 1880 and in 1935 a massive disproportionality between nominal religious membership and actual practice. There were some five thousand seats in Amsterdam synagogues in 1880, and some three thousand in 1935, in either case sufficient for fewer than 10 percent of Amsterdam Jewry only. Even so, already in 1880 some one thousand or more seats usually remained

[23] Abraham S. Rijxman, *A. C. Wertheim, 1832–1897: Een bijdrage tot zijn levenssgeschiedenis* (Amsterdam, 1961), 97–98; Isaac Lipschits, *Honderd jaar NIW: het Nieuw Israëlitisch Weekblad, 1865–1965* (Amsterdam, 1966), 90ff.

[24] Gans, *Memorbook*, 370–77.

[25] Jacob Meijer, *Hoge hoeden, lage standaarden: De Nederlandse Joden tussen 1933 en 1940* (Baarn, 1969), 27; cf. Rijxman, *Wertheim*, 92ff., 227ff.

empty on the sabbath.[26] There was also a sharp decline in Jewish instruction.[27] In the beginning of the nineteenth century there had been a number of (admittedly poor) private Jewish schools or teachers, and even some publicly financed Jewish schools. These disappeared rapidly after 1857 when Jewish children flocked massively to the government schools (even though in the phraseology of the Education Act these were to educate children to "Christian and social virtues"). At a time when Catholics and Calvinists began to rebel against these government schools, demanding full financial support for separate denominational schools of their own, Jews on the whole embraced the public schools with alacrity. Only a few isolated voices called for attempts to establish Jewish denominational schools on a par with Catholics and Calvinists, including J. H. Dünner in his later life and also the Portuguese chief rabbi, I. de Juda Palache. Although a few Jewish schools were established, most vested interests in the Jewish communities went against this trend. Only in 1939 did a minority report on the schools issue raise the banner for a massive expansion of separate Jewish schools—much too late and too little to turn the tide of mass alienation.[28] Some attempt was made to fill the gap by the organization of special Jewish schools, held on Sundays or after school time. But these were often of low quality, and they were very poorly attended.

Until as late as the early 1930s, the existing religious organizations did prove able to resist the establishment of separate Reform communities.[29] This was partly due to a curious *mariage de raison* between the Orthodox and leading liberal elements. It was the very liberal president of the Ashkenazi *Kerkgenootschap,* A. C. Wertheim (1832–97), who at a critical moment in 1897 prevented the ousting of an Orthodox majority from the governing boards of the Amsterdam community.[30] He set an example that was followed later by many leaders, such as Abraham Asscher, who occupied positions of authority in the religious governing bodies, notwithstanding the fact that they had themselves little actual identification with traditional religion in private life. Thus official Jewry was both

[26] Meijer, *Hoge hoeden,* 42 ff.; cf. also Kruijt, "Jodendom," 222–23.

[27] Jozeph Michman, who was himself the son of a teacher at a Jewish school, holds that the dominant liberal Jewish leaders in the Netherlands put charity before education in expressing their Jewish identity; cf. his contribution, "The Netherlands," in *Encyclopaedia Judaica* (Jerusalem, 1971), 12:983. On Jewish schools, see also Dan Michman, *Joods onderwijs in Nederland, 1616–1905: Geschiedenis samengesteld ter ere van de opening van nieuwe gebouwen van de Stichting Joodse Scholengemeenschap* (Amsterdam, 1973).

[28] Meijer, *Hoge hoeden,* 80–81.

[29] But see Dan Michman, *Het Liberale Jodendom in Nederland 1929–1943* (Amsterdam, 1988).

[30] Cf. Rijxman, *Wertheim,* 226.

liberal and supportive of orthodoxy in official Jewish life, and in most cases very definitely bourgeois—the work of some individual rabbis notwithstanding.[31]

Jews in Dutch Political and Social Life

What place did Jews attain in Dutch political life? Immediately after 1796 there were some seemingly remarkable breakthroughs. Some historians claim that the first two Jews elected to any national assembly in western European countries were H. L. Bromet and H. de H. Lemon, who became members of the Second National Assembly of the Batavian Republic in 1797. Twice a Jew became a member of the Amsterdam town council in 1798, but not for long. There was the remarkable career of Jonas Daniel Meyer, whose name is inextricably bound to a well-known Amsterdam square—now practically destroyed by new traffic provisions—near the large Sephardi and Ashkenazi synagogues. At sixteen a doctor of Leiden University, Meyer was admitted in 1796 as barrister to the Court of Holland. He became a leading counselor to both Louis Napoleon and King William I. Perhaps the most interesting of his many appointments was that of secretary to the committee that drafted the Constitution of 1815. This committee consisted of twelve Protestants and twelve Catholics. The King gave it a Jewish secretary. In the nineteenth century the law[32] provided employment to numerous other prominent Jewish lawyers, such as A. de Pinto, who became Crown Counsel (*Landsadvocaat*). There were two famous dynasties of jurists: the Asser family, beginning with Mozes Salomon Asser (who had been one of the founding members of Felix Libertate) and ending with Tobias Asser, who won the Nobel Prize and became an apostate, and the Van Nierop family. Typically, the only two professing Jews who became cabinet ministers before 1940 were ministers of justice, and had it not been for their own refusal two others might have served in the same office. L. E. Visser was a well-known Jewish president of the Supreme Court, from which he was

[31] One might offer the hypothesis that the somewhat official character of the Jewish religion under liberal influence in the Netherlands, and the absence of strong sectarian conflicts within the Jewish community, may have been factors in alienating the Jewish proletariat from all religion. For a parallel analysis explaining the early success of Socialist propaganda in East Groningen in the light of the dominance of liberal Church leaders in the Dutch Reformed Church, which, unlike a more orthodox pietistic Calvinism in other parts of the same province, had offered no solace to a starving proletariat, see Evert W. Hofstee, *Het Oldambt* (Groningen, 1937).

[32] Cf. Benjamin M. Telders, "De Joodse geest en het recht," in Pos, *Anti-Semitisme,* 107–29.

dismissed during the German occupation. (After 1945 another two Jewish cabinet ministers, including the later burgomaster of Amsterdam, Ivo Samkalden, were to serve as ministers of justice.)

On the basis of a Leiden University computer file of all members of the Dutch parliament,[33] one can arrive at a clear picture of the successive election of Jewish deputies, first as Liberals—"uniting Thora and Thorbecke," as the phrase went in those days (Johan Rudolf Thorbecke being the leading constitutional Liberal of the third-quarter of the nineteenth century)—then as Radicals, then as Socialists. Out of 100 members composing the Dutch Lower House in 1940, eight were of Jewish descent (four Socialists, two Radicals, one Liberal, one Communist). At the same time, the computer file also exposes anew the sensitive problem of whom to define as Jews. What about agnostics? What about apostates? If of some 1,600 members of parliament in the file, we located thirty Jews—three sons of a rabbi, one of a shammash, one of a ritual slaughterer (*shochet*)—we know of at least another twenty politicians of Jewish descent not registered as Jewish (including Samkalden, just mentioned, and Ed van Thijn, leader of the Socialist Group in parliament, a one-time minister of the interior, and, like Samkalden, later mayor of Amsterdam).

Should one conclude from this that there was something of a bar against professing Jews in Dutch politics? Some symptoms might be adduced in evidence. How often did one not encounter the view that Jews should not seek public office, lest they expose themselves to anti-Semitism? In 1933, that eminent example of the Dutch Yellow Press, *De Telegraaf,* condemned the fact that four Jewish aldermen were simultaneously holding office in Amsterdam (although they represented different political parties). Jews were very definitely underrepresented in numerous public offices: few if any Jews were ever appointed mayor of a local community before 1940, and not a single Jew was a prosecutor in that year, to take only two examples.[34]

We can expand this statement further, to other parts of society. Even in the professions that have often attracted prominent Jews, such as law, medicine, or journalism, Jews never surpassed the 5 percent figure. Marx's famous, and infamous, anti-Semitic description of Amsterdam *haute finance*—which he described as better in finding their way about

[33] A scanning of the Leiden computerized biographical file of over 1,600 members of Parliament since 1848 finds eleven Liberals, six Radicals, ten Socialists, two Communists, and one dissident Socialist. This number could probably be doubled if one were to include those who are known to be of Jewish descent, but who no longer considered themselves to belong to either of the two Jewish religious communities.

[34] Henri Polak, *Het wetenschappelijk anti-semitisme: Weerlegging en vertoog* (n.p., n.d.); idem, in *Volksblad voor Gelderland* (27 December 1938), quoted in Kruijt, "Jodendom," 206ff.

other people's cash than the smartest highwayman in the Abruzzi[35]—was far off the mark, even in his day. In the 1930s there were some small Jewish banks. Two larger Dutch banks had one or two Jewish directors. But Jews were absent from the board of all other large banks. Not a single Jew even worked in the Bank of the Netherlands. Jews found absolute bars against them in such worlds as insurance or shipping. Even in the universities, the number of Jewish professors was far from numerous, with the possible exception of the law faculties.

Against such facts one might pose a long list of successful apostates in Dutch society: Marx's uncle, Lion Philips, who was to become the founder of the Philips dynasty; the founder of the largest cigar-making factory, Van Abbe, in whose name the now famous Van Abbe museum was established in Eindhoven; the president of the Jewish Seminary, S. P. Lipman, who converted to Catholicism in 1852; famous Calvinists such as the poet Isaac da Costa (1798–1860) and the physician Abraham Capadose (1795–1874); and the Ephraim family of Tiel, who as Tilanus were to end as leaders of the Protestant party, the Christian-Historical Union, and many others. Does this mean that baptism was vital as an entrance ticket in Dutch society? It is a hazardous statement. Many of the apostates remained known for their Jewish origin, and most did little to hide that fact. A former Sephardi like that famous apostate to Calvinism, Isaac da Costa, even prided himself on his Jewish descent and essential Jewishness,[36] thus strengthening the myth of the "Hebrew coloration"[37] of Dutch society, and of Dutch Calvinists as representing the "Israel of the West." Many Calvinists regarded themselves as united to Jews by a bond between two chosen people. Although such sentiments did not prevent anti-Semitic utterances—not least those of the famous Calvinist leader Abraham Kuyper[38]—this factor may have contributed to making the Calvinists the single most important communal group that was to harbor Jews in hiding after 1941. A certificate of baptism was also not of great interest, because the census, as well as people generally, soon began to regard "agnostics" of whatever earlier background as perfectly respectable members of society.[39]

[35] Marx's statement is only one of many in the same vein; cf. William H. Chaloner and William O. Henderson, "Marx, Engels and Racism," *Encounter* 45 (July 1975): 20.

[36] Cf. Martinus J.P.M. Weijtens, *Nathan and Shylock in de Lage Landen: De Jood in het werk van de Nederlandse letterkundigen in de negentiende eeuw* (Groningen, 1971), 81ff.

[37] The phrase is Conrad Busken Huet's, quoted by Kruijt, "Jodendom," 193.

[38] See Ivo Schöffer, "Abraham Kuyper and the Jews," in Jozeph Michman and Tirtsah Levie, eds., *Dutch Jewish History* (Jerusalem, 1984), 137–59.

[39] After the German occupation the share of Jews in various sectors of society became visible through imposed registration orders. In October 1940 all government personnel were ordered to sign a so-called *Ariër-verklaring*, testifying to the best of their ability that they were *not* Jewish; some 2,500 Jews were subsequently dismissed from government

Dutch Jews in a Segmented Society

What to conclude about the position of Dutch Jews, after about a century and a half of emancipation initiated in 1796? One might single out a few main themes: first, the vague atmosphere of provincialism that characterized Dutch Jewry in its relation toward world Jewry; second, the marked contrast between the assimilatory tendencies of Dutch Jews on the one hand and the simultaneous growth of powerful isolated subcultures of Dutch Calvinists and Catholics on the other; and finally, the somewhat deferential attitudes of many Dutch Jews toward public authority.

1. The provincialism of Dutch Jewry may be illustrated both by its relation toward other religious centers in the world, and by the somewhat special nature of the Dutch Zionist movement.

As we have seen, both the Ashkenazi and Sephardi communities were successfully "Netherlandized" in the course of the nineteenth century, even within their own day-to-day religious services and practices: by their successful integration into Dutch society, they partook of the provincial outlook that was characteristic of the Netherlands in world affairs generally. Both the Ashkenazim's loss of Yiddish[40] and the clear atmosphere of self-satisfaction among Dutch Jews alienated them from the great talmudic centers in eastern Europe, and also made them virtual strangers to the new centers of Judaism across the Atlantic. Very often, Jewish intellectual and religious leaders found their chief intellectual frame of reference more easily in secular Dutch or European culture than in living Jewish culture in other lands.

A similar proposition may also be maintained with regard to the Zionist movement. On the whole, the religious establishment, and also the Jewish press, such as the *Nieuw Israëlitisch Weekblad*,[41] came down strongly against political Zionism, as did a meeting of chief rabbis in a later much-criticized statement in 1904.[42] There were some early and notable exceptions among the rabbinate: again J. H. Dünner and partic-

positions (de Jong, *Koninkrijk der Nederlanden*, 5:510). This practice was later followed in numerous other professional bodies, leading to the singling out of Jews who were then forbidden to treat non-Jews; this affected some 667 medical doctors, 80 dentists, 4 veterinarians, 177 dispensing chemists, 9 public notaries, 75 official translators, and 7 office keepers of the state lottery (de Jong, *Koninkrijk der Nederlanden*, 5:545–46).

[40] However, in a personal communication to me in 1975 the late Dr. Leo Fuks qualified this assertion, arguing that in any case eastern Jews would not normally have understood the western Yiddish spoken by Ashkenazi Jews in the Netherlands.

[41] Cf. Lipschits, *Honderd jaar NIW*, 228–53; Meijer, *Hoge hoeden*, 59–86.

[42] Cf. Ludy A. M. Giebels, *De Zionistische beweging in Nederland, 1899–1941* (Assen, 1975), 35ff.

ularly S. Ph. de Vries of Haarlem. There was a Dutch branch of Mizrachi, which sought to combine Orthodoxy with Zionism, from 1911. But when young Mizrachi activists introduced innovations such as using the modern Hebrew pronunciation in prayers, they were officially condemned by older Mizrachi and other religious leaders for acting against Jewish law.[43]

The Dutch Zionist movement similarly failed to strike root among the large Jewish proletariat in the Netherlands. When Herzl walked the Amsterdam Jewish quarters, he had expressed the hope that its children would soon sing Zionist hymns.[44] This was not to be. The Jewish proletariat of Amsterdam followed Socialism rather than Zionism. In its initial emancipation, so it has been said, it even found in Henri Polak its own rabbi and in the General Diamond Workers' Union a secular substitute for a chevra synagogue. A Dutch Poale Zion branch was established only in 1933, and it was never to acquire a massive following. One of its leaders, Salomon Kleerekoper, was to rationalize its failure to develop a mass following by insisting that this particular brand of Zionism demanded more comprehension than any other ideology: a full understanding of the proletarian and of the national issue, both combined in a living synthesis. Presumably, only the elect could thus be counted upon.[45]

Zionism thus was mainly a movement of the secular younger intellectuals of bourgeois descent. The membership of the *Nederlandse Zionistenbond* (Netherlands Zionist Society) stood at a little over four thousand in 1939, and the actual number of Dutch Jews who had departed to Palestine must have been around 1,500.[46] In as far as Dutch Zionists were of significance to the International Zionist Movement this was mainly through the activities of particular individuals (who were often in opposition to the international Executive, for that matter). One can single out three outstanding figures by way of example: the banker Jacobus Kann, who purchased the land on which Tel Aviv was to be built;[47] Fritz (later Perez) Bernstein, who became a cabinet minister in Israel in 1948; and Nehemia de Lieme, who was prominent in the international as well as the Dutch Zionist movement. De Lieme's special outlook has been described by one of his lieutenants in the following terms:

> No participation in religious organizational activities. No authority in the organization for those who supported the Zionist cause only with money.

[43] Meijer, *Hoge hoeden,* 72.

[44] Gans, *Memorbook,* 600, 607.

[45] Salomon Kleerekoper, "Het Joodse proletariaat in het Amsterdam van de eerste helft der twintigste eeuw en zijn leiders," *Studia Rosenthaliana,* 3,2 (1969):216; cf. Giebels, *Zionistische beweging,* 184–92.

[46] In October 1939 the *Nederlandse Zionistenbond* put its membership at 4,246. Cf. Giebels, *Zionistische beweging,* 171.

[47] Gans, *Memorbook,* 611–12.

> Immigration not for those who seek refuge in Palestine, but only for those who could contribute actively by their own labor to the economic development of the country—not quantity, but quality. Buying of land only in as far as financially responsible, and only if a profitable exploitation were guaranteed. Rejection of any political proposition which did not start from the idea of exclusive Jewish control of the whole country.[48]

Chaim Weizmann dubbed Dutch Zionism a *Geschäftszionismus* (commercial Zionism)—a view provoked not least by De Lieme's financial strictures against the policies of the Jewish Agency in Israel.[49] One foreign Jewish observer who was approached during the Second World War in Switzerland about the plight of Dutch Jews cynically remarked: "All I know about Dutch Jewry, alas, is that the guilder was always good."[50]

2. The development of Dutch Jewry in the nineteenth and twentieth century stands in considerable contrast with developments in the same period of the orthodox Calvinists and the Catholics. The emancipation movements of the more militant Calvinists and Catholics expressed themselves in a strengthening of Orthodoxy and a rapid development of a tight organizational network to buttress their particular systems of faith, their interests and social bonds. The typical mechanisms of the politics of *verzuiling* could have been used to some extent by Jews as well, for instance by the establishment of a network of denominational Jewish schools, and of state-subsidized welfare organizations. But Dutch Jews used such potential instruments only sparingly. Some explanations may be advanced as to why they did not follow the example of other Dutch religious groupings:

• From the outset, the Jewish community may have been too divided: originally, between Ashkenazim and Sephardim; within the elite, between the traditional *parnassim* and the emancipationists of 1795 and later years; and between the elite on the one hand and the proletarian mass on the other. Moreover, such sense of identity as history had initially created was eroded to a great extent once social modernization resulted in increased physical and social mobility.

• There was the comfort of existing Jewish religious institutions that were always there, although they exerted few real claims. Judaism differed from Calvinism and Catholicism, moreover, in that it provided less of a dogmatic-ideological system, and more of a shared tradition of com-

[48] Izaak Kisch, "Een bespreking, maar eigenlijk een bosje mémoires," review of *Het Koninkrijk der Nederlanden*, by Louis de Jong, *Studia Rosenthaliana*, 3,2 (1969): 264.

[49] Gans, *Memorbook*, 613. Cf. Giebels, *Zionistische beweging*.

[50] Gans, *Memorbook*, 627.

mands and customs. The latter lent themselves less easily to a process of defensive politicization than did Calvinist or Catholic dogma.

• There was a persistent fear on the part of many Jews to press Jewish claims, even in such a relatively favorable environment as Dutch society seemingly offered. The importance of this factor may be compared to similar anxieties, found among that other minority grouping in the Netherlands which had suffered even more resolute discrimination in the past: Catholics. But in the case of the Catholics, large numbers, and strong regional bastions, eventually overcame clear qualms and fears, although even this process took in practice a century or more.

• There was always the possibility of the individual way out: baptism only rarely, agnosticism more frequently, indifferent Jewishness more naturally.

• There was the rival attraction of political creeds: of Liberalism and Socialism above all (but also in the 1930s of the strong-man Calvinist Anti-Revolutionary Hendrik Colijn). Though Liberals and Socialists often took Jewish support too easily for granted, without a strong need for repayment in kind, they did make room for influential politicians of Jewish descent: for example, I. A. Levy, who was practically the founder of the Liberal Union in 1885; Henri Polak, who helped establish the Social Democratic Labour Party (SDAP) in 1894; and David Wijnkoop, one of the triumvirate who headed the beginning of the Dutch Communist movement in 1909. One could argue that Jewish *verzuiling* was obviated, exactly because the Jewish bourgeoisie integrated successfully into the Liberal segment, the Jewish proletariat (and also a number of Jewish intellectuals of bourgeois descent) into the Socialist subculture.

• Sheer size was another factor. Catholics and Calvinists also had to fight the indifferent and the antagonistic in their midst, but the core of committed remained always credibly large. This was never true of the Dutch Jewish community—so very much smaller in numbers in proportion to the rest of the Dutch population. The number of Jewish leaders was almost too few to man the manifold Jewish religious organizations, let alone to build these into an independent comprehensive subculture of its own.

• A final factor may have been the heavy concentration of Jews in Amsterdam. There they could feel self-sufficient, in a way Jews in other parts of the country could not. Jews outside Amsterdam were never strong enough in comparison to Amsterdam Jews to go it alone. If Amsterdam lacked the incentive, Jews in the provinces lacked the infrastructure for anything more than somewhat introspective Jewish life.

3. As well as a certain provincialism, and an unwillingness to press minority status on a par with Catholics and Calvinists, a third charac-

teristic trait of leading Jews in the Netherlands was an overtly trustful—not to say deferential—attitude toward public authority. The force of this attitude may be illustrated, for instance, by the particularly strong adulation of the House of Orange in Jewish circles. One need only compare the tone of Menasseh ben Israel's elocution in the Portuguese synagogue to Frederick Henry and the English Queen Henrietta Maria in 1642 with the speech of Chief Rabbi A. S. Onderwijzer when he welcomed Queen Wilhelmina, her husband, and daughter to the large Ashkenazi synagogue in 1924,[51] to find a consistent attitude.

A more portentous example can be found in the respectful attitude toward the Dutch authorities, demonstrated by the leaders of the Committee of Special Jewish Affairs, with Abraham Asscher and Professor David Cohen as its main leaders since 1933. There is a direct link between this organization and its attitude—at the moment when hell had already broken loose on the other side of the Dutch border—with the later attitudes of the Joodse Raad (the Jewish Council) under Asscher and Cohen after 1941.

It is the bitter paradox of the combination of assimilatory and deferential attitudes that they could not prevent the forceful reimposition of a Jewish collectivity once "the Jewish problem" began to make itself felt in the Netherlands. A number of events foreshadowed the coming Holocaust. Was there not already visible in the treatment of immigrants and refugees by Dutch and Jewish authorities alike something of a coalition of all the known against the nameless? Should one not regard the banning of all immigration of foreigners in May 1938, based on the alleged need to avoid economic competition and *Ueberfremdung,* as a first sign of discrimination against the truly unprotected?[52] And should one be allowed to forget that the later notorious camp of Westerbork was built by the Dutch government, originally as a camp for Jewish refugees, far from the urban centers of the country, at the expense of Dutch Jewry and Jewish organizations? Most Dutch Jews thought themselves secure in the Netherlands, and they respected the authorities placed over them. Many would continue to do so, when the new German rulers began to use Dutch authorities—both Jewish and non-Jewish—as instruments in the registration of the Jews first, then of their isolation, and finally of their deportation and death.

[51] Ibid., 632.

[52] Cf. Ben A. Sijes, "The Position of the Jews during the German Occupation of the Netherlands: Some Observations," *Acta Historiae Neerlandicae* 9 (The Hague, 1976): 173.

THREE

FROM "*SCHUTZJUDEN*" TO "*DEUTSCHE STAATSBÜRGER JÜDISCHEN GLAUBENS*": THE LONG AND BUMPY ROAD OF JEWISH EMANCIPATION IN GERMANY

Werner E. Mosse

THE SITUATION of German Jewry and its relation with "the state" differed from that of other countries in one important respect. Until the creation of the German empire in 1871, there existed no national German state. Instead, at the time when the emancipation debate began in earnest in 1781, the Imperial Diet contained the representatives of 324 principalities, temporal and spiritual.[1] After the Congress of Vienna (1815), with varying degrees of emancipation in the different German states, there were still thirty-eight separate territorial units (excluding Austria). "The process of emancipation," the leading German historian of the subject has written, "was greatly impeded by the existence side by side of very diverse concepts and developments, and to this day the work of the historian is made harder by this multifariousness when he seeks to tell and to analyze the history of Jewish emancipation in Germany."[2]

Two attempts, in 1815 and 1848–49, to introduce uniform arrangements for German Jewry ended in failure. The process of piecemeal emancipation, a consequence of the multiplicity of sovereignties, would extend over the better part of a century. Two additional reasons have been assigned for the length of the process. One is the widely adopted concept of a gradual and phased emancipation to be considered presently. Another is the problem of Jewish emancipation in (and into) a society itself only partially emancipated.[3] To these might be added the

[1] Reinhard Rürup, "The Tortuous and Thorny Path to Legal Equality: 'Jew Laws' and Emancipatory Legislation in Germany from the Late Eighteenth Century," *Leo Baeck Institute Yearbook* [*LBY*] 31 (1986): 5.

[2] Ibid., 9–10.

[3] Reinhard Rürup, "Jewish Emancipation and Bourgeois Society," *LBY* 14 (1969): 86.

sheer diversity in religion, political structure, social and economic development, and Jewish presence in the different German states and the consequent variety of attempts to deal with the Jewish problem.

In the long, drawn-out process of Jewish emancipation a number of different phases or stages are traditionally (if somewhat artificially) distinguished. The first of these, extending from 1781 to 1815, witnessed the initial debates on the "Jewish Question" accompanied by some early legislative enactments. This is likely to have culminated in the abortive attempt in 1815 to achieve an all-German solution. The next phase, extending to 1847, to the accompaniment of continued debate, saw a series of retrograde measures. The revolutions of 1848–49 then became the occasion of a second unsuccessful attempt at general emancipation. During the following period extending to 1871, initial political setbacks, accompanied, however, by rapid economic advance, were followed by a period of Liberal ascendancy that saw the completion of legal emancipation. The different phases must now be considered in turn.

The State of the "Jewish Nation"

To understand the course of Jewish emancipation in Germany it is necessary first to consider the situation of what was then called the "Jewish nation" in the second half of the eighteenth century. This has been done by Rürup in terms that cannot be bettered:

> The Jews constituted a minority inexorably set apart from the majority by its religion, its language, culture and customs, its ancestry and its economic practices. They were looked upon as aliens whose residence in the country was of limited duration and in principle revocable, even where they had been settled for generations in one and the same locality. Wherever they lived they were—in the words of one of the official reports that paved the way towards emancipation—"living merely on sufferance as subjects who, while enjoying the protection of the state, are not members of civic society."[4]

"Jews and non-Jews lived in two worlds apart, with economic relations forming virtually the only link between them."[5]

As so-called *Schutzjuden*[6] (Jews enjoying legal protection), they were subject to the territorial ruler and his *Judenordnung* ("Jews Statute"). As

[4] Rürup, "Tortuous Path," 4–5.

[5] Ibid., 5.

[6] See especially Hrsg. Monika Richarz, *Jüdisches Leben in Deutschland: Selbstzeugnisse zur Sozialgeschichte 1780–1871* (Stuttgart, 1976), 20–21.

such, they were tolerated in a majority of German states.[7] They had to pay *Schutzgeld* (protection money) and a price for every privilege granted to them. They were, effectively, taxable at will. The better-off in particular constituted a welcome economic resource for every needy ruler. They were employed also to develop or conduct a variety of commercial activities. In a number of territories therefore every attempt was made to attract wealthy Jews. The settlement of poor ones, who formed the great majority, was, on the other hand, severely discouraged. The increase in Jewish numbers was often restricted by legislative enactment. In many states only one son per family was permitted to marry, two in the case of better-off families.

In return for their economic services, Jews received an at-times precarious protection. The authorities, whether from an extension to Jews of the prevailing estates organization or simply from indifference, allowed Jewish communities on their territories a large measure of internal autonomy. Not only did they enjoy the right to unimpeded practice of their religion, but they could freely set up and administer their synagogues and cemeteries, schools and charitable institutions. There was no outside interference in communal affairs. In inner-Jewish matters, rabbinical authority prevailed.

Within this legal framework, severe restrictions were placed on Jewish economic activity. Jews were barred from land ownership and farming and from crafts administered by *zünfte* (guilds). In a predominantly rural society still largely with a natural economy, Jews were thus by law effectively confined to trade. Even here, a variety of regulations forced them in the main into activities disdained by Gentiles. As *Hausierer* (petty ambulatory traders) they were often obliged to cross the numerous frontiers of German mini-states. Each time, they were liable not only to payments in respect of their goods but also to a demeaning *Leibzoll,* a payment for their person that assimilated them to cattle.

It was in such unpropitious economic circumstances that a distinctive social stratification had developed within German Jewry in the course of the eighteenth century. Frequently incomplete or unreliable data suggest that, at the end of the century, at least three-quarters of German Jews earned a precarious living as *Hausierer* or *Trödler* (hawkers). Their major function was to supply village dwellers with a variety of minor manufactured articles.[8] The dream of most—a majority, though ambulatory

[7] During the eighteenth century Jews were still excluded altogether from some of the more important German states, notably Bavaria, Saxony, and Württemberg. Rürup, "Tortuous Path," 5.

[8] For a detailed account of the Jewish *Hausierer* and his important place in rural life, see Arthur Prinz, *Juden im deutschen Wirtschaftsleben 1850–1914* (Tübingen, 1984), 23ff.

had a fixed residence—was to open a small shop. This would enable them to escape the drudgery of carrying their wares over miserable roads. A number, with time, had succeeded in achieving this ambition. Through credit transactions, money lending, pawnbroking, or involvement in the cattle trade, they scraped together some modest capital. In due course, they joined a small middle class of somewhat better-off shopkeepers and petty bankers. This also included a number of bakers and butchers serving primarily the Jewish communities as well as some artisans specializing in nonguild crafts.[9]

Below the petty traders on the social scale were beggars, and in between an underworld of thieves, receivers of stolen goods, pimps, and even robbers. This "underclass," with the two groups shading into each other, may have constituted approximately a fifth of the Jewish population.[10]

At the opposite end of the social scale were to be found the *Hofjuden* (Court Jews), the agents and factors of princes, and a number of wholesale merchants. These, together with their dependents, may have formed some 2 percent of the Jewish population.[11] Their importance in the present context lies in their role as links between capitalism and Jewish emancipation. Such Court Jews, in fact, could acquire considerable if precarious fortunes and on occasion transmit them to their heirs. Freed as a rule from "normal" Jewish disabilities, they constituted a highly privileged group. Their status and position have been described by Jacob Katz:

> As a result of their important economic role, these rich Jews acquired positions of influence with those in power—the emperor, king, princes and bishops whom they served. . . . In return for their services, they often secured privileges for themselves. Some of them were exempted from paying the *Schutzgeld* . . . that was a basic condition of the Jew's right to toleration in a certain place. The court Jew might also secure the right of residence for his family, his widow or his sons-in-law. More than that, communities were founded or enlarged owing to the influence of a court Jew. In addition court Jews were exempted from the jurisdiction of both Jewish and Gentile Courts. . . . Indeed, the court Jew's status resembled that of high officials in other respects as well. He was appointed to his post by his lord; he bore the title *Hoffaktor* or *Hofagent* . . . and received a salary. Finally the court Jew also demonstrated his high standing by outward appearance. He is clad, if not entirely in the fashion followed by one of the other estates, then, in any

[9] Richarz, *Jüdisches Leben,* 33–34.

[10] For details, see Prinz, *Juden,* 20–21.

[11] For the Court Jews, see Selma Stern, *The Court Jews: A Contribution to the History of the Period of Absolutism in Central Europe* (Philadelphia, 1950); Henrich Schnee, *Die Hochfinanz und der moderne Staat: Geschichte und System der Hoffaktoren an deutschen Fürstenhöfen im Zeitalter des Absolutismus,* 6 vols. (Berlin, 1953–67); and Francis L. Carsten, "The Court Jews: A Prelude to Emancipation," *LBY* 3 (1958): 140ff.

case, differently from his Jewish brethren. In his household, his attire and his equipage exhibit his wealth and influence.[12]

The role of Court Jews in the early phases of Jewish emancipation has been the subject of controversy.[13] In Katz's judicious summary,

> [Court Jews] were active in the struggle for Jewish rights—at least in the first phase of the era of emancipation—and the whole process could therefore be easily attributed to their weight and influence. This was done in a most consistent fashion by the German historian Heinrich Schnee, who more than anyone else contributed to our knowledge about the activity of court Jews. According to Schnee, the "emancipation of the Jews was the work of the Hoffactoren." Not the Enlightenment, nor the message of 1789 were decisive for the emancipation of the Jews, but the numerous court Jewry (*Hoffactorentum*).[14]

"That court Jews," Katz qualifies Schnee's assessment, "or better their descendants or those that inherited their wealth and influence, pulled their weight in the negotiations that resulted in acts of legislation favorable to Jews cannot be denied. But not all legislation in favor of Jews was supported by court Jews nor owed its origin to their influence."[15]

There did indeed exist a second privileged group involved in the early campaign for Jewish emancipation for which the term *Adelsbürger* has been coined.[16] These were men (and their families and dependents) who were beneficiaries of mercantilist policies adopted by states and bureaucracies.[17] Under these, the importation of luxury goods was considered harmful while their manufacture and especially export were highly desirable. Whoever produced goods such as gold or silver embroideries, silken fabrics, jewelry, and china was welcome, even though a Jew. So were so-called *Münzjuden,* men conversant with matters of bullion and coinage. Under the impact of such mercantilist policies, Jews were able to enter several branches of industry and commerce, notably in Berlin.[18] Such

[12] Jacob Katz, *Out of the Ghetto: The Social Background of Jewish Emancipation, 1770–1870* (Cambridge, Mass., 1973), 29.

[13] See ibid., 227 n. 5; Rürup, "Tortuous Path," 12 n. 19; Richarz, *Jüdisches Leben,* 21; and Avraham Barkai, *Jüdische Minderheit und Industrialisierung* (Tübingen, 1988), 13–14. It is difficult to escape the conclusion that assessment tends to be colored by ideological preconceptions.

[14] Katz, *Out of the Ghetto,* 29.

[15] Ibid., 30.

[16] For details of *Adelsbürger,* see Jacob Toury, "*Der Eintritt der Juden* ins Deutsche Bürgertum," in Hrsg. Hans Liebeschütz and Arnold Paucker, *Das Judentum in der Deutschen Umwelt, 1800–1850* (Tübingen, 1977), 154ff.

[17] See Prinz, *Juden,* 28.

[18] See Hugo Rachel and Paul Wallich, *Berliner Grosskaufleute und Kapitalisten* (Berlin, 1939).

early entrepreneurs had since the mid-eighteenth century received on occasion extensive privileges, assimilating their status to that of their Christian counterparts.[19] Thus, in a striking instance in 1791, the Berlin banker Daniel Itzig received on the petition of his son, "Senior Court Banker and Highway Construction Inspector" Isaac Daniel Itzig, "for himself and his legitimate progeny of both sexes," a Patent of Naturalization granting them "all rights possessed by Christian citizens" in the entire Prussian state. The patent covered no fewer than eleven Jewish households and marked, in the words of the then-minister of finance, "a total revolution in the entire administration of Jewish affairs and in the position of this nation not only *vis-à-vis* the state, but also *vis-à-vis* the other inhabitants of the land."[20]

In effect, under the *ancien régime* a number of both *Hoffaktoren* and *Adelsbürger* thus achieved what might be called a proto-emancipation in recognition of outstanding economic performance. The combination of economic achievement and privileged position indicates the close link between early capitalism, usefulness to rulers and governments, and the early stages of the emancipation process. It was a linkage never entirely to disappear.

The majority of the "Jewish nation" lived, like the rest of the population, predominantly in villages or towns of fewer than twenty thousand inhabitants. Jewish communities in the major cities were relatively small. Thus Hamburg in 1816 had 7,000 Jews, Breslau 4,409, Frankfurt 4,309, and Berlin 3,373.[21]

The proportion of Jews differed in the several German states, as of course did the size of their populations. Prussia in 1821 contained 141,762 Jews (1.23 percent), Bavaria in 1818 53,208 (1.45 percent), and the Grand-Duchy of Hesse in 1818 some 20,000 (3.04 percent). The figure for Baden in 1825 was 17,577 (1.60 percent), while for Württemberg in 1828 approximately 9,000 (0.55 percent) Jews were unevenly distributed within states. The largest concentrations were to be found in the Free Cities of Hamburg and Frankfurt, in Hesse and in the territories incorporated in Prussia as a result of the Polish partitions. Of a total of 153,498 Jews counted in Prussia in 1825, 65,123 lived in Posen, 19,721 in Silesia, and 21,036 in the Rhineland. There were 15,350 in West Prussia, 11,142 in Westphalia, and 4,079 in the city of Berlin. Areas of regional concentration were thus the eastern provinces of Posen, West Prussia, and Silesia (100,203), and the Rhineland and Westphalia (32,178).

[19] Toury, "*Eintritt*," 154ff.

[20] Rürup, "Tortuous Path," 11. The borderline between *Hoffaktoren* and *Adelsbürger* could at times be fluid. While the senior Itzigs were Court bankers, the numerous members of their extended family emancipated with them were prosperous *Adelsbürger*.

[21] Richarz, *Jüdisches Leben*, 28.

Such was the state of German Jewry on the eve of the emancipation debate.[22]

Integration by Assimilation

In 1781, a Prussian official, Christian Wilhelm Dohm, published the first volume of his epoch-making book, *Über die bürgerliche Verbesserung der Juden.* Dohm, not accidentally, was close to Berlin Enlightenment circles and, like Lessing, a friend of Moses Mendelssohn.[23] Mendelssohn was the key figure in a small group of Jewish intelligentsia overlapping with members of prominent business families. Accultured during the second half of the century, these formed part of a wider "mixed" intelligentsia. Here "Jews and Gentiles mingled as though the barriers separating the two societies had already been torn down."[24] What emerged during the 1780s and 1790s in learned societies, salons, and Masonic Lodges has been described as a "semi-neutral" society.[25] Confined almost entirely to Berlin, this formed the background to Dohm's pioneering work.

The Jew, Dohm claimed, was a human being even more than he was a Jew.[26] He was endowed by nature with the same capacity as the Christian for becoming a better and happier human being and a more useful member of society. Here, at the start of the debate, Dohm adopted the approach that would underlie much of the subsequent discussion. An optimistic view of human perfectibility was combined with turning people, in this case Jews, into more "useful" members of society. Jews, Dohm argued, might be "morally more degraded" than other nations. They might be guilty of a comparatively larger number of offenses than Christians. Their character, on the whole, was more inclined to usury and sharp trading practices. Their religious prejudices were more exclusive and unsociable. However, this "admitted greater moral degradation" was a necessary and natural consequence of the oppressive conditions under which they had lived for so many centuries.[27] Abolish these by removing all legal disabilities and enabling Jews to enter civil society, and the result would be their "civil betterment" and eventual fusion with the

[22] The population figures belong to a somewhat later date, as these are the earliest statistics with any degree of reliability.

[23] For Mendelssohn's part in the emergence of the "mixed" intelligentsia of the Enlightenment, see Katz, *Out of the Ghetto,* 47ff.

[24] Ibid., 47.

[25] For the effective limits of Jewish integration, see ibid., 50–51.

[26] C. W. von Dohm, *Über die bürgerliche Verbesserung der Juden,* (Berlin, 1781), 28. Also see Rürup, "Jewish Emancipation," 71–72.

[27] Ibid., 71.

Christians. In a second book in 1783 Dohm asserted that better treatment of the Jews was "*dictated* by common sense and general humanity, as well as by the self-interest of civic society."[28]

If Dohm's motives were thus mixed, so also were the remedies proposed.[29] In principle, Jews should receive "complete equality of rights with all other subjects." However, their necessary "civil betterment" could only be the fruit of a prolonged process of education under the supervision and guidance of the state. Through the direction of educational policy, Jews must be weaned away from both religious segregation and from an excessive occupation with trade. The necessary "recasting of an entire people," Dohm believed, could be undertaken only by the state. It was therefore

> the great and noble business of government . . . to attenuate the exclusive principles of all those various societies that the common link that embraces all of them is not impaired . . . and that all of them are resolved in the great harmony of the state. Let the government allow to each of those special groupings to indulge in its pride, even in innocuous prejudices; but let it also strive to instil yet more love in each of its members, and it will have achieved its great task when the nobleman, the peasant and the scholar, the Christian and the Jew is, beyond and above all that, a *citizen*.[30]

Such was the vision of the "statist" post-estate, Enlightenment bureaucrat. Jews, like all others, while perhaps persevering in "innocuous prejudices," would merge their particularisms in a common sense of citizenship. Jewish integration in civic society could not be envisioned otherwise than as "a process of assimilation to the mentality and life-style of the non-Jewish majority."[31]

From the long drawn-out polemics provoked by Dohm's writings, three different schools of thought emerged. What may be called the ideological view, to which Dohm himself partly subscribed, advocated full Jewish integration into civil society, possibly by a single enactment. With equal rights, Jews would progressively shed their peculiarities and particularism. They would abandon their separate institutions. They would also become acculturated. Becoming increasingly similar to the rest of the citizenry, many would, in the end, convert to Christianity and be absorbed in the general population. Improvement in their condition must, of necessity, produce an improvement in the Jews themselves. The "Jewish question" would, in this manner, be solved.

28 Rürup, "Tortuous Path," 7.
29 See Rürup, "Jewish Emancipation," 71–72.
30 Ibid., 72.
31 Rürup, "Tortuous Path," 7.

Somewhat different in approach though not in aim was the bureaucratic view to which Dohm, in part, also subscribed. This started from the premises that the majority of Jews were unready at one stroke to assume the full responsibilities of citizenship. Only a minority spoke the German language adequately. Sabbath observance and ritual laws prevented the performance of military duties. Often outlandish appearance and sometimes negative attitudes toward their Gentile surroundings also militated against instant citizenship. So did the Jews' distinctive educational institutions as well as rabbinical jurisdiction. The "Jewish nation," moreover, was something of a state within the state, raising the issue of double loyalty. Before naturalization, therefore, Jews must undergo a process of moral regeneration. Petty ambulatory trade, pawnbroking, and money lending must be replaced by productive occupations. They must learn to use the German language and shed some of their more outlandish characteristics. They must progressively adopt the values, customs, and manners of surrounding society. It was the responsibility primarily of the state to turn the misfits into useful citizens. Citizens' rights should be granted only *pari passu* with moral regeneration. This, of necessity, would prove a lengthy process. Such was the bureaucratic-statist view that would on the whole prevail.

A third school of thought could, according to taste, be described as anthropological, Christian, or anti-Jewish. History, religion, and tradition, it claimed, had given Jews distinctive characteristics that, with time, had become ineradicable. No radical change or improvement was possible. Jews inevitably were and must remain a distinctive nation within what was seen by many already as a Christian society. As heretofore, they should continue to enjoy a wide measure of administrative autonomy under what would, in modern parlance, be a system of apartheid. Some argued that Jews should be given a status of tolerated aliens with possibly municipal but without wider political rights. These were arguments tending to something like the maintenance of the status quo. They reflected views that at least until 1848 were not unacceptable to many among the more conservative Jews. Only a handful of eccentrics, pointing to the Jewish longing for Palestine, raised the possibility of expulsion.

While all three schools stressed in different ways the role of the state, an eccentric but prophetic voice drew attention to the limitations of state power. F. V. Schuckmann argued for a policy of gradualism on grounds that in retrospect appear strangely prescient. A sudden mixing of the Jews with the rest of the citizens, he considered, "would probably fail to relieve their situation of its oppressiveness. . . . [D]riven by deep-rooted prejudice, the citizens would still not accept them as brothers, a large part of the authorities would still not treat them on equal terms with the others, and no decree, however strict, however wise, would protect them against such conduct."

What, Schuckmann asked, could decrees avail against prejudice? What could they achieve if the spirit of their execution had not yet ripened in the nation? "So long then, as the nation as a whole looks upon the Jews as an inferior kind of people and takes offence at being treated on a par with them; so long as prejudice against them rules the hearts of the greater part of the constituted Christian authorities and of the clergy who guide the people; for so long it will be impossible to protect them entirely from oppression by promulgating laws."

The inner content of human actions—tone and gesture—could not be challenged before a court of laws. Moreover at the present stage the large majority of the newly accepted Jews would undeniably be lacking the requisite civic capabilities, so that acts of discrimination would rarely be without a semblance of justification, "and in the end the Jewish cause would be set back further and brought lower than where it stands today."[32] Much, though not all, of the subsequent history of Jewish emancipation in Germany would be a comment on these words.

The Napoleonic Era

Against the background of the emancipation debate, governments were taking the first tentative steps toward improving the legal position of at least certain groups of Jews. Although members of the Jewish intelligentsia were bombarding the authorities with petitions for change, the driving forces in the matter were the civil servants.[33] Legislative reform had begun when, between 1781 and 1783, the Emperor Joseph II had issued a series of "patents" or statutes for different parts of the Habsburg monarchy. These, inspired by a desire to promote "civic betterment" without, however, introducing fundamental change, had removed a number of Jewish disabilities. In Germany also, before the end of the century, some piecemeal steps had been taken. Thus the degrading *Leibzoll* had been abolished in Prussia in 1787 and in Bavaria in 1799. An ordinance on Jewish affairs, promulgated in Breslau in 1790 to promote "civic betterment" of Jews and help them to "come closer to the rest of the citizens," had brought improvements. A "Jew Statute" issued in 1797 for provinces acquired by Prussia in the Polish partitions permitted the qualified admission of Jews to civil trades and professions and free access to all "regular" occupations. This was accompanied, however, by a ban on

[32] F. V. Schuckmann, "Über Judenkolonien. An Hrn. Geheimen-Rath Dohm," in *Berlinische Monatsschrift,* 1785, 54. Quoted in Rürup, "Jewish Emancipation," 72–73.

[33] Ibid., 74.

"hawking" and restrictions on petty trade and money lending. Jews were instructed to adopt fixed names and to keep commercial records in German. Their children could join Gentile schools. The changes were designed, as one of the statutes phrased it, to "foster among the Jews the qualities needed to become good and useful subjects."[34]

Emancipation received a major impetus from the effects of the French Revolutionary and Napoleonic Wars. In territories that either directly or indirectly fell under French control, Jews received full emancipation. Thus in 1798 they were granted full civil rights in territories on the left bank of the Rhine annexed to France. In 1808 a law gave Jews complete civic equality in the kingdom of Westphalia ruled by Napoleon's brother Jérome. Two years later, following annexation to France, Jews in the Hanseatic cities obtained full citizen rights. Restrictions on petty trade and usury, however, imposed in 1808 on Jews in France by the so-called "décret infâme," were three years later extended also to northwestern Germany. Nonetheless, a large number of German Jews had, thanks to French legislation, been given a taste of full civic rights.

The indirect effects of the turmoil of the age were scarcely less significant. In the resulting restructuring, numerous petty principalities were incorporated in larger surrounding or neighboring states. Bavaria, Württemberg, and Hesse-Darmstadt, among others, were considerably enlarged. In the first two, no Jews other than some isolated individuals had, until then, been permitted to reside. After 1815, however, Bavaria suddenly found itself with some fifty thousand Jews. For states acquiring new Jewish subjects governed by a variety of "Jew-Statutes," a measure of codification had to become necessary. The ongoing emancipation debate, combined with the example of French-inspired legislation, ensured that the new arrangements would in general improve the Jewish situation. Thus between 1807 and 1809, the grand duchy of Baden granted its Jews full state citizenship though retaining some elements of discrimination. Uniform Bavarian regulations in 1813 equally extended Jewish rights. Codification in Württemberg was delayed until 1828 while some other states, notably Saxony and Hanover, hung back. Only a few ministates of central Germany conceded what amounted to full citizen rights.

Prussia, the leading German state with the largest number of Jews, had, like the rest, experienced the impact of French hegemony. Following a crushing defeat at the hands of Napoleon in 1806, reform-minded ministers embarked upon an extensive program of modernization. This included also new arrangements for the monarchy's Jewish subjects. Thus a municipal statute of 1808 extended to all Jews municipal rights previously reserved for isolated individuals. Jewish notables, henceforth,

[34] Rürup, "Tortuous Path," 11.

would play a significant part in municipal affairs, notably in the eastern provinces, where they held the balance between Germans and Poles.[35]

Prussia's "modernizing" legislation regarding the Jews, due largely to the personal engagement of the state-chancellor Hardenberg, culminated in the "Edict concerning the civic condition of Jews in the Prussian state" promulgated on 11 March 1812.[36] By this edict, Jews received the status of "natives and citizens of the Prussian state" with "the same civic rights and liberties as those enjoyed by Christians." An exception, however, was made for admission to "public services and state offices" in respect of which a decision was deferred. On the other hand, Jews would in the future be admitted to "academic and other teaching posts as well as to local government offices." In matters such as taxation, military service, or the ban on hawking and peddling, their position would be the same as that of Christians. Not least important in practice, Jews were given a free choice of residence, the right to own land, and, within the framework of the general laws, the right to choose their occupation. As a condition of their new citizenship, Jews would have to present a Protective Letter Patent (*Schutz-brief*) or "concession" and adopt a hereditary family name.

As part of the broader policy of transforming the *ancien régime* of absolute princes, estates, and corporations into a modern society of citizens under the state, many corporate functions hitherto exercised by Jewish communal authorities and notably rabbinical jurisdiction were abolished. At the same time, regulations to determine the status of organized religion "and to improve educational instruction of the Jews" were deferred to a future date. Meanwhile, "men of the Jewish faith who enjoy public trust on account of their knowledge and probity" would be permitted to testify in the courts.

While the Edict still bore traces of educational intent, and while it fell short of complete emancipation, it nonetheless greatly extended the sphere of Jewish rights.[37] "Not since the Austrian Edict of Tolerance," Katz has noted, "had any legislation concerning Jews elicited such enthusiasm."[38]

The Napoleonic era, and with it the first phase of Jewish emancipation in Germany, ended with the Congress of Vienna in 1815. In connection with the decision of four Free Cities to rescind French-imposed legislation, the plenipotentiaries reviewed the legal situation of Jews within the

[35] See Stefi Wenzel, *Jüdische Bürger und Kommunale Selbstverwaltung in Preussischen Städten* (Berlin, 1967).

[36] See Rürup, "Tortuous Path," 14–15.

[37] Rürup, "Jewish Emancipation," 76.

[38] Katz, *Out of the Ghetto*, 70.

Germanic Confederation. Austria and Prussia, represented respectively by Metternich and Hardenberg, pressed for a uniform solution in a liberal spirit. Their proposals, however, foundered on the opposition of some lesser German states and, notably, the Free Cities. Article 16 of the Confederate Charter merely stated that the Federal Diet would "deliberate on the question as to how best to act in a uniform manner so as to bring about the civic betterment of adherents of the Jewish faith in Germany."[39] In the meantime Jews would retain "the rights already conceded to them by the individual Confederate States." In replacing "in" of the original draft with "by," the delegates thus sanctioned the annulment of the full emancipation introduced in the formerly French territories and the kingdom of Westphalia. The uniform legislation envisaged by Article 16 of the charter was destined never to materialize. Metternich and Hardenberg before long gave up the hopeless struggle. Jewish policy, as before, remained the responsibility of the separate states.

The legislation of the Napoleonic era had in fact reflected an incomplete transition under the direction of groups of enlightened bureaucrats from the patrimonial state of the *ancien régime* to a modern citizen-state. With a widespread anti-French, anti-Enlightenment, and antirationalist reaction, however, the Christian religion, abetted by political and nationalist Romanticism, became the hallmark of antirevolutionary politics. Resulting ambiguities in state policy affected the position of the Jews. Where the residual influence of enlightened officialdom (and occasionally rulers) persisted, they preserved the status of second-class citizens that had been conceded. The attitude of the state continued to be that of progressive "betterment." The improvements in rights of residence and choice of occupation brought by general "modernization" were, on the whole, preserved. At the same time, in the face of determined opposition from vested interests seconded by protagonists of the "Christian state" and a Christian society, the new legislation everywhere had stopped short of full legal emancipation. Nor was the bulk of the German population sympathetic to Jewish emancipation, a fact that in turn reinforced the anti-Jewish prejudices of the members of elected chambers. The political climate, from 1812 onward, had become increasingly unfavorable to emancipation. The process of political "modernization" was arrested, leaving an ambivalent practical situation. While Germans, rather than becoming *Staatsbürger* (citizens), remained *Untertanen* (subjects), Jews emerged as second-class citizens with limited rights. They had, during the Napoleonic era, been partially emancipated into a partially emancipated society.

[39] Rürup, "Tortuous Path," 15.

Economic Mobility

Following the Congress of Vienna, retrograde tendencies prevailed. In an unfavorable economic climate, Jews, through their role in the rural economy and their involvement in money lending, were caught up in wider social and economic tensions. In the summer of 1819 incidents in the city of Würzburg set off a wave of anti-Jewish riots, the so-called "*Hep-Hep* movement."[40] Nothing of this sort had been seen in Germany for centuries. The effect in slowing down if not indeed partially reversing the process of Jewish emancipation was dramatic. In fact, during the decades that followed it became axiomatic—and not without justification—that the bulk of the population, particularly in rural areas where most Jews resided, disliked them and was hostile to their further emancipation. It was an argument that henceforth lay at hand for all who opposed emancipation on other grounds. It would color public debate and influence the attitude of elected chambers. Deputies to the lower chambers representing predominantly rural areas would have their own anti-Judaism (or neutrality) reinforced by the prejudices of large parts of their electorate.

Economic and social problems, moreover, coincided with changes in the intellectual climate. With the defeat of France the enlightenment rationalism that had partly inspired the movement of Jewish emancipation had had its day. Restoration, the Holy Alliance, and the onset of the Romantic movement ushered in a Christian conservative reaction that would presently receive its ultimate ideological sanction at the hands of the Jewish convert Friedrich Julius Stahl. The concept of the "Christian State," propounded since the Dohm debate, gained a wider currency thanks to his formulation. In vigorous public debate on the "Jewish question" after 1815, "in contrast to the preceding decades the general trend of the arguments put forward by national-progressive as well as by conservative authors was critical of emancipation and anti-Jewish."[41]

It was in these conditions that a number of states withdrew concessions previously granted or gave them restrictive interpretations. The policy of Prussia, which in 1816 counted 123,938 Jewish inhabitants,[42] may be taken as an example.

Frederick William III, king of Prussia since 1797, was ill-disposed toward Jews and Jewish emancipation. Ministers in their correspondence would refer to "the categorical aversion of His Majesty the King to the

[40] The meaning of the "battle cry" of the rioters is obscure.

[41] Rürup, "Tortuous Path," 16.

[42] Ibid. The Jewish inhabitants of Prussia were then just under half the total of all Jews resident in the territories that would later form the German Reich without Alsace-Lorraine.

admission of Jews into the service of the state."[43] In 1816 and again two years later it was declared that "for the time being" the Edict of 1812 would not apply in the new or regained provinces. Finally, following some uncertainty, its operation was officially confined to the "old provinces" of Brandenburg, Saxony, Pomerania, East and West Prussia, and Silesia. As each of these provinces, however, contained new or retained territories where the Edict would not operate, Prussia until 1847 would have almost two dozen different "Jew Laws." While in 1816 68,023 Jewish citizens in old Prussia and Rhineland-Westphalia benefited from the provisions of the Edict, a majority in Posen, 58,500 did not.[44]

A "Provisional Ordinance concerning Jewish affairs in the grand duchy of Posen" was promulgated in 1833.[45] It created two Jewish categories. To qualify as a "naturalized" Jew it was necessary to have a clean police record, to know the German language, to have adopted a hereditary family name, and to exercise either a civil occupation (science and learning, the arts, agriculture) or "a specific permanent craft practiced in a town." Naturalization could be the reward also of a large fortune or of special services rendered to the state through "patriotic actions" (meaning support of the German element against the Poles). Though deprived of a number of political rights, naturalized Jews would in all other respects enjoy equality with Christians. Non-naturalized Jews, however, who did not speak High German, were unacculturated, and preserved a traditional way of life were confined to towns, forbidden to marry under the age of twenty-four, and severely restricted in their occupational choices. On acquiring the necessary qualifications they could obtain Patents of Naturalization, which, however, were not hereditary. In 1847, of approximately 80,000 Jews living in Posen, some 14,500 (18 percent) would be naturalized.[46]

The ordinance set up Jewish corporations in which membership was compulsory. These were to control taxation and communal finances. Their functionaries were to see to the regular education and vocational training of Jewish youths and to ensure that none should be employed in any itinerant trade or craft. It was an extreme and somewhat belated instance of the state policy of Jewish "betterment."

Prussian policy, in fact, was moving in a retrograde direction. An abortive "Jew Statute" in 1830 would have divided Jews into "citizens of the state" and "protected Jews" with even the former denied the full rights conferred in 1812. In 1841 Frederick William IV, who had come to the throne the year before, sought to annul altogether the policies of 1812.

[43] Ibid., 17.

[44] Ibid.

[45] See ibid., 18–19.

[46] Ibid., 19 n. 32.

"The endeavor . . . to seek a betterment of the social condition of the Jews by way of their individual fusion in civic relations with the country's Christian population," he wrote, "stands in contradiction to their national type, and can therefore never be fruitful and beneficial for the mutual relationship of Christians and Jews." It was the king's wish, the minister of the interior explained, that the "national peculiarity" of the Jews and the "urge for segregation inseparably bound up with it" should henceforth be "the guiding consideration in determining their civic relations." This ruled out "the civic fusion of the Jewish with the Christian population," severed its municipal bonds, and put an end to its obligation of military service. Despite protests from several directions, these ideas underlay the draft "Jew Law" submitted to the United Diet of 1847. Jews were to be organized in *Judenschaften* (compulsory corporations) responsible for internal Jewish affairs and for training boys in "useful trades." Jewish participation in municipal affairs would, unlike that of Christians, be collective, not individual. The description of Jews as *Staatsbürger* (state-citizens) was abandoned. The bill in fact conveyed the impression that Jews were henceforth to live primarily in their own communities and only secondarily to participate in the general social and political life of the population.[47] It was nothing less than a return to the pre-emancipation view of the Jews as a distinctive "nation." A draft bill of 1830 had actually described them as "aliens."[48]

In the chamber, however, the bill underwent substantial modifications. The proposed *Judenschaften* were whittled down to *Synagogengemeinden* (synagogue congregations) with functions strictly confined to the religious sphere. While, except for some sixty-five thousand unnaturalized Jews, civic equality with Christians was reaffirmed, they were to be excluded from all matters involving the state, "the exercise of judicial, policing and executive authority." They would be ineligible for all teaching appointments and the status of *Staatsbürger* would be denied them. While their freedom particularly in the economic sphere was confirmed, their exclusion from the state domain was uncompromisingly reasserted. It was the practical expression of the ideology of the Christian state, to which the king and conservative opinion subscribed and under the sway of which Jews, *per definitionem*, were excluded from equal citizenship.[49]

If between 1815 and 1847 the movement toward legal emancipation was, if anything, retrograde, that of economic and social ascent was at the same time proceeding apace. It was during this period that Jews in increasing numbers were able to enter the German *Bürgertum*, in important respects the key to Jewish emancipation. Favored by earlier civic

[47] Ibid., 25–26.
[48] Ibid., 24.
[49] Ibid., 26.

emancipation and by new economic opportunities, they did so largely as private entrepreneurs without direct involvement of the state. While legal emancipation lagged, economic advance accelerated. With it came changes in the economic and social structure of German Jewry favorable to "betterment" and to ultimate legal emancipation. While the Jewish *haute bourgeoisie* grew in numbers and a larger middle-class developed, the old "underclass," recently a majority, entered a process of steady shrinkage. Developments were under way by which a majority of German Jews would acquire a measure of economic security, middle-class status, and, with it, a degree of respectability and acceptance at least in part of the wider community.

Already at the beginning of the nineteenth century, a number of Jews in isolated commercial centers had succeeded in establishing themselves as bankers, merchants, and entrepreneurs. This had been the case most notably in Berlin.[50] Here, the Directory of Industry for 1807 had listed thirty Jewish as against twenty-two Christian bankers. The naturalization registers (*Einbürgerungslisten*) of Jews for 1809 had recorded fifty-three bankers, fifteen money changers, and sixteen financial agents and jobbers. Significantly, forty-six had come from smaller towns outside Berlin. The Berlin Stock Exchange (*Bürse*), founded in 1803, had been set up on a basis of parity of Jew and Christian. Two of its four elders (*Vorsteher*) had been Jews, as had, after 1805, five of the ten sworn jobbers (*vereidigte Makler*) charged with certifying the official list of quotations. In 1809, shortly after his naturalization, the banker Salomon Veit had become Berlin's first elected Jewish municipal councillor.

Some Berlin Jews, moreover, had acquired substantial fortunes. This is shown by the assessment lists for the forced loans of 1812–15. Of the thirty-two most highly rated banking houses, seventeen belonged to Jews, and a further six to men of Jewish origin. In trade and industry, similarly, nine of the twenty-six most heavily assessed firms were in Jewish hands, and another in those of a baptized Jew. In 1814, some 60 percent of all Berlin fortunes over 200,000 thaler belonged to Jews or people of Jewish origin.

Nor had the emergence of small capitalist groups been confined only to Berlin. Of some one hundred banks of varying importance in the financial center of Frankfurt am Main around 1800, a majority were probably Jewish, including with one exception all the most important. Jewish bankers had also flourished in Hamburg, led by the wealthy Salomon Heine (uncle of the poet). Of five leading banks involved in 1809 in floating a Danish loan, two had been Jewish.

Numbers of the nascent Jewish bourgeoisie had of course been small.

[50] See Toury, "*Eintritt,*" 162ff.

Data for the year 1834, when not a great deal had yet changed since 1815, show (in the somewhat vague categories of Prussian statistics) the wider occupational distribution.[51] Of Prussian Jews 51 percent (60.8 percent) earned their living by "trade and credit," 17.7 percent (9.8 percent) by "crafts and industry." While 13.6 percent (13.7 percent) were classed as day laborers or domestics, 10.6 percent (6.2 percent) were beggars or in receipt of charity. The poorest stratum, thus, accounted for 24.1 percent (19.9 percent).[52]

Such had been the position on the eve of Germany's industrial ascent, conventionally dated from the year 1835. In fact, from the mid-1830s, under the growing stimulus of railway construction, the sluggish pace of German economic life quickened.[53] Commerce and banking expanded. Growing urban populations required increasing numbers of shops. So did the countryside, due to a decrease in self-sufficiency combined with improved transport facilities. Living standards were rising somewhat, with Germany's growing involvement in international trade stimulating demand for colonial products like coffee, cocoa, and tea. Gradually, shops were beginning to replace the ambulatory trader. Jewish *Hausierer* profited from the new opportunities to open shops whether in town or country. The Jewish underclass was depleted in the process.

From the forties onward, the class of "poor Jews" was reduced further by young men joining in the wider exodus to the United States.[54] Precise figures of Jewish emigration for this time are unavailable, but contemporary descriptions and comments indicate that it was in the main

> a movement of the young, the unmarried and the poor. Many of them had their fares paid by the charities, taking advantage of the eagerness of communities to get rid of migrants in transit. . . . Youngsters set out in their teens as journeymen after concluding their apprenticeship and earned their transport in stages, working their way to the ports. Many of them travelled by the cheaper sailing ship long after steamships had started to cross the ocean.[55]

Most of the emigrants came from villages and small towns mainly in the south and southwest, though presently more urbanized Jews from Posen would join in the exodus. A particular reason for emigration were the restrictions on the marriages of poorer Jews, notably in Bavaria. Many

[51] Figures in parentheses relate to Prussia without Posen.

[52] Prinz, *Juden,* 19.

[53] See ibid., 25 and 37.

[54] See ibid., 39–40; and Avraham Barkai, "The German Jews at the Start of Industrialization: Structural Change and Mobility, 1835–1860," in Werner E. Mosse, Arnold Paucker, and Reinhard Rürup, eds., *Revolution and Evolution: 1848 in German-Jewish History* (Tübingen, 1981), 127ff. and 146ff.; Avraham Barkai, "German-Jewish Migration in the Nineteenth Century," *LBY* 30 (1985): 301ff.

[55] Ibid., 311.

betrothed couples would marry almost as soon as they set foot on American soil.

The migration, fed mainly by the poorest strata of Jewish society, assisted the economic progress of the rest. Many "from the other shore" would later send remittances to remaining relatives in Germany. Their departure, moreover, tended to relieve competitive pressures in overcrowded occupations or localities. It contributed, as already indicated, to a marked shrinkage of the Jewish underclass.[56]

The shrinkage was accompanied by the steady growth of a middle class of shopkeepers and merchants. Thus the Prussian census of 1843 recorded 21,739 independent Jewish traders.[57] Of these, 1,140 were involved in wholesale trade and banking. 6,003 were shopkeepers (*Kaufleute mit offenen Läden*). With them might be ranked 1,358 commission agents of various kinds. There remained 13,238 petty traders (excluding 650 assistants), constituting 61 percent of the total.

When the next census was taken in 1861, the total number of those engaged in commerce had risen to 38,683, of whom 59 percent could be described as regular merchants. The number of bankers and wholesale merchants had risen from 1,140 to 3,335, that of shopkeepers from 6,003 to 9,736. There were 2,035 agents, jobbers, and pawnbrokers. A new category of commercial employees numbered 7,665. As against this, there remained 14,974 petty traders, including assistants and 938 horse dealers difficult to classify. Members of the underclass had become a minority.

Overall, while at mid-century the underclass still remained numerous, there is evidence to suggest that many, perhaps a majority, had been rising into the "respectable" middle class of the German *Bürgertum*. Favored by the removal of restrictions on their economic activity and by the general quickening of economic life, they had been taking advantage of unprecedented opportunities. Assisted by large and industrious families and notably wives, endowed with commercial expertise, an entrepreneurial spirit, and varying amounts of capital, they had risen not only into the rising German *Bürgertum* but also within it. Upward economic mobility had preceded the completion of legal emancipation.

Social and Cultural Integration

A measure of legal and economic enfranchisement had, as some of the early emancipators had hoped and anticipated, been accompanied by a process of rapid acculturation. Both the politics of German states and the

[56] Prinz, *Juden,* 39–40.
[57] See ibid., 59–60.

efforts of the Jews themselves had contributed to this result. The "educational" efforts of governments had in part borne fruit. Jews on their part had, in this respect, fulfilled their side of what had been widely considered an emancipation compact or bargain.

Although some Jews, Moses Mendelssohn among their number, had been largely self-taught, while others had received a private education, the decisive impetus had come from the introduction of compulsory secular education. This, from the start, had been the core of the state policy for Jewish "improvement." It had been welcomed also by many Jews. Indeed the initiative in setting up "modern" schools for Jewish children mainly from the poorer classes had come from members of the Jewish Enlightenment intelligentsia.[58] After a pioneering venture in Berlin in 1781, several schools had been founded elsewhere around the turn of the century. Most were started with state encouragement and support. A common feature of the new schools was the use of High German as the language of instruction and religious teaching based on Mendelssohn's translation of the Pentateuch. Compared to traditional Jewish schools, there was a predictable shift to secular subjects, arithmetic, French, handicrafts, or the classics.

The impact of such pioneering ventures could only be limited. Of greater importance for the Jewish "masses" was the insistence of governments on compulsory education whether in Jewish or general schools.[59] Dates of the relevant enactments reflect the progress of Jewish acculturation in the different German states. The pacesetter here was the "progressive" duchy of Baden (1809) followed by Bavaria (1813) and the Hessian principalities (1817–19, 1816–23, and 1823). There followed Prussia (1824) and Württemberg (1825) with retrograde Saxony and Hanover (both 1837) bringing up the rear. In nearly every instance compulsory education was accompanied by readiness to admit Jewish children to public schools. As a rule, Jewish communities were also authorized to found and run their own schools. Arrangements with regard to religious instruction varied. In Prussia, which lagged behind, this was made compulsory only in 1847.

Well before the acculturation of the majority, members of the Jewish intelligentsia had acquired a growing familiarity with German and European culture. In numbers of cases, at the start, they had benefitted from the encouragement of Christian patrons.[60] Eager to acquire a secular culture, more and more young Jews flocked to schools and universities. Medical faculties in particular had adopted early a liberal admissions

[58] See Katz, *Out of the Ghetto,* 126ff.

[59] See Toury, *Soziale und Politische Geschichte der Juden in Deutschland, 1847–1871* (Dusseldorf, 1977), 166ff.

[60] For a number of instances, see Toury, "*Eintritt,*" 179.

policy with regard to Jews, while medical studies were congenial to Jewish students. Of fifty-four medical doctorates conferred by the University of Berlin in 1826, four to six went to Jewish students, another to a baptized Jew. There were no impediments to Jewish medical practice.[61]

Acculturation against a background of growing prosperity had resulted in a limited social and cultural integration in Gentile society. Some Jewish women of the upper class presided over mixed salons frequented by luminaries of the Gentile *Bildungsbürgertum* (there is no English equivalent), such as Wilhelm von Humboldt or the historian Leopold V. Ranke. At the same time, selected "accultured" Jews were admitted to the debating societies, clubs, and institutions of the educated middle classes and were able to share their interests and activities. The process is described, perhaps overenthusiastically and in a somewhat generalized form, in an account dating from the year 1833: "Let us consider," it began,

> the immense changes that have taken place in language, apparel, way of life, in requirements and amusements, in manners and customs. . . . Already their external appearance, how it has changed since those times. Who would not previously have recognized a Jew instantly by his clumsy oriental dress, his loose dark kaftan, by the fur cap pressed low on his brow and by the beard disfiguring his face, who would not have recognized a Jewish matron by her silver-embroidered headgear, her severe forehead, devoid of adorning coiffure?[62]

How many Jews were still to be seen in this guise unless relics of the past or of Polish origin? How anxiously they then clung to the pettiest customs. Which Jews only thirty years ago would have ventured to open his shop on a Saturday or to follow his commercial avocations, to write, or to travel? Would one have found Jews thirty years ago in inns or restaurants joining the common table d'hôte, to converse unconstrainedly with Christians, to share with them food and drink? Now Christian schools in every town received Jewish children, especially older ones. Only in a few homes did older family members still use the Jewish jargon. Both children and dwellers in the larger towns now spoke the same language as their Christian fellows both at home and in public. Many alive in the last century could bear witness if in their youth they had ever seen a Jew finding pleasure in concerts, soirées, balls, or popular entertainments or studying the daily press in coffee houses or the lobbies of exchanges. Had

[61] Matriculation in universities had been and remained easier for Jews than entry into gymnasia. Already in the eighteenth century the number of Jews enrolled in medical faculties had run into three figures. Ibid., 180–81, 184.

[62] M. B. Lessing, *Die Juden und die öffentliche Meinung im preussischen Staate* (Altona, 1833), 129ff. The quotation is from Toury, "*Eintritt*," 199. The translation is my own.

they found any interested in theater, music, or the arts? Had they ever encountered in scientific circles or among educated people a Jew the equal of the rest of the company in either manners or knowledge? The profound changes thus described the author attributed to the combined effects of the Prussian Edict of 1812 and the conscious endeavor of Jews to become "productive."

The picture presented by Lessing requires some modification. Clearly, it applied mainly to urban dwellers. Cultural interests in all probability were confined to a small minority. Social intercourse with Christians, even within the parameters described, remained almost certainly exceptional. Yet the terms of social relationships between Jews and Christians had been undergoing a change.[63] The rapid growth of cities meant that Jewish "immigrants" found there growing numbers of Christians, strangers like themselves to the established municipal oligarchies and more willing to accept Jews as equals. The new relationships, however, were no longer the intimate personal ones that had characterized the salons of an earlier age. Instead, contacts were largely confined to the semi-public realm of a variety of clubs and associations frequented by the rising Liberal *Bildungsbürgertum.* Secular Liberalism provided a common ideological basis for *rapprochement,* while democratic radicalism did the same for members of a younger intelligentsia regardless of religion or ethnicity.

Such social relations, however, were confined to limited intellectual and bourgeois circles mainly in the larger towns. Elsewhere, "integration" was confined to an exchange of mutual assurances of respect in political and cultural societies and associations. In the middle layers of Gentile *Bürgertum,* the Jew remained a social outsider. In the petty bourgeoisie and in smaller towns and villages also, there was little intimacy, notwithstanding occasional acts of good-neighborliness. Many Jews, and perhaps most Christians, according to Jacob Katz,[64] ignored prohibitions with regard to eating each others' food or in one another's company. However, the abandonment of ritual restrictions, while it made social contact between Jew and non-Jew possible, did not necessarily encourage or promote it. Meetings between the two continued to be regarded as encounters between members of separate societies that differed both in status and quality. Special motivation was needed for such meetings and when they occurred, they were accompanied by "self-consciousness evaluation of the event." "All things being equal, the Jew was the one who gained when a Gentile of similar cultural and economic standing deigned to meet him just for the meeting's sake. The non-Jew

[63] See Lessing, *Juden,* 237ff.

[64] See Katz, *Out of the Ghetto,* 203–4.

was at once suspect, an ulterior motive was immediately ascribed to him and the meeting robbed of whatever ease or innocence it might have had."[65] In any case, the chances of a Jew knowing a fellow Jew really intimately were statistically greater than his chances of knowing a non-Jew. His social separation from non-Jewish society was conditioned by his professional preferences and religious affiliation. The social exclusiveness of the Jew, at the same time, reinforced his disposition for certain professions and strengthened this affiliation to his community. Above all, "an inclination for endogamy," in Jew and Gentile alike, "reinforced the Jewish tendency to remain a society apart."[66]

The Modernization of Judaism

Acculturation, secular education, and the attempt to shed distinctive Jewish traits had a profound influence on the religious practices of Jewish communities.[67] As state schools replaced the *heder* and *yeshiva*, features of traditional Jewish life and ritual were abandoned. Expressions of Jewish nationalism were toned down or disappeared altogether from religious services. The prescriptions of the Talmud gave way to those of the Decalogue. What had been a way of life was progressively transformed into a confession analogous to Protestantism. Rabbis, from having exercised quasi-judicial functions, became primarily preachers. Such at least is the conventional picture of religious reform in Germany. It is in need of qualifications.

In the first place, Jewish communities, membership in which would remain compulsory until 1876, enjoyed a wide measure of autonomy in religious and communal matters. In the absence of a central Jewish authority (except in Baden) they were able, in a form of "congregationalism," to shape the ritual of their synagogues to their taste. In consequence, both the pace and degree of reform differed from one community to the next with infinite gradations ranging from the modernized traditionalism of neo-orthodoxy to the "quasi-Protestantism" of radical reform. In general, the larger and more urbanized a community, the stronger its propen-

[65] Ibid.

[66] Ibid., 204.

[67] For the religious transformation of German Jewry, see ibid., 124ff. and 207ff.; Ismar Schorsch, "Emancipation and the Crisis of Religious Authority—The Emergence of the Modern Rabbinate," in Mosse et al., *Revolution and Evolution,* 205ff.; Steven M. Lowenstein, "The 1840's and the Creation of the German-Jewish Religious Reform Movement," in Mosse et al., *Revolution and Evolution,* 255ff.; Pinchas E. Rosenblüth, "Samson Raphael Hirsch: Sein Denken und Wirken," in Liebeschütz and Paucker, *Judentum,* 293ff.; Julius Carlebach, "The Foundation of German-Jewish Orthodoxy: An Interpretation," *LBY* 33 (1988): 67ff.

sity for change. Smaller and more rural communities, on the other hand, would incline to conservatism in matters of ritual. There were problems in communities where, as was not infrequently the case, reformers clashed with conservatives. In such clashes, the authorities would tend to adopt a neutral stance.

Overall, the evidence would seem to suggest that the progress of reform may have been slower and more uneven than is sometimes suggested. The larger and more reform-minded communities would receive disproportionate attention from both contemporaries and posterity.

It may, moreover, be questioned whether there existed, except among extreme ideologues in either camp, a clear-cut ideological distinction between reform and neo-orthodoxy. There were numerous gradations, compromises, and intermediate forms with communities of rabbis opting for greater or lesser elements of either one or the other. Moreover, the neo-orthodox would presently become no less accultured and, to some extent, denationalized than the reformers. Both, in fact, were different representatives of a modernized and partially emancipated Jewry.

What helped modernization was that the interests of the state coincided on the whole with those of moderate reformers. Religious reform, from the start, had formed an element in the educational policies adopted for the "betterment" of the Jews. It would tend to assimilate them to the rest of the population. States with Catholic majorities, though, might favor religious Orthodoxy.

At the same time, a measure of reform reflected the preference of a growing number of Jews. Some considered that, as part of an unwritten bargain, they had agreed to abandon "particularist" features of their religious practice and way of life in exchange for civil equality with Christians. Indeed emancipation and modernization, both incomplete, had been parallel developments.

In any case, with changes in the socialization of Jewish youth, features of talmudic Judaism had come to be considered as antiquated with little relevance to contemporary life. They would also be dysfunctional in both economic and social terms. Strict observance of the sabbath and adherence to the dietary laws were, respectively, obstacles to any form of public activity and to social intercourse with Gentiles. There appeared to be economic and social rewards attached to reform. Again, a modernization of Jewish religious practice was not unrelated to a quest for respectability in the eyes of the Gentile world.

The modernization of Judaism was welcomed also by Gentiles. Some, from the start, had envisaged the progressive assimilation of Jews, culminating, they hoped, in their ultimate conversion. Such indeed had been the hidden agenda of many protagonists of Jewish emancipation. With progressive secularization, conversion was coming to be advocated on civic rather than religious grounds. "It is not baptism that counts," an opponent of Judaism declared, "but that the Jews, by saying 'Baptize me,' says at the same time: I obey the laws of the country, I submit myself to the institutions you have created, I fulfill all the obligations laid upon me at all times."[68] It was an argument also advanced by Jews seeking to justify their conversion or that of their infant children. Conversion, where it was not purely opportunistic, was fast becoming a civic rather than a religious gesture. At the same time the convert, spurned by Jews, ceased also to be highly regarded by growing sections of the Gentile population. Many preferred Jews who remained faithful in whatever form to the traditions of their fathers. Others had always believed that baptism could not alter the essential nature of Jews and was therefore meaningless. The convert in search of worldly advantage was for many an object of derision.

Fundamental Rights

The Revolution of 1848–49 has been considered—with questionable justification—as marking a turning point in the history of Jewish emancipation.[69] In the "revolution of the intellectuals"[70] it fell to representatives of the *Bildungsbürgertum,* including a number of Jews, to tackle the Jewish question on an all-German plane as part of a wider emancipation movement. Following prolonged discussions, parliamentarians in the *Paulskirche* in Frankfurt adopted a law defining the "Fundamental Rights of the German people." Article 5, without specific reference to Jews, declared the enjoyment of civil and political rights to be "neither dependent on nor restricted by religious creed."[71] This was the formulation followed by individual states when adopting the "Fundamental Rights." It was also incorporated in new constitutions, notably in Prussia and Austria. An all-German emancipation of the Jews might thus appear to have been achieved by German intellectuals as part of a wider application of Liberal principles.

The attempt was to have little practical effect. Even as the Frankfurt Parliament was proclaiming the Fundamental Rights, the revolutionary

[68] Quoted in Katz, *Out of the Ghetto,* 95. On the general issues of conversions and mixed marriages and the numbers involved, see Katz, *Out of the Ghetto,* 104ff., and Toury, "Soziale Geschichte," 51ff.

[69] See Mosse et al., *Revolution and Evolution,* and Jacob Toury, "Die Revolution von 1848 als Innerjüdischer Wendepunkt," in Liebeschütz and Paucker, *Judentum,* 359ff.

[70] Lewis Namier, "1848: The Revolution of the Intellectuals," in *Proceedings of the British Academy* 30 (1944).

[71] Quoted in Rürup, "Jewish Emancipation," 83.

tide was beginning to ebb. Soon individual governments were reasserting their authority. With few exceptions, they returned to their traditional Jewish policies. A period of partial reaction followed, comparable to after 1815.

Evaluations of the significance of the episode—the German attempt at a "French solution"—differ. Thus while Mosse considers the legislation of 1848–49 a "flash in the pan,"[72] Rürup, with some hesitation, opts for an opposite view.[73] Toury sees the importance of 1848 mainly in the effects of the revolution on Jewish attitudes and inner-Jewish developments.[74] To some extent, the view taken depends on the definition of emancipation adopted.[75] Whatever the conclusion, however, while inner-Jewish change was a gradual process, externally the great majority of Jews after 1848–49 would notice little difference from what had gone on before.

Legal Emancipation

In the postrevolutionary Prussian constitution of 1850, Article 12 laid down that differences of religious belief could not justify inequality in civic and citizen rights. Article 14, however, partly negated the general principle by declaring that "notwithstanding the freedom of religion guaranteed in Article 12, the Christian religion shall form the basis of all institutions of the state concerned with religious practice."[76] The interpretation of the clause lay largely in the eye of the beholder. In fact, it would be used in a restrictive sense debarring Jews from most public office whether in the judiciary or in education, as village elders and even as surveyors. Thus the concept of the "Christian State" prevailed. The establishment of a regency for the incapacitated king and the subsequent adoption of somewhat more liberal policies in the so-called "New Era"

[72] W. E. Mosse, "The Revolution of 1848: Jewish Emancipation in Germany and Its Limits," in Mosse et al., *Revolution and Evolution,* 389ff.

[73] "[E]ven though the development was not completed it must be noted as significant advance that things everywhere had been set in motion and that in actual fact the issue of Jewish emancipation had indeed been decided in principle." Rürup, "Tortuous Path," 28.

[74] "Jedenfalls lässt sich . . . aus der Revolution von 1848 das Fazit einer jahrzehntelangen Entwicklung ablesen, an deren Schlusspunkt der politisch liberalisierte, wirtschaftlich und kulturell integrierte, gesellschaftlich (wenigstens teilweise) akzeptierte, aber religiös und gruppenmässig disorganisierte Jude steht. Die Revolution des 'Tollen Jahres' bezeichnet damit das Ende der Ghetto-Existenz aber auch den Schlüsselpunkt einer Wandlung im jüdischen Sein." Toury, "Die Revolution von 1848 als innerjüdischer Wendepunkt," in Liebeschütz and Paucker, *Judentum,* 376.

[75] Frank Eyck, "The Revolution of 1848—A Comment," in Mosse et al., *Revolution and Evolution,* 403ff.

[76] For this and the following see Rürup, "Tortuous Path," 30.

did not bring an early change. To the end of the sixties, the Prussian Diet would confine its activities to endless debates on Jewish disabilities in the Lower House where Liberals were in the majority. As late as 1862, the Upper House threw out a modest proposal to abolish the degrading oath *more judaico.*

However, while Prussian reactionaries (with Bismarck as prime minister from 1862) were still able to block attempts at full legal emancipation, the tide, elsewhere in Germany, was turning. Hamburg had led the way in granting Jews full citizenship rights in 1860. It was followed by Württemberg (1861, with the removal of a few remaining residual restrictions left over until 1862–64). In 1861, with only some minor Jewish disabilities remaining, Bavaria had at last repealed the notorious *Matrikelgesetz* of 1813. The following year, Baden conceded full equality of rights.[77] Despite Prussian recalcitrance, the battle for legal emancipation was steadily being won.

What caused the change of heart of rulers, ministers, and chambers can be illustrated from the well-documented case of Baden.[78] There the grand duke early in 1860 had formed a Liberal government under First Minister Lamey. Although he knew that Jewish emancipation would not be popular, Lamey told the grand duke that it was both a necessary demand of justice and a political necessity. The whole structure of the state, he argued, no longer permitted that a class of subjects should remain excluded from a number of legal competences for a characteristic so little relevant as their formal religious allegiance. Even if Jews stood morally below the Christian population, their exclusion from the operation of the common law would be an injustice. It would hit the educated, the honorable, and the hard-working due to the bad ones, whereas among the Christian population numerous brutal and immoral people enjoyed equal rights for the sake of the better ones.[79] Partial solutions were no longer possible. The end result of new legislation could only be complete emancipation. Withal, Lamey confessed, one had to overcome a certain repugnance in having to accept Jews as equals. There was about them "for us

[77] Ibid., 32.

[78] Rürup, "Die Judenemanzipation in Baden," *Zeitschrift für die Geschichte des Oberrheins,* Band 114 (1966): 241ff.

[79] "Die ganze Anlage unserer staatlichen Zustände verträgt es nicht mehr, dass eine Klasse von Untertanen um eines so wenig zutreffenden Merkmals willen, wie der äusserlich bekannte Glaube es ist, von einer Reihe rechtlicher Befugnisse ausgeschlossen bleibt. . . . Ja stünden sie selbst menschlich tiefer als die christliche Bevölkerung, so bliebe ihr Ausschluss vom gemeinen Recht eine Ungerechtigkeit, denn er träfe auch die Gebildeten, Redlichen, Fleissigen um der Schlechten willen, während bei der christlichen Bevölkerung die doch zahlreich genug vorhandenen Rohen und Unsittlichen um der Besseren willen mit gleichen Rechten versehen sind." Lamey to the grand duke of Baden, probably 3 August 1860, quoted ibid., 294.

Germans," something "alien . . . of a disagreeable nature."[80] They were, however, citizens, and they were considered Germans and Badeners, and from this the conclusions had to be drawn.[81] In the course of the last decade, Lamey added, people had lost the courage to oppose Jewish emancipation in principle. All that opponents now based their arguments on was opportuneness and timing.[82]

It was, in fact, on these latter issues that the government dwelt in introducing its emancipation bill in the second chamber early in 1862.[83] Earlier political ferment, it argued, had now given way to calmer and more considered views about the reciprocal rights of estates and individuals existing within the state. It had come to be increasingly felt that only the freest development of individual forces could achieve the greater perfection of the whole. Again, the average well-being of the population had reached a point where possible economic misgivings no longer need carry decisive weight. The freedom of movement in commerce and crafts to be legally established by the present *Landtag* must include the Israelites. This would open to them a new path to the development of their forces. It would pave the way for an assimilation to Christian customs and ways of life and thereby contribute mightily to the removal of "remaining isolated prejudices and passions."[84] Such were the arguments that eventually carried the day.

It is reasonable to assume that considerations such as these underlay Jewish emancipation in German states other than Baden at this time. Noteworthy is the "emancipator" Lamey's exposition of his personal aversion to Jews on account of their "alien" and uncongenial nature. However, as a good Liberal, he is nevertheless rationally convinced of the injustice of continuing discrimination. Moreover, there hangs over Lamey's argumentation an element of fatalist resignation. Emancipation, demanded by the nature of a modern state, can no longer be resisted. Jews at the same time are referred to as subjects, not citizens. There is,

[80] "Aber freilich, eine gewisse Abneigung muss jedermann überwinden, um sie sich gleichzustellen. Sie haben eben für uns Deutsche etwas uns Fremdes von unangenehmer Beschaffenheit." Ibid.

[81] "Dagegen sind sie aber Staatsbürger; wir betrachten sie als Deutsche, als Badener und müssen die Konsequenzen daraus ziehen." Ibid.

[82] "Seit den letzten zehn Jahren ist der Mut verschwunden, der Juden-emanzipation in Prinzip entgegenzutreten. Allein, was man nicht mehr von der rechtlichen Seite zu negieren gewagt hat, das sucht man von Seiten der Zweckmässheit in Frage zu stellen. Die Frage, so sagt man, muss zu Gunsten der Juden gelöst werden, allein es ist jetzt nicht an der Zeit." Ibid., 295 n. 219.

[83] The chamber, coincidentally, contained the first Jewish deputy, Dr. Rudolf Kusel from Karlsruhe. Ibid., 294.

[84] Ibid., 295.

moreover, an implication of their moral inferiority to Christians. Still, for the sake of the "good Jews," emancipation must be granted also to the less deserving. Lamey's feelings in the matter clearly were ambivalent, as probably were those of the grand duke.

Following the spate of emancipatory acts of the early 1860s that appeared to make general legal emancipation a mere matter of time, the movement once more lost momentum. Governments were concerned with the problems of unification. Some continued to prevaricate in an attempt to stave off the inevitable. However, with the founding of the North German Confederation in 1866–67, the "Jewish Question" was once more placed on the agenda.[85] Immediately after the convocation in 1867 of its lower chamber, the *Reichstag,* 371 Jewish communities petitioned for a law to abrogate all remaining limitations of municipal and state rights resulting from differences of religious confession. A bill to this effect introduced by one of the deputies was passed the same year by a large majority. When the second chamber, the *Bundesrat,* had failed to act on the bill for a year, the *Reichstag* passed a second identical bill. In the *Bundesrat,* a rearguard action by the Mecklenburgs, the most recalcitrant and reactionary German states, further delayed proceedings. In part thanks to the intervention of Bismarck, however, resistance was finally overcome. The law, promulgated on 3 July 1869, declared that, for the territory of the Confederation, "All remaining restrictions on civic and citizenship rights imposed on the grounds of differences of religious profession are herewith abolished. In particular, eligibility or participation in representative bodies at both communal and state level and the holding of public offices shall be independent of religious profession."[86] The full legal emancipation of all Jews north of the river Main was an accomplished fact. By means of an imperial law (1870) and interstate treaties (1871), the North German law was then extended to the southern states. In law and on paper, at any rate, Jewish emancipation in Germany was complete.

There is no evidence to suggest that the completion of the long drawn-out process of legal emancipation was greeted by German Jewry with particular joy or excitement. De facto emancipation had been, for many of them, an accomplished fact for some time. Economic and especially social and cultural processes were not amenable to legislative acts. Neither were administrative procedures. In fact, the practical effects of the legislation from which complete Jewish emancipation is conventionally dated were minimal. It had been little more than a tidying-up operation.

[85] See Ernest Hamburger, *Juden im öffentlichen Leben Deutschlands* (Tübingen, 1968), 28–29.

[86] Rürup, "Tortuous Path," 32.

The "Jewish Question"

Jewish emancipation in Germany had been completed, not accidentally, under favorable economic auspices. The years since 1867 had seen a hectic boom, the so-called *Gründerjahre,* when the "typical figure" had been the *Gründer* (promoter) "hawking the shares of any kind of company, safe, risky or downright fraudulent, to a population seized with a mania for reckless investment."[87] Among the promoters had been many Jews, the precise number or proportion of whom it is impossible to determine.

The year 1873 saw a sharp reversal of the long economic trend period with the onset of the Great Depression that would last until the mid-1890s.[88] Share prices on the Berlin Stock Exchange collapsed as many of the newly founded companies went out of business. Numerous middle-class savers lost the whole or part of their investments. Anticapitalist resentment found a ready target in the Jews, widely blamed for fraudulent manipulations of the so-called *Gründungsschwindel.* Court preacher Adolf Stoecker and his Christian Social Party inaugurated a vicious anti-Jewish campaign, the so-called "Berlin movement." In 1881, anti-Semites (the term is conventionally dated from its use in 1879 by an anti-Semitic publicist, Wilhelm Marr) presented to the German government a petition bearing some 250,000 signatures.[89] This demanded the exclusion of Jews from all responsible state positions. Only in exceptional circumstances should they be admitted to teaching posts. They must not sit as single judges. A separate religious census should be introduced. Restrictions must be placed on Jewish immigration. An accompanying document spoke of "Jewish racial characteristics" that seriously threatened the well-being, culture, and religion of the German people. Jewish influence must be combatted by effective measures. The "Jewish danger" was in fact referred to in a manner that suggested that the authors' ultimate objective was the repeal of emancipation.

The authorities, which meant essentially the imperial chancellor Bismarck, adopted an ambivalent attitude in the face of the anti-Semitic campaign. While "restoring order" when confronted with anti-Jewish riots and attempted pogroms that threatened public tranquillity, they did nothing to counteract the anti-Jewish campaign itself. Indeed Bismarck, whose personal attitude toward Jews was ambiguous and opportunistic, was ready to utilize it for tactical political purposes. During 1878–79, while the campaign was reaching a first peak, he was jettisoning his erst-

[87] Peter Pulzer, *The Rise of Political Antisemitism in Germany and Austria* (London, 1988), 19.

[88] For the effects of the Great Depression on the anti-Semitic movement in Germany, see Hans Rosenberg, *Grosse Depression und Bismarckzeit* (Berlin, 1967).

[89] See Wanda Kampmann, *Deutsche und Juden* (Frankfurt, 1979), 254.

while (National) Liberal free-trade supporters in favor of an alliance with protectionist Conservatives and anti-Liberal Catholics of the Centre Party. His new majority would be anti-Liberal, protectionist, and, in consequence, inevitably unsympathetic to Jews. The state, while maintaining the letter of the law in the matter of Jewish citizenship rights, would now reverse the more liberal trend of the previous period in the matter of administrative practice. Jewish social integration, at the same time, would receive a major setback. There was a general anti-emancipatory and anti-Jewish atmosphere. It might be noted in passing that this was part of a wider European trend marking the age of the Great Depression.

It was in this broadly anti-Jewish climate of opinion that one of Germany's most highly regarded historians, Heinrich von Treitschke, professor at the University of Berlin, wrote a polemic on the "Jewish Question" that forms a suggestive counterpart to the writings of Dohm on the same subject a century earlier. In November 1879 in the *Preussische Jahrbücher,* which he edited, Treitschke published a brief statement, "Ein Wort über unser Judentum" ("A Word about Our Jews").[90] In response to numerous objections, he elaborated his arguments further the following year. Treitschke made clear that he did not advocate the revocation of emancipation, which, he said, would be a breach of the law. However, he maintained that the Jews should demonstrate gratitude for the civic equality granted freely by the state that was not a natural right. The "unfinished" German nation lacked instinctive pride and a distinctive cultural physiognomy. It was defenseless against alien influences. Of the Jews it must be demanded that they either become unreservedly Germans or emigrate. It was only in this expectation that emancipation had been ceded to them. In the same breath, however, Treitschke raises doubts whether Jews could in fact become "true" Germans. A gulf, he contended, would always remain. Why, he asks, had so many noble and talented nations throughout history directed the diabolical forces hidden in the "depth of their souls" against the Jews and against them only? His answer is that the Jews of the Diaspora were a people without a state, without history, without a language of their own. They lived scattered all over the world without abandoning their separate identity, at one and the same time beneficiaries of their host countries and a strictly separate nation. They were thereby responsible in part also for the brutality of the "justifiable" popular feeling that was once more rising against them. Although there was in Treitschke's argumentation little that was new, his academic standing would make his views the gospel of a rising generation of students and academics. His ideology of integral German nationalism in fact effectively implied the negation of Jewish emancipation.

[90] Ibid., 265ff.

While the anti-Semitism of the imperial period contained much that was traditional, some novel features have been noted.[91] Whereas previously anti-Judaism had been directed mainly against unassimilated and unintegrated Jewish groups, the new anti-Semitism had as its principal target precisely emancipated and "assimilated" Jews. Moreover, ethnicity and "racial origins" (*Abstammung*) were now more important than religion. The "Jewish Question" could henceforth be defined as one of race rather than religion. A further innovation was the emergence of anti-Semitic political parties, of anti-Semitism as a political movement. Finally, anti-Semitism was being transformed from an anti-Jewish program into a philosophic-historical worldview, a key to the understanding and solution of general social problems.

In practice, the eighties and early nineties witnessed the virtual elimination of Jews from German public life, not by the revocation of emancipation but by administrative means. The state, meanwhile, taking its stand formally on law and constitution, maintained a specious neutrality in the conflict between anti-Semite and Jew. There can be little doubt that without that neutrality and the maintenance of law and order, where necessary by force, a wave of pogroms would have swept Germany with incalculable results.

At the same time, despite a radical reversal of economic policy, the state, in the interest of economic development and expansion, continued to favor Jewish enterprise. Attempts by interest groups to introduce thinly disguised anti-Jewish legislation in the shape of special taxes on stock-exchange transactions or department stores produced little practical result. In matters of fiscal and commercial policy, governments might have been inclined to favor agricultural interests and those of heavy industry in which the Jewish role was small as against those of finance, commerce, and light industry where it was considerable; nevertheless some balance, under the influence of rival pressure groups, was maintained. Nor did the state interfere with uncongenial cultural pursuits in which Jews played a prominent part. Rather, there developed a cultural dualism with an official nationalist culture favored by the ruling class confronting a liberal, internationalist, and largely (if by no means exclusively) Jewish counterculture.[92] Thus, during the great antiliberal and anti-emancipatory reaction, the division was once again reinforced: Jews,

[91] See Reinhard Rürup, "Emanzipation und Antisemitismus: Historische Venbindungslnien," in Hrsg. Herbert A. Strauss and Norbert Kampe, *Antisemitismus* (Frankfurt and New York, 1984), 95.

[92] See W. E. Mosse, *The German Jewish Economic Elite: A Socio-Cultural Profile, 1820–1935* (Oxford, 1989), 297ff., and idem, "Wilhelm II and the Kaiserjuden: A Problematical Encounter," in Jehuda Reinharz and Walter Schatzberg, eds., *The Jewish Response to German Culture* (Hanover and London, 1985), 164ff.

all but completely excluded from official positions in the state, were compensated through opportunities in other fields and received consistent protection against mob violence in the streets and, if at times hesitantly, against insult and defamation in the courts. If neither side had obtained all it had hoped for in the emancipation "bargain," each had achieved at least a part of its objectives.

German society, meanwhile, had manifested its pervasive anti-Jewish sentiments through the progressive exclusion of Jews from the bulk of voluntary associations (*Vereine*) to which they had been selectively admitted in slowly increasing numbers during the preceding period. Interethnic social intercourse languished. Jews as a result were thrown back on their own resources. Wherever they were debarred from membership, conspicuously in student fraternities or corporations, they created their own organizations. There developed a system of apartheid (the process has been described by Shulamit Volkov as "dissimilation"),[93] which, ironically, contained aspects of a pluralist society. It was a process deplored by some Jews, accepted by others as an inescapable fact, and welcomed by a small but growing number. Whether from necessity, choice, or previous indifference to matters Jewish, a mark of increasing integration (even the term "assimilation," which, on the whole, has been deliberately avoided here, may be appropriate) gave way to growing Jewish awareness and self-assertion.

The organized Jewish response to the challenge of anti-Semitism was the founding in 1893 of a defense organization, the Centralverein Deutscher Staatsbürger Jüdischen Glaubens (Central Association of German Citizens of the Jewish Faith), known as the C.V.[94] The day of its foundation, 26 March 1893, has been described as a historic landmark in the history of German Jewry.[95] Whatever the evaluation of the organization by later historians, its founding marked a turning point in the evolution of German-Jewish self-consciousness. The first section of its programmatic declaration contained its response to Treitschke and the anti-Semitic challenge: "We German citizens of Jewish faith stand firmly on the ground of German nationality. Our community with Jews of other countries is not different from the community of German Catholics and Protestants with the Catholics and Protestants of other countries. We

[93] Shulamit Volkov, "The Dynamics of Dissimilation," in Reinharz and Schatzberg, *Jewish Response,* 195ff.

[94] For the C.V., see Arnold Paucker, "Zur Problematik der jüdischen Abwehrstrategie in der deutschen Gesellschaft," in W. E. Mosse, ed., *Juden im Wilhelminischen Deutschland 1890–1914* (Tübingen, 1976), 479ff.; Ismar Schorsch, *Jewish Reactions to German Antisemitism, 1870–1914* (New York, 1972); Jehuda Reinharz, *Fatherland or Promised Land: The Dilemma of the German Jew, 1893–1914* (Ann Arbor, Mich.: 1975); and Marjorie Lamberti, *Jewish Activism in Imperial Germany* (New Haven and London, 1978).

[95] Paucker, "Zur Problematik," 484.

happily fulfill our duties as citizens and keep to our constitutional rights."[96]

The overall tone of the statement, clearly addressed mainly to non-Jews, is defensive. Several points are significant: the definition of Jewishness in terms of the Jewish faith, and the comparison of solidarity with one's coreligionists in other countries. This is the reply to the traditional charge of dual loyalty. As regards the relationship with the German state, the key term employed is "citizen." To Treitschke's demand that they should become "Germans and nothing but Germans," Jews assert that their adherence to the Jewish faith is similar to the religious allegiance of Catholics or Protestants (whose Germanness, especially for the latter, is not called into question thereby). A consideration of the position of secularized Jews would, in terms of the C.V. statement, have posed insuperable problems. With regard to their religious affiliation—the feature distinguishing them from their "fellow Germans"—the authors of the C.V. declaration take their stand on the rights guaranteed by the constitution. In fact the C.V., run largely by lawyers, would see as one of its major tasks throughout its existence the defense of Jewish rights in the courts.

Finally the founding fathers of the C.V. tried to confront as best they could what had become (or been made) in the eyes of perhaps a majority of Gentiles the crux of the "Jewish Question": could a Jew ever be a true German, a member of the German *Volk?* No Jew, by definition, could form part of the German race. But could they belong to the *Volk,* an emotion-charged term in vogue among nationalists and anti-Semites? The C.V. statement, carefully avoiding the use of "Volk," states somewhat lamely (but what other answer was possible?) that it stood firmly "on the ground of German nationality." The choice of this term, devoid of meaning ("nationality" in the technical sense is not applicable here; in a much looser sense, it is something approaching "ethnicity"), betrays the fundamental Jewish dilemma when confronted with *völkisch,* let alone racialist ideology. Jews could indeed claim to be German citizens and to be of the Jewish faith. But how indeed could they establish membership of the German people denied them by their opponents?

From this time onward, whatever the weaknesses of its ideology, the C.V. to the bitter end would remain the representative body of emancipated German Jewry. Its membership would grow from around two thousand in 1894 to some forty thousand at the outbreak of World War I. It

[96] "Wir deutschen Staatsbürger jüdischen Glaubens stehen fest auf dem Boden der deutschen Nationalität. Unsere Gemeinschaft mit den Juden anderer Länder ist keine andere als die Gemeinschaft der Katholiken und Protestanten Deutschlands mit den Katholiken und Protestanten anderer Länder. Wir erfüllen als Staatsbürger freudig unsere Pflicht und halten fest an unseren verfassungsmässigen Rechten." Ibid., 488.

would become a "genuine representative institution of the Jewish religious community."[97] Ideologically and organizationally it may be considered the end product of the century-long process of Jewish emancipation in Germany. In the apt formulation of Jacob Toury, "the tradition-bound, primarily religious Jew had become a new, secularized, German-acculturea citizen of the Jewish faith."[98]

[97] Ibid., 489–90. For minority groups not represented or underrepresented in the C.V., see ibid., 490–91.

[98] "Der traditionsgebundene, primär religiös orientierte Jude hatte sich zu einem neuen säkularisierten, im Deutschtum akkulturierten Bürger jüdischer Konfession gewandelt." Toury, "Die Revolution von 1848," 376.

FOUR

BETWEEN SOCIAL AND POLITICAL ASSIMILATION: REMARKS ON THE HISTORY OF JEWS IN FRANCE*

Pierre Birnbaum

THE ENTRY of the Jews of France into modernity unfolded in a dramatic context. It began with the French Revolution and the difficult Napoleonic epoch and extended through the numerous revolutionary periods of the nineteenth century, all the while undergoing relatively violent periods of crisis. For a long time, the different types of Jewish communities throughout the nation, particularly the important concentrations in eastern France, including Bordeaux, Bayonne, and the Contat Venaissin, had had little means for communication that would allow for a minimum of coordination and solidarity. Each community's particular notion of Jewish identity and fate produced divergent strategies.[1] To understand why many Jews emerged from the social process of assimilation while others turned away from the emancipatory measures taken by the state, we must briefly evoke the long-term effects of the Revolution itself, for its primarily long-term consequences would shape the strategies for future generations of Jews in France until contemporary times.

A comparative focus on the Jews of southwestern and eastern France enables us to understand the extent to which profound differences alienating these communities from each other gave rise to altogether different strategies. Let us simply recall here that the so-called Portuguese Jews and those from Bordeaux and Bayonne benefitted from formal residency status, which gave them nearly all the same rights as other citizens. Since the eighteenth century they had taken part in some of the most important economic activities. They were involved in arms exportation, even in colonial expeditions that enabled them to become plantation owners in Santa Domingo and Martinique. Belonging to the local upper classes, they comprised a closed sphere whose unity was continually reinforced

* Translated by Jacqueline Kay.

[1] Pierre Birnbaum, "Les Juifs entre l'appartenance identitaire et l'éntrée dans l'espace public: la Révolution française et le choix des acteurs," *Revue Française de Sociologie* 3 (1989).

by endogamous matrimonial strategies. Important families such as Gradis, Rabas, Peixotte, and Furtado would play a critical role in the events of the revolutionary emancipation. Yet though most Bordeaux Jews remained loyal to their community of origin, participating regularly in local philanthropic politics, Catholic conversions affected nearly every family.[2] The Portuguese Jews furthermore maintained close ties with their Amsterdam and London counterparts, facilitating economic ties. They adhered to the rationalism of the eighteenth century and rejected the Talmud and Midrash, following only the Bible. Throughout the French Revolution there was "nothing to be gained"[3] by drawing attention to particularisms they felt no longer existed. As a full-fledged citizen, Gradis would almost be appointed to the Etats Généraux, just as Furtado was nominated to be the Conseil Général de Bordeaux before becoming Napoleon's principal interlocutor during the session of the Grand Sanhédrin meetings on assimilation. Bordeaux and Bayonne Jews were only interested in "entering" society as equal citizens; they aspired to an assimilation that would dissolve the communitarian links they considered anachronistic in favor of a Jewish identity because they were grounded solely in religion. Their success was all they had hoped for, including their appointment as Court Jews.

The Alsatian Jews, in contrast, were still living in close-knit communities in ghettos similar to the shtetls of the Jewish communities in eastern Europe. Most were very poor and earned a living from simple trades such as peddling or as lace and animal merchants. Their dense social networks, based upon a very Orthodox way of life that respected tradition and was centered entirely around the synagogue, reinforced the sentiment of a common destiny.[4] The Jacobin emancipation and the violent processes of centralization that accompanied it could only destroy this communal life, just as it attacked all the regionalisms, peripheral affiliations, and provincial dialects. Abbot Grégoire, a supporter of Jewish emancipation who favored the "regeneration" of the Jews, and who fervently and courageously upheld their cause, also initiated a policy for full

[2] Paul Butel, *Les négociants bordelais: L'Europe et Les Iles au 18è siècle* (Paris: Aubier, 1974).

[3] See Frances Malino, *The Sephardic Jews of Bordeaux: Assimilation and Emancipation in Revolutionary and Napoleon France* (Tuscaloosa: University of Alabama Press, 1978). See also Pierre Guillaume, *La population de Bordeaux au 19è siècle: Essai d'histoire sociale* (Paris: Armand Colin, 1985).

[4] Erwin Schnurmann, *La Population juive en Alsace* (Paris: Libraire du Recueil Sirey, 1936); Freddy Raphael and Robert Weyl, *Juifs en Alsace* (Toulouse: Privat, 1977); Vicki Caron, *Between France and Germany: The Jews of Alsace-Lorraine, 1871–1918* (Stanford: Stanford University Press, 1988), chap. 1; Françoise Job, *Les Juifs de Nancy* (Nancy: Presses Universitaires de Nancy, 1991); and Paula Hyman, *The Emancipation of the Jews of Alsace* (New Haven: Yale University Press, 1991).

cultural unification within France, one that could only reinforce the prudent hostility of eastern European Jews concerned about defending their group as well as their culture. These Jews attempted to protect their communitarian structures, rabbis, syndics, and particular laws that would assure the harmony of the "Jewish nation." In their lengthy "Petition of the Jews settled in France addressed to the National Assembly" of 28 January 1790, the Alsatian Jews claimed the right to preserve their own collective structures within revolutionary France:

> Would they form, we wonder, a Jewish colony? Will we never grow accustomed to the idea of separating the Jew from the citizen? We'll see the Jew everywhere and the citizen nowhere! No, not a Jewish colony but a colony of citizens should be established in Alsace. There could therefore easily be a greater number of Jews as citizens here than there. . . . In the way that the Protestants are the most numerous and wealthy in Languedoc than in other provinces? Yet there are no Protestant colonies; there will be no further Jewish colonies.[5]

The Jews of France thus indirectly confronted the general revolutionary upheaval. The cost of an individual "exit" for an eastern Jew was high enough to defy the rationality of such a choice, even for someone who otherwise would be willing to take risks. In general, "loyalty" to the community, serving both as a kinship group and a reference group, is a rational choice. However, solidarity is never automatic and always requires a commitment from the one testifying to its validity.[6] In adverse circumstances, the Jews of eastern France decided to stand by each other.

It would later be noted that such a choice would have an unexpected effect on their relationship with French citizens and citizenship. Note that under restraint, as they were, for example, in Alsace, the Jews considered themselves to be essentially "loyal" to their community and traditions. This was in a region dominated by agriculture, to which they did not have access, and in which most big cities, such as Strasbourg and (though less systematically) Nancy or other cities like Metz, barely tolerated their presence.

When they did "voice" their grievances through the forum of the Constituent Assembly of 1789, they did so mainly to defend their particular vision during the Revolution. They had hoped to develop a strategy based upon a more communitarian vision than that conceived of by Jews in cities such as Bordeaux, Bayonne, Avignon, or even (perhaps especially)

[5] *Pétition des Juifs établis en France adressée à l'Assemblée Nationale* (Paris: Editions d'histoire sociale, 1968), 5:82.

[6] For a general discussion of this, see Michael Hechter, *Principles of Group Solidarity* (Berkeley: University of California Press, 1987).

Paris. The Jews in these cities tended to embrace strategies of "exit," transferring their "loyalty" to this new, developing, "open" society. Yet, as we will see, the future can never really be predicted. "Disappointments" can actually provoke a return to even more particularist forms of "loyalty."[7] In other words, as in all social acts, the Jews of France strove to develop strategies adapted to the great changes affecting the state as much as to the rapid social and economic changes developing in French society.

In the days following the revolutionary emancipation, the Jews became active citizens. Yet this activity was limited to a local level; their entry into national politics was slow. There were few unconverted Jewish deputies, and even fewer ministers before the July Revolution and the Second Empire. At this time, Achilles Fould was elected as a deputy in 1834 before becoming, once converted, a minister under Napoleon III. In 1842, Adolphe Crémieux and Max Cerfberr were elected, as were Benoit Fould, David Raynal, and Michel Goudchaux in the period from 1846 to 1848. During the Second Empire, the Pereires were also elected: Javal in Yonne and Koenigswater in the Seine region. But it would take the eighty years following the emancipation of 1791 and the advent of the Third Republic before Jews were elected with any frequency.

Previously, active Jewish participation at high levels in a strong and politically institutionalized state proved difficult.[8] During the formative discussions of emancipation, the issue of Jewish entry into public function had of course been raised. The Declaration of the Rights of Man of 1789 stated that "the law is the expression of the general will. . . . All citizens, being equal in her eyes, shall be equally eligible to all high offices, public positions and employments, according to their ability and without other distinction than that of their virtues and talents." As Abbot Grégoire proclaimed, "Let us give Jews every opportunity to make their talents and virtues flourish; let us link them to the state in the hopes of procuring public consideration and access to all functions within the various classes. We are not [however] suggesting that Jews be admitted as procurators; we can sense why."[9] Thiery, who would later receive recognition along with Abbot Grégoire and Hourwitz at the Metz Academy

[7] Albert Hirschman, *Exit, Voice, and Loyalty* (Cambridge: Harvard University Press, 1970); idem, *Shifting Involvements* (Princeton: Princeton University Press, 1982). For a comparative perspective, see Zygmunt Bauman, "Exit Visas and Entry Tickets: Paradoxes of Jewish Assimilation," *Telos* 77 (Fall 1988).

[8] See David Cohen, *La Promotion des Juifs de France à l'époque du Second Empire* (Paris: Librairie Honoré Champion, 1980), vol. 2.

[9] Abbot Grégoire, *Essai sur la régénération physique morale et politique des Juifs* (Paris: Stock, 1988), 131. See Pierre Birnbaum, "Sur l'étatisation révolutionnaire: le rôle de l'Abbé Grégoire et le destin des Juifs," *Le Débat* 53 (January–February 1989).

gathering in 1788, explained: "How could they fill a position that displays our religion in all of its greatness and majesty?"[10]

Even though they were finally regarded as citizens, certain Jews who had hoped to be selected for public office according to meritocratic and universalistic criteria would quickly be in for a "disappointment" in so far as their "exit" to the state proved perilous. This is illustrated, for example, in the story of Isidore Cahen, a graduate of the Ecole Normale Supérieure, who performed brilliantly on his philosophy-teaching examination and subsequently was appointed to a position at the Lycée Napoléon in La Roche-sur-Yon in the Vendée in October 1849. Yet on October 14, the Bishop Luçon was able to oppose this appointment. He further registered surprise that "wise and prudent statesmen could even have conceived of sending a Jewish teacher devoted to the teaching of philosophy to one of the most religious [Catholic] and traditional regions in France." In the name of universalistic principles, Cahen refused to accept any other teaching appointment and instead became the talented director of Archives Israélites.[11] As Hirschman's hypothesis in *Shifting Involvements* suggests, this "disappointment," experienced by a number of Jews connected to the state in some capacity, demonstrates a retreat to "private interest" and, in this particular case, a permanent return to the community. There were other similar incidents, some in girls' high schools, until the end of the nineteenth century.[12]

Prior to the Second Empire but primarily during the Third Empire, which considerably reinforced the elite and further imposed a reign of secularism, few Jews could enlist in the army or the prefectorial without converting. This was the case, for example, with Lambert, who became a prefect after changing his last name from Cain and converting. Likewise, Alfred Vieyra-Molina (whose mother was born in Bordeaux and had connections to the Gradis family, the famous negotiators and shipowners) was appointed to the Conseil d'Etat under the Second Empire only after converting to Catholicism.[13]

Thus, in spite of the state-led emancipation of the Jews, the real political integration of Jews in France was quite limited. This can further be attributed to the fact that under the Restoration, Catholicism was the official state religion until 1848. Jews therefore could employ assimilation strategies of social mobility only by leaving the ghetto[14] or by aban-

[10] M. Thiery, *Dissertation sur cette question: Est-il des moyens de rendre les Juifs plus heureux et plus utiles en France?* (Paris: Editions d'histoire sociale, 1968), 84.

[11] See Cohen, *La Promotion des Juifs*, 161.

[12] Françoise Mayeur, *L'enseignement secondaire des jeunes filles* (Paris: Armand Colin, 1977).

[13] See Cohen, *La Promotion des Juifs*, 391–97.

[14] Jacob Katz, *Out of the Ghetto* (Cambridge: Harvard University Press, 1973).

doning the collective structures that had been preserved in some major cities. These strategies would allow them to join the middle and sometimes upper classes in which the ambiguous title "Court Jew" would be bestowed on them.[15]

As Werner Sombart rightly points out, it is because so many openings to the state remained closed to them (in France as in Germany) that certain Jews "were forced to devote all their efforts to the world of trade and industry."[16] The first chapter of his book on the state bears emphasis. He believes that one cannot conceive of Colbert, Richelieu, Mazarin, Cromwell, or Frederick the Great without considering the role of the Jews: "It would be like Faust without Mephistopheles. Arm in arm the Jew and the ruler stride through the age which historians call modern. To me this union is symbolic of the rise of capitalism and consequently of the modern state."[17] Though his overall assumption is quite objectionable, not taking into account, for example, the particular nature of each state, it is also taken up indirectly by Hannah Arendt. She argues that "the seventeenth and eighteenth centuries witnessed the slow development of nation-states under the tutelage of the absolute monarchs. Individual Jews everywhere rose out of deep obscurity into the sometimes glamorous and always influential position of court Jew who financed state affairs and handled the financial transactions of their princes."[18]

Without dwelling upon the almost anti-Semitic slant to certain formulas found in one of these authors, we can see that they both shared a very similar understanding of the links between Jews, the state, and capitalism. Nevertheless, while these observations might seem convincing if applied in a more nuanced manner, they are generally misleading for an understanding of all countries and eras.

This variation is precisely one of the main points of this study. In Germany, for example, the very nature of the state denied nonconverted Jews access to the highest state functions until the beginning of the twentieth century. The state further obliged some to remain Court Jews (others joined the ranks of the working class and the Socialist party or, later, the

[15] Selma Stern, *The Court Jew* (New Brunswick, N.J.: Transaction Books, 1984).

[16] Werner Sombart, *The Jews and Modern Capitalism* (New Brunswick, N.J.: Transaction Books, 1982). We reject, however, this author's further psychological theories that lead him straight to Nazism because of his support (contrary to that of Max Weber) for the idea that the Jews' sexual repression predisposed them to money trade and at the same time distanced them from brotherhood. For a recent critique of Sombart, see Paul Mendès-Flohr, "Werner Sombart and Modern Capitalism: An Analysis of Its Ideological Premises," *Leo Baeck Institute Yearbook* [*LBY*] 21 (1976), and Werner Mosse, "Judaism, Jews and Capitalism: Weber, Sombart and Beyond," *LBY* 24 (1979).

[17] Sombart, *Jews and Modern Capitalism,* 49.

[18] Hannah Arendt, *The Origins of Totalitarianism* (New York: Harcourt, Brace and World, 1951), 14.

Communist party.)[19] In France, however, Jewish statesmen succeeded the Court Jews (few Jews joined worker organizations at this time). However, proficient in their understanding of the state order, the Jewish statesmen rose very quickly from the time of the Second Empire and still more during the Third Republic, all the way to the upper ranks of the state.[20] The interpretation put forth as much by Sombart as by Arendt can thus only be used to understand the eighteenth and early nineteenth century. Finally, contrary to Arendt's claim, the Jews of France actually linked their own fate to that of the state itself.

During the first half of the nineteenth century, the Jews of Bordeaux and Bayonne, and wealthy arms dealers such as Gradis or Raba, were the ones who for a long time had been benefiting from the status of quasi-citizenship and had enthusiastically adhered to the rationalism characteristic of this period. They "entered" society, and at the same time "exited" from what remained of their own communitarian structures to become closely linked to bourgeois circles in Bordeaux, which participated in foreign trade and the opening of new markets. These big-city Jews would become actively involved in France's economic modernization by taking part in, among other things, the Saint-Simon movement so favorable to industrialization. Thus did Emile and Isaac Pereire, both born in Bordeaux and belonging to the Portuguese "nation," and Olinde and Eugène Rodriguès, both Sephardic Jews related to Emile Pereire. In his discussion of the Pereire brothers, about whom, unfortunately, no serious biographical work exists as yet, a historian commenting on this period highlights the fact that "it is extraordinary that the science of banking has remained outside of Catholicism for the last century. Sixty years ago we had Genevan Protestants; today, it's the Bordeaux Israelites."[21] In their desire to join a rationally conceived modernity, the Pereires, Olinde Rodriguès, and Eichtal (also a native of Bordeaux) converted to the Christianity that they now perceived as the transposition of ancient messianic messages onto modern industrial society. At the same time, the Pereire, Rodriguès, and even Eichtal families would play a critical role in the implementation of Saint Simonian industrial ideology, a

[19] See, for example, Ernest Hamburger, *Juden im Offentlichen Leben Deutschland* (Tubingen: J. C. B. Mohr, 1968); idem, *Juden im Wilhelminischen Deutschland, 1890–1914* (Tubingen: J. C. B. Mohr, 1876); and idem, "From the Wilhelmian Era to the Third Reich," *LBY* 31 (1986).

[20] See Pierre Birnbaum, *Anti-Semitism in France: A Political History from Léon Bloom to the Present* (Oxford: Blackwell, 1992). See also Perrine Simon, *Contribution à l'étude de la bourgeoisie juive à Paris entre 1870 et 1914* (master's diss., Institut d'Etudes Politiques, 1982).

[21] Hyppolite Castille, *Les Frères Pereire* (Paris: B.N.G. 21088, 1861), 40. See also Frédéric Barbier, *Finance et politique: La Dynastie des Fould, XVIIIè–XXè siècle* (Paris: Armand Colin, 1992).

worldview hostile to politics itself, one that expected the new industrial order to bring a consensus capable of guaranteeing solidarity among men.[22]

This type of social emergence into modernity for some Jews took place during France's slow and continuous process of modernization, one whose continuity historians have often underestimated. Between 1815 and 1830, influenced by the Saint Simonism of the time, Lafitte conducted his first banking endeavors, involving certain Bordeaux Jews. Among them were the Pereire brothers, who would later create the Crédit Mobilier in 1852. The industrialization of France followed a different rhythm than that of Great Britain or Germany, although the principal explanation for its "lateness" has been rejected by most historians of the French economy, as Richard Rohl writes: "France was the first industrialized nation to attempt to move in this direction."[23] This "lateness," as Jean-Charles Asselain observes, can be attributed to banking structures that limited more innovative initiatives among general conservative banking practices that were too cautious in terms of the long-term real estate transactions necessary for industrialization; he believes the Central Bank was incapable of keeping up with industrial development.[24]

The connection between the Central Bank and industry was at the heart of the conflict that was to divide Jewish bankers and ultimately lead to the dismal crash of the Crédit Mobilier. Since the early part of the nineteenth century the Rothschilds had played a considerable role in this important French bank. They also figured into the heart of modernity in major cities, thus transposing a reconstituted type of Court Jew to the center of the urban system. However, as had been the case with most German Court Jews, they did not convert and thus remained faithful to their community of origin, never really "exiting" except as a means for attaining the highest social levels of the upper classes. Very close to the ultra-reactionary Villèle government in 1825, James de Rothschild managed Louis Philippe's personal fortune under the July Monarchy and worked closely on a daily basis with government leaders such as the banker Casimer Périer. In 1840 James wrote to one of his female friends, "I know all the ministers, I see them every day and when I realize that the path they're taking runs contrary to the interests of the state [James also

[22] Michel Graetz, *Les Juifs en France au 19è: De la Révolution française à l'Alliance israélite universelle* (Paris: Le Seuil, 1989), chap. 4.

[23] See Richard Rohl, "L'Industrialisation française: Une remise en cause," *Revue d'histoire économique et sociale* 3 (1976), 415. See also Rondo E. Cameron, *La France et le dévellopment économique de l'Europe: 1800–1971* (Paris: Le Seuil, 1971), 188; originally published as *France and the Economic Development of Europe, 1800–1914: Conquests of Peace and Seeds of War* (Princeton: Princeton University Press, 1961).

[24] Jean-Charles Asselain, *Histoire économique de la France,* vol. 1, *De l'Ancien Régime à la Première Guerre Mondiale* (Paris: Le Seuil, 1984), chap. 5.

meant: to that of his own people] I alert the king, whom I see whenever I want."[25] In 1840 he obtained Thiery's dismissal from the king. The following day the newspaper *Le Constitutionnel* asked, "By what right and under what pretext can this king of finance meddle in our affairs?"[26]

Under the July Monarchy, the Rothschilds played a considerable role in the formulation of debt policy and negotiation: as Court Jews they helped frame financial policy for the Central Bank, and, slowly and cautiously, became involved in the implementation of an industrial policy that tended to restrict the movement of long-term capital. Nevertheless, in 1833, under the very influence of the Pereires who were also working for him, as well as that of Eichtal, ever a Saint-Simonien, James de Rothschild launched himself into the construction of the first railroad built in France, the Paris-St. Germain line. Their relationship soon deteriorated, however, because Pereire and Eichtal advocated a more vigorous industrialization, requiring another kind of bank open to public capital. A merciless fight began at the time of the Second Empire, with the emperor favoring a rapid industrialization of France, linking himself to the Pereires, and employing a strategy of rapid expansion implemented throughout all of Europe by Crédit Mobilier, which they themselves had created along with the Foulds. We know that this battle of the titans was to end with the defeat of the Pereires, for whom economic policy still expressed a quasi-messianic and rationalist industrialization based upon the Saint-Simonian message. The Jews of Bordeaux, assimilated and often converted, favoring industrialization as the source of a new form of solidarity, did not ultimately master the new financial policy of the Rothschilds: namely, of "Court Jews" remaining close to their community of origin and still practicing a fairly traditional form of Judaism but who could also count on the aid of most of the other members of the Central Bank, who themselves had little desire to engage in an industrial process that could upset the social hierarchies.[27] It is hard to imagine two more opposing notions of social emancipation, even though both were diametrically opposed to a radically different state-led emancipation that would ultimately create a significant number of Jewish statesmen.

It is worth noting that at this time Jules Isaac Mirès, a Jewish banker also born in Bordeaux in 1809 who had participated in the founding of the Crédit Mobilier before initiating his own financial and industrial agenda, took part in the construction of blast furnaces near Marseille,

[25] Jean Bouvier, *Les Rothschild* (Paris: Club Français du Livre, 1960), 101, 76–95.

[26] Ibid., 102.

[27] See Bertrand Gille, *Histoire de la Maison Rothschild* (Paris: Droz, 1965). See also Bouvier, *Les Rothschilds,* 145. On the conflict between the Rothschilds and the Pereires see Bertrand Gille, *La Banque en France au 19è siècle* (Geneva: Droz, 1970), 125; and Jean Bouvier, *Un Siècle de banque française* (Paris: Hachette, 1973), 207.

investing in mines, among other things. In this way, he benefited from Napoleon III's continuous support, as had Pereire. He recorded his reflections on the distinction between the Rothschilds and the Pereires and himself in a little-known work entitled *A mes juges.* Mirès, a banker favoring rapid industrialization who was brought to the heights of national glory and economic success only to lose everything in the dismal crash that would cost him lawsuits, stated the following:

> We must distinguish the northern Jews from the Midi ones. The northern European Jews, otherwise known as German Jews, are cold and methodical. The social organization of Germany has excluded the Jews from all levels of society. . . . In Germany Jews do not, therefore, associate their fortune and wealth with that of the state they live in. [However] the Midi Jews known as Portuguese Jews have drawn on their Latin roots whence reside their more noble instincts: and the bestowal in France of all citizens' rights has developed their inherent tendency that ultimately drove them to pursue, by associating their wealth with the public interest, an increase in their own esteem; it is as though they wanted to gain recognition for the services they have received from what they have done for the state. The Rothschilds' interest has never corresponded to the French interest. . . . They have rebelled against all assistance to industry or the state. . . . Along with the Pereires, however, the Midi Jews have made the general interest their main goal by obtaining all the benefits of credit and industry.[28]

It is hard to imagine a better expression, nearly anti-Semitic, of the different approaches toward emancipation among Jews still anxious to achieve social emancipation. Let us further recall that James de Rothschild, who played a critical role in French society and lived in a sumptuous salon in which he received members of the upper, even aristocratic, classes of French society, could never hope to become French. On the other hand, members of the Pereires, Rodrigues, and Eichtal families had been French by birth since even before the French Revolution and had extended their assimilation through conversion to both rationalism and Christianity. As with Bleichroder[29] in Germany, it was as though the still very Catholic French society of this era would accept a fusion so complete as to dissolve this particularism.

In this way, the real power of the Rothschilds actually was circumscribed, in that their control of the Central Bank was quite limited. Their influence on industrial society itself was even more restricted. Nonetheless their role in the Central Bank was well known and their fortune one of the largest in France. During the Second Empire only two of the thirty-

[28] J. Mirès, *A Mes Juges* (Paris, 1861).

[29] Fritz Stern, *Gold and Iron: Bismarck, Bleichroder, and the Building of the German Empire* (New York: Vintage Books, 1979).

seven seats in the Conseil de la Banque de France were occupied by Jews. These seats were held, though not at the same time, by Halphen, a jeweler, and by Alphonse de Rothschild, James's son. Alphonse would remain there for a long time.[30] Upon his death in 1905 his inheritance was by far the largest of the period, estimated at 250 million francs.[31] However, as Jean Bouvier points out, the Rothschilds remained the products of the era preceding industrialization, steel works, and bank notes.[32] They had remained Court Jews and never really became capitalists adapted to the modern world and industrialization. Ultimately the Rothschilds played only a limited role in the Central Bank, which would thus be increasingly dominated by the great aristocratic Catholic families, such as those of the Count d'Argout, the Count of Germiny, or by representatives of top Protestant banks such as the Mallets, the Hottinguers, and the Schlumbergers, who were powerful and mutually supportive.[33] This group kept themselves apart from the Jews and often displayed an anti-Semitism similar to that displayed by the Catholic national bank.[34] The Jewish bankers also played no role in the new banks that emerged in the nineteenth century that were better adapted to industrial expansion and the growth of capitalism. These banks, which relentlessly asserted themselves and accompanied the current economic development by attracting a significant part of the national wealth, this time reinvested in industrialization; they included the Crédit Foncier, Crédit Agricole, Comptoir d'Escompte de Paris, and especially the Société Générale. Finally, the Crédit Lyonnais was created in 1863; its founder, Henri Germain, along with the Bank of Paris and the Netherlands (created in 1872), actively intervened in the saga of the industrialization of French society.[35]

[30] Alain Plessis, *Régents et gouverneurs de la Banque de France sous le Second Empire* (Geneva: Droz, 1985), 44, 265. In the same way, few Jews figured among the two hundred shareholders of this bank, with the exception of the Eichtals and the Foulds, who had converted, and the jeweler Halphen. However, the Dollfus family, J. Périer, H. Germain, the Lemerciers of Nerville, the De Germigys, the Lafittes, as well as Berthier, Prince of Wagrams, Sauvaire de Barthélémy, Pillet-Witt, Ackerman, Viscount of Argout, and many other members of the bourgeois and aristocratic milieu primarily dominated. Alain Plessis, *La Banque de France et ses deux cents actionnaires sous le Second Empire* (Geneva: Droz, 1982), 81.

[31] Adeline Daumard, *Les Bourgeois et la bourgeoisie en France* (Paris: Aubier, 1987), 102.

[32] Bouvier, *Les Rothschild,* 11.

[33] Herbert Lûthy, *La Banque protestante en France* (Geneva: SEVPEN, 1965); and J. Nére, "La Haute Banque Protestant de 1870 à 1885," in Nére, ed., *Les Protestantes dans les débuts de la Troisième République* (Paris: Editions Protestantes, 1978).

[34] Plessis, *Régents et gouverneurs,* 268.

[35] See Guy Palmade, *Capitalismes et Capitalistes français au 19è siècle* (Paris: Armand Colin, 1961).

Industrial expansion thus occurred with practically no Jewish participation.[36] The aristocrats or the bourgeoisie, still the holders of immense landed property, or occasionally even craftsmen, all Catholic or Protestant and assisted by long-established local Catholic banks, often were the ones who were truly responsible for the capitalist industrialization taking place in French society in the latter half of the nineteenth century. They were further assisted by the powerful national banks named above. The principal property holders, former ironmasters, turned to iron and steel or industrial textiles. Thus the de Wendels, inheritors of a solid banking and industrial dynasty, would control the iron and steel mines in northeastern France from this time to the present;[37] the Schneiders would create a giant iron and steel empire in Creusot, as would Peugeot. In the developing chemical sector Saint Gobain generated a family effort benefiting from support of local employers and the banking system. In much the same way Péchiney was created with the help of Lyons' capitalists, as was the Kullman company in the north.[38] Excepting two rare occasions—two Jewish negotiators from Metz, Mayor Dupont and Myrtil Dreyfus, founded Pompey blast furnaces[39] in the Lorraine region in 1850—it was nearly always members of the solidly rooted provincial bourgeoisie who built true industrial empires in the heart of the French provinces, far from Paris and the Central Bank. These included Flavigny in Elbeuf, Fauchille in Lille, Colcombet in Saint-Etienne, Berliet in the Lyon region, and many other industrialists backed by the local banks, always Catholic, whose names economic historians have not always remembered. In Grenoble, Nancy, Tours, Reims, Maubeuge, Château-Thierry, or Bar-le-Duc, they truly took charge of the industrialization of French society. Often distanced from the Central Bank, working jointly on a local level, Catholic industrialists and bankers shared a solid traditionalism and actually played a crucial role in the industrial development of French society.

Because of this considerable assistance, the Catholic bourgeoisie, with uniform values, gained power over elected local employees far from Paris, where some Court Jews could still act like noblemen who had been uprooted during the history of modern France.[40] Furthermore, among

[36] One might qualify this remark by highlighting the role played by the rather exceptional Javal dynasty. See Emmanuel Chadeau, *L'Economie du Risque* (Paris: Orban, 1988), and, in the example of the Dreyfus family, Michael Burns, *Dreyfus: A Family Affair, 1789–1945* (New York: HarperCollins, 1991).

[37] Jean-Noel Jeanneney, *François de Wendel en République: L'argent et le pouvoir, 1914–1940* (Paris: Le Seuil, 1976).

[38] Palmade, *Capitalismes et Capitalistes français,* 178–82.

[39] Louis Bergeron, "Vers un renouvellement des entreprises et des hommes," in Yves Lequin, ed., *Histoire des Français, 19è–20è siècles* (Paris: Armand Colin, 1983), 2:281.

[40] Louis Bergeron, *Les Capitalistes en France (1780–1914)* (Paris: Gallimard, 1978).

the general councillors elected in 1870 with revenues exceeding 300,000 francs a year, only Alphonse de Rothschild, Pereire, and Fould had converted to Christianity, to join the ranks of Duc de la Rochefoucauld-Doudeauville, the Marquis de Talhouet, the Baron de Gaffenried, the Marquis de Vogue, the Marquis de Chasseloup-Laubat, the Prince of Beauvau, and many other Catholic aristocrats linked by exogamous strategies to the *grande bourgeoisie* itself.[41] The Court Jews, primarily upholding a strategy of endogamy, were not admitted to this locally organized upper class, but nevertheless gradually penetrated the ranks of national power,[42] thereby threatening the very differentiation of a state that seemed to lose little of its haughtiness, at the same time that industrialization was exploding.

The eighteenth- and nineteenth-century industrialization of French society also owed a great deal to the actions taken by foreigners, often of Protestant origin. Dutch investors built refineries in Rouen while others founded the largest wool industry in Abbeville; Wilkinson, from England, created the metallurgy of iron and steel in Creusot, the epitome of capitalist expansion. Similarly, Oberkampf, from Württemberg, the Swedish baron Oscar d'Adelswald, some Swiss, and a number of Belgians played an essential role in the creation of potential French industry, from which Jews actually were quite absent.[43] In Mulhouse in eastern France, Koechlin founded a iron and steel metallurgy industry and, as the head of Dullfus-Mieg (a Protestant family), created one of the most important companies of contemporary capitalist France.[44] In much the same way, Waddington, of English and Protestant origin, built textile and iron and steel metallurgy industries along with other German and Swiss Protestants in Rouen, further supported by the local Catholic bourgeoisie. Not until the end of the century would the Jews who had left Alsace after the defeat of 1870, having abandoned the textile companies they had created in places like Mulhouse or Bischwiller,[45] found textile firms such as the one in Elbeuf.[46]

There were numerous examples throughout France of industrialization spurred locally by Catholic, and sometimes Protestant, capitalists. The

[41] Louis Girard, Antoine Prost, and Remi Gossez, *Les Conseillers Généraux en 1870: Etude statistique d'un personnel politique* (Paris: Armand Colin, 1967).

[42] Jean L'Homme, *La grande bourgeoisie au pouvoir: 1830–1880* (Paris: Presses universitaires de France, 1960).

[43] See J.-P. Poussou, "A l'école des autres," and Yves Lequin, "La trace de l'Ancien Régime," in Yves Lequin, ed., *La mosaique France* (Paris: Larousse, 1988).

[44] See Cameron, *La France et le développment économique de l'Europe,* 118.

[45] See Caron, *Between France and Germany,* 64.

[46] Jean-Pierre Chaline, *Les Bourgeois de Rouen: Une élite urbaine au 19è siècle* (Paris: Presses de la Fondation Nationale des Sciences Politiques, 1982). Let us further note that at the dawn of World War I the greatest negotiator in silk and ribbons in Paris was the Brach, Blum, et Cie company. Lequin, *Histoire des Français,* 253.

textile industry in northern France was entirely controlled by a traditional body of employees, and the bankers of the region were all deeply Catholic.[47] The textile industry belonged almost completely to solidly established local Protestant families (although very traditional Catholic families did dominate the northern Alsace region), all having exclusive dealings with their own local banks. A complementary proof of this is that the Catholic and occasionally Protestant banks' stranglehold in this region, as in others, was such that not until 1865 would a small Jewish company be established in the region—the Herzog-Dreyfus-Lantz firm in Mulhouse.[48] In the same way, northern French collieries that had played a critical role in its general industrialization were dominated by local bankers of long familial traditions, such as the Pereires or the Dupont banks, which would be privatized by the Socialist government of 1981. These local families controlled the celebrated blast furnaces, as well as Denain-Anzin's forges and steelworks that had demanded baptismal and church marriages from prospective employees for a long time. There are numerous examples that unambiguously demonstrate how greatly the locally established Catholic and Protestant bourgeoisie had mastered the capitalist and industrial expansion of nineteenth-century France, in which a new dominant bourgeoisie was formed alongside the traditional and still-substantial land fortunes that continued to be partially controlled by the aristocracy.[49] Let us further note that it was often the France of the *ancien régime* that was more adaptable to the nineteenth century in that it allied itself with the newer bourgeoisie. The former aristocracy, at least throughout the first part of this century, continued to make up a significant part of the wealthy nobles established in the industrial world.[50]

As we have pointed out, Jews were almost completely excluded from the dominant industrial bourgeoisie. Of course, the Rothschilds and Pereires and, for a few years, J. Mirès were almost singlehandedly responsible for the installation of the very dense railway system that eventually spread throughout all of France. This contribution appears to have been an essential part of an industrialization that literally transformed not only the modes of industrial production, but the role of the city itself.[51] As noted above, the Rothschilds were more than hesitant about joining

[47] Jean Lambert-Dansette, *Quelques familles du patronat textile de Lille-Armentières (1789–1914)* (Lille: Presses de l'Université de Lille, 1954).

[48] Claude Fohlen, *L'Industrie textile au temps du Second Empire* (Paris: Plon, 1954), 436.

[49] See Adeline Daumard, ed., *Les Fortunes françaises au 19è siècle* (Paris: Mouton, 1973).

[50] Adeline Daumard, *La Bourgeoisie parisienne de 1815 à 1848* (Paris: SEVPEN, 1963).

[51] See Louis Girard, *La politique des Travaux Publiques sous le Second Empire* (Paris: Armand Colin, 1952); François Caron, *Histoire de l'exploitation d'un grand réseau: la Compagnie du Chemin de fer du Nord, 1846–1937* (Paris: Mouton, 1973).

the industrial venture; though they did participate in the Denain-Anzin iron and steel industries and other industrial companies, they refused to join the ranks of the great captains of industry. However, the Pereires, whose prompting of James de Rothschild to participate in railway construction was inspired by their adherence to Saint-Simonian beliefs, nevertheless hoped (as did the assimilated Bordeaux Jew, Mirès) through the support of Napoleon III to promote the policy of the industrialization and urbanization of France, one that would guarantee the new order, permanently turning away from the *ancien régime*.

The Rothschilds ultimately would play only a limited role at the Central Bank, as the Catholic and Protestant bankers restrained their influence. At the same time, the Pereires and J. Mirès were brutally and deliberately forced into bankruptcy and disappeared from public life. Zealous propagators of a new notion of a bank that would be more open to the public and in the interest of all,[52] the Bordeaux Jews failed miserably, while the Rothschild family remained so much a symbol of the power of the Central Bank that henceforth its members would be the target of extreme right-wing and left-wing anti-Semitic pamphlets, made to represent capitalism's ever-ruthless domination. While the Rothschilds were excluded from industrial power and their influence within the Central Bank was diminished (compared to the rise, for example, of Crédit Lyonnais,[53] Société Générale, or the Bank of Paris and the Netherlands), they were, throughout the nineteenth century until contemporary times, subject to popular condemnation that associated capitalism with Jewish power. The legend of the "bigwigs" that the Rothschild family came to symbolize for large portions of public opinion was so firmly rooted that it gave rise to an outbreak of violence rarely seen before in France.[54]

The list of anti-Semitic writings entirely devoted to the supposed clandestine and terrifying powers of the Rothschilds in the nineteenth century until today is endless. It affected nearly all political trends; this family was truly demonized, seen as the visible face of a perpetual Jewish conspiracy that used capitalism to make itself master of Christian French society. In 1846 Georges Dairnwaell (known as Satan) published his cele-

[52] According to David Landes, there was not, on the contrary, a true opposition between the traditional bank symbolized by the Rothschilds and the Pereires's conceptions. Landes, "Vielle Banque et banque nouvelle: La Révolution financière du Dix-neuvième siècle," *Revue d'histoire moderne et contemporaine* 3 (July 1956).

[53] René Girault's portrayal of the businessman in 1914 compares Henri Germain, creator of Crédit Lyonnais who played a critical role in industrialization and whom he considers to be the "master of his generation in the banking world," to Alphonese de Rothschild, who, according to Girault, "remains the master." For a new portrayal of the French businessman around 1914, see *Revue d'histoire moderne et contemporaine* 16 (July–September 1969): 343.

[54] Pierre Birnbaum, *Le Peuple et les gros: Histoire d'un mythe* (Paris: Grasset, 1979).

brated *Histoire édifiante et curieuse de Rothschild I, Roi des Juifs* ("The edifying and curious story of Rothschild I, King of the Jews"); Toussenel and Auguste Chirac, as well as Pierre Leroux, Jules Guesde, Fourier, and many other thinkers of the nineteenth-century Left relentlessly denounced the Rothschilds by associating capitalism with Jewish misdeeds.[55] We know that their racist and purely imaginary message found an attentive audience in the populist thinkers of the extreme right already hostile to capitalism, who hoped for a return of a Catholic France whose organic nature was supposedly crushed by the French Revolution, as well as by the industrial and urban revolutions. Edouard Drumont, the celebrated author of *La France juive,* which sold millions of copies, devoted most of its ferocious pages to Jewish bankers such as the Rothschilds. They were also the object of ridicule in Balzac's equally conservative political opinions.[56] For Zola and so many other authors, the Jew was portrayed as the "king banker" oppressing the helpless French people; Rothschild stood for "all of Jewry" that personified the evil power of money. The hope was to replace the Jew, incarnated by the Court Jew of declining power (such as James de Rothschild), with a new interclass alliance of all Frenchmen. The alliance would transcend class differences, extending from workers to Christian capital holders who shared the rejection of the Jews, themselves stateless.

This true anti-Semitic hatred, which would swell to such proportions as to result in the tragic consequences of Vichy, concentrated on the Rothschilds. But the Pereire brothers, who were at the very heart of national economic and political life, at least during the Second Empire when the Crédit Mobilier reached the height of its glory, proved to be the object of similar derision. It is true that both descended from a long line of highly assimilated Jews, some of whom had pushed the consequences of their "entry" into French society to the extreme limits by converting to Catholicism. The fact that James de Rothschild never became French

[55] Georges Dairnwaell, *Histoire édifiante et curieuse de Rothschild I, Roi des Juifs* (Paris, 1887). See also Georges de Pascal, *La Juiverie* (Paris, 1887); Jacques de Biez, *Les Rothschild et le péril* (Paris: 1891); and Jules Guesde, "A mort, Rothschild," in *Etat, politique, et morale de classe* (Paris: Girard, 1901) 444–47.

[56] There also exists a great deal of high quality literature on this theme. See for example Robert Byrnes, *Anti-Semitism in Modern France* (New Brunswick, N.J.: Rutgers University Press, 1950); Stephen Wilson, *Ideology and Experience: Anti-Semitism in France at the Time of the Dreyfus Affair* (London: Associated Press, 1982); Paul Kingston, *Anti-Semitism in France during the 1930s: Organizations, Personalities, and Propaganda* (Hull, England: University of Hull Press, 1983); Frederick Busi, *The Pope of Anti-Semitism: The Career and Legacy of Edouard Drumont* (Lanham, Md.: University Press of America, 1986); Jeanne Verdès-Leroux, *Scandales financiers et antisémitisme catholique: le krack de l'Union Générale* (Paris: Le Centurion, 1969); Pierre Sorlin, *"La Croix" et les Juifs* (Paris: Grasset, 1967); and Michel Winock, *Edouard Drumont et Cie: Antisémitisme et fascisme en France* (Paris: Le Seuil, 1982).

(though his son and successor, Alfred, would) reinforced in the anti-Semitic mind the illusion of errant and cosmopolitan Jews who "swarm about our country," as *La Croix* put it,[57] tarnishing its true nature. Thus, like the Rothschilds, the Jews of France, from the poorest to the wealthiest, the most conservative to the most revolutionary, the most politically integrated within the state to those who still continued to lead a fairly marginal existence in the very closed communities of eastern France, were all definitively seen as manipulative financiers of unproductive money that sterilized the very wealth of the nation.[58] By the mid-nineteenth century, French Jews, although emancipated for more than fifty years, had never been fully admitted to the state; they did not truly have access to high office. Moreover, they almost completely failed to gain admission to the new bourgeoisie that was gradually coming to power. Political assimilation was not yet open to them, while social emancipation had come to an impasse. Worse still, the Rothschild myth —of the omnipotence of the unassimilated Court Jew, loyal to his religious convictions and kinship community, engaging in hidden conspiracies with his coreligionists abroad, ultimately to dominate the good people of France—was widely perpetuated. This myth demonstrates the unexpected arrival of an anti-Semitism of rejection and extreme negation utilized by numerous anti-Semitic doctrinaires to legitimate the exclusionary behavior that lead to the Dreyfus affair and finally to Vichy.

In this context, social assimilation beyond emancipation remained very fragile during the latter part of the nineteenth century. The Jewish population grew from forty thousand at the time of the French Revolution, being essentially concentrated in eastern France (over twenty-five thousand) and the southwest (twenty-five hundred in Bordeaux),[59] to eighty thousand according to an 1861 census. At this time, there were considerable interior migrations from one region to another and within each region from the country to the city, as industrialization induced population growth in the large cities. Perhaps more than the rest of the French population, the Jews tended to gravitate toward large metropolitan areas, especially to Paris. Furthermore, with the transfer of the Rabbinical School of France from Metz to Paris in 1859, national religious life henceforth was organized in the capital, to the detriment of the old Orthodox tradi-

[57] Cited in Sorlin, "*La Croix*" *et les Juifs,* 105.

[58] See Pierre Birnbaum, "Anti-Semitism and Anti-Capitalism in Modern France," in Frances Malino and Bernard Wasserstein, eds., *The Jews in Modern France* (Hanover, N.H.: University Press of New England, 1985).

[59] See David Feurwerker, *L'émancipation des juifs en France de l'Ancien Régime à la fin du Second Empire* (Paris: A. Michel, 1976); G. Nahon, "Sefardes et Askenases en France, La conquête de l'émancipation (1789–1791)," in M. Yardeni, ed., *Les Juifs dans l'histoire de France* (Leiden: E. J. Brill, 1980).

tions in eastern France. These communities increasingly shut themselves off from the rest of the world. After the loss of Alsace and Lorraine to German occupation, fifteen thousand Jews left this area for the Paris region, where nearly forty-five thousand Jews resided by the mid-1880s.[60] France rarely had experienced a high rate of emigration. However, after the loss of Alsace and Lorraine, a significant number of Jews, often from the countryside, not wishing to belong to the German empire (whose anti-Semitism was even more openly pronounced), emigrated to the United States.[61] Nonetheless, this movement was marginal compared to the Jews who came from eastern Europe. After the Russian pogroms of the 1880s, nearly eight thousand Russian, Galician, and Romanian Jews headed to Paris, where they settled primarily in the Marais and formed an ethnic island. The creation of such a distinct identity ran counter to the more general movement of the destruction of particularist kinships that had so considerably transformed the Jews of Bordeaux and Paris.

This ultimately temporary renaissance of an openly ethnic nature (from both a cultural and religious perspective) is even more astonishing in that it took place in an urban environment, in the same neighborhood, the Marais (under the name of Pletz) and later in Belleville, in the north of Paris, where eastern European immigrants rallied and who were, unlike their French coreligionists, often workers or even craftsmen. Though there were thirty thousand immigrants between 1881 and 1914, there were fewer than had gone to the United States or Great Britain during this period. Their arrival in France would not radically alter the general nature of the Jewish population, in that by running counter to the great emancipation movement that encouraged independence, they revived numerous communitarian associations. They further organized their own synagogues and religious life and formed, as they had in their own countries, particularly active unions.[62] They created mutual aid organizations, *landsmanshaften*, which allowed them to rally according to place of origin, thereby building a specifically Jewish milieu in which religious

[60] Michel Roblin, *Les Juifs de Paris: Démographie, économie, culture* (Paris: A. Picard, 1952); Doris Bensimon-Donath, *Socio-démographie des Juifs de France et d'Algérie* (Paris: A.L.C., 1976); Michael Marrus, *Les Juifs de France à l'époque de l'affaire Dreyfus* (Paris: Calmann-Levy, 1972), 45; originally published as *The Politics of Assimilation: A Study of the French Jewish Community at the Time of the Dreyfus Affair* (Oxford: Clarendon Press, 1971); and Béatrice Philippe, *Les juifs à Paris à la Belle Epoque* (Paris: Albin Michel, 1992).

[61] See Caron, *Between France and Germany,* chap. 4. The author shows (85), for example, that in Hagenau between 1873 and 1898, of the 309 emigrating, 30 percent headed to France and 56 percent to the United States, especially to New York or New Orleans.

[62] Paula Hyman, *From Dreyfus to Vichy: The Remaking of French Jewry, 1906–1939* (New York: Columbia University Press, 1979); Nancy Green, *Les Travailleurs immigrés juifs à la Belle Epoque* (Paris: Fayard, 1986); originally published as *The Pletzl of Paris: Jewish Immigrant Workers in the "Belle Epoque"* (New York: Holmes and Meier, 1986).

services, medical aid, loan services, and funeral arrangements could take place. Immigrant associations also rallied around the Federation of Jewish Societies of Paris in 1913. Unlike their coreligionists, emancipated since the Revolution, they primarily looked to political organizations of both Marxist and anarchist tendencies, on the extreme left: numerous political Communist, Bundist, and Socialist groups were born at this time, groups whose differences were often publicly displayed in either the strong and active press or numerous public meetings.

These left-wing groups clashed with anti-Communist immigrant groups, and both maintained very conflicting relations with the Zionist movements that flourished first among the immigrants and then among some of their more assimilated coreligionists. Often using Yiddish in their press (*Naya presse, Parizer haynt, Unzer Shtime, Die Neye tsayt, Der Yidisher arbeter*) and in their collective demonstrations, these immigrants further became actively involved in the trade union struggle. Like the French Trade Union, they organized themselves according to profession and often led, alone or with all French workers, militant strikes in the *couture* industry, even against a Jewish body of employers. It is hard to understand how much the Jewish population had changed since the beginning of the century, a period in which the very assimilated Portuguese Jews made up more than half the population of Jews living in Paris.[63] From this moment, the emancipated Jews would reside in Parisian neighborhoods far apart from each other. The differences between the so-called Portuguese Jews and eastern French Jews tended to diminish, in that the Portuguese Jews, whose emergence into French society was complete when they ceased to comprise a specific sector of the Jewish population, were now secondary. Both a conflicting and paternalistic rapport now existed between the French Jews. Their Alsace or Lorraine origins were distant from the Jewish immigrants who were not of French nationality, and who tended to embrace a more traditional Judaism.

In 1913, during the General Assembly of the Paris Consistory, Edmond de Rothschild, heir to the Court Jew, declared, "These new [Jewish] arrivals do not understand French customs . . . , they remain among themselves, retain their primitive language, speak and write in jargon." In the same way, Jules Meyer, who had played an important role in the consistorial organization that had included the Jewish population since Napoleon, believed that "the walls of Paris must no longer be covered with Hebrew characters; Paris must cease being flooded with Yiddish newspapers, books, films, and plays."[64] Similarly, the Paris Consistory

[63] Christian Piette, *Les Juifs de Paris, 1808–1840: La Marche vers l'assimilation* (Quebec: Presses de l'Université de Laval, 1983), 63.

[64] These two quotations are from Hyman, *From Dreyfus to Vichy*, 118.

did their utmost to oppose the creation of new traditional synagogues in the Pletz. Thus, once again, just as during the French Revolution and contrary to all the myths, solidarity was not automatic among all Jews; as the *Archives Israélites* somewhat sadly observed on 1 May 1913, "This Tunic of Nessus that comprised Jewish solidarity in that these anti-Semitic gentlemen understand it has fallen from our shoulders since the day when (in law as in equity) collective responsibility made way for individual responsibility."[65]

The arrival in France of Jews who openly took on intense cultural and religious practices and a particular language in the service of a profound sense of community contributed to the considerable transformation of anti-Semitic campaigns by radically modifying the Rothschild myth: Jews could no longer simply be feared as rich and powerful lords of the cosmopolitan banks, since they were now obviously poor and exploited. From now on anti-Semitism strongly clung to the legend directly excerpted from *The Protocols of the Elders of Zion,* abundantly translated and commented upon in current terms according to which Jews were both opulent capitalists and impoverished revolutionaries. This allowed them to seize power by way of a double strategy. Drumont continuously employed this language in his writings, including those in *La Libre Parole;* the widely circulated *La Croix* addressed this idea and further helped create a language consistent above all with the ideas of the extreme Right.

The most immediate effect of the arrival of European Jewish immigrants was to radically undermine the largely mythical image of the Court Jew assimilated with the haute bourgeoisie, ostensibly a part of the most brilliant aristocracy, frequenting salons and so on. However extreme their social assimilation, the Jews continued to give the impression of being an inassimilable ethnic group. This trap ensnared the Court Jews and even those who had converted. It happened at the time of the final institutionalization of the Third Republic. The Jews, nearly a century after their formal emancipation, finally entered the public sphere and had access to the state offices that during the revolution Abbot Grégoire or even the lawyer Thiery had seen as strictly reserved for the Catholics. Contrary to the analyses of Werner Sombart or Hannah Arendt, the Jews of Republican France could in fact become statesmen and could no longer be satisfied with their (largely exaggerated) status of Court Jew. Yet at almost the very same time, political assimilation would be challenged by the explosion of anti-Semitism, whose excuse was the arrival

[65] *Archives Israélites,* 1 May 1913. And, as Nancy Green remarks, "the individualism of the 'every man for himself' ethic . . . established the community against the threat of immigrants." Green, *Les travailleurs immigrés juifs,* 86.

of the Eastern Jews, but which nevertheless condemned all the Jews, whether assimilated socially or politically.

In France, the centennial of the Revolution brought numerous memorial services in all the synagogues. For Chief Rabbi Zadoc Kahn it was "our exodus from Egypt. . . . It is our modern Passover."[66] Nearly a century after their emancipation the Jews did complete their political victory in the republic by entering the "new layers" that Gambetta had announced and whose arrival he so anxiously awaited. The Jews shared Gambetta's admiration for "French centralization" and favored the reinforcement of a "strong" state to defend the equality of citizens, a "state with its high tutelage, perfected police, and endless train of functionaries." Like Gambetta, the new Jewish statesmen developed the idea that "the Republican party is not a party of revolution but of conservation." In the manner of this true founder of the republic, most Jews perceived socialism as a "chimera," or else a "utopia" that "horrified" them. They were further grateful to Gambetta for having unambiguously confirmed that "the state must be secular," thus supporting the idea that "if there is a clerical problem, neither the Protestants nor the Jews have anything to do with it: the conflict is stirred up only by agents of ultramontanism." To drive his point home Gambetta added, "If it were just a question of Jewish and Protestant religions we would have no objection to make. . . . But with the Catholic Church, it is no longer just a minority religion but one which has inscribed 97 percent of the children of this country on its lists of baptism, an immutable, disciplined, and all-powerful church."[67]

It is therefore understandable that in these circumstances a certain number of future Jewish statesmen began their political careers with the assistance of Gambetta, with whom they had become intimate friends. Let us cite Joseph Reinach, for example, who represented the ideal type of Jewish statesman playing a critical role in the Gambetta government and throughout the Third Republic. He would also figure centrally in the Dreyfus affair, along with Zola, Clemenceau, and Bernard Lazare, and Gambetta would entrust him with what was the ultimate sign of trust, the possibility of publishing his correspondences and articles in a definitive edition. In much the same way Ferdinand Dreyfus, a deputy of great influence, would be close friends with him, as would E. Millaud, who became minister of public works, or Paul Strauss, who became minister of health and social welfare. David Raynal was elected deputy of Bordeaux because of Gambetta's direct intervention, and in turn he nominated E. Lisbonne as prefect of the Hérault in 1871. He would later

[66] Quoted in Marrus, *Les Juifs de France,* 11.

[67] Quoted in Pierre Barral, *Les Fondateurs de la Troisième République* (Paris: Armand Colin, 1968), 162, 178, 185, 232, 258, 263, and 319.

become deputy, then senator of this department. There would be even more Jewish statesmen close to Clemenceau (Georges Wormser, Georges Mandel, L. Klotz, Georges Ignace) and to Poincaré and, later, to de Gaulle (from Pierre Mendès France to Jules Moch and René Cassin).[68] In this way, the great political figures in French political life, who played a considerable role in the defense of a legitimate republican order, were considered quasi-hostages to Jewish statesmen who were grounded in purely meritocratic and universalistic principles. Gambetta, born in France to a mother who came from a long line of French but to an Italian father, would be the first politician considered by the anti-Semitic press to be a Jew protecting his coreligionists; for Drumont, Gambetta was a "Jew from Württemberg" who would install a "corner of the Jewish empire" in France.[69] Clemenceau also would wind up violently criticized in the extreme-right press for being too close a friend of the Jews.[70] Later, the Vichy press unrelentingly attacked de Gaulle, accusing him of being a traitor who aimed for both Jewish-French and Anglo-American revenge. This furthermore was the origin of the myth in contemporary France of a "Jewish republic" standing behind the great statesmen.

Between 1870 and 1936, when the last legislative elections took place, fifty-two Jews figured among the deputies, senators, or ministers, thus benefiting from oft-renewed mandates that gave them a stronghold locally as well as nationally. This figure is hardly a considerable part of the nearly 6,000 people that made up the political staff at this time, but it is nevertheless quite impressive for a number of reasons. First, in no other country in the world were there as many Jews exercising political functions so crucial to the implementation of the state and the general control of society; in addition, even if this figure is not itself very impressive, it takes on more significance when taking into account the type of functions, such as ministries, that Jews held each time. They thus appeared as Jews in favor of maintaining the republican order par excellence, and they participated very actively in the implementation of the "strength" of the state. Six Jews became minister of the interior, with control of the public order by means of their control over the police and the administration: Adolphe Crémieux in 1870, David Raynal in 1883–84, L. Klotz in 1913, Abraham Schrameck in 1925, and Georges Mandel in 1940; later, Jules Moch, already minister under the Third Republic, would become

[68] See Pierre Birnbaum, *Les Fous de la République: Histoire politique des Juifs d'état, de Gambetta à Vichy* (Paris: Fayard, 1992). See also idem, "Particularism versus Universalism within a Strong State: The Case of the French Jewish Civil Servants," in Rolf Torstendahl, ed., *State Theory and State History* (London: Sage, 1992).

[69] Edouard Drumont, *La France Juive* (Paris: Flammarion, 1938), 1:534ff.

[70] Barnett Singer, "Clemenceau and the Jews," in *Jewish Social Studies* (Winter 1981). See also Jean-Baptiste Duroselle, *Clemenceau* (Paris: Fayard, 1988), 455.

minister of the interior in 1953. The six continued to appear to be ministers especially repressive of the extreme Right movements, such as the Nationalists Leagues and French Action (e.g., Schrameck, Mandel), but also fighting just as fiercely the extreme Left movements (thus, Raynal ran a round-up of anarchists, and later, during the Cold War in 1952, Jules Moch ordered the police to open fire on workers in a national strike led by the *Confederation generale du travail* [CGT] and the Communist party).

In the same way, as undersecretary to the court of military justice, E. Ignace also exercised an important role in the maintenance of order amidst often defeatist troops in World War I. Until the period between the two wars, the Jewish statesmen were more than moderate, attached as they were to the defense of a strong republic; they refused any form of conflict that could threaten it. Thus, for Joseph Reinach, "the enemy is Socialism"; for him, Marx would carry us off to the "shades of night. The sons of the revolution encourage it like the destruction of essential works in 1789."[71] Similarly, Ferdinand Dreyfus, also a close friend of Gambetta, felt that socialism was simply a "call to crime."[72] Not until the period following World War I, once the republic became permanently legitimate in almost everyone's eyes, would the Jews who weren't recent immigrants actively join the extreme Left parties and adhere to socialism and the theory of class struggle conducted within the Republican sphere. Thus, Léon Blum, Jules Moch, E. Ignace, and Salomon Grumbach would become deputies of the Socialist party by playing a very active role during the Tours Congress; only one deputy, G. Weil, was elected to the ranks of the Communist party, harboring a perspective too revolutionary for the Jewish statesmen who were still so attached to the meritocratic and emancipating Republican order.

These Jewish statesmen, as Joseph Reinach said, "worship the religion of the French Revolution in their hearts."[73] Even Alfred Naquet, at one time in favor of anarchism or Boulangism (a right-wing popular movement led by General Boulanger) also congratulated the "Constituent Assembly to have been so bold as to grant Jews the title of French citizen."[74] There were numerous examples of the Jewish statesmen's cries of enthusiasm about the French Revolution. In 1889 Camille Dreyfus was the one to propose a law to commemorate its centenary at the Chamber of Deputies. Ferdinand Dreyfus, Gambetta's close friend, declared, "Modern France, the France of the revolution, is calling to its children,

[71] Joseph Reinach, *Démagogues et Socialistes* (Paris: 1886), 4, 9.

[72] Ferdinand Dreyfus, *Misère sociales et etudes historiques* (Paris: 1901), 164.

[73] 29 January 1891 speech of Joseph Reinach to the Chambre des Députés, *Journal Officiel,* 30 January 1891.

[74] Alfred Naquet, *La Republique radicale* (Paris, 1873), B.N. 8 Lb 57 4079b.

all of her children, to partake in civil and civic rights."[75] And in 1928, another deputy, Henry Torrès, pleaded in favor of Samuel Schwartzbard, who two years earlier in Paris had killed Petlioura, the head of the 1919 Jewish pogroms in Ukraine: "Ladies and gentlemen of the Jury, Schwartzbard's trial touches on the purest French instincts since it touches on the ideas of this great Revolution of which no living man does not claim to be more or less the son. By a magnificent gesture, the French Revolution intended for the Jews to exist in equality and dignity."[76]

The French Revolution and its final accomplishment under the Third Republic made state-centered emancipation possible by way of Jewish access to the national political and administrative staff. This universalistic type of emancipation further encouraged the entry of Jewish statesmen into higher public office, where they would henceforth hold the positions of prestige and authority that even Abbot Grégoire had wanted to deny them. Beginning with the institutionalization of the Republic, a number of Jews transcended an exclusively social emancipation and the outmoded status of Court Jew to bring themselves to the summit of the state based on purely meritocratic criteria, thus incarnating public power in action. The strong French state[77] was the only one in modern history, indeed in all history, to open its various *Grands Corps* to Jewish statesmen. Paradoxically, at the same time that France was undergoing so many major social and ideological crises, they became prefects or underprefects, state councillors, presidents of courts of appeal, judges in the most important court, first president of the Supreme Court of Appeal, or even generals without being obliged to convert, as they were in Germany or Austria-Hungary. Within the limited framework of this study, it is not possible to examine in detail their social origins, careers, the modes of insertion in different institutions, values, ways of thinking, or their affinities with society in general and with their coreligionists. Such analyses of practices and behavior nevertheless are indispensable to a reflection upon how the Jews were emancipated within a particularly institutionalized and differentiated type of state. Thus, before analyzing the well-known problem of the fate of ethnicity, of the maintenance of particularist sentiments throughout the processes of political emancipation, let us evoke a few specific cases of this mode of entry into a "strong" state.

Within the political arena, the example of the Reinachs comes to mind as the embodiment of Jewish statesmen who had won various competi-

[75] Ferdinand Dreyfus, *Misères sociales,* 257.

[76] Henry Torrès, *Le Procès des Pogromes* (Paris: Editions de France, 1928), 48.

[77] On this notion, see Bertrand Badie and Pierre Birnbaum, *The Sociology of the State* (Chicago: University of Chicago Press, 1983) and, more recently, Peter Evans, Dietrich Rueschemeyer, and Theda Skocpol, eds., *Bringing the State Back In* (New York: Cambridge University Press, 1985).

tions during their schooling to the surprise of their contemporaries.[78] Their academic successes were characteristic of numerous Jews who henceforth turned to the Grandes Ecoles, the royal path to the state. *L'Univers Israélite* noted that during the year 1897–98 twenty Jews were received at the Polytechnique, and four others at the Ecole Normale Supérieure.[79] Having attended such prestigious schools, including the Ecole des Mines and that of Ponts et Chaussées for many generations, they could become, with the triumph of the republic, and soon after of secularism, Jewish statesmen.

Herman Reinach, the father of three future advanced diploma holders, was a German Jew who was naturalized French in 1870 and had married Julie Buding, the daughter of a Jewish banker from Cassel. His family settled in one of the most beautiful neighborhoods, Saint Germain en Laye. Reinach remained loyal to this Jewish community and was a frequent donor to it. Upon his death in 1889, *L'Univers Israélite* lamented the loss of "one of our most dignified and charitable coreligionists." Of his sons, Théodore was admitted to the Ecole Normale Supérieure and became a great orientalist at the Collège de France; Joseph studied law and, in Gambetta's wake, began work at the *République française,* a newspaper created and directed by Gambetta, which Reinach would ultimately head, that was very influential on the course of national political struggles. Joseph participated in the fight against Boulangism and even fought a duel with a member of the League of Patriots in 1887. In 1889 he was elected deputy of Digne. Confronted with severe anti-Semitic attacks he retorted, "I've been reproached for being born to a religion which is not the Catholic religion. . . . It is true that I am not Catholic but this is perhaps what gives me greater strength and authority to defend the cause of tolerance since it affects me."[80]

Reelected continuously, Joseph Reinach would serve as secretary general to the Great Ministry formed by Gambetta and play a principal role in the fight for Alfred Dreyfus. He fervently defended the French Revolution and came across as a vibrant patriot. However, touched by the scandal of Panama (although he had done nothing wrong), he once again became the object of very violent anti-Semitic attacks; he was probably the Jewish statesman most savagely caricatured in the partisan but widely circulated French press. The *Journal des Basses-Alpes* received the following letter addressed to the minister of the interior: "You are no doubt

[78] Julien Benda declared that "Reinach's triumphs during the competitions strikes me as one of the essential sources of the anti-Semitism that would reverberate fifteen years later." Quoted in Marrus, *Les Juifs de France,* 59.

[79] *L'Univers Israélite* (August–September 1899).

[80] Cited in Jean El Gammal, *Joseph Reinach et la République* (Ph.D. diss., University of Paris X, Nanterre, 1982), 152.

aware, Mr. Minister, that we are represented by a Jewish deputy called Joseph Reinach. He is not one of us. . . . Without being the bastions of the church we have our children baptized, we send them to mass, to the catechism, we make them take their first communion, we get married in the church and we bury our own in blessed earth with the assistance of a parish priest. Being represented by a Jew hardly accommodates this."[81]

Reinach took part in all the struggles for the republic, against Boulangism and socialism and in favor of secularism, education, and social welfare. He was a major player in the political game for many years, along with Gambetta, Jules Ferry, and Clemenceau, and exercised a considerable influence in the formation or failure of successive governments. The Dreyfus affair nevertheless was a turning point in the life of this Jewish statesman, so removed from religion and profoundly tied to universalist values. Of Captain Dreyfus he observed, "He was Jewish, from Mulhouse and of humble origins, who left the rich factories for a military career. A student of the Grandes Ecoles, he could never have committed this most wretched of crimes. These Alsatian Jews, treated so roughly, humiliated for such a long time, suspected, proved themselves during the war to be equal in devotion and courage to the oldest of the French."[82]

Along with Bernard Lazare, Zola, and Clemenceau, Reinach participated in the fight for Dreyfus amidst reverberating cries of "death to the Jews." He became the favorite target of all the anti-Semitic pamphlets in France. For Drumont, "this Reinach truly appears as the personification of the false Frenchman. . . . He's really the type of the German Jew, of the invading Jew."[83] Unruffled, Reinach, who momentarily feared that this violence throughout the territory[84] would lead to the "massacre of the Jewish vespers, the Saint Barthelemy of Israel,"[85] would fulfill his destiny as an emancipated Jewish statesman, later requesting to enlist, like Drey-hfus, in the ranks of the French army during World War I, performing many courageous acts during the long and terrible war.

Endogamy was strong among the Reinachs. Only one of the three brothers would marry a non-Jew; from information available to us nearly all the children of the next two generations until the Third Republic married Jewish women, nearly always in a synagogue.[86] Even though they all sought to adapt Judaism to the rationalism of the Enlightenment by

[81] Ibid., 222–23.

[82] Ibid., 261.

[83] Edouard Drumont, in *La Libre Parole,* 27 January 1889.

[84] See Wilson, *Ideology and Experience,* chap. 3.

[85] J. Reinach, *Histoire de l'Affaire Dreyfus* (Paris: 1901–8), 3:230.

[86] Simon, *Contribution à l'étude de la bourgeoisie juive,* 149. See also Corinne Casset, *Joseph Reinach avant l'Affaire Dreyfus: Un example de l'assimilation des Juifs de France au début de la Troisième République* (Ph.D. diss., Ecole des Chartres, 1982), 77, 281.

abandoning its more traditional dimensions, the Reinachs remained both Jews and important members of the state. For example, Joseph Reinach was elected in February 1883 to the central committee of the *Alliance universelle israélite* (of which other Jewish ministers or deputies were also president or vice president, such as Crémieux, Javal, or later René Mayer). Joseph then was primarily concerned with the lot of the eastern European Jews subject to violent pogroms. However, Théodore Reinach, an intellectual, a specialist in ancient Greece, and a very active deputy reelected in the Chambéry's first electoral constituency, who was "resolutely opposed to the anarchy and the diminishing of the nation and wanting the intangible maintenance of the principle of secularism,"[87] upheld a liberal Judaism that he wanted to adapt to a Christian society. Founder of the Liberal Jewish Union, he hoped to introduce organs, decorated with figures, into new synagogues in order to distinguish them from the "German or Polish synagogues where duties without beauty are performed amidst a deafening brouhaha, in a sometimes indecent confusion."[88] He wrote, "Judaism, now released from its former chains to the earth and to nationality, aspires to a true universal belief." He further expressed his support for mixed marriages and belief that circumcision was "an obsolete demand,"[89] even suggesting that Sunday become the sabbath in order to be "in harmony with the milieu" of the open society,[90] a measure actually applied for a while. For him, "emancipation and equality affect everything, not only the laws but the morals and ideas; the Jewish sentiment will lose more and more of its sharpness and will ultimately be extinguished. The Jews are gradually becoming absorbed into the general mass of their fellow citizens of other religions. . . . They will disappear into a more or less receding future . . . in order to give birth to the religion of humanity."[91]

However, as distant as he was from Orthodox Judaism, and as favorable as he was to the transformation of Jews into Israélites that little distinguished Jews from their fellow citizens in a society in which "the beautiful" reigned, Théodore Reinach would still not go so far as to convert, as certain Court Jews had. Rather, his Judaism lost all its specificity. It is furthermore understandable that, contrary to his brother Joseph, he

87 "Profession de foi de Théodore Reinach aux élections de Savoie de 1910," *Receuil de textes authentiques des programmes et engagements électoraux des députés proclamés élus* (Paris: Imprimerie Nationale, 1910), 902.

88 Théodore Reinach, "Beauté et religion," Temple de l'Union Libérale Israélite, 21 May 1922, B.N. A 23855.

89 Théodore Reinach, "Israel et le Prosélytisme," Paris, Union Libérale Israélite, 1920, B.N. 23846.

90 Théodore Reinach, "Ce que nous sommes," Paris, Union Libérale Israélite, Copernic, 1927, B.N. 1 23833.

91 Théodore Reinach, "Juifs," in *Grande Encyclopédie* (Paris, 1894), 91.

hoped to answer Drumont's anti-Semitic attacks with only a "silence of disdain." As Léon Blum would later observe, exaggerating only slightly, "The Jews of the Dreyfus era, . . . who belonged to the same social stratum, who, like him, had passed difficult tests, were introduced to the cadres of state officers or in the most sought-after civil administration corps, exasperated by the idea that hostile prejudice could limit their irreproachable careers."[92]

This interpretation of the consequences of political emancipation, which radically opposed Jews to "Israélites," must be very nuanced.[93] Numerous Jews belonging to the political staff did not abandon their particularism in the public sphere. There is no shortage of examples of loyalty to Jewish identity, even for those who did not truly practice Judaism. Out of the fifty-two Jewish members of the political staff, only three deputies or senators married Catholic women. Funeral chronicles also frequently indicate the presence of a rabbi: even the chief rabbi, Zadoc Kahn, officiated and pronounced official funeral discourses.[94]

Between 1870 and 1940, there were nearly fifty Jewish prefects and underprefects in France, of which the first, Lisbonne, was named at the foundation of the Third Republic by Gambetta himself. A number of them deserve to be mentioned as well. The great Reinach family's role in the political staff was paralleled by the Hendlé dynasty within the high administration, in that its fathers and sons would be prefects and underprefects. Ernest Hendlé created this administrative family: very active in the administration of the National Defense Government, he was named prefect in the north in 1871 by Jules Favre, then in Creuse; he became one of the great prefects of the Third Republic. His son Albert would become underprefect in 1893, then prefect in 1907 in Calvados, and finally state counselor in 1921. Albert's son also joined the prefectorial administration in 1930 and became secretary general in 1936 of the prefecture of Lot and Garonne; he died in 1938 from his many wounds he suffered during World War I, for which the Croix de Guerre, the Croix du Combattant, and numerous other related awards were bestowed upon him.[95]

The three Hendlé generations believed in the state and were devoted to public service: as high functionaries they were, like all members of the prefectorial body, placed at the heart of the political-administrative system. Let us give two examples of a purely symbolic nature: upon the

[92] Léon Blum, *Souvenirs sur l'Affaire* (Paris: Gallimard, 1981), 520.

[93] Dominique Schnapper, *Juifs et Israélites* (Paris: Gallimard, 1980), and Phyllis Albert Cohen, "Israelite and Jew: How Did Nineteenth-Century French Jews Understand Assimilation?," in Jonathan Frankel and Steven Zipperstein, *Assimilation and Community: The Jews in Nineteenth Century Europe* (Cambridge: Cambridge University Press, 1992).

[94] Rabbi Zadoc Kahn, *Souvenirs et Regrets* (Paris: 1898).

[95] Archives Nationales, F1B1 784.

death of Ernest Hendlé in February of 1900 creped flags furled at half-mast. The funeral was attended by the president of the general counsel and numerous prefects, by Waddington, senator and former president of the counsel, by the general commander of the third army corps, and by the first president of the court of appeals, as infantry troops and cavalry marched along. In such a display of the republic's pomp, in the presence of many thousands of people, the chief rabbi performed the funeral oration.[96] A period of deep mourning was declared, and the flag was at half-mast for many days.[97] At the wedding of Albert Hendlé's son, then underprefect, to Marthe Ricqlès, daughter of an industrialist, in the synagogue on the Rue de la Victoire on 1 March 1893, the state itself attended through its elite: the president of the counsel was there, as were numerous ministers, Jules Simon, the head prefect of the police, numerous prefects, and distinguished men in political life.[98]

From father to son, the three Hendlés actively defended the republic, fought the influence of the Church, and reinforced the role of the state, secularism, and the Jacobin structures of the departmental administration. Jewish statesmen par excellence, true professional administrators, they nevertheless upheld endogamous marital practices, not without consequence. Thus, Albert Hendlé's confidential administrative file of 1901 contains this surprising remark: "Held in high esteem despite his Jewish origin that has alienated certain sympathies."[99] In other words, the republican and universalist state was not above making anti-Semitic remarks even within its own administration! Outside, things were worse. Like the Reinachs, the Hendlés, at the upper echelons of the state, were the prey of anti-Semitic pamphlets: for example, *La Libre Parole* unrelentingly attacked the "powerful Yids who are Hendlé father and son."[100]

As noted, in the finally triumphant republic, certain Jews had access to the top of the state but nevertheless witnessed the unleashing of a political anti-Semitism as ferocious as the economic anti-Semitism once directed against the Court Jews. This new anti-Semitism was applied to all the Jewish statesmen, especially to those who had had familial relationships that marked them for still more anti-Semitic criticisms: thus, Ernest Handlé's daughter Rachel married Jules Simon's friend Léon Cohn, who became prefect of the Loir et Cher in 1877 before settling for a long period in the Haute Garonne, where he ran the whole département from Toulouse with an iron hand. Let us further note that in 1889 the *An-*

[96] Archives de la Préfecture de la Police, B.A. 1114.

[97] Archives Départmentales Seine-Maritime, carton 1M371.

[98] Archives de la Préfecture de la Police, B.A. 1114.

[99] Archives Nationales, F1B1 569.

[100] *La Libre Parole,* 24 July 1899. The newspaper consistently blamed the "Jewish prefectorial" that Hendlé represented. See the 20 November 1897 issue.

nuaire de la Société des Etudes Juives counted Cohn among its members. He was also explicitly designated as *"Israélite,"* even in the written and confidential in-house reports of the administration. Outside, the local press attacked him unrelentingly as "the Jew from Toulouse."[101] There are numerous other examples and analyses of the careers of Abraham Schrameck, who would be minister of the interior, and of Isaie Levaillant, who would become director of security (La Sureté)—in other words, chief of police—before quitting and being named editor of *L'Univers Israélite* and gaining access to the Central Consistory, where he played an absolutely crucial role beginning in 1905.[102] Others like Eugène See also played an active role in the *Grand Corps* of the administration: his 1877 nomination as prefect in the Haute Loire region nevertheless would be received in the local newspaper *Le Reveil de la Haute Loire* as follows: "So the Minister wants to turn the département into a synagogue."[103]

In the area of justice, certain Jews also reached the highest levels of the administration. In 1862 Philippe Anspach was named president of the Chambre de Paris before becoming counselor of the Supreme Court of Appeal. His brilliant career enabled him to join the *haute bourgeoisie;* his daughter married a Rothschild in an elaborate ceremony.[104] Gustave Bedarrides, throughout his long career, would be named substitute procurator to the King in 1840 and would become president of the Supreme Court of Appeal and doyen of all the magistrates in France. Married to Joséphine Crémieux, he therefore was related to Adolphe Crémieux, the minister of justice who would favor his career. Having worked their way up to the highest level in the hierarchy, these Jewish statesmen were still linked to the Jewish world: both were elected to the Central Consistory and had headquarters in this enclosed part of French Judaism.[105] Bedarrides's personal administrative report in 1849 contained the following: "He belongs to the Jewish religion, he has the manners, the ideas of Christian society";[106] in 1880, however, another in-house report reads: "Like all of his Jewish coreligionists he has a head for business and a sense of diplomacy in his conduct."[107]

Other magistrates would work their way up the judiciary hierarchy, including A. Bloch, who became president of the Chambre de Paris in 1897; Charles Berr, who married Pauline Levy, was successor to this crucial post in 1903 and would become leader of the Chambre presidents.

[101] Archives Nationales, F1B1 321.

[102] Consistoire Centrale, deposition, 27 June 1905.

[103] Archives Nationales, F1B1 523.

[104] Ibid.

[105] Archives du Consistoire Central, no. 6 1E6.

[106] Archives Nationales, B.B. 6 II 26.

[107] Ibid., B.B. 6 II 663.

La Libre Parole exclaimed, "Here is the man proposed for one of the most coveted posts of the magistrature; this is yid insolence."[108] Shortly thereafter, in 1925, Eugene Dreyfus proceeded to the post of first president of the court of appeals of Paris.[109] There are numerous examples here of other Jews named to the counsel of state, the other most important judiciary structure of public law in the public order: Camille Sée to his headquarters in the foundation of the Third Republic, Camille Lyon, Georges Saint-Paul, Jacques Helbronner, Georges Cahen-Salvador, Paul Grunebaum-Ballin, Léon Blum, and others would be named section presidents in this important moment of the state. At the turn of the century and again during the two world wars, some of these high state magistrates, such as Camille Lyon, would also have headquarters at the Central Consistory or, like Georges Saint-Paul and Jacques Helbronner, in the commissions of the Paris Consistory.

This rapid overview would not be complete without a short mention of Jews in the army. From the beginning of the nineteenth century Jews had access to officers' posts, and by mid-century a number of them were promoted to the rank of captain or colonel. At this time, the army was probably a privileged place for political mobility as well as access to the state. In France, access to the state for Jews passed by way of the army first, a phenomenon that has been underestimated for a long time because of purely ideological interpretations of the effects of the Dreyfus affair. This is not the place to retrace this element in detail, though it was essential and is nearly always neglected when considering political emancipation. Consider the Naquets. Born in 1843 in Carpentras, Samuel Paul Naquet-Laroque, son of Isaac Naquet, entered the Ecole Polytechnique in 1863, married Myriam Milhaud, became colonel in 1894, then general in 1900. After many brilliant campaigns against the Germans in 1870, then in the war of 1914–18, and after also distinguishing himself in the conquest of Algeria and Tunisia, he died in 1921. His son Elie was a student at St. Cyr and went into the army.[110] His brother Louis David Naquet married Laure Elisabeth Vidal-Naquet, president of the Consistoire Israélite of Marseille. He was made lieutenant in 1893 and captain in 1902, and he participated in the Tonkin campaign, dying a heroic death in September 1914.[111] Their sister Naomi Naquet married Adrien Brisac, born in Metz. Their son Pierre Salomon Isaac Brisac enlisted in the army in 1915, fought throughout the war, and was wounded at Verdun. He later entered the Ecole Polytechnique. Altogether he participated in a number of campaigns, from Morocco to Levant, joined the French resistance in

[108] Palmade, *Capitalismes et Capitalistes français,* 178–82.

[109] Archives Nationales, B.B. 6 II 824.

[110] Services Historiques des Armées, G.D. 3è série, 386.

[111] Ibid., G.D. 3è série, 95 652.

1940, and served as chief of state under General de Lattre before becoming a general himself and the commander of the Ecole Polytechnique. He married Edith Crémieux, a very religious young woman, in the Marseille synagogue. In 1945, while head of the Ecole Polytechnique, he participated in the activities of the Paris Consistory. He accompanied his children to the Temple of Victory, and during his son François's bar mitzvah he gave an official reception at the Ecole Polytechnique itself. When he died in 1975, the chief rabbi pronounced the funeral oration. His son Michel, graduate of St. Cyr, would ultimately become a brigadier general in 1985.[112]

From the mid-nineteenth century to contemporary times, this great family of army servants at the highest level would witness the political assimilation of the Jews of France, who would nevertheless remain loyal to their particularist origins. One might evoke further examples of this essential social fact, which provides yet another illustration of the particularity of the strong French state built upon meritocratic and secular foundations. Thus, Eugène Abraham Lévy was promoted to general in 1880 and throughout the Dreyfus affair pursued a brilliant career as division general,[113] an epoch in which Lt. Colonel Emile Dreyfus, son of Moyse Dreyfus and Rosette Lévy, also led a peaceful career.[114]

The anti-Semitism that was openly expressed in the rapports among the military was rarer than in other state institutions. Thus, in 1876 it was noted that "General Léopold Sée belonged to the Jewish sect that maintained distant though honorable relations," an observation that bears witness to the care with which people almost always forced themselves to limit all official expressions of anti-Semitism, even in the army, even if its members did not hide their anti-Semitic sentiments.[115] Not only had a certain number of Jews become generals, but some of them had married Jewish women; some, such as General Pierre Brisac and, even earlier, Generals Weiler and Abraham Sée, were very active in the Paris Consistory. General Geismar was even president of Keren Keyemeth LeIsrael. It is clear that many prefects, judges, or generals became atheists or distanced themselves in other ways from Judaism; there are numerous other examples. However, though some rejected all links with their community of origin, there were few who converted or even changed their names. They nevertheless were forced to regularly confront anti-Semitic mobilizations from outside the state, ones that challenged their legitimacy in various cities throughout France: prefects or judges

112 Personal interview with General Michel Brisac.

113 Services Historiques des Armées, G.D. 3è série, 81.

114 Ibid.

115 Ibid., G.D. 2è série, 1615. On the open anti-Semitism in the French army see William Serman, *Les officiers français dans la nation: 1848–1914* (Paris: Aubier, 1982), chap. 6.

were unrelentingly mocked in the local press and sometimes were targets of demonstrations that were both anti-Semitic and anti-republican. To the cries of "France for the French!" the demonstrators tried to impose a very limited provincialism in the recruitment of high functionaries in order to better represent their fellow citizens, often Catholic. Further, as noted above, even within the state and after its separation from the church, observations of a strongly anti-Semitic slant appeared regularly in the administrative files of these high functionaries: their superiors were even brought to challenge "the Jewish race," "the physique of the Jews," "the traditional Jewish shortcomings." It was as though the republic showed two faces, a visible and noble one, emancipatory and meritocratic, and another, hidden one that manifested itself in anti-Semitic practices within the state trying so hard to be strong. That prejudices and hatreds penetrated state barriers to such an extent reveals that universalist state institutionalization hardly was realized and, further, that the ideal type of the strong state was far from corresponding to the concrete world of the republican state of the Third Republic.

Beyond assimilation and entry into civil society on an egalitarian basis, what was unique was the linkage between Jews and a particularly strong and elaborated state structure. It has been a commonplace to assume that in consequence French Judaism was a nonentity, devoid of ethnic sentiment out of place in a universalism directed toward citizenship and the state. On the contrary, other scholars today assert the persistence of ethnic particularities throughout the nineteenth century. At the same time one of the unintended consequences of the new links between Jews and the state, beyond the creation of the *Alliance isréalite universelle* in a universalist perspective, was paradoxically the exposure of a politics seen by non-Jews as Jewish, leading to a form of Zionism to which French Jews were often explicitly opposed.[116] What mattered most in the creation of a specifically Jewish identity in France was, on the one hand, the extreme character of assimilation derived from social mobility arising from economic expansion, and, on the other hand, the more limited effects of contact with the state. In consequence, French Jews often remained more loyal to their particularism than the modern Court Jews.

The "divine surprise" of 1940, as Maurras termed the birth of the

[116] Phyllis Albert Cohen, "L'intégration et la persistance de l'ethnicité chez les juifs dans la France moderne," in Pierre Birnbaum, ed., *Histoire politique des Juifs de France: Entre universalisme et particularisme* (Paris: Presses de la fondation nationale des sciences politiques, 1990); Michael Graetz, *Les Juifs en France au 19è siècle*, 430. Also see Catherine Nicault, *La France et le sionisme, 1897–1948: Une recontre manquée?* (Paris: Calmann-Lévy, 1992), 139–53, describing the "hostility" and the "anti-Zionism of French Jews." In addition, see Aron Rodrigue, *De l'instruction à l'émancipation: Les enseignants de l'Alliance israélite universelle et les Juifs d'Orient, 1860–1939* (Paris: Calmann-Lévy, 1989), 186–93; and Michel Abitol, *Les Deux terres promises* (Paris: Orban, 1989).

Vichy regime, brought about a profound shock among French Jews, who had considered their state an inclusionary republican one. From October 1940, the Jewish Laws excluded them from public service, dismissed Jewish members of parliament, and cost others far more, including their French nationality.[117] French emancipation, which had been rapid and fruitful as Jews had assumed the highest responsibilities in the name of the general interest, reached its limits here, at least provisionally. France was covered with camps in which thousands of Jews were incarcerated, after being arrested by Vichy and delivered to the Nazis. Certain prominent Jews were brought to Drancy, where one could see four Jewish members of the council of state wearing their yellow Stars of David and being subjected to a harsh regime imposed by the French police, prior to deportation and an almost certain death.

This image captures well the French Jews' rise to the summit of power and their fall from it. Jewish prefects and generals wrote to Marshal Pétain in disbelief at the state's treason; their letters show how profound was their bewilderment. Jews were numerous in the resistance, once again in the name of the republican state in which they continued to place their hopes and which, after the Allied victory, would restore them to their positions and prestige. For most Jews, the Vichy episode would only be just that, an episode at the limits of comprehensibility. At the same time, however, another impulse appeared. The deportation and death of tens of thousands of Jews, often organized by the French police—a "second Inquisition," a St. Bartholomew's night for the majority of the Jewish population less directly tied to the values and legitimacy of the state—produced a more inward looking development, toward the enhancement of the collective character of Jewish civil society, a process that was enhanced greatly by the creation of the State of Israel as well as by the return of North African Jews to France in the 1960s in the aftermath of decolonization.

[117] See Michael Marrus and Robert Paxton, *Vichy et les Juifs* (Paris: Calmann-Lévy, 1981); Serge Klarsfeld, *Vichy-Auschwitz* (Paris: Fayard, 1985); Bernard Leguerre, "Les denaturalises de Vichy, 1940–1944," *Vingtième Siècle* (October 1988); and Pierre Birnbaum, "Grégoire, Dreyfus, Drancy, et Copernic," in Pierre Nora, *Les Lieux de mémoire,* vol. 3, *Les France,* part 1: *Conflits et Partages* (Paris: Gallimard, 1992).

FIVE

ENGLISH JEWS OR JEWS OF THE ENGLISH PERSUASION? REFLECTIONS ON THE EMANCIPATION OF ANGLO-JEWRY

Geoffrey Alderman

STUDENTS of Jewish emancipation in Britain must focus their attention at several different levels more or less simultaneously if they wish to obtain a reasonably accurate measure of the interplay of forces that acted upon the object of study. They must also exercise extreme vigilance in relation to the definition of terms. "Emancipation" is usually taken to mean the setting free from legal, social, political, or intellectual disabilities. In some of these senses the emancipation of British Jewry can be traced with comparative ease: for example, the release from legal constraints or the granting of full political equality. Social and intellectual (not to mention economic) emancipation are much less tangible concepts and there is, in any case, much less agreement about what these terms actually mean.

An example will illustrate the kind of difficulty involved. Strictly speaking, professing Jews were prohibited from voting in British parliamentary elections until 1835 (for males aged twenty-one and over who could fulfill the necessary property and residence qualifications). But this did not mean that until 1835 no professing Jews could—in practice—exercise the right to vote. Before that date the returning officers who supervised constituency election arrangements had the right to demand the swearing of a Christian oath by all intending voters, but this was not a right they were obliged to exercise, and it is clear that in particular localities election officials deliberately chose not to discriminate against Jews in this way. In May 1830 Sir Robert Wilson told the House of Commons that Jews habitually voted in parliamentary elections in Southwark (south London) because no one bothered to insist that they take the Christian oath.[1] In December 1832 Rabbi Asher Ansell of Liverpool was clearly able to vote in the general election without hindrance.[2]

[1] *The Mirror of Parliament,* vol. 2, col. 1781 (17 May 1830).

[2] Liverpool Poll Book of 1832, in the Institute of Historical Research, University of London.

These instances tell us something also about the nature of the British state, in its relations with its Jewish inhabitants, during the late eighteenth and early nineteenth centuries. Social and economic emancipation preceded by a half-century and more the granting of full civic equality; the former, indeed, was a precondition of the latter. In contrast to the situation to be found in the major countries of western Europe, Anglo-Jewish emancipation did not proceed from the top downward, by some great single act of emancipation emanating from the highest levels of the state and imposed upon society as a whole. Rather, it grew, as a process, out of a mosaic of changing social, economic, and religious circumstances over which the Anglo-Jewish community as a whole had relatively little control.

The Anglo-Jewish community of the Cromwellian Resettlement did indeed inhabit a ghetto, but one that had no physical dimension and was partly of its own making. The granting of entry to the House of Commons (1858) was merely the culmination of a movement the origins of which may be traced back certainly until the second half of the eighteenth century, and which was accelerated by the onset of that period of rapid economic growth known as the Industrial Revolution. In particular, the growth of religious toleration in the late eighteenth and early nineteenth centuries was bound to affect the status of British Jewry, elements of which (such as the Goldsmid brothers and the English Rothschilds) had by then acquired for themselves important places in the financial and commercial life of the nation. The Jews (of whom there were about thirty-five thousand living in Britain in the 1850s, with about twenty thousand in London) had much in common with other, larger, "dissenting" minorities, such as the Unitarians and the Quakers, whose members were also conspicuous in banking, finance, brokering, and underwriting. Legally the Jews were, as they felt themselves and declared themselves to be, merely a section of nonconformist society.[3]

During the eighteenth and early nineteenth centuries, the belief that heresy (the holding of religious views at variance with those of the established Protestant Church of England) was tantamount to treason was finally laid to rest. In 1828 and 1829 most dissenting groups in Britain were admitted to full political equality. These groups, however, were all Christian. Henceforth the United Kingdom of Great Britain and Ireland was a Christian realm, even if it was no longer a Protestant one. Jews, especially if they were born in the United Kingdom, already enjoyed a wide measure of toleration and legal protection. Lord Chancellor Brougham put the matter thus in 1833: "His Majesty's subjects professing the Jewish religion were born to all the rights, immunities and privileges of His Maj-

[3] Israel Finestein, *Post-Emancipation Jewry: The Anglo-Jewish Experience* (Oxford: Oxford Centre for Postgraduate Hebrew Studies, 1986), 8.

esty's other subjects, excepting so far as positive enactments of law deprived them of those rights, immunities and privileges."[4]

Doubts as to whether Jews could legally dwell in England had been resolved by the end of the seventeenth century. The right of foreign-born Jews to become naturalized was conferred (incidentally) by Act of Parliament in 1825. By the end of the 1840s there were no legal restraints upon the right of Jews to worship freely, to own land, and to seek the protection of the courts of law for themselves and their property; indeed, in 1818 the right of a synagogue to take proceedings to recover dues owed to it was recognized.[5] The ability of professing Jews to vote in parliamentary elections was, as noted, made explicit in 1835 though it had in practice been exercised much earlier.[6]

In general, entry of Jews into the major professions (especially the law) from which Jews had been barred hitherto had been effected through the repeal of the Test and Corporation Acts (1828); the first Jewish barrister, Francis Goldsmid, was called to the Bar in 1833.[7] The right of Jews to engage in retail trade within the square mile of the City of London had been conceded in 1830 (though it had almost certainly been exercised before then). The right to hold any and every municipal office was granted by Act of Parliament in 1845—but there are numerous examples of Jewish involvement in local government prior to the passage of that legislation.[8] The Registration Act of 1836 had given statutory recognition to the London Committee (subsequently known as the Board) of Deputies of British Jews. Originally the records of the Board had been kept in Portuguese; from the 1770s they were kept in English, and it is also noteworthy that sermons in English were introduced into the Spanish and Portuguese Synagogue in 1829, by which time they had ceased to be unusual in Ashkenazi congregations.

Thus by the mid-nineteenth century, through an incremental process, the legal equality of Jewish with non-Jewish citizens of the United Kingdom was substantially complete. There were as yet no professing Jews in the House of Lords (then a totally hereditary body), and any professing Jew brave enough to secure election to the House of Commons was legally precluded from taking his seat by virtue of the require-

[4] Quoted in Michael C. N. Salbstein, *The Emancipation of the Jews in Britain* (London: Associated University Presses, 1982), 44.

[5] Cecil Roth, *A History of the Jews in England* (Philadelphia: Jewish Publication Society, 1979), 113.

[6] Todd M. Endelman, *The Jews of Georgian England* (Philadelphia: Jewish Publication Society, 1979), 113.

[7] See generally Phyllis S. Lachs, "A Study of a Professional Elite: Anglo-Jewish Barristers in the Nineteenth Century," *Jewish Social Studies* 44 (1982): 125–34.

[8] Geoffrey Alderman, *Modern British Jewry* (Oxford: Oxford University Press, 1992), 53.

ment to swear a Christian oath. But this disability was not one about which the Jewish community itself was particularly agitated. To begin with, the acknowledged lay and religious leaders of the community were much more concerned with the maintenance of traditional (i.e., orthodox) Jewish values and practices than with entry into Parliament. Moses Montefiore, who became president of the Board of Deputies in 1835 (and who was to remain president, almost without a break, until 1874), confided to his diary in 1837 his resolve "not to give up the smallest particle of our religious forms and privileges to obtain civil rights."[9] The recognition of the Board of Deputies as the competent authority to certify Jewish places of worship for marriage purposes was valuable, of course. But two years earlier Parliament had, as part of a general enactment, curtailed the total autonomy the community had enjoyed—uniquely—hitherto to marry within degrees of kinship permitted by rabbinical authority. In like manner, religious autonomy in matters of divorce was irrevocably compromised by the Matrimonial Causes Act of 1857, which gave the civil courts, for the first time, the power to dissolve a religiously sanctioned marriage.

Equal treatment had thus been obtained, but at a price considered by many to be too high. Two issues were involved. The first concerned, obviously, the religious freedoms of the community, which (it was argued) were being eroded in the name of equality before the law.[10] Second, and no less important, this equality threatened to disturb the structure of power within a community that had been until then almost entirely self-governing.

We need to remember that in the 1840s the communal structure of Anglo-Jewry was far from settled. Until Montefiore's elevation to its presidency, the Board of the Deputies—in effect, at that time, merely a committee of representatives of the four largest London congregations (three Ashkenazi and one Sephardi)—had met very infrequently. Montefiore, by nature an autocrat, was concerned that the board should become the sole medium of communication between the community and the government, and be acknowledged as such on both sides. This necessitated a more formal structure (including a written constitution) and a widening of its membership, to include provincial congregations. The

[9] Quoted in Lloyd P. Gartner, "Emancipation, Social Change and Communal Reconstruction in Anglo-Jewry, 1789–1881," *Proceedings of the American Academy for Jewish Research* 54 (1987): 90.

[10] In 1911 Lord Rothschild defended Chief Rabbi Hermann Adler's recommendation to a Royal Commission on Divorce, that "foreign rabbis" who authorized "irregular divorces" (i.e., divorces conforming to rabbinic precept but not recognized by the state) should be rendered liable to prosecution. Rothschild argued that emancipation implied, on the part of Anglo-Jewry, a renunciation of "*imperium in imperio.*" Finestein, *Post-Emancipation Jewry,* 2.

very small Jewish communities of Scotland (principally Glasgow), Wales (principally Cardiff), and Ireland (principally Dublin) were, in every sense of the word, peripheral: the great provincial Jewries of Victorian England (Manchester alone excepted) did not develop and flex their muscles until the 1880s. This is not to say that challenges to the hegemony of London were until then nonexistent; rather, provincial leaders lacked the numerical support and the communal status to overcome the predominance of the large London congregations. By 1858 there were fifty-eight deputies, of whom only twenty-six represented six London synagogues; but six of the provincial deputies also lived in London and, in practice, those who dominated communal affairs in the capital dominated also the affairs of the board.[11]

Montefiore shared the view then prevailing among the communal grandees that the well-being and reputation of the community necessitated a continued measure of intracommunal discipline, which might also be put to use to defend traditional Orthodoxy against the depredations of the Reform movement. The 1836 Registration Act gave the board, in the person of its president, a mighty weapon to use against Reform congregations trying to establish themselves in Britain; the first, the West London Synagogue, opened its doors in 1842. Montefiore refused to grant the necessary certificate for marriage registration purposes to this congregation, and he refused to admit to membership of the board any adherent of the Reform persuasion. In 1853, when four provincial congregations elected Reformers as their deputies, Montefiore used his casting vote to keep them out; in 1856 a special Act of Parliament had to be passed to provide the West London Synagogue with a marriage secretary of its own.

From 1845 Montefiore had a staunch ally in Nathan Marcus Adler, elected that year as (Ashkenazi) Chief Rabbi following Solomon Hirschell. Adler, who came from Hanover, could claim an allegiance that his predecessors could not, for his was the first election in which provincial communities as well as London congregations had participated. It was during his tenure as Chief Rabbi (1845–90) that the office developed along the broad path it was to follow for the next hundred years. He used the power to certify congregations to the Board of Deputies (so permitting them to be represented there and to obtain marriage registration) in order to reinforce his authority over provincial congregations, and to prevent Reformers from becoming deputies.[12] He laid down the form of worship

[11] Aubrey Newman, *The Board of Deputies of British Jews, 1760–1985* (London: Board of Deputies of British Jews, 1987), 17.

[12] See generally Israel Finestein, "The Anglo-Jewish Revolt of 1853," *Jewish Quarterly* (Autumn/Winter 1978–79): 103–13; the first Reform deputies were not admitted to the board until 1886.

for "all the Synagogues in the British Empire" (1847) and conducted pastoral visitations of his provincial communities. He claimed and exercised the power to license all synagogue officials and *shochtim* (ritual slaughterers of meat).[13] In short, Nathan Adler believed that the Orthodox structure in Britain was too weak to permit the growth of self-governing communities—as existed in Germany, Poland and Russia—and that what was needed was strong centralization under his aegis.

The approach of Montefiore, Adler, and their allies to questions of communal organization and power was bound to inform and color their attitude also toward political emancipation. The founders of the West London Synagogue, and in particular the Mocattas and the Goldsmids, were among the most energetic workers for emancipation, which at one level was argued simply in terms of taxation and representation: Jews who paid their local and national taxes were entitled to exercise the concomitant rights of representation. Such rights were also being denied to Reformers (in respect of marriage registration and seats on the Board of Deputies) and—it should be noted—to newer immigrants within the Orthodox fold who found that the synagogues they joined were controlled (apparently in perpetuity) by a class of well-to-do "free" members whom it appeared impossible to unseat. The "rotten borough constitution" of the Great Synagogue, London, was denounced by the scholar immigrant S. M. Drach, who pointed out that "whilst its leading members are publicly striving for the extension of . . . civil and religious liberty . . . they themselves keep up the old restrictive and select vestry system."[14]

David Salomons, the leading emancipationist (also the first Ashkenazi President of the Board of Deputies [1838–40] and the first professing Jew to sit, literally, in the House of Commons [1851]), though not a Reformer himself, nonetheless found himself at odds with the Orthodox establishment because he viewed the Orthodox-Reform rift within Anglo-Jewry as a hindrance to the removal of civil disabilities. Salomons argued that the Jews could not demand equality with the Gentiles while denying it to their fellow Jews who happened to be Reformers; he did not regard the Reform controversy as being by any means the most pressing problem facing the community; and he resented Nathan Adler's attempts to assert the Chief Rabbi's authority in this matter and in others, such as education.[15]

So it was that the quest for political emancipation became bound up,

[13] Geoffrey Alderman, "Power, Status and Authority in British Jewry: The Chief Rabbinate and Shechita," in Geoffrey Alderman and Colin Holmes, eds., *Outsiders and Outcasts: Essays in Honour of William J. Fishman* (London: Ducksworth, 1993), 14–16.

[14] *Jewish Chronicle* (hereafter *JC*), 1 November 1844, 15.

[15] Geoffrey Alderman, *The Jewish Community in British Politics* (Oxford: Oxford University Press, 1983), 16.

inextricably, with the Reform controversy, with the sporadic secessions from the major London congregations incited by the cloying oligarchic modes of governance to be found within them, with the growing authority of the Ashkenazi chief rabbinate, and with the claim of the Board of Deputies to speak—and to speak without challenge—for the whole of British Jewry. For as long as no professing Jew could gain admission to Parliament, perhaps to articulate there "Jewish" opinions at variance with those of the lay and religious leaderships outside, the authority of these leaderships could be maintained reasonably intact. Conversely, once the claim for civil equality had been met, the very fact of its having been granted would be used within the community (so it was said) to bring about drastic alternations in the structure of communal power and in the exercise of communal authority.

To these arguments two others were added. The first was a fundamentalist one, derived from the thesis that although Jews could dwell among other nations, they were not permitted to sink their identities within those of the nations among whom they dwelled: the Jew was not an Englishman and, if he tried to become one, his Jewish identity—and destiny—would be lost.[16] This viewpoint was admittedly extreme. But it was espoused by a number of religious authorities, on the severely practical ground that political emancipation might lead to assimilation and complete loss of religious identity. Such spokesmen publicly repudiated the quest for political equality and did not shrink from identifying themselves with Christian opponents of emancipation in this regard.[17]

Nathan Adler, it must be said, was not of this view. But he had no enthusiasm for the emancipation campaign. Moses Montefiore viewed emancipation as a desirable objective, but not one that had to be given the highest communal priority. Moreover, he was (inevitably) highly critical of the attempts of the leading emancipationists to bypass the Board of Deputies in their dealings with the government on this issue. Partly in consequence, the board did not stir itself in regard to emancipation until the very final stages of the struggle. In this matter, as in so many others, the attitude evinced by the board was entirely reactive: in general, it did not desire a close relationship with the British state and was generally suspicious of the motives of those who sought a Jewish presence in the Westminster legislature.

Here a second argument came into play. For it could not be denied that most Jews neither desired the right of election to Parliament for themselves nor thought it important for the community as a whole that efforts

[16] Salbstein, *Emancipation of the Jews*, 78–84.

[17] Israel Finestein, "Anglo-Jewish Opinion during the Struggle for Emancipation (1828–1858)," *Transactions of the Jewish Historical Society of England* 20 (1959–61): 116–17; see also Ursula R. Q. Henriques, *Religious Toleration in England 1787–1833* (London: Routledge, 1961), 182–83.

should be expended in pursuit of such a privilege. To comprehend the full force of this viewpoint we must bear in mind that only the wealthiest elements of British society could contemplate a political career. Election contests cost money; members of Parliament were unpaid. Given the highly decentralized nature of the British state in the mid-nineteenth century, the role of Parliament could hardly be said to be critical to the everyday life of the nation: what *practical* advantages, therefore, could possibly accrue to British Jewry from the presence in the House of Commons of a handful of identifying Jews?

The right of entry into the professions had a general application. The ability to deliberate upon the affairs of local authorities was undoubtedly beneficial, especially in areas of high Jewish concentrations, such as London. The right to vote might be said to open a necessary dialogue between Parliament and Jewry—though it is worth noting that there was never a Jewish "campaign" on this particular issue. But the right of election to the House of Commons did indeed strike many Jews as utterly peripheral to the real interests of the community, more particularly in view of the fact that not even the most strident Jewish protagonists in the struggle for entry into Parliament harbored any intention of creating a Jewish "lobby" at Westminster. Thus in 1830 the entrepreneur Lewis Levy (the renowned farmer of turnpike tolls) petitioned the Commons in favor of a declaratory law on the right of Jews to own land, but insisted that he desired neither the franchise nor the right of election to Parliament, adding that his Jewish acquaintances were of a similar opinion.[18] Researching in the 1850s, Henry Mayhew, the chronicler of London life, had this to say about the attitude of the Jewish "man in the street" to the question of Jewish political emancipation:

> I was told by a Hebrew gentleman (a professional man) that so little did the Jews care for "Jewish emancipation," that he questioned if one man in ten, activated solely by his own feelings, would trouble himself to walk the length of the street in which he lived to secure Baron [Lionel de] Rothschild's admission into the House of Commons. . . .
>
> When such is the feeling of the wealthier Jews, no one can wonder that I found among the Jew street-sellers and old-clothes men with whom I talked on the subject . . . a perfect indifference to, and nearly as perfect an ignorance of, politics.[19]

The quest for Jewish political emancipation was not one in which British Jewry, as a collective, took part. Rather, it was undertaken by a few leading members of the community, acting partly out of personal or communal ambition as well as out of pure idealism and principle. After Li-

[18] *Mirror of Parliament*, 29 April 1830, 1423.

[19] Henry Mayhew, *London Labour and the London Poor* (1861–62; reprint, London: Cass, 1967), 2: 126–27.

onel de Rothschild's victory, the number of Jewish members of the House of Commons rose quickly, to six MPs by 1865. But this was, in large measure, simply a function of Jewish overrepresentation in the social groups from which the political classes were drawn. During his entire parliamentary career (1858–74) Rothschild never once made a speech on the floor of the House of Commons; indeed, few of these early Jewish MPs (Salomons and Sir John Simon are important exceptions) could be relied upon to put their parliamentary positions at the service of the Jewish community.

Of course, the saga of Lionel de Rothschild's attempts to gain admission to the Commons as an MP for the City of London (for which he was elected five times between 1847 and 1857) acquired epic proportions; it was a saga in which the city's Jewish electorate played a central part. But the overriding factor here (as in other constituencies, such as Greenwich, which returned Salomons in a by-election in 1851) was the favorable attitude of the Liberal party, anxious to win Jewish voters to its side, to bring about a further disengagement between Church and State through an alteration in the Christian character of Parliament, and to exploit whatever issues came to hand in another campaign, aimed at the subordination of the unelected, hereditary House of Lords to the elected House of Commons. Once Rothschild had been elected, his right to take his seat as a professing Jew became nothing less than a struggle to convince their Lordships that they had no business meddling in the affairs of the Lower House. In these two respects (Lords versus Commons and State versus Church), Jewish emancipation occupied a small but nonetheless exotic corner of two much more elaborate mosaics.

The legislation of 1858, which gave the Commons and Rothschild their victories, did not quite mark the end of the battle for emancipation in its legal and political phases. Strictly speaking, the right of professing Jews to enter either House of Parliament was not definitively conferred until the passage of the Parliamentary Oaths Act of 1866. The right of election to Fellowships at Oxford and Cambridge did not come about until 1871, the same year in which (by virtue of the Promissory Oaths Act) Jews acquired the right to hold almost all offices of state, and in which the first appointment of a Jew (the Liberal MP Sir George Jessel) as a Minister of the Crown (Solicitor-General) was made. In 1885 Queen Victoria was prevailed upon to confer on Lionel de Rothschild's son, Nathan, the peerage she had declined to give to Moses Montefiore.[20]

On 16 June 1887 Heinrich Graetz, the leading Jewish historian of his time, visited the Anglo-Jewish Exhibition at the Royal Albert Hall and

[20] Vivian D. Lipman, "The Age of Emancipation, 1815–1880," in V. D. Lipman, ed., *Three Centuries of Anglo-Jewish History* (Cambridge: Heffer, 1961), 82. *JC* (6 April 1883) had described Jessel's life as "a justification of the Emancipation" (9).

heaped praise upon the Anglo-Jewish achievement. "I have no wish to pay you mere compliments," he confessed. "I desire only to establish the fact that a new birth, full of bright hope, has again come to despised and powerless Israel."[21] In the epilogue to his *History of the Jews in England* (1949), the late Dr. Cecil Roth waxed lyrical upon these achievements, regarding them not merely as the culmination of the process of emancipation, but as the incontrovertible proof that it had come about. Before considering the condition of British Jewry in the subsequent period, I should like to introduce into the equation certain terms and factors omitted from Roth's conventional evaluation.

In 1917, during the stormy debates between Zionist and anti-Zionist Jews in Britain that surrounded the efforts of the former to obtain the Balfour Declaration, and of the latter to thwart its promulgation, leading anti-Zionists argued that the battle for Jewish emancipation, sixty or so years before, had been fought and won on the ground that an English Jew was different from an English Christian merely and only by virtue of his religion; admit the Zionist claim to Jewish nationhood (so the argument went) and you admitted, too, that the Gentiles had been deceived at the time emancipation had been granted.[22]

Organized Jewish opposition to Zionism was small, but it was led and articulated by a highly influential group that included D. L. Alexander (president of the Board of Deputies, 1903–17), C. G. Montefiore (president of the Anglo-Jewish Association), the second Lord Swaythling (Louis Montagu, president of the Federation of Synagogues), and the Unionist MPs Lionel de Rothschild and Sir Philip Magnus. These notables were but a couple of generations (at most) removed from that of the emancipation, and it is clear that the "Contract" argument—that the Jews of England had given up any claims to nationhood in return for civil equality—had a powerful impact upon them. A pseudonymous article on Zionism that appeared in the *Fortnightly Review* in November 1916 stressed the existence of this bargain and pointed to T. B. Macaulay's famous essay advocating Jewish emancipation that had appeared in the *Edinburgh Review* in January 1831 as proof of its contention.

Macaulay had relegated the Jewish attachment to restorationism to the level of "a pious dogma"[23] and, in trying to prove that the English Jew could be regarded as a sound patriot, had asked rhetorically: "Does the expectation of being restored to the country of his forefathers make [the

[21] Finestein, *Post-Emancipation Jewry*, 5.

[22] Harry Sacher, *Jewish Emancipation: The Contract Myth* (London: John Murray, 1917).

[23] Israel Finestein, "Some Modern Themes in the Emancipation Debate in Early Victorian England," in Jonathan Sacks, ed., *Tradition and Transition* (London: Jews' College, 1986), 142.

Jew] insensible to the fluctuations of the stock exchange? Does he, in arranging his private affairs, ever take into account the chances of migrating to Palestine?" At the time these sentiments had attracted from the community considerable praise, even adulation. But with the passage of years they acquired a more sinister aspect. When, in July 1897, Chief Rabbi Hermann Adler (Nathan's son) denounced the forthcoming First Zionist Congress as an "egregious blunder" and condemned the idea of a Jewish state as being "contrary to Jewish principles," he was demonstrating, in a remarkable way, that the forebodings of religious fundamentalists as to the consequences of emancipation had had substance, after all.

Hermann Adler insisted that the Jews had ceased to be a nation once the Second Temple had been destroyed. This sentiment was not far removed from the insistence of Claude Montefiore, the founder of Liberal Judaism, that Judaism was a "denationalised" creed.[24] There can be little doubt that, without the mass immigration of eastern European Jews to Britain in and after the closing decades of the nineteenth century, the bulk of Anglo-Jewry would willingly have paid the ransom (in terms of withdrawal of support from the Zionist movement) that had been agreed during the period of emancipation.

But the implications of Macaulay's arguments went much further than this and had an impact more immediate still. Macaulay had put forward in favor of emancipation contentions that were clearly ambiguous; he emphasized and exaggerated Jewish financial power and expressed the hope that this might be used for the good of British society: "Jews are not now excluded from political power. They possess it; and as long as they are allowed to accumulate property, they must possess it. . . . What power in civilised society is so great as that of the creditor over the debtor?" Opponents of Jewish emancipation claimed that "it would be impious to let a Jew sit in Parliament. But a Jew [Macaulay pointed out] may make money, and money may make members of Parliament. . . . The scrawl of a Jew on the back of a piece of paper may be worth more than the royal word of three kings . . . but, that he should put Right Honourable before his name, would be the most frightful of national calamities."[25]

As Bryan Cheyette has pointed out, the widespread acceptance of these sentiments scarred the Anglo-Jewish consciousness.[26] The immediate

[24] Finestein, *Post-Emancipation Jewry,* 7.

[25] G. T. Bettany, ed., *Essays Historical and Literary from the "Edinburgh Review" by Lord Macaulay* 2d ed. (London: Ward, Lock, Bowden and Co., n.d.), 171–72. Macaulay's private (and therefore authentic) view of Jews was far from adulatory: see his letter to his sister, Hannah (8 June 1831) quoted in Abraham Gilam, *The Emancipation of the Jews in England, 1830–1860* (New York: Garland Publishing, 1982), 68–69.

[26] Bryan Cheyette, "From Apology to Revolt: Benjamin Farjeon, Amy Levy and the Post-Emancipation Anglo-Jewish Novel, 1880–1900," *Transactions of the Jewish Historical Society of England* 29 (1982–86): 255.

post-emancipation generations felt that they were on trial, that they had to prove, and to continue to prove, that they were worthy of the rights and freedoms Anglo-Christian society had extended to them, and that they must somehow conform to what they felt were Gentile expectations of acceptable Jewish behavior. Inevitably, therefore, post-emancipation Anglo-Jewry was "dominated by considerations of public image."[27]

In the cultural sphere this preoccupation—almost obsession—had a stultifying and dehumanizing influence. Jewish writers were expected to produce material that would project images designed to counterbalance those drawn by anti-Semites.[28] Samuel Gordon's *Sons of the Covenant* (1900) was praised because its idealized portrait of recently arrived Jewish immigrants to London's East End, wishing for nothing better than to marry into the assimilated Jewish gentry of the West End, represented "all that is best and most typical in Jewish life and thought."[29] Benjamin Farjeon's literary output (especially *The Pride of Race,* also published in 1900) extolled the virtues of the "English Jewish gentleman" and idealized them: "the spirit of the English-born Jew, whose parents are also English-born," Farjeon explained, should be contrasted with the outlook of the "foreign Jew who, of late years, has overflooded the East End Ghetto."[30]

It is difficult to find in these works much that corresponded to the reality of Anglo-Jewish existence at the end of the nineteenth century. For a true account of the unashamed nepotism and deep, irreverant materialism of the Jewish middle classes in London at this time we must turn to *Reuben Sachs,* written by Amy Levy and published in 1888. The novel was condemned by the *Jewish Chronicle* and castigated by Rabbi Edward Calisch in his survey of *The Jew in English Literature* that appeared in 1909.[31] But its brilliance, conceptually and stylistically, cannot be denied.

"Much neglected" and "ignored" by Anglo-Jewry,[32] the tragic Amy Levy (who died by her own hand, in 1889, at the age of twenty-seven) was nonetheless a major influence on Israel Zangwill, whose *Children of the Ghetto,* the first realistic literary portrait of Jewish immigrant life in the East End, appeared in 1892. "She was accused," Zangwill recalled in 1901, "of course, of fouling her own nest; whereas what she had really done was to point out that the nest was fouled and must be cleaned

[27] Finestein, *Post-Emancipation Jewry,* 6.

[28] *JC,* 20 May 1892, 9.

[29] Ibid., 25 January 1901, 17.

[30] Ibid., 8 February 1901, 8.

[31] Ibid., 2 August 1889, 12; 13 September 1889, 6; 6 December 1889, 16; and Edward Calisch, *The Jew in English Literature as Subject and as Author* (Richmond, Va.: Bell Book and Stationery Company, 1909), 159.

[32] Beth Zion Lask, "Amy Levy," *Transaction of the Jewish Historical Society of England* 11 (1924–27): 168.

out."[33] When, in response to Zangwill's strictures, Samuel Gordon published *Each Man His Own* (1904), its jarring descriptions of West End Jewry evoked communal outrage; such an approach, one correspondent told the *Jewish Chronicle*, was bound to do "incalculable mischief to the community and to Jewry in general."[34]

The perceived need to project images of "good" citizenship had a predictable effect, too, upon the public policies of the communal leadership in the post-emancipation era. In no sphere was this more apparent than in relation to social problems, especially those pertaining to the condition of the Jewish poor. Jewish pauperism was a source of concern to communal leaders less on account of the inequality of wealth it reflected, or of the sickness and distress in which it resulted, than because of the dangers it posed to the safety and standing of the community as a whole. At one end of the Anglo-Jewish social scale were Jews of wealth and substance, the objects (without doubt) of much popular envy and some popular derision, whose ever-closer contacts with the British ruling classes seemed nonetheless to be not merely a vindication of emancipation but a guarantee (so to speak) that hard-won victories would not be reversed. But at the other was an underclass of Jewish peddlers and old-clothes dealers, some of whom, as receivers of stolen property, moved easily within the criminal fraternities of the city slums.

The existence of a Jewish pauper class caused deep communal anxiety, made worse by the relative ease with which foreign Jews could gain entry into Britain. On the eve of the Russian pogroms, when the total number of Jews living in Britain had reached perhaps sixty thousand, the statistician Joseph Jacobs estimated that in London alone there were over ten thousand paupers—slightly more than one-fifth of the total Jewish population of the capital.[35] Every effort was made to ensure that these unfortunates (no matter whether British-born or alien) did not enter the workhouses established under the provisions of the Poor Law Amendment Act of 1834, or otherwise obtain or even seek maintenance and relief from the secular authorities. This policy culminated, in March 1859, in the establishment by the leading Ashkenazi synagogues in London of the Jewish Board of Guardians.[36]

The foundation and early work of the Board of Guardians can be viewed from two perspectives. On the one hand, it was undeniable that entry into the statutory workhouses, grim enough for the Victorian poor

[33] *JC*, 25 January 1901, 19.

[34] Ibid., 29 January 1904, 8; the correspondent called on Gordon to withdraw the book from publication.

[35] Joseph Jacobs, *Studies in Jewish Statistics* (London: D. Nutt, 1891), 11–13.

[36] Vivian D. Lipman, *A Century of Social Service, 1859–1959: The Jewish Board of Guardians* (London: Routledge, 1959), 1.

in general, was certain to be grimmer still for the Jewish poor, because of the splitting up of families and the near impossibility of observing the dietary laws, the Sabbath, and other Holy Days; the "outdoor relief" afforded by the Jewish Guardians was infinitely preferable. On the other hand, the very existence of the Board gave tangible expression to the view that the Jewish poor must not become a burden on the state. Jewish ratepayers were, like all ratepayers, assessed by the Poor Law Guardians for the maintenance of workhouses and other forms of relief to which all paupers might have access; they were then assessed again, through synagogue contributions, to provide for the work of the Jewish Guardians.

That this was an exercise in freedom cannot be doubted. But did it not also serve to mark the Jew still as a person apart, actually erecting the walls of a new ghetto when the old ones had so recently been pulled down? Interestingly, it does not seem to have occurred to the Jewish leadership that an alternative method of helping to relieve Jewish poverty might have been found through supplementing and supporting the work of the secular authorities in Jewish areas. Instead, a completely separate apparatus was brought into operation.

In its first twenty years or so these questions (if asked at all) did not seem to matter very much. So long as immigration remained at relatively modest levels, the schemes of cash and medical relief, loans and apprenticeships operated by the Jewish Board of Guardians could—it was hoped—eventually lift most of the Jewish poor beyond the level at which they would need to call upon its services. The problems of the Jewish poor were (in short) regarded as finite, and the Anglo-Jewish gentry looked forward to a time, not far distant, when these problems would for all intents and purposes disappear. There was all the more reason, therefore, for generosity and open-mindedness.

The mass immigration that began in the 1880s "rendered all these calculations abortive."[37] Between 1881 and 1914 about 150,000 Jews from eastern Europe settled in the British Isles; most found their way to London. Merely from a demographic viewpoint this amounted to a revolution. Between 1851 and 1881 London's Jewish population had grown at an annual rate of about 4 percent. But between 1881 and 1900 London's Jewish population expanded to approximately 135,000 (an annual rate of growth of 10 percent); of these it was estimated in 1899 that roughly 120,000 were living in the East End.[38] A London Jewry that had been dominated, numerically, by the lower-middle classes had now become largely working class in composition. The Jewish character of London's

[37] Ibid., 75.

[38] Samuel Fyne, "London's Jewish Population," *JC,* 14 October 1955, 34; see also Stanley Waterman and Barry Kosmin, *British Jewry in the Eighties* (London: Board of Deputies of British Jews, 1986), 6.

East End was magnified a thousandfold, and the Jewish presence in London—and in a specific area of London—was emphasized as a result. The same type of trends, on a reduced scale, characterized the Jewries of the major provincial cities, such as Manchester, Birmingham, and Leeds. Anglo-Jewry also became identified in the popular mind with certain occupations—the garment trade, furniture making, and leather work—and even though Jews constituted a minority of all those who worked in these occupations, the perceived occupational idiosyncrasies and spatial locations of these Jews made them easy targets for those of a xenophobic and anti-Semitic inclination.

Only then did the inherent bankruptcy of mid-nineteenth-century Anglo-Jewish social policy become evident. The working-class immigrant presence strained beyond all expectations the resources of the middle-class Jewish Board of Guardians. In 1880 the number of applications for relief processed by the board was less than 2,500; by 1894 this number had more than doubled. Measured over the entire period of 1881–1914, the number increased by an annual rate of up to 200 percent.[39] Those who controlled the affairs of the Guardians knew that they could not themselves cope with this influx. In addition, there were grave doubts as to the wisdom of encouraging the growth of an Anglo-Jewish proletariat. Yet the Guardians were too imbued with the prevailing ethos of "emancipation" to contemplate turning to the statutory authorities for help. So it was that the Board of Guardians advertised in the Jewish press in eastern Europe, making it known that Jews who sought to escape persecution by coming to Britain would face many hardships and would not obtain relief during the first six months of residence—when (of course) they needed it most.

Those refugees who did reach Britain were encouraged to continue their journeys to America or South Africa, and some were even persuaded to return whence they had come. In 1885, in the heart of Jewish East London, matters reached a head when F. D. Mocatta, a vice president of the Board of Guardians, and Lionel Alexander, the board's honorary secretary, prevailed upon the authorities in Whitechapel to close down a "Home for the Outcast Poor" that had been established by a local folk hero, the pious baker Simon Cohen. Cohen (a refugee himself from Poland) had had the audacity to set up a hostel for Jewish immigrants. Mocatta and Alexander declared it to be "unhealthy," adding with remarkable candor that "such a harbour of refuge must tend to invite helpless Foreigners to this country, and therefore was not a desirable institution to exist."[40]

An ugly confrontation between the newer Jewish immigrants and the

[39] Lipman, *Century of Social Service,* 81.

[40] Geoffrey Alderman, *The Federation of Synagogues, 1887–1987* (London: Federation of Synagogues, 1987), 8.

sons of the emancipation was only averted through the farsightedness of a group of more sympathetic grandees, led by the banker, Liberal politician, and Orthodox Jew Samuel Montagu (later first Lord Swaythling), who agreed that Cohen's home should close, but who arranged for a new and more formalized establishment, the Poor Jews' Temporary Shelter, to be opened later in the year. This shelter served two meals a day, gave no financial assistance, and did not allow anyone to remain under its roof for longer than two weeks. Even so, the Board of Guardians refused for fifteen years to become reconciled to it, demanding (*inter alia*) that it should only admit adult males and that those who did not find work after leaving the shelter should be referred to the Guardians for repatriation.[41]

Thus emancipation, to those who had lived through it and who regarded themselves as its guardians and heirs, meant, above all, the fostering and preservation of the image of an assimilated and acculturated community, as indistinguishable from that of the host society as it was possible for the Jews to possess in Christian Britain. David Salomons's opposition to Nathan Adler's scheme to establish a college that would both train an Anglo-Jewish clergy and act as a high school to educate, to university-entrance standard, an Anglo-Jewish middle-class elite sprang from a deep-seated belief that such an institution must act as a barrier to social equality. Jews' College opened its doors in 1855, but the school that formed part of the original plan failed to attract a clientele of sufficient size and was closed in 1879.[42]

It was true that there existed a miscellany of Jewish voluntary schools, both in London and in the major provincial centers.[43] It had been necessary to establish these due to the total absence of any system of state schools prior to 1870, a gap filled by a variety of Christian institutions. The Jews' Free School (JFS), Spitalfields, London, was by far the largest of the Jewish schools, but its avowed purpose was as far removed from educating an Anglo-Jewish elite as could be imagined.

The *raison d'être* of the JFS, founded in 1817 and sustained largely by Rothschild money, had originally been to provide merely a religious education for the children of poor Jews in order (it was said) to help combat the activities of Christian missionaries but also to counteract the attractions of criminal life.[44] By 1870 the JFS had no less than 1,600 boys on its roll and one thousand girls, taught by a staff of seventy, including

[41] Ibid., 9.

[42] Gartner, "Emancipation, Social Change and Communal Reconstruction," 102; Salbstein, *Emancipation of the Jews*, 121.

[43] They are listed in Vivian D. Lipman, *Social History of the Jews in England, 1850–1950* (London: Watts and Co., 1954), 45–46.

[44] Geoffrey Alderman, *London Jewry and London Politics, 1889–1986* (London: Routledge, 1989), 16.

student teachers; presiding over them all was the redoubtable Moses Angel, headmaster for fifty-one years. Even before the great immigration Angel had made no secret of his belief that the school's overriding purpose must be to anglicize the children entrusted to its care. "Their parents," Angel told the newly established London School Board in 1871, "were the refuse population of the worst parts of Europe"; "until they [the children] had been Anglicised or humanised it was difficult to tell what was their moral condition. . . . [They] knew neither English nor any intelligible language."[45]

Yiddish was thus defined as "unintelligible"! Once in the JFS, immigrant youngsters and the children of immigrant parents were weaned away from Yiddish as quickly as possible; their Yiddish-based cultural background and lifestyle were derided. "They enter the school Russians and Poles," a Board of Trade Report noted with evident satisfaction in 1894, "and emerge from it almost indistinguishable from English children."[46] An editorial in the *Jewish Chronicle* in 1888 supporting an appeal for funds in aid of the JFS made the following observations:

> The perplexing problem growing out of the presence in our midst of a large number of foreign poor can only be resolved by Education. To raise the parents in the social and intellectual scale is a task in which at best only partial success can be hoped. The children offer a much more promising field of effort. . . . They, at least, may be taught and helped to practise self-reliance and self-restraint; they may be made into good and industrious citizens and a source of positive strength to the body politic. . . . The work is clearly educational; and the Free School does the bulk of it. Of the three thousand children within its walls the great majority enter it practically foreigners; they leave it potential Englishmen and women, prepared to take their part in the struggle of life in the spirit of English citizens.[47]

The reaction of the established community to the refugees from tsarist persecution and economic discrimination proved to be the ultimate test of the true meaning of emancipation. Leaving aside entirely the questions of restorationism and nationality, had Jews been emancipated in order to contribute to the development of society "in the spirit of English citizens" (to use the *Jewish Chronicle*'s significant phrase), or to provide a specifically Jewish dimension to the society of which they were now declared to be fully a part? The *Jewish Chronicle* in September 1888 had no doubt that "multiculturalism" (as it would now be called) was thoroughly reprehensible:

[45] Quoted in Lloyd P. Gartner, *The Jewish Immigrant in England, 1870–1914* (Detroit: Wayne State University Press, 1980), 223.

[46] Quoted in Lipman, *Social History,* 147.

[47] *JC,* 20 April 1888, 9.

> If poor Jews will persist in appropriating whole streets to themselves in the same district, if they will conscientiously persevere in the seemingly harmless practice of congregating in a body at prominent points in a great public thoroughfare like Whitechapel or Commercial Road, drawing to their peculiarities of dress, of language and of manner, the attention which they might otherwise escape, can there be any wonder that the vulgar prejudices of which they are the objects should be kept alive and strengthened?[48]

Accordingly, once the immigrant flow had begun to reach British shores, a veritable battery of devices (of which the JFS was but one) was brought into play with the object of anglicizing the newcomers as quickly as possible. These ranged from the provision of English-language classes for adults to the establishment and fostering of a network of clubs and societies catering for both adults and young people. In these, not only was the learning of English encouraged, but the new arrivals were introduced to the panoply of English cultural and leisure pursuits, such as swimming, soccer, and cricket.

Typical of these organizations were the Jewish Working Men's Club (1872), the Jewish Girls' Club (1886), the West Central Jewish Club (1895), and the Brady Boys' Club (1896). The Jewish Lads' Brigade, founded in 1895 by Colonel A. E. W. Goldsmid, was "substantially modelled" on the Church Lads' Brigade, in whose quasi-militaristic and religiously patriotic spirit it unashamedly followed.[49] We should also note that in the mid-1880s "it became established communal policy, with the firm approval of Hermann Adler, to regard Jewish day-schools [generally] as appropriate only for the areas of the foreign poor. . . . The declared aim of the new policy was the prevention of narrow-mindedness and the stimulation of mutual understanding between different sections of English society."[50]

By far the most ambitious instrument of anglicization was the Federation of Synagogues, founded in 1887 by Samuel Montagu as a means of bringing structural order and communal discipline into the multitude of *chevrot* (independent synagogue fraternities) that the immigrants were then establishing in East London. I have elsewhere examined in detail the miscellany of motives that caused Montagu (by then the member of Parliament for Whitechapel) to take this step.[51] Montagu was a strict sabbath-observant Jew, and he clearly felt himself, spiritually, closer to the immigrants than to many of his assimilated and irreligious relatives

[48] Ibid., 28 September 1888, 9.

[49] Chaim Berman, *Troubled Eden: An Anatomy of British Jewry* (London: Vallentine, Mitchell, 1969), 88–89.

[50] Finestein, *Post-Emancipation Jewry,* 15.

[51] Alderman, *Federation of Synagogues,* chap. 1.

and business associates within the "cousinhood" that comprised the Anglo-Jewish ruling classes. It is clear, however, that he shared the establishment's view that the immigrant presence constituted a threat to the entire Jewish community.

The immigration from the Pale of Settlement created a vibrant and remarkably self-confident Jewish proletariat in the East End and in some other urban concentrations, such as Manchester and Leeds. This proletariat was the target of a great deal of malicious and frankly mischievous anti-Jewish propaganda; the fact that the proletariat offered itself as a breeding ground for the propagation of socialism, anarchism, and Zionism merely compounded the dangers that accrued thereby. The allegations that the Jewish immigrants deprived their English-born neighbours of work, by accepting lower wages and tolerating a generally inferior standard of life, were largely without foundation. The immigrant Jews were as much the victims of cut-throat competition as anyone else but—pre-eminently in the garment trades—they actually created new employment opportunities.

Yet however ill-informed and malevolently motivated, the hue and cry directed against the Jewish immigrants frightened the Anglo-Jewish leadership into taking countermeasures. Montagu, as one of the few members of this leadership who could be considered *persona grata* in immigrant eyes, willingly took up this burden. In 1886 he established a nonsocialist Jewish Tailors' Machinists' Society, which repudiated the use of the strike weapon. In 1887 he and F. D. Mocatta attempted (unsuccessfully) to suppress the Jewish socialist newspaper *Arbeter Fraint* ("Workers' Friend").

Montagu feared socialism not so much in a religious sense, but because of the bad name he felt would attach to Anglo-Jewry through the favorable reception of socialist ideas within the immigrant community. The *Jewish Chronicle* (of which Montagu was part-owner) had for some time been stressing the necessity of anglicizing "the foreign contingent," which it saw as "the great task before the London Jewish community."[52] The *chevrot,* the newspaper had declared at the beginning of 1880, "originate partially in the aversion felt by our foreign poor to the religious manners and customs of English Jews. . . . The sooner immigrants to our shores learn to reconcile themselves to their new conditions of living, the better for themselves. Whatever tends to perpetuate the isolation of this element in the community must be dangerous to its welfare."[53] A week later the paper was even more strident in its tone: "To form 'wheels within wheels,' or little communities within a great one, is to weaken the general body. They have no right, if permanent residents, to isolate them-

[52] *JC,* 11 February 1887, 11.
[53] Ibid., 30 January 1880, 4.

selves from their English coreligionists. . . . They should hasten to assimilate themselves, completely, within the community amongst whom they dwell."[54]

That this assimilation could not take place in the short term was patently obvious. The staunchly Orthodox immigrants who conversed in Yiddish, who shunned the cold formalism and cathedral-like structures of the United Synagogue (into which the major Ashkenazi congregations in London had formed themselves by Act of Parliament in 1870), and who regarded with great suspicion the Orthodoxy of the United Synagogue's chief rabbinate, nonetheless now constituted the majority in Anglo- and London Jewry. The authority and status of the established community, Montagu argued, could best be preserved and (he frankly admitted) the less desirable features of *chevrot* life (such as the proliferation of very small, makeshift, and unsafe places of worship) best be controlled by providing the *chevrot* with a communal framework of their own that would leave them a reasonable amount of autonomy in religious affairs, but would at the same time bring them within the ambit of the already existing communal infrastructure.

The Federation of Synagogues was, to be sure, a separate body, quite distinct from the United Synagogue and in some respects a rival to it. But its wheels were oiled by Montagu's money, its titular president was none other than Lord Rothschild (the president of the United Synagogue), and its rabbis and members had to acknowledge the ultimate jurisdiction of Dr. Hermann Adler, whose very office ("Chief Rabbi") was a concept quite unknown to the Jewries of Russia and Poland.

So it was that emancipation, deflected by successive waves of immigration between 1882 and 1906, turned to introspection, to an obsession with communal organization and power and, ultimately, to a grotesque inversion of the concept *Kol Yisrael Chaverim*—"All Israel Are Brothers." There is no need to repeat here the oft-recounted story of Anglo-Jewish responses to the "anti-alien" agitation that resulted in the passage of the Aliens Act in 1905. As eventually passed into law the legislation was certainly less draconian than had been intended by those who had campaigned for it. In any case, by 1905 pre-1914 Jewish immigration to Britain had passed its peak. The number of immigrants dropped sharply, from over eleven thousand in 1906 to under four thousand in 1911; the main impact of the 1905 legislation was undoubtedly psychological.[55]

What is relevant to the present discussion is that the Act of 1905 was supported by a number of Jewish MPs, including Harry Samuel (the Member for Limehouse), Louis Sinclair (Romford), and the then-president of

[54] Ibid., 6 February 1880, 9.
[55] Alderman, *Jewish Community*, 77.

the Board of Guardians, Benjamin Cohen (Islington); that at the 1900 General Election two of the most notorious political anti-Semites (Major Evans-Gordon at Stepney and David Hope Kyd at Whitechapel) had been able to boast the official support of Lord Rothschild; and that even Chief Rabbi Adler refused to condemn the legislation as it made its way through Parliament.[56]

The chickens that hatched on the morrow of the emancipation victory had indeed come home to roost. Advocates of Jewish entry to Parliament had pledged that they harbored no desire to create a Jewish lobby, and they had promised that Jewish MPs would conform to a strictly Burkeian concept of representation. When Parliament assembled after the General Election of 1859 (at which three Jewish MPs had been returned) the *Jewish Chronicle* protested, "We are interested in it as citizens, not as Jews."[57] And in 1872 (the number of Jewish MPs having meanwhile doubled) the English-born patent agent and poet Michael Henry, who had been installed as editor of the *Chronicle* following its purchase by Samuel Montagu, his brother-in-law Lionel Louis Cohen (a founder of the Board of Guardians and of the United Synagogue), and their friend Lionel Van Oven, had reassured his Gentile readers: "The House [of Commons] may have its Roman Catholic party, its Presbyterian party, its Evangelical party; but if of the six hundred and fifty-six gentlemen who compose the House of Commons, one third were members of the Jewish community, there would be no such section as a Jewish party."[58]

Even so able an advocate of Jewish causes as Bertram Straus, who as Liberal MP for Mile End (adjacent to Whitechapel), from 1906 to 1910, might be regarded as the leading Jewish spokesman in the House of Commons at that time, rejected the idea of any formal organization of Jewish MPs, "as the Jewish members must remember that they represented their constituents and not their co-religionists."[59] The community had recoiled from organizing the Jewish vote, even though both major political parties had, without embarrassment or hesitation, made specific appeals to Jewish voters. Now, in 1904–5, when Jewish support in Parliament was urgently needed, it was nowhere to be found. Even David L. Alexander, the president of the Board of Deputies, was moved in December 1905 to condemnation: "I have for some time past felt . . . that this Board on many occasions does not receive that cooperation and assistance from some of the Jewish members of Parliament, which it has a right to expect . . . and, further, that its efforts to procure the adoption

[56] Ibid., 78; Alderman, *Federation of Synagogues,* 5.

[57] *JC,* 27 January 1860, 5.

[58] Ibid., 9 August 1872, 262; the total number of MPs in the Commons at that time was actually 658.

[59] Ibid., 23 November 1906, 17.

of provisions and amendments, safeguarding Jewish interests are not infrequently hampered—if not rendered altogether abortive—by the want of unanimity amongst the Jewish members of Parliament."[60]

Outright opposition to the 1905 Act had indeed been left to a group of radical Liberals (none of whom were Jewish) and to the immigrants themselves. For it was not at the Board of Deputies that the principle of the legislation was condemned, but at the Jewish Working Men's Club and by the socialist-Zionist Poale Zion organization in Whitechapel.[61] The elder statesmen of the board conceded that the community might campaign for the act to be modified; they would not countenance an agitation for its repeal. Under Leopold Greenberg, a Liberal and a Zionist who became editor of the *Jewish Chronicle* in January 1907, just such an agitation (ultimately unsuccessful, it is true) was begun. Greenberg made no secret of his belief that an orchestrated Jewish vote should be used to protect Jewish interests.[62] "The political emancipation of the Jews is reduced to a sham," he argued, "when its representative body feels that because an Act specifically affects Jews, Jews must put up with it."[63]

It was indeed in the ghettos created by the immigrant generations that the assimilationist view of emancipation met its greatest and, in fact, its only credible challenge. That these immigrants were different from the Gentiles among whom they dwelled was obvious, but that these differences extended beyond mere religious beliefs and practices to embrace an entire spectrum of customs and lifestyles (that we would nowadays classify under the label of "ethnicity") seemed to the ghetto dwellers a source of pride rather than of embarrassment. A culture—and a newspaper press—flourished behind a linguistic barrier that marked the Jews out as a people apart. This, however, did not prevent immigrant participation in national life. The major Yiddish newspapers, such as the *Arbeter Fraint* and the *Idisher Ekspres,* carried news of domestic affairs and of politics as well as of events in eastern Europe. The immigrants sought to participate in the life of their adopted country in a way (they hoped) that would enable them to preserve their distinctiveness rather than to smother it.

The major avenue for such involvement, and one which did not depend upon the granting of British nationality, was that provided by working-class movements, especially trade unions. There were never separate branches of the Conservative and Liberal parties; occasional attempts to establish such outlets locally were invariably short-lived and much

[60] Ibid., 8 December 1905, 11.

[61] Ibid., 19 May 1905, 7, 26 May 1905, 16–17.

[62] Ibid., 17 July 1908, 8.

[63] Ibid., 17 January 1908, 7.

frowned upon by communal leaders.[64] But within the international fraternity of labor different criteria prevailed. In 1884 a Society of Jewish Socialists was established, and it in turn founded an International Workers' Educational Club, with premises at Number 40 Berner Street, in London's East End. We know that the Berner Street Club, as it was popularly called, was visited by some of the leading British socialists of the day, including William Morris and H. M. Hyndman, the founder of the (Marxist) Social-Democratic Federation.[65] Similar clubs were in due course set up in Manchester, Leeds, Liverpool, Hull, and Glasgow.

These clubs stimulated contacts between Jewish workers and British socialists, from which sprang Jewish branches of Hyndman's Federation and, in September 1905, a League of Jewish Social-Democratic groups.[66] In Leeds, prominent members of Morris's Socialist League involved themselves in Jewish labor problems in the city with a surprising result, for in February 1890 the Jewish tailors amalgamated with the non-Jewish gasworkers to fight for shorter hours.[67] The Leeds Jewish Tailors' Machinists' and Pressers' Union (established 1895) was regularly represented at the Trades Union Congress and became an early affiliate of the Labour Representation Committee, the forerunner of the Labour party.[68]

In London a similar if less dramatic coming together of Jewish and English workers can be observed. A strike organized in the summer of 1890 by Lewis Lyons, the English-born leader of the East End garment workers, received financial support from the London dockers and the London Society of Compositors.[69] Lyons was a member of the Executive Committee of the London Trades Council, a body representing all trade unions in the metropolis; in 1891 the Council established its own political party, the Labour Representation League, in order to contest School Board and London County Council elections. In 1912 Lyons stood unsuccessfully as a Labour candidate for Stepney Borough Council; in 1914 the Executive Committee of the newly formed London Labour party included the Jewish Bundist Joe Fineberg and Dr. Marion Phillips, who in 1929 became the first Jewess to be elected to Parliament.[70]

In this way elements of London's Jewish proletariat were drawn firmly into the world of Labour politics, a coalescence of interests that was

[64] Ibid., 10 September 1909, 14.

[65] Edmund Silberner, "British Socialism and the Jews," *Historica Judaica* 14 (1952): 38.

[66] *JC,* 13 October 1905, 28.

[67] J. Buckman, "The Economic and Social History of Alien Immigration to Leeds, 1880–1914" (Ph.D. diss., University of Stratclyde, 1968), 282, 291–92.

[68] Ibid., 322; Colin Holmes, "The Leeds Jewish Tailors' Strikes of 1885 and 1888," *Yorkshire Archaeological Journal* 45 (1973): 165.

[69] Gartner, *Jewish Immigrant,* 124.

[70] *East London Observer,* 9 November 1912, 2; Alderman, *London Jewry,* 76.

bolstered by the spread of the Poale Zion movement in England. In February 1904 this movement in London opened permanent headquarters in Whitechapel Road; British Poale Zion was formally constituted at a meeting in Liverpool on 25 December 1906.[71] The full impact of this working-class alliance was not to be felt until after the First World War, with the formal adhesion of Poale Zion to the Labour party (1920) and the entry, into both the House of Commons and the major local authorities, of substantial numbers of Jewish candidates elected on the Labour ticket. By the late 1920s the Labour party was regarded as the major political vehicle for the articulation of Jewish interests and concerns; it was primarily through Labour that the political integration of the immigrant generations came about in and after the First World War.

A further aspect of emancipation as seen through immigrant eyes was the willingness to use Jewish voting strength as a means of effecting an input into public affairs. As we have seen, one of the central tenets of emancipation had been the assurance that Jews would conduct their political behavior as "Englishmen." The understandably close relationship between Anglo-Jewry and the Liberal party, based upon Liberal support for emancipation, came to be regarded as a liability thereafter. The argument was that Jews could only claim to be fully integrated into British society if they supported—and were seen to support—both of its great political coalitions; otherwise, as the young Lionel Louis Cohen had pointed out in 1865, Anglo-Jewry might obtain for itself a bad name as a selfish and "separatist" collection of citizens.[72] Cohen joined the Conservative party partly on broad grounds of policy and class interest, but partly also on grounds of communal welfare, for he spent the best years of his life fighting (as he put it) "the domination so long exercised by the so-called Liberal party over the Jews, and the monopoly of the Jewish vote which they have exercised and even yet claim to enjoy."[73]

By the late 1880s, through a combination of political calculation and generational change, the Jewish middle classes finally cut the umbilical cord that had tied them to Liberalism hitherto. It was a conscious and deliberate act and was seen by them as a necessary demonstration of political maturity and (no less important) of social integration and acceptance.[74] The Jews, the *Jewish Chronicle* proclaimed in 1885, "are too powerfully dominated by the desire to see that party controlling affairs

[71] *JC*, 26 February 1904, 30; Schneier Levenberg, *The Jews and Palestine: A Study in Labour Zionism* (London: Poole Zion, 1945), 126–27.

[72] *JC*, 11 August 1865, 5.

[73] Ibid., 1 July 1887, quoting a letter dated 8 February 1874.

[74] Ibid., 30 March 1894, 7; letter from the Jewish Liberal MP H. S. Leon. See generally Alderman, *Jewish Community*, 35–42.

which each considers the more calculated to perform the task successfully, to allow mere considerations of racial pride or interest to influence them."[75]

This was not a view shared by the immigrants and their offspring. From the mid-1890s we can cite a number of instances in which Jewish electorates created largely by the more recent immigrant arrivals chose to behave in idiosyncratic ways. In 1895 the Jewish Conservative Morris Abrahams, well-known in the East End as the highly successful manager of the Pavilion Theatre and as an accomplished social worker, won for the "Moderates" (i.e., Conservatives) their only victory in the Whitechapel division of the London County Council, in a result strongly reflective of the operation of a Jewish "personal" vote. Two years later a County Council by-election occurred in the same division. To fight this seat in the "Progressive" (Liberal) interest, the local MP, Samuel Montagu, imported Harry Lawson, the Christian grandson of Joseph Levy, founder of the *Daily Telegraph*. The record of the Progressive-controlled London County Council in slum clearance was the major theme of the contest, which Lawson won handsomely.[76]

In 1904, as a result of a combined Jewish-Catholic revolt against Liberal opposition to the Conservative policy of making ratepayers' money available to finance denominational schools, Henry Herman Gordon, son of the cantor of the Great Synagogue, won a London County Council seat from the Progressives by standing as an Independent. Gordon boasted the support of Lord Rothschild and Rabbis Moses Hyamson and Susman Cohen, two *dayanim* (judges) of the chief rabbi's Ecclesiastical Court. Armed, according to one local newspaper, with "the great bulk of the Jewish and the whole of the Roman Catholic vote," Gordon's position was indeed unassailable.[77]

Examples relating to parliamentary elections are admittedly harder to come by. But we are surely justified in pointing to the Conservative defeats at Leeds Central and Manchester North-West in the General Election of January 1906 as evidence of the willingness of Jewish electors to go out of their way to punish a candidate pledged (as Gerald Balfour was in the Leeds constituency) to the maintenance of the Aliens Act, and to reward a candidate (Winston Churchill in Manchester North-West) whose opposition to the legislation was very well known.[78] Churchill foolishly promised that an incoming Liberal government would either repeal or amend the 1905 Act. In fact the Liberal government had no intention of sweeping away or modifying what it knew to be a generally

[75] *JC*, 13 March 1885, 11.

[76] Alderman, *London Jewry*, 30–32.

[77] *East London Advertiser*, 12 March 1904, 8.

[78] Alderman, *Jewish Community*, 75–76.

and genuinely popular measure. In April 1908, following his elevation to the Cabinet, Churchill was obliged to resign his seat and fight a by-election. There was a Jewish revolt against him, due to both his failure to fulfill his pledges as to the Aliens legislation and Liberal opposition to ratepayers' funding of Jewish schools, and he lost the seat.

The realization that many Jewish voters had cast their votes—or had simply but deliberately abstained—so as to secure the defeat of a Cabinet minister came as a shock to the community. But when the shock had subsided more robust sentiments prevailed. Preaching at the Birmingham Synagogue the Reverend G. J. Emanuel expressed his approval of what the Jews of Manchester had done.[79] An unnamed correspondent told the readers of the *Jewish Chronicle,* "Jews are expected to act as no other section of the population ever dreams of acting. . . . The Jew will always vote as an Englishman, but, if he is true to his Judaism, he will vote as *an Englishman who is a Jew.* We Jews do not know our own power; the sooner we realise it and exert it in the interests of our political freedom the better it will be."[80]

In the years immediately preceding the First World War, therefore, two views of Jewish emancipation enjoyed an uneasy coexistence. According to one, emancipation meant—and demanded—a submerging of Jewish identity within the host community. I use the word "submerging" deliberately, for I am far from suggesting that according to this view Jews had to yield up their separateness in its entirety: we are not dealing here with a conversionist view of Jewish assimilation. This view did imply, however, that the characteristics that marked out the Jews as a distinct and distinctive people had to be kept to a minimum, and that emancipation would permit full freedom to Britain's Jews only so long as they played out their roles within this framework. Jewish voters were voters who happened to be Jews. Jewish MPs were MPs who happened to profess Judaism. Jewish writers would describe a deserving and grateful community, while the Jewish poor and underprivileged would be looked after at no expense to the state and—again at no expense to the state—would be relocated away from the large city centers, in small, discreetly positioned provincial locations.[81]

We might add that a situation was almost reached in which Anglo-Jewish clergymen were clergymen who happened to be Jewish. Under Hermann Adler, "delegate" chief rabbi from 1880 and chief rabbi in his own right from 1891 until his death in 1911, the community acquired a religious leader who, though born in Hanover, felt himself to be totally English. In urging his claims upon the communal conference summoned

[79] *JC,* 15 May 1908, 13.
[80] Ibid., 1 May 1908, 15.
[81] On attempts to disperse East End Jewry, see Gartner, *Jewish Immigrant,* 149.

to appoint a new chief rabbi, Benjamin Cohen referred to Adler as "the head of our Church." Adler himself referred more than once to the community over which he presided as "our communion."[82] His sermons were models of elegant Victorian prose. He adopted Anglican clerical garb (complete with gaiters) and styled himself "The Very Reverend," the form of address used of deans of the Church of England.[83] He was "chief" rabbi, but until 1901 he would neither grant the rabbinical diploma to any other minister of religion within Anglo-Jewry, nor permit the title of rabbi to be used by those who had gained such diplomas abroad. Instead, Jews' College produced a succession of "reverends," complete with white clerical collars, who could minister and preach within their congregations but who were in no sense recognized as competent to give rulings on religious matters.

Under Hermann Adler, Chaim Bermant writes, the United Synagogue "seemed to be the Jewish branch of the Anglican establishment."[84] King Edward VII referred to him as "my Chief Rabbi." This, according to the Anglo-Jewish gentry, was what emancipation was all about: acceptance by the Gentiles. But to the immigrants of the 1880s and 1890s Hermann Adler was an object of hatred and derision. Adler's petulant refusal to address as "rabbi" those eminent talmudic scholars whom the refugees from eastern Europe brought with them was a calculated insult, which was repaid in kind. The immigrants refused to adhere to the religious institutions that operated under Adler's aegis, questioned his certification of kosher food and ritually slaughtered meat, and established their own synagogues (both in London and the provinces) in preference to those that operated under his authority.

The manners and lifestyle no less than the language and politics of the newcomers emphasized and reinforced their determination to seek an accommodation with British society that differed fundamentally from that of the established community; for theirs would be a coexistence based upon the mutual recognition of differences rather than of similarities. Whether the tensions (both within and beyond Anglo-Jewry) to which this determination was bound to give rise could have been overcome, to produce in the 1920s, perhaps, a multicultural interface that was recognized and respected by all, is impossible to say. At all events, a convergence of factors during the First World War frustrated whatever

[82] Finestein, *Post-Emancipation Jewry,* 16.

[83] Adler adopted this title "at the suggestion of his friend the Bishop of Bath and Wells," Ruth P. Lehmann, "Hermann Adler: A Bibliography of His Published Works," in D. Noy and I. Ben-Ami, eds., *Studies in the Cultural Life of the Jews in England* (Jerusalem: Hebrew University, 1975), 101.

[84] Chaim Bermant, *The Cousinhood* (London: Eyre and I. Spottiswoode, 1971), 370.

longer-term purposes either the Anglo-Jewish middle classes or the immigrant-Jewish working classes might have had in mind.

Here these factors can only be mentioned in the barest outline. One was anti-Semitism. Racial, religious, economic, and xenophobic prejudice against Jews had been whipped to an unprecedented frenzy during the "aliens" agitation at the beginning of the century, was kept alive through agitation against ritual slaughter of meat, and was to be seen at work in a particularly violent form in South Wales in 1911, when "rich Jew" and "poor Jew" anti-Semitism were combined in a terrifying manner through the instrumentality of the manual working classes.[85] During World War I qualitative evidence suggests that the general level of anti-Jewish prejudice in British society rose sharply, more especially after the Bolshevik Revolution.[86]

At precisely the same time, however, the Zionist movement achieved a momentous breakthrough—the Balfour Declaration—and the labor and trade-union movements gained respectability through participation in government. It was now much more difficult for the Anglo-Jewish establishment to argue that it was un-English to be a socialist, or that it was unpatriotic to be a Zionist. These concessions were often made grudgingly, and only after fierce intracommunal struggles. David Lindo Alexander's anti-Zionism cost him the presidency of the Board of Deputies (1917), while Louis Montagu's anti-Bolshevism, added to his anti-Zionism, cost him the presidency of the Federation of Synagogues (1925).[87]

Within a decade of the overthrow of tsarism, elements of the Jewish refugees who had fled from Russia to seek refuge in Great Britain had either taken control of the major Anglo-Jewish communal institutions or were in a position to do so whenever they chose. But they too had made or were making accommodations with the society into which an increasing number of them had lived from birth. Anxious to escape as quickly as possible from the poverty and squalor in which they had grown up, they embarked upon a voyage of upward social mobility, into the ranks of the petty bourgeoisie and even of the professional classes, and of outward

[85] Geoffrey Alderman, "The Anti-Jewish Riots of August 1911 in South Wales," *Welsh History Review* 6 (1972): 190–200; Colin Holmes, "The Tredegar Riots of 1911: Anti-Jewish Disturbances in South Wales," *Welsh History Review* 11 (1982): 214–25.

[86] Colin Holmes, *Anti-Semitism in British Society, 1876–1939* (London: Edward Arnold, 1979), chap. 10; David Cesarani, "Anti-Alienism in England after the First World War," *Immigrants and Minorities* 6 (1987): 5–29. Also see generally S. Kadish, "Bolsheviks and British Jews: The Anglo-Jewish Community, Britain and the Russian Revolution," Ph.D. diss., University of Oxford, 1986.

[87] Alderman, *Federation of Synagogues*, 51–55; Stuart A. Cohen, *English Zionists and British Jews: The Communal Politics of Anglo-Jewry, 1895–1920* (Princeton: Princeton University Press, 1982), chaps. 7, 8.

physical mobility, away from the inner-city slums. The immigrants spawned their own establishment, more left-wing, certainly, than that of the pre-1914 period, but just as anxious to prove its worth in the eyes of the Gentiles. Religious observance became diluted in the process.

Both in the East End and West End of London these movements resulted in the emergence of a younger generation of Jews who belonged—and who felt themselves to belong—neither to the Yiddish-based, synagogue-going existence of their parents nor to the culture and lifestyle of a Gentile society in which anti-Jewish prejudice was becoming evermore fashionable. The Reverend Israel Brodie (the future chief rabbi) observed, prior to his departure for Australia in 1923, that in the East End "betting, boxing and gambling" had replaced synagogue attendance, while in 1931 Maurice Pearlzweig, minister of the Liberal Synagogue, noted the problem of intermarriage at all levels of Anglo-Jewish society.[88]

It was this society that suffered—almost without protest—the anti-Jewish policies of the London County Council in the spheres of education, employment, and housing,[89] which acquiesced—almost without protest—in the anti-Jewish prejudice inherent in the Slaughterhouses Act of 1933 and the Sunday Trading Act of 1936, and which—entirely without protest—accepted and operated the restrictions upon Jewish immigration to Britain from Nazi Germany.[90]

British society had assimilated its Jewish newcomers in a manner of which the emancipationists of the mid-nineteenth century would have been exceedingly proud.

[88] *JC*, 13 March 1923, 10; 27 February 1931, 14.

[89] Alderman, *London Jewry*, 63–68.

[90] Geoffrey Alderman, "Anglo-Jewry and Jewish Refugees," *AJR Information* (June 1987): 3.

SIX

BETWEEN SEPARATION AND DISAPPEARANCE: JEWS ON THE MARGINS OF AMERICAN LIBERALISM

Ira Katznelson

> There may be something of separateness in their social life among us, but this should be naturally expected among those who are not altogether free from the disposition born of persecution and the loss of nationality, to seek in a common devotion to their peculiar religious creed the strongest bond of their social fellowship.
>
> —"Address by Ex-President Grover Cleveland," *The Two Hundred and Fiftieth Anniversary of the Settlement of the Jews in the United States: Addresses Delivered at Carnegie Hall, New York, on Thanksgiving Day, 1905* (New York: The New York Cooperative Society, 1906, 15).

> The effect of our liberal institutions upon the Jewish race has been undoubtedly beneficent. Liberty has done for them what the hard repression and persecution of other nations has failed to accomplish. They are in the undoubted process of an unreserved assimilation into the citizenship of the country. They have conquered to a great extent their own prejudices and ours.
>
> —"The Jews in America," *The Philadelphia Record,* 30 November 1905; reprinted in ibid., 229.

F*ORTUNE,* the country's leading business publication, devoted much of its February 1936 issue to a special section on "Jews in America." It sought to confront "a situation dangerous to the State," when "fearful minorities become suspicious minorities and suspicious minorities, their defensive reactions set on the hair trigger of anxiety, create the animosities they dread." The magazine worried that because "the apprehensiveness of American Jews has become one of the important influences in the social life of our time," their reactions to perceived slights risked promoting a level of anti-Semitism that did not exist. Jews were in danger of authoring the realization of their fears.[1]

This treatment of the Jewish condition reminds us that the usual success narratives of American Jewry are far too linear and assured. Even as *Fortune* sought to give comfort to its Jewish and non-Jewish readers by demonstrating the comparatively tame attributes of anti-Semitism in the United States while affirming the confined role Jews played in the higher reaches of the economy, the magazine established that the engagement of Jews with America took place in a zone of interaction charged with ambiguity and contradiction. More implicitly, it showed how the boundaries and content of this zone were distinctive to the American experience. Yet insofar as the United States condensed some of the most significant features of the Enlightenment and its liberal progeny, the relationship forged between Jews and the American milieu also can clarify important aspects of the situation facing Jews elsewhere under the impact of emancipation.

By the mid-twentieth century, the United States had become the most populous and, arguably, the most important center of world Jewry. Notwithstanding its archetypical status, this place of Jewish settlement was unlike any other in the diaspora. Jews could secure legal and political emancipation merely by entering. In spite of the country's Protestant hegemony and doleful record with respect to race and its treatment of indigenous minorities, the United States was attractive to Jews as the western nation that gave the most sustained expression to the universal and instrumental values of the Enlightenment. Undergirded by popular sovereignty, the United States was broadly liberal in politics and economics from the start, democratic in its practical and vernacular culture, relatively secular in orientation, and polyglot in its human composition.

In these circumstances, did Jews come to be "at home in America" or "strangers at home"?[2] Both, of course. The central puzzle this essay ad-

[1] "Jews in America," *Fortune* 13 (February 1936).

[2] Deborah Dash Moore, *At Home in America: Second-Generation New York Jews* (New York: Columbia University Press, 1981) (Moore dedicates her book to "a second generation Jew committed to the ideals of America"); Jacob Neusner, *Stranger at Home: "The Holocaust," Zionism, and American Judaism* (Chicago: University of Chicago Press, 1981). Neusner used the phrase to describe his own experiences in Israel, but he might well have used it to describe Jews in the United States. Yet another attempt to play with this trope is Leonard Dinnerstein, *Uneasy at Home: Antisemitism and the American Jewish Experience* (New York: Columbia University Press, 1987). In his classic study of emancipation, Jacob Katz treats the subject in terms of "the transformation of strangers into citizens." Here, I want to inquire about the degree to which citizens remained strangers. Jacob Katz, *Out of*

dresses is why, under such favorable conditions, they became strangers *and* at home simultaneously. I should like to explore how the American regime's doctrinal and institutional liberalism, including its Enlightenment premises and the naturalness of markets and citizenship, produced a setting for Jewish emancipation that managed at once to be welcoming and menacing.

The United States presented Jews with the nearly total absence of formal barriers to choice about places of residence, occupations, and political participation. Their status as insiders, however, was put in question by far more than the episodic instances of social, economic, and institutional anti-Semitism they experienced, or by the more pervasive nativism that challenged Catholic as well as Jewish newcomers. The situation Jews discovered in the United States exemplified some of the most important systematic tensions inherent in the Enlightenment concerning tradition and difference. These tensions entailed costs to Jewish identity and culture. If the United States provided the location for the single greatest success story of the diaspora, a place where issues of legal and political emancipation did not even arise as matters of politics and public policy, it also furnished a site where the outer limits placed upon entry into the Enlightenment by outsiders were revealed with unusual clarity.

Inserted by migration into this environment, Jews discovered they could possess only highly imperfect information about the qualities of welcome and permeability in American society. With some regularity, they were reminded they could not enter American life unimpeded, whether they chose to downplay or emphasize their identity as Jews. Either move, as it were, was encumbered with risks whose dimensions were difficult to discern. What American Jews sought, therefore, was an orienting stance that could protect them while they probed actually existing possibilities.

The Jews who came from Germany and eastern Europe discovered just

---

the Ghetto: The Social Background of Jewish Emancipation, 1770–1870 (New York: Schocken Books, 1978), 7.

The shelves of the relevant library stacks bulge, of course, with monographs, revised dissertations, and such grand syntheses as those provided by Arthur Hertzberg, *The Jews in America: Four Centuries of an Uneasy Encounter* (New York: Simon and Schuster, 1989); and Howard M. Sachar, *A History of the Jews in America* (New York: Alfred A. Knopf, 1992). Unfortunately, there have been far too few analytical treatments of American Jewish history that seek to construct the American case in a manner susceptible to comparative analysis. A notable, and most welcome, exception is Benjamin Ginsberg, *The Fatal Embrace: Jews and the State* (Chicago: University of Chicago Press, 1993). For a treatment of Canadian Jewry, including their ties to the United States, see Michael Brown, *Jew or Juif? Jews, French, Canadians, and Anglo-Canadians, 1759–1914* (Philadelphia: Jewish Publication Society, 1986).

such a strategic stance in a multifaceted institutional enclosure. Underneath the immense variations in the responses of Jews to the American version of modernity in the period appraised by this book, it is possible to discern a shared sensibility, style, and orientation for grappling with opportunities and pitfalls. This strategy of "city niches" allowed Jews to straddle the demarcation between strangeness and belonging.

This particular solution resembled that of other ethnic immigrants, but with differences I will try to identify. One of these was the relatively intense urban character of the Jewish stance. Jews connected with American politics, economics, and society from the atypical locations of a small number of dense city neighborhoods and from a limited selection of occupations and places of work. Launched into America from these bounded sites, Jews fashioned dispositions and patterns of individual and collective behavior, combining gratitude and wariness, which made sense as a coherent repertoire.

Enlightenment and Exceptionalism

The relationship of the Enlightenment to European Jewry was contradictory from the start. As Jonathan Israel argues in his treatment of the reintegration of the Jews into early modern western and central Europe, reversing a long period of expulsions, the Enlightenment threatened the cohesion of Jewish life and culture by its anti-Judaism and by the stresses it placed on traditional structures of authority and belief within the Jewish community. The declining hegemony of Christianity in Europe in the aftermath of the stalemate between Reformation and Counter-Reformation, the elaboration of skeptical models of state, culture, and society, the rise of speculative philosophy and modern science, and the growth of *raison d'état* and mercantile economics transformed the possibilities of European Jews, paving the way for their corporate reconnection to a rapidly changing Europe. With some of the underpinnings of ghettoization that had been designed to insulate Christians from the contamination of Jew and Judaism now removed, Jews and their neighbors began to transact with and impinge on each other far more regularly.[3] But on what terms?

If the Enlightenment softened the animus of European societies toward their Jews, it also was deeply hostile to Judaism. "The notion that Judaism was a tenacious, as well as ancient, superstition, a device of priests to promote their own power, which, in some measure, still held modern minds in thrall, so thoroughly permeated Enlightenment thought that it

[3] Jonathan I. Israel provides a superb synthetic overview in his *European Jewry in the Age of Mercantilism, 1550–1750,* rev. ed. (Oxford: Clarendon Press, 1989).

may, without exaggeration, be described as one of its fundamental principles."[4] The personal anti-Semitism of an Erasmus or a Voltaire is less significant than the constitutive anti-Judaism of Enlightenment ideas.

When Jews in central and western Europe took advantage of the economic roles that opened to them with the decline of guilds, the importance of finance in periods of war, and the rapid increase in trade of various distances, Enlightenment ideas and values profoundly affected the hierarchies, institutions, and social integration of their communities. Lifestyles liberalized. Rabbinic authority weakened. Religious observance, and respect for Jewish tradition, declined. "The prevailing characteristic of the western European Jewish mind from the second quarter of the [seventeenth] century onwards was one of increasing rejection of its own intellectual culture and tradition."[5] This collective erosion of the oligarchical and solidaristic structure of Jewish communities that had occupied well-defined locations in the medieval Christian world was accompanied now by individual exit options, the most extreme of which was conversion. As Zygmunt Bauman has put it, Jews now had exit visas by virtue of their changed collective condition, even if their access to entry tickets as individuals was hardly assured.[6] Thus, even before the moment of political emancipation in the aftermath of the French Revolution, traditional Jewish communities and ways of life were buffeted by the anti-Judaic impulses of the Enlightenment, impulses many Jews themselves found irresistible. Even where the new universalism and liberality were resisted, attempts to withstand the new seductions, like that of the Vilna Gaon, had to take account of them. The Enlightenment set dynamics of both welcome and rejection with which Jews had to contend. After Spinoza, who shared in the Enlightenment's scorn of Jewish traditionalism, the Jewish community almost inexorably divided into a modernist camp that in quite diverse ways sought to find formulas for involvement with a rapidly changing Europe and a traditionalist camp that became increasingly defensive and casuistic. Later, the process of legal and political emancipation simultaneously liberated Jews from onerous restrictions while contributing to the breakdown of the capacity of communal authorities to impose a bounded and intense traditional way of life, but this double process was grounded in the pre-emancipation character of the Enlightenment itself.

Even for Orthodox immigrants, engagement with the United States took place on the Enlightenment's multifaceted terms. Like its other offspring, the United States transformed the meaning of what it meant to be

[4] Ibid., 232.

[5] Ibid., 257.

[6] Zygmunt Bauman, "Exit Visas and Entry Tickets: Paradoxes of Jewish Assimilation," *Telos* 77 (Fall 1988).

a minority. As Ernest Gellner has observed, the emerging societies of the modern West (of which the United States was in some of the most important ways a condensation and a harbinger), were "not only due to be more rational than the *ancien régime*. . . . [They were] also destined to be more mobile, *open*. (Karl Popper's famous phrase, whatever important functions it also performs, contains an implicit justification of the abandonment of minority communities.) This being so, the new order absolutely needed a *shared* cultural idiom, rather than a multiplicity of in-group jargons. It was only natural that this idiom should be that of the majority group, especially if it *already* contained a powerful literature of Enlightenment."[7] None of the newcomers could avoid the challenge of arriving at a synthesis that would permit them to be both Jewish and at home in America where the promises, enticements, and contradictions of the Enlightenment proved even more inescapable than elsewhere.

Elsewhere, in their various European communities, the most severe and threatening challenges to Jews were not those of the dilemmas posed by the Enlightenment, acute as they were, but those posed by the Romantic reaction to the Enlightenment as a bloodless cosmopolitanism. Ironically, the very Jews whose ties to the Enlightenment were problematic came to be identified as its exemplars. Jews had no access to the folk cultures and histories exalted by the Romantics. Where this impulse was strong, they were compelled to choose between playing a losing game of trying to join the dominant culture and its *Gemeinschaft* or leaving the game by exiting entirely, as in the solutions of Zionism and emigration. After emancipation, the more common approach of Europe's Jews was a rejection of these options in favor of a fervid embrace of the values and opportunities proffered by the Enlightenment.

American Jews largely were spared intense conflicts between the Enlightenment and reactionary romanticism. On North American shores, they discovered a country marked by a not quite decisive resolution of this battle in favor of liberal outcomes, where the clash between romanticism and the Enlightenment by comparison was less stark.[8] In the United

[7] Ernest Gellner, *Culture, Identity, and Politics* (Cambridge: Cambridge University Press, 1987), 78.

[8] This statement could not possibly describe the slave and post-slave experiences of blacks or those of native Americans. Further, I certainly do not mean to imply that the treatment of minorities, including European Catholics and Asian immigrants, was benign.

The quite wonderful but also terrible possibilities inherent in the Enlightenment provided the starting point for Horkheimer and Adorno's consideration: "In the most general sense of progressive thought," *Dialectic of Enlightenment* (1944) begins, "the Enlightenment has always aimed at liberating men from fear and establishing their sovereignty. Yet the fully enlightened earth radiates disaster triumphant." Max Horkheimer and Theodor W. Adorno, *Dialectic of Enlightenment* (New York: Herder and Herder, 1972), 3. Similarly, Gellner observes that "It was Heine who foresaw that the anti-semitism of the pagans would be worse than that of the Christians" (*Culture, Identity and Politics*, 80).

States, many of the most pressing issues and problems of minority status were placed within the embrace of Enlightenment liberality, rather than between the Enlightenment and its antagonists. Jews already in the United States lived the tragedies of European Jewry vicariously. Many of their experiences of anti-Semitism seemed as much a product of Jewish difference as the result of the inaccessibility of a majority folk culture.

The particularities of the American state, economy, and culture made it especially permeable to Jewish, and other white, newcomers, albeit not without a price. It was not only the hegemony of the Enlightenment that set the United States apart; it was also the distinctive qualities of the regime set in the universe of the other emergent modern states, economies, and civil societies of the late eighteenth and nineteenth centuries that established the most felicitous setting in the West for Jewish entry into modernity. It is the formation of Jewish identities, dispositions, institutions, and patterns of behavior in these special circumstances that defines the content of the question of *how* Jews came to be at home in America, and why it was nevertheless that their "strangeness" remained integral to their learning to be at home.

For the British during the colonial period, the American problem was one of defining a relationship between the metropolis and the colonies that could balance the goal to make the periphery more dependent on the center while accommodating to pressures for autonomy by the colonists. The American Revolution was testimony to the failure of the various constitutional attempts to manage such a relationship. After the Revolution, Jack Greene has stressed, the newly independent colonies found themselves faced with the need to construct a state with precisely the same dilemma to solve, now appearing in the guise of the problem of a Republican empire. A way had to be found to reconcile the claims of independent state governments in a situation of popular sovereignty with the desire to create a national entity of potential continental reach. The 1787 Constitutional Convention discovered a workable allocation of authority between center and periphery by creating a national state that was less a centralized "strong" apparatus in the Weberian sense than a framework capable of securing a workable balance. The founders utilized the notion of popular sovereignty as a way of overcoming old debates about the location of sovereign capacity to create a doctrine of coordinated sovereignty. The result was as much a state of representation and rights characterized by a protected boundary between the state and civil society and by federalism's institutional complexity and diffusion of authority.[9]

By inventing such a state, and by securing the consent of the governed

[9] Jack P. Greene, *Peripheries and Center: Constitutional Development in the Extended Polities of the British Empire and the United States, 1607–1788* (Athens: University of Georgia Press, 1986).

through a popular ratification process, the United States also invented the American people. Unlike other national entities, the requirements for entry into this peoplehood were relatively thin, lacking (with the notable and fateful exception of race) tests of national origins, religion, social class, or region. From the start, citizenship was liberal. No group, including Jews, was placed on probation.[10] Access to positions of military and political leadership likewise was officially disconnected to social structural standing or to an established church. To the contrary, the abundance of land made English-style aristocracy irrelevant, and the fragmentation of Protestantism into a multiplicity of denominations relaxed the outlying positions of Catholics and Jews. Further, the absence of social and religious tests came to be taken for granted as natural, especially after the franchise was extended to all white males without regard to property by the early 1830s.[11]

So, too, did market capitalism. The Constitution organized a coherent framework for property rights and markets. Through the transformations of law and the provision of national and regional infrastructures, both the national and state governments maintained relatively unencumbered and uncontested access to free capital and labor markets. In this setting, Jews, like other whites, faced no barriers of entry to real estate and labor markets.[12]

The scale of the new federated republic and its commercial economy, relentless western march, secularization, and heterogeneous population helped shape a national democratic culture to which access was easy and regular. The very existence of the United States, as Philip Fisher points out, challenged every theory of nationalism extant at the time of the republic's founding. A patchwork of peoples, Americans lacked a common history, religion, racial origins, customs, conventions, and civil institutions. They were not a *Volk*. Nor was America a land sharing climatic or geographic traits. It lacked a sense of culture or language in the deep Romantic sense. Fisher argues, persuasively in my view, that within the framework of a liberal state, but especially a liberal capitalism, America solved its problems of national identity through the creation of a common democratic, homogeneous social space that was atomistic and cellular, broadly similar from place to place. The South aside, everywhere

[10] Katz observes that after emancipation in the various European countries, "Jews were on probation. Improvement of their situation was the bait dangled before their eyes—should they live up to expectations" (*Out of the Ghetto,* 192).

[11] This discussion is indebted to Edmund P. Morgan, *Inventing the People: The Rise of Popular Sovereignty in England and America* (New York: W. W. Norton and Company, 1988).

[12] Morton J. Horwitz, *The Transformation of American Law, 1780–1860* (Cambridge: Harvard University Press, 1977). Also see James Willard Hurst, *Law and Economic Growth* (Madison: University of Wisconsin Press, 1964). A discussion of the economic structure of European Jewry under more restrictive conditions can be found in Israel, *European Jewry,* 171–82.

across the continent that whites settled similar constitutions, institutions, and even spatial grid designs were replicated. The uniformity of this social space across the continent made it seem uncoded and transparent. This kind of social space did not contain oppositional positions; all participants were insiders. Further, unbounded and porous, it invited entry and mobility. "Open to immigration and equally to expatriation or internal mobility—that continuation of immigration into later generations—it has no natural or final size."[13] The map of American society, politics, and culture thus was a relatively abstract design for the accommodation of variations within civil society provided they could coexist on the same plane of institutions and utterance, and provided they were intelligible and not hidden from view.

If the characteristic discourse of modern European politics concerned antinomies of the secular and religious, divine right and popular sovereignty, feudalism and capitalism, and modernity and tradition, American political language assumed a decisive tilt in favor of the secular, the democratic, the capitalist, and the modern. Likewise, whereas Jewish emancipation in Europe often was bitterly contested, in the United States it was no real issue at all.[14] The language and debates of American social and political life took place within a framework that was limited in this way. Not that there were no differences, even fundamental ones, in American debates. Lockean liberalism, republicanism, work-ethic Protestantism, religious fundamentalism, and theories of power and sovereignty vied with each other in a proliferation of idioms and vigorous debates about virtue, power, and rights.[15] But most of these assumed the likely solutions to exactly those questions entailed in European debates about the emancipation of the Jews.

The dilemmas of American Jewry were the product of a double exceptionalism. American Jews never were emancipated in the European sense, because there was no need. Yet the bulk of American Jews came to North American shores from places that either had produced the most contingent and limited instances of emancipation, or none at all. Only when they set foot in the United States did they experience the wider world in terms of both the opportunities afforded by a liberal economy and liberal citizenship and an episodic anti-Semitism.

[13] Philip Fisher, "Democratic Social Space: Whitman, Melville, and the Promise of American Transparency," *Representations* 24, (Fall 1988): 75.

[14] See Katz, *Out of the Ghetto*, 198.

[15] A fine discussion of political language in late-eighteenth century America can be found in Isaac Kramnick, "The 'Great National Discussion': The Discourse of Politics in 1787," *William and Mary Quarterly* 45 (January 1988). Also see the growing body of relevant work by Rogers M. Smith, including "The 'American Creed' and American Identity: The Limits of Liberal Citizenship in the United States," *Western Political Quarterly* 41, no. 2 (1988), and "Beyond Tocqueville, Myrdal, and Hartz: The Multiple Traditions in America," *American Political Science Review* 87 (September 1993).

Jews possessed important advantages in colonial America. They were a tiny minority of newcomers among newcomers. Puritan culture induced respectful treatment. There were virtually no restrictions on Jewish admission to universities or to various occupations and crafts. With the exception of state-level religious tests for office directed principally at Catholics, Jewish men had full voting rights and were eligible for office. In the early settlement of New Amsterdam, Jews had been excluded from being "fellow-soldiers," but, after protesting, Asher Levy was permitted to stand guard in 1655. Oscar Handlin treats as emblematic of the political tolerance of pre-independence America the fact that South Carolina elected a Jewish planter, Francis Salvador, to the provincial Congress, in spite of the negligible number of Jews in the state. With only a bit of hyperbole, he describes the situation of Jews in the colonies as that of "total equality." Jews also were very active in the Revolution, attracted by the promise of "all men created equal."[16]

[16] Oscar Handlin, *Adventure in Freedom: Three Hundred Years of Jewish Life in America* (Port Washington, N.Y.: Kennikat Press, 1971), chaps. 1, 2. Throughout his book, and in the section on colonial America in particular, Handlin underscores the positive and considerably downplays the more unpleasant features of the American Jewish experience. As David A. Gerber notes, in *Anti-Semitism in American History* (Urbana: University of Illinois Press, 1986), "Nowhere in the British colonies did Jews receive equal status with professing Christians in law, and . . . much informal prejudice and negative imagery surrounded colonial Jewry" (13–14). The limitations placed on Jews with respect to rights of naturalization (only after 1740 did Jews have such rights by virtue of an act of Parliament), settlement, voting in elections for colonial legislatures, office holding, legal practice, and service on juries, however, rarely were directed at them exclusively, but at other religious minorities as well, including deists, atheists, Catholics, and nonconformist Protestants. In some ways, Jews were advantaged compared to non-Protestant Christians. The 1740 statute permitting the naturalization of Jews, for example, excluded Catholics for failing to meet a sacramental test. The various legal disabilities Jews and other minorities faced were unevenly applied from state to state and from time to time. And even within this context of discrimination, Jews never experienced forced exile or a deprivation of freedom of religion. Nonetheless, it is wrong to simply treat the era of independence as a simple continuation of the colonial period, because the civil and political equality of the new country represented a break of important dimensions. This is attested to by the century-long period it took from independence for all the states to eliminate restrictions on Jewish officeholding and voting, New Hampshire being the last to repeal them in 1877. See the discussion in David A. Gerber, "Anti-Semitism and Jewish-Gentile Relations in American Historiography and the American Past," in Gerber, ed., *Anti-Semitism in American History*. A balanced treatment of the colonial period, stressing the distinctive character of the religious tolerance Jews secured in spite of their civil and political disadvantages, can be found in the synthetic history by Henry L. Feingold, *Zion in America: The Jewish Experience from Colonial Times to the Present* (New York: Twayne Publishers, 1974), chap. 11. For a comparison between the circumstances of Jews and non-Protestant Christians in colonial America, see James H. Kettner, *The Development of American Citizenship, 1608–1870* (Chapel Hill: University of North Carolina Press, 1978), 113–17. The best portrait of post-independence, antebellum Jewry, focusing on immigration, population growth, occupational distribution, and spatial location within cities, as well as Jewish slaveholding, is Ira Rosenwaike, *On the Edge of Greatness: A Portrait of American Jewry in the Early National Period* (Cincinnati: American Jewish Archives, 1985).

The American Constitution does not mention Jews, nor to my knowledge does any specific Act of Congress. Jews do not exist as a statutory entity in American life. The census, ever since its initiation in 1790, has not enumerated Jews as such, but has included them in such categories as "Germans," "Poles," or "Russians." If elsewhere in the West the emancipation of the Jews "formed part of that general process of emancipation of bourgeois society,"[17] and if it thus entailed the self-conscious destruction of legal and social constraints inherent in the old order, there was no emancipation in America.

Of course, the Constitution, as one interpreter who sees it as an unabashed liberal document has recently insisted, does not mention women or blacks either (slavery, of course, does occupy a central place, but the Constitution refers to the role of slave, not to blacks as such). But, *de facto,* their situations were dramatically different. All women and virtually all blacks were not eligible to be citizens in the full sense of participation in the franchise. For Jews, by contrast, the Constitution, without ever referring to them by name, was empowering in a way that was historically unprecedented. "No religious test shall ever be required as a qualification to any office or public trust under the United States" is the language of Article 6, section 3. Together with the First Amendment's stark separation of church and state, this single mention of religion in the Constitution inserted Jews, as individuals and without the limits, constraints, or contingencies common to other early Jewish experiences of emancipation, directly into the radical new world of liberal citizenship.[18]

Nonetheless, when they arrived in the United States, Jews did pass through the portals of emancipation because they virtually all came from situations that either were entirely or partially mired in pre-emancipation

[17] Reinhard Rurup, "Jewish Emancipation and Bourgeois Society," *Leo Baeck Institute Yearbook* (hereafter *LBY*) 14 (1969): 67–68.

[18] Robert A. Goldwin, "Why Blacks, Women and Jews Are Not Mentioned in the Constitution," *Commentary* 83 (May 1987).

The entry of Jews into the world of liberal citizenship did not occur entirely without constitutional impediments. With the exception of New York, all the original states of the Union barred Jews from holding high political office; as late as 1787, only Virginia had joined New York to emancipate its Jews. Some states, like South Carolina, applied a Protestant test; others a Christian standard. By the early 1790s, Pennsylvania, Delaware, and Vermont, as well as the Northwest Territories, retracted Jewish political disabilities; and by 1840, all but New Hampshire, Rhode Island, New Jersey, and North Carolina had done so. Only North Carolina and New Hampshire preserved the exclusion of Jews from office after the Civil War. North Carolina removed its restrictions in 1868; hence the state's blacks were emancipated by the Fourteenth Amendment before the state's Jews. New Hampshire emancipated its Jews only in 1877. A discussion of the tensions embodied in this history between competing visions of American citizenship, including the view that the United States is a Christian country, can be found in Morton Borden, *Jews, Turks, and Infidels* (Chapel Hill: University of North Carolina Press, 1984).

practices. The growth of the American Jewish community from a mere three thousand in 1790 to over a quarter million by 1881 was largely the result of exit decisions taken by Jews from the various German states. Later, between 1881 and the First World War, approximately 2.5 million Jews left their European countries and moved to the West. While some had resided in the Habsburg Empire, the vast majority came from the western parts of Russian rule, and of these, a large preponderance crossed the North Atlantic. Of course, as we know, this movement of Jews was an aspect of a much broader population shift. Between 1881 and 1914, nearly twenty-two million immigrants arrived in America, of whom about 9 percent, or just over two million, were Jews; three-quarters of these immigrants came from tsarist Russia.[19]

Thus, each new generation of Jews experienced emancipation directly as a tangible life experience. Just as it is a mistake to think that because there was no feudalism in America, Americans did not undergo the transition to a postfeudal world, so it would be an error to cast American Jewish history as unembedded within the recurring catastrophes of European Jewry in the age of emancipation. American Jews, once they had arrived, did not experience the full force of the anti-Semitism of the romantics. At the same time, the recurrent pattern of immigration brought both the tangible experience and memory of the worst of anti-Jewish persecutions in the modern world directly into the consciousness of American Jews. In this way, their situation was fundamentally different from that of the other newcomers who had come from majority Christian cultures, and thus had much less problematic access to the Enlightenment and the romantic reaction to it. If to be a Jew in America certainly was one way to be an American, whereas in Europe to be a Jew frequently meant not to be a European, to be a Jew in America also meant to be an

[19] For excellent overviews, see H. G. Reissner, "The German-American Jews (1800–1850)," *LBY* 10 (1969), and Simon Kuznets, "Immigration of Russian Jews to the United States: Background and Structure," *Perspectives in American History* 9 (1975). The population numbers are taken from Jacob Rader Marcus, *To Count a People: American Jewish Population Data, 1585–1984* (Larham, Md.: University Press of America, 1990), 237–43; and from Salo Baron, "United States, 1880–1914," in Salo Baron, *Steeled by Adversity: Essays and Addresses on American Jewish Life* (Philadelphia: Jewish Publication Society, 1971). Jewish demographic data rest on quite a variety of methods and conjectures because, as noted above, the census did not specifically count Jews. Thus, reliable sources often disagree about the size of the Jewish population. Different issues of the *American Jewish Year Book,* for example, have reported the Jewish population for the United States in 1917 quite differently, ranging from a low of 3,012,141 to a high of 3,389,000. Reissner estimates there were only 1,500 Jews in the United States in 1790, rather than the more conventional figure of three thousand. Feingold, *Zion in America* (68–69), beginning with the latter figure, puts the population in 1830 at six thousand, 1840 at sixteen thousand, 1848 at twenty thousand, then a great leap to 150,000 by 1860 in the aftermath of the 1848 revolutionary failure.

unusual, and rather vulnerable, kind of American. In turn, Jews confronted America not by demanding full entry into all its spatial and institutional spheres but through a strategy of selective involvement, one that rendered them ever more visible in certain cities, regions, and occupations, but made them rather invisible, even mythical, for much of American society.

The standard exceptionalist reading of the American Jewish experience (as concretized, for instance, in Oscar Handlin's celebratory *Adventures in Freedom,* a book that treats this history as a linear narrative of the successful exploitation of opportunity and insertion into the larger culture and society), by celebrating America's Enlightenment liberality and by stressing the unimpeded access of Jews to it, misses both those dilemmas of American Jewry integral to the Enlightenment itself, as well as the ways in which anti-Semitism, though unsanctioned by the country's liberal regime, nevertheless played a role in shaping the consciousness and actions of American Jews. Handlin-style interpretations have dominated the historiography of American Jews. Remarkably coherent as stories because of their verisimilitude, they also are insufficient to the task of understanding not just the sometimes ugly underside to the entanglement of Jews with America, but also of specifying the precise contours and character of the more dominant motif of successful integration.

The emigrés from Germany in the early-to-middle nineteenth century had witnessed a state-centered process of emancipation that had produced full emancipation only in the territories captured by Napoleon. In the main, the situation in the German states, as Werner Mosse in this volume shows, was one of fitful, partial emancipation. This process took place very unevenly across the various states, often by local option within the states. It was not a linear process of the extension of liberality; rather, it also included the revocation of rights, including access to academic posts and other civil service positions, that had already been granted. Until the 1830s, even most German liberals thought of Jews as a premodern people disqualified as candidates for full rights. Only in 1848, with the passage of the Fundamental Rights of the German People by the National Assembly, was Jewish emancipation enfolded within the larger inclusionary goal of access to German citizenship irrespective of religion. With the quick collapse of the Revolution, however, it was not until 1871 that Jews throughout Germany no longer faced legal disabilities to citizenship.[20] In short, the central feature of the first two-thirds of the nine-

[20] This discussion draws mainly from Rurup's excellent article, "Jewish Emancipation and Bourgeois Society." See also Michael A. Meyer, *The Origins of the Modern Jew: Jewish Identity and European Culture in Germany, 1749–1824* (Detroit: Wayne State University Press, 1967), for an account of the situation of German Jews at an earlier moment, and Ismar Schorsch, *Jewish Responses to German Anti-Semitism, 1870–1914* (New York:

teenth century for the Jews of Germany, the period of major Jewish emigration to the United States, was that of a contingent and uncertain emancipation process.

For the Jews of Russia and eastern Europe, the second main source of American Jewry, the nineteenth century was an era of punctuated and uneven policies, but the general trend was toward a serious deterioration of condition, turning toward violence, enhanced limitations on occupations, and increasing segregation in space, with a concentration in the Pale of Settlement, consisting of the western rim of the Russian empire. Further, Jews came to see that the increasingly harsh policies of the regime found resonance in what Kuznets believes to have been a majority of the Christian population and in a willingness by members of the majority to direct violence (sometimes encouraged, sometimes organized by, the tsarist regime) against Jews.[21]

In sum, emancipation for American Jews took place not by the passage of new laws or the removal of existing legal debilitations, but by crossing a great ocean. Emancipation thus was a self-generated act, individual by individual, family by family. This process was not characterized by an even flow of migrants, but in jumbo clusterings, each with its own demography, that differed in terms of timing with respect to the development of American capitalism, the qualities of state building, and the extensiveness of anti-Jewish reactions. As a consequence, the fine-grained character of access to a post-emancipation condition the newcomers experienced depended on when they came. Those in each first generation did, however, share in the tangible experience of menacing pre-emancipation situations. This history, together with the harsh aspects of the welcome they received from the host society, produced recurring reminders that the Jewish condition, even in the unusually favorable circumstances of the United States, continued to be defined by an unremitting, if now far more soft, precariousness.[22]

Columbia University Press, 1972), for a treatment of a later period. For important treatments of the economic situation of German Jewry and of the economic aspects of emancipation, see Werner Mosse, *Jews in the German Economy: The German-Jewish Economic Elite, 1820–1935* (Oxford: Oxford University Press, 1987); and Werner Mosse, *The German-Jewish Economic Elite: A Socio-Cultural Profile, 1820–1935* (Oxford: Oxford University Press, 1989). Also see Mosse's essay in this volume.

21 Kuznets, "Immigration of Russian Jews," 92. For a fuller discussion, see the essay by Michael Stanislawski in this volume.

22 On the new voluntaristic situation of post-emancipation Jewry, see Arthur Hertzberg, "The Emancipation: A Reassessment after Two Centuries," *Modern Judaism* 1 (September 1981). The main theme of this paper is that of a profound pessimism about the future. After the Holocaust, virtually all Jews live in voluntary communities, with the main exception being those of the Soviet Union, where significant changes in condition now seem plausible,

German Incorporation

The four decades between the American Revolution and the end of the War of 1812 defined a period of international upheaval within which these two conflicts were but a part. Travel was uncertain and unsafe. In these four decades, the movement of European migrants to the United States virtually stopped, averaging about six thousand each year. After 1815, the peopling of America began again in earnest, with most of the migrants (250,000 between 1815 and 1830) coming from England, Ireland, Scotland, Germany, and Scandinavia. On the whole, this was a movement of craftspeople, farmers, and laborers. Very few professionals were part of this stream.

To a labor-starved country, this new population, especially in the rapidly growing cities of the east coast, formed the core of the new working class, whose emergence went hand in hand with a basic shift in immigration patterns for which the year 1815 was a watershed: it marked the virtual end to indentured immigration and its replacement by immigration driven by market forces of the supply and demand for labor. From that point forward, one of the special hallmarks of American capitalism was that it secured its labor by importation from abroad, rather than from its own rural hinterlands, peopled so heavily by Native Americans and slaves, plantation owners and homesteading farmers. The country's large pool of unskilled labor was to be found on the other side of the Atlantic. There were numerous consequences to this method of securing a labor supply, including a striking ethnic segmentation within the working class (and between classes), with the general pattern that most skilled craft workers were natives, and the more unskilled were immigrants. The phenomenal pace of American industrialization, which went hand in hand with the spatial extension of the country westward and the formation of new industrial cities such as Buffalo, Pittsburgh, Chicago, and St. Louis, was made possible by this overseas labor reservoir, in part because

---

and outside the religious tradition. The experience of the past two centuries demonstrates, he argues, that third-generation post-emancipation Jews intermarry at a rate of one in three, a figure that has held remarkably constant. Through this route, and that of indifference, the Jewish community erodes; it is no longer necessary to convert to effectively leave the Jewish fold. Only the most ghettoized Jews, those who reject modernity and its emancipation entirely, remain a coherent community. And further, in this rendering, there comes the reminder that the sources of first-generation experiences with emancipation—the populations of east central Europe—are no more. For an entirely different, far more optimistic reading about the prospects for Jewish survival, albeit on a new basis, see the popular book by Charles E. Silberman, *A Certain People: American Jews and Their Lives Today* (New York: Summit Books, 1985).

it facilitated, even demanded, a capital-intensive strategy of industrialization. In turn, the technical innovations of American industrialization further fueled the demand for labor. In this reinforcing process, the periods of large-scale immigration coincided with breakthrough moments of inventions in technology.[23] In turn, both the relative shortage of labor and the capital-intensive quality of American industrialization kept wages relatively high, thus attracting new migrants from abroad.

It was also the acceleration of capitalist development in Europe that extended the numbers of people who were available to make the move across the Atlantic. As Charles Tilly puts it, "The separation of households from their means of production, the spread of wage-labor, the rising labor productivity of agriculture, and the concentration of capital in cities combined to establish long-term, long-distance migration as an increasingly common response of Europeans to contraction at home and expansion elsewhere."[24] The search for opportunities in the cities of Europe in a period of substantial population growth was supplemented increasingly in the nineteenth century by cross-Atlantic migration.

Immigration, however, is not merely a matter of economic rationality. It is embedded within large-scale political and social processes. States control borders; they must decide to permit entry as well as exit. In the United States, recurring nativist pressures have opened and closed the gate at different moments to different kinds of entrants, but, on the whole, the gate has been open relatively wide.[25] Understood socially and culturally, migrations generally, and the American immigration in particular, are marked by two aspects underscored by Tilly. First, the American migration "was extraordinarily selective by origin and type of migrant. Second, on the whole it did not draw on isolated individual decision-makers, but on clusters of people bound together by acquaintance and common fate." These clusters, moreover, were not composed of categories, but of networks (as he puts it, "networks migrate, categories stay put; and networks create new categories"). The central point is this: "The

[23] For discussions, see Rowland Berthoff, "The Working Class," in John Higham, ed., *The Reconstruction of American History* (London: Hutchinson Books, 1962), and Aristide Zolberg, "How Many Exceptionalisms?," in Ira Katznelson and Aristide Zolberg, eds., *Working Class Formation: Nineteenth-Century Patterns in Western Europe and the United States* (Princeton: Princeton University Press, 1986). For the last point, Zolberg draws on Brinley Thomas, *Migration and Economic Growth: A Study of Great Britain and the Atlantic Economy,* 2d ed. (Cambridge: Cambridge University Press, 1973).

[24] Charles Tilly, "Transplanted Networks," New School for Social Research, Center for Studies of Social Change, Working Paper 35 (October 1986), 2.

[25] For a fine consideration of these issues, see Aristide Zolberg, "International Migration Policies in a Changing World System," in William H. McNeill and Ruth S. Adams, eds., *Human Migration: Patterns and Policies* (Bloomington: Indiana University Press, 1978).

effective units of migration were (and are) neither individuals nor households but sets of people linked by acquaintance, kinship, and work experience who somehow incorporated American destinations into the mobility alternatives they considered when they reached critical decision-points in their individual or collective lives." Further, these networks made the strategic choice of exit and entry an interdependent one by reducing information costs, providing mutual assistance, and organizing migration chains that structured and allocated opportunities for newcomers.[26]

All these considerations apply to the movement of German Jews to the United States, but not just these, because they also had to deal with the special precariousness of the uneven experiences of emancipation in the various German states. For German Jews, economic considerations were imbricated with the emancipatory promises of liberal citizenship in the United States, especially after the debacle of 1848. The resulting complex matrix of economic, political, social, and religious considerations prompted a small, if significant, minority of the Jews of Germany to join the larger stream of Germans to American shores.

Early American Jewry mainly was Sephardic. By 1850, by far the largest subgroup was German. In the first half of the nineteenth century, German Jewish immigrants moved across the United States in the direction of the more general German flow. By mid-century, some four-fifths of the eighty-five Jewish congregations that had been established in forty-eight towns and cities had been founded by immigrants from German-speaking Europe.[27]

Before 1815, during the period of diminished immigration, the number of Jewish newcomers from Germany was small; what information we have about motivations indicates a pastiche of economic circumstance and political rationale that frequently was highly idiosyncratic. Certainly not by intent, these forerunners who immigrated mainly from Posen and from southwest and northwest Germany became the first links in what came to be a robust pattern of mass chain migration in the 1830s. Then, the profile of the immigrants took on a proletarian aspect. A declining economic situation in Germany as well as anti-Jewish discrimination appear as the most proximate causes, together with the lowering of immigration costs as a result of the information and assistance furnished by the pre-1830 cohort. More than fifty books about the early experiences

[26] Tilly, "Transplanted Networks," 3.

[27] Reissner, "German-American Jews," 57–59. The following overview draws heavily from this text and from the pointillist overview of nineteenth-century German Jewry provided by Jacob Rader Marcus, *United States Jewry, 1776–1985*, Vol. 2: *The Germanic Period* (Detroit: Wayne State University Press, 1991).

of the immigrants circulated in Germany between 1815 and 1850, and the experiences of the migrants were reported regularly in the *Allgemeine Zeitung des Judenthums,* which began publication in 1837.

The German immigration can be sharply demarcated from the later Russian pattern by virtue of its organic links to more general German population movements. Whereas the Russian Jews concentrated in a handful of cities, and within them in a handful of neighborhoods with determinate characteristics, the German Jews moved to areas that previously had been settled by German Gentiles, including Michigan, Wisconsin, Ohio, upstate New York, Pennsylvania, South Carolina, and Maryland.[28] New York City, later to become the city of the great major-

[28] The place of Jews in the South deserves, but will not get, an extended discussion in this essay because of space constraints and the secondary place of southern Jewry in the larger American experience. It merits one, however, in spite of the relatively small number of Jews in the region (W. J. Cash observes in his classic work *The Mind of the South* [New York: Alfred A. Knopf, 1941] that the South never had enough Jews "to constitute a Jewish Problem under any rational view of the case" [305]), because of the significant peculiarities and variations imposed on Jews by the character of the South's distinctive racial civilization and political economy. If I were to develop a treatment of southern Jewry I would stress the parallels in its mercantile position to Jews in pre-emancipation early modern Europe and to their later interstitial places in Russian and Polish estates and towns as economic mediators between different positions in the economic structure, in this case between whites and blacks. As Abraham J. Peck observes, the surprisingly warm welcome German Jews received in the South was in part due to the fact that they "represented a numerically and politically powerless substitute for the independent middle-class feared by the plantation owners as a potential rival for economic and political power" ("That Other 'Peculiar Institution': Jews and Judaism in the Nineteenth-Century South," *Modern Judaism* 7 [February 1987]: 102). The dispersed southern Jews thus were able to play an important economic role in a quasi-feudal society without an indigenous commercial class. The least liberal region of the United States and the one least marked by the universalist credos of the Enlightenment, the nineteenth- and early twentieth-century South was marked by a quite pervasive and diffuse anti-Semitism (Cash writes that Jews "were usually thought of as aliens even when their fathers had fought in the Confederate armies" [345]; the anti-Semitism they faced had a pre-Enlightenment character, as Jews were considered Christ-killers and as the Eternal Alien); nevertheless, these sentiments were cushioned by anti-Catholic and especially anti-black prejudice. Thus the situation of Jews was less sinister than might have been anticipated. Individual Jews found a decent level of tolerance, and an opening to a limited kind of assimilation that produced an identification with the South, even with its aristocratic myths. Southern Jews were distinguished from their northern brethren in other ways as well. In part because of the lack of religious leadership and in part because of the absence of many concentrated communities and institutional networks, southern Judaism was less entrenched as a set of religious practices. Yet however much Jews closed the cultural gaps between themselves and the region's other whites, they were not accepted on equal terms, as displayed by the upsurge in evangelically based intolerance in the late nineteenth and early twentieth centuries, as well as the rise of the Ku Klux Klan, whitecapping against Mississippi's Jews, anti-Semitic strains in southern populism, and the lynching of Leo Frank in Atlanta. In response to their complex and vulnerable situation, the South's Jews, Peck observes, "distanced themselves from the racial question, but made

ity of Russian Jews, held on to about one-fifth of the Germans who came through its port. In 1855, when the city's population had reached 630,000, nearly ninety-six thousand of its residents had been born in the German states, of which just over ten thousand were Jews.[29]

Where the Jews differentiated themselves from the Gentiles was in their occupational profile. Most non-Jewish German immigrants worked in skilled crafts or on farms; a large majority of the Jews earned their livings as peddlers, clothing merchants, and employees in retail food and clothing operations. There was a small number of Jewish laborers and craftsmen, with many examples of movement from wage labor to small business status. The figure of the entrepreneurial German Jew, catering to the wholesale and retail consumer requirements of the new economy, could be found virtually everywhere on the rapidly expanding frontier. In the pre-1850 period, a handful of Jews entered the world of finance, most acting as local agents of the Rothschilds. Another larger but still small group of immigrants worked as lawyers, physicians, rabbis, architects, teachers, and other professionals.[30]

---

every effort to see that religious and economic freedoms were not harmed by an overt distaste for the system of segregation and a too-visible reaction against the entire oppressive nature of Southern society" (110). Other useful treatments include L. Dinnerstein and M. D. Palsson, eds., *Jews in the South* (Baton Rouge: Louisiana State University Press, 1973); Eli Evans, *The Provincials: A Personal History of Jews in the South* (New York: Atheneum, 1974); Leo and Evelyn Turith, *Jews in Early Mississippi* (Jackson: University of Mississippi Press, 1983); Nathan Kaganoff and Melvin Urofsky, eds., *Turn to the South: Essays on Southern Jewry* (Waltham, Mass.: Brandeis University Press, 1979); Mark Elovitz, *A Century of Jewish Life in Dixie: The Birmingham Experience* (Tuscaloosa: University of Alabama Press, 1974); and Steven Hertzberg, *Strangers within the Gate City: The Jews of Atlanta* (Philadelphia: Jewish Publication Society, 1978). See also the fine-grained discussion on "slavery and wealth" in Rosenwaike, *On the Edge of Greatness,* 65–75.

[29] The New York data is drawn from Amy Bridges, *A City in the Republic: Antebellum New York and the Origins of Machine Politics* (Cambridge: Cambridge University Press, 1984), chap. 3. Also see Diane Lindstrom, "Economic Structure, Demographic Change, and Income Inequality in Antebellum New York," in John Mollenkopf, ed., *Power, Culture, and Place: Essays on New York City* (New York: Russell Sage Foundation, 1988). The much lower propensity of German Jews to settle in large American cities as compared to the post-1881 Russian newcomers in part reflects the fact that urbanization of European Jewry came largely in the second half of the nineteenth century. For a discussion, see Arcadius Kahan, "The Urbanization Process of the Jews in Nineteenth-Century Europe," in Kahan, *Essays in Jewish Social and Economic History,* ed. Roger Weiss (Chicago: University of Chicago Press, 1986). In 1850, the German Jewish populations of Berlin and New York were virtually identical.

[30] "An overall picture of the occupational structure of American Jewry—whose backbone, by 1850, was formed by immigrants from Germany, would look roughly as follows: in the port cities of the East and in New Orleans on the Mexican Gulf there were importers who sold to wholesale distributors in the interior and on the West Coast, besides a host of recent immigrant arrivals awaiting final redistribution, and a sprinkle of professionals and intellectuals. Major distributing and manufacturing centres had entered, or were emerging,

The modest size of the German-Jewish contingent, its dispersion, and its interstitial role in urban and frontier economies in an age of economic liberalism facilitated its entry into an emancipated world virtually free from legal disabilities with regard to citizenship and economic activity. Further, the positioning of the Jews within the much larger German Gentile influx supplied the Jewish newcomers with the spatial and institutional advantages of an ethnic identity within which they could maintain a distinctive religious orientation. The German community taken together endowed the Jews with an economic base for their commercial pursuits significantly larger than the Jews alone could have sustained. Further, the economic and social situation of the Germans was buffered by the Irish, who were the principal targets of the period's nativists and who disproportionately were located at the bottom of the occupational structure as unskilled laborers or domestics. By contrast, very few of the Germans were in this least-advantaged section of the working class, in the building trades, on the docks, and in the factories as laborers, porters, cartmen, draymen, teamsters, and boatmen, or as laundresses and housekeepers. Rather, about half the economically active Germans were in the upper reaches of the working class, working as printers, bakers, glassworkers, hatters, tailors, cabinetmakers, dressmakers, and shoemakers. About one in six German workers were mechanics or artisans in skilled trades; most of the others were small proprieters, mainly in clothing, dry goods, tobacco, and food stores. Within this location of Germans in the ethnically tilted class structure, the German Jews were disproportionately found in the ranks of the proprieters.[31]

Between 1848 and 1881, the number of Jews in the United States, still principally from Germany, quintupled. They entered a pre-existing ethnic infrastructure, characterized by economic liberalism, spatial dispersion, and interdependent linkages to the wider German immigration. The institutional legacies of the pre-1848 immigrants helped blunt the period's anti-Semitism, established a model for the further elaboration of Jewish religious and secular communal institutions, and defined a formula for Jewish identity consistent with an insertion into America mediated by the larger German population.

---

in strategic locations in the interior, such as Buffalo, N.Y.; Rochester, N.Y.; Cincinnati, Ohio; Chicago, Ill.; St. Louis, Mo. There, Jewish resident wholesalers served local stores in smaller places as well as itinerant peddlers; some had taken up the manufacturing of clothing for sale through the same outlets. In smaller local trading centres all across the continent, Jewish retail stores attended to consumers' needs (clothing, textiles, dry goods, groceries). Finally, there were the rural areas from the New England states to Michigan, Wisconsin, and Minnesota in the north; Mississippi, Alabama, and Texas in the south; Colorado and Utah in the West, where itinerant peddlers continued to eke out a precarious livelihood." Reissner, "German-American Jews," 74. Also see Feingold, *Zion in America,* chap. 5.

[31] Bridges, *City in the Republic,* chap. 3.

The dispersion of Jews in the founding period of frontier cities and towns, as well as their economic role as merchants and businessmen in places where many settlers lacked worldly experience or even basic literacy, made it possible for them to emerge as non-negligible political actors. "Thus, by 1880," Jacob Rader Marcus observes, "transmississippi Jews were found frequently in municipal and state offices. They were mayors, legislators, judges, and attorney generals. In the late nineteenth century a professing Jew from Oregon was sent to Turkey as a minister; the first Jewish governors in the country were in Plains states." Jews, moreover, gained robust access to the military, though not to its highest echelons. The Navy proved especially resistant to Jewish mobility, but even in this branch Jews were able to secure officer status. The well-known case of Uriah Levy, who enlisted after 1812 from a position in the merchant marine, only to undergo a history of being repeatedly court-martialed for pugnacious behavior and snubbed by senior and junior officers, is often cited as emblematic of the barriers to Jewish success in the military. Less often noted is that Levy, despite his difficult set of experiences, was promoted from the ranks to become the commanding officer of a squadron. The breakthrough for Jewish military participation came during the Civil War, when Jews secured prominent positions in the forces of both sides. Whereas only forty-six Jews had served in the Continental Armies during the Revolutionary War, forty-four during the War of 1812, fifty-eight in the Mexican War, and just ninety-six in the Regular Army and seventy-eight in the Navy between the Mexican and Civil Wars, 7,935 Jews, out of a total Jewish population of approximately 150,000, served in regiments of the Union and Confederate armies. Of these, "we know of 9 Generals, 18 Colonels, 8 Lieutenant-Colonels, 40 Majors, 205 Captains, 325 Lieutenants, 48 Adjutants and 25 Surgeons." Just as American participation in the First World War accelerated the incorporation of eastern European Jews into American institutions and culture, so the Civil War provided German Jews with access to the central symbols and associations of the Union and the Confederacy. Their participation as citizen-soldiers proved a substantive marker of political incorporation, even as it was accompanied on both sides by discriminatory barriers and harassment in the ranks.[32]

[32] Marcus, *United States Jewry,* 2: 195. Marcus notes (117–18) that Jews often succeeded in attempts to secure political office quite soon after their arrival. Between 1850 and 1852, there was a Jewish alderman, county treasurer, and representative to the state assembly in fledgling San Francisco, as well as an unsuccessful Jewish candidate for the United States Senate in 1850, who was elected to the California Supreme Court a year later.

The data on Jewish military participation appears in Simon Wolf, *The Jew as Patriot, Soldier, and Citizen* (Philadelphia: Levy Type Co., 1895), 424; and on Jewish officers in Sydney G. Gumpertz, *The Jewish Legion of Valor: The Story of Jewish Heros in the Wars of the Republic* (New York: Sydney G. Gumpertz, 1934), 97. He claims "these figures are extremely conservative." Also see Bertram Korn, *American Jewry and the Civil War* (Philadelphia: Jewish

Early-to-middle nineteenth century anti-Semitism largely took the form of an anti-Jewish cosmology. The traditional Christian discourse of the Jew as apostate and Christ-killer was quite common. Jewishness continued to be defined by the majority society in sacral terms, with religion rather than race as the heart of the matter. Given the protections of the Constitution and the very limited functions and size of government in Washington, this impulse found almost no political expression. Moreover, theologically grounded anti-Judaism at this post-Enlightenment moment that preceded the invention of racial anti-Semitism was so lightweight that new sanctions could not easily latch on to it; and Jews were by no means the only nonconformists. Jews also were not terribly vulnerable in economic terms because they did not enter crowded labor markets, but participated in economic activities consistent with their economic background in Germany. Accordingly, the only significant behavioral manifestations of anti-Semitism were social, in the episodic exclusion of Jews from hotels, resorts, clubs, and fraternities. The main result of this apolitical anti-Semitism was to supply a goad for the development of an independent Jewish civil society with its own institutional alternatives. This pattern intensified later in the century.[33]

Publication Society, 1951), which includes discussions of divisions in the rabbinate over slavery and the Union; the wartime controversy, resolved positively, concerning whether Jews could serve as chaplains in the Union Army; and ties between Lincoln and the Jews.

The most significant and visible statist act of anti-Semitism during the Civil War was the order promulgated by General Ulysses Grant in November 1863 to expel all Jews from the Department of Tennessee, which included northern Mississippi and parts of Kentucky as well as Tennessee west of the Tennessee River. He did so in order to curb trade with the Confederacy and to put a stop to speculation in cotton and bullion, activities he associated with Jews. As soon as President Lincoln was convinced the order was authentic, he revoked it. Reporting on a visit to the president by a Jewish delegation to discuss the matter and to thank Lincoln for his swift action, Rabbi Isaac Mayer Wise, who had come to the United States in 1846, served congregations in Albany and Cincinnati, and was one of the key founders of Reform Judaism, wrote, "The President, we must confess, fully illustrated to us and convinced us that he knows of no distinction between Jew and Gentile, that he feels no prejudice against any nationality, and that he by no means will allow a citizen in any wise be wronged on account of his place of birth or religious confession." *The Israelite,* 16 January 1863; reproduced in Morris Schappes, *A Documentary History of the Jews in the United States* (New York: Schocken Books 1971), 474. A useful overview of the situation of Jews during the Civil War, including their difficulties in the military, can be found in Sachar, *History of the Jews in America,* 72–80.

[33] See Michael Dobkowski, *The Tarnished Dream: The Basis of American Anti-Semitism* (Westport, Conn.: Greenwood Press, 1979), chap. one; Lee Levinger, *Anti-Semitism in the United States: Its History and Causes* (New York: Bloch Publishing, 1922), 11; John Higham, *Send These to Me: Jews and Other Immigrants in Urban America* (New York: Atheneum, 1975), chaps. 7–9; Alan Ryan, "Letting Them Live," *London Review of Books,* 4 August 1988; and, on the lightweightedness of religious anti-Semitism after the Enlightenment, Gellner, *Culture, Identity, and Politics,* 80.

The Jews of Germany who had crossed the Atlantic had belonged to Jewish *Gemeinden,* corporations chartered in state law from which they could depart only by an explicit statement of intent in court or by conversion to Christianity. The Jewish community as an institutional network provided for religious services such as the synagogue, kosher food, and ritual baths, assistance to paupers, burial needs, and social interactions. In the United States, by contrast, all these functions, when they were to be performed at all, had to be acquitted on a voluntary basis. The result was a dense but chaotic and ever-changing organizational structure. Each synagogue possessed an independent status, its autonomy regulated only by the preferences of its members, with the result that even small Jewish communities divided into separate synagogues based on liturgical divisions. Until the 1860s, the majority of synagogues lacked a rabbi. Even where there was one he served at the pleasure of the membership without the possession of the kind of religious sovereignty that had prevailed in European synagogues. Given this decentralized community structure that mirrored the more general voluntarism of secondary secular and religious associations in the United States, other specific community functions, such as burial, credit, and support for the sick, were institutionalized in specific, autonomous associations, each with its own task.

This diffuse organizational structure promoted two significant goals. It permitted German Jews to identify with the larger German population and form a distinctive section of it (much as the Germans also were divided between Protestants and Catholics); and it facilitated the spatial extension of the Jewish communities into all the regions with significant German populations (and in some cases, beyond). In short, organizational diffuseness reduced the visibility of the Jews and promoted their integration through the mediation of the larger German community into American society.

At this point in American Jewish history, the secondary associations to which Jews belonged were as likely to be German as exclusively Jewish, and Jews were distinguished from fellow Germans mainly on the basis of religion. Over the period that spanned the three decades from 1850, when the number of German Jews expanded dramatically as part of the larger migration of Germans to the United States, their situation altered in two partially contradictory ways. Jews became more institutionally self-enclosed as a distinctive ethnic community, and their dominant theology, not without some irony, developed greater affinities with the mainstream of liberal Protestantism. Put another way, the Jewish community moved from its envelopment within the social, cultural, and economic milieu and institutions of the German-American community and toward the creation of a German-Jewish ethnicity. This process of separation was marked by a mimetic process of "separate but similar." German Jewish secular and religious institutions differentiated just as German Jews came to behave much as the majority of Americans, not just as a subgroup of Germans.

Before 1848, German Jews nested within the German community. They lived where other Germans did, spoke German a good deal of the time, read German newspapers, and joined German social and cultural organizations such as the German Society of the City of New York and the German Friendly Society of Charleston, South Carolina. German voluntary associations were characterized by a cross-religious integration; two of the five-person leadership of the Committee in Aid of the German Political Refugees that was founded in 1850 were Jews, for example. Jews also joined the elite fraternal lodges of the Masons and the Odd Fellows in significant numbers.[34] As Meyer observes,

> The Christians who took the initiative to leave Germany were less likely to have harbored anti-Jewish prejudices than those who remained, and once they arrived most of them readily accepted the American value of social equality. When Jews with German professional training reached America, having fled German discrimination, they were, ironically, hailed as representatives of superior German university training. With few exceptions, Gentiles welcomed Jews into German cultural societies whose counterparts in Germany would have most likely excluded them. In San Francisco in 1852, a Jew headed a cultural and social club that included the most distinguished Germans of the city. German Jews could feel like insiders in these groups while they still remained outsiders in America.[35]

The watershed of 1848 ushered in Jewish immigration on an unprecedented scale. Jews now constituted a much more defined and visible population group. Their synagogues no longer were led by a lay leadership, but by an exceptional group of rabbis who sought to create intercommunity Jewish institutions and new networks of communications between Jews in different parts of the country. B'nai Brith, a society of Jewish lodges modeled on the Odd Fellows, was created in 1843 in response to a number of instances of exclusion; it grew to become a national network with lodges in virtually every area of German Jewish settlement. Strengthened by political refugees with considerable organizational experience after 1848, the B'nai Brith became the preeminent Jewish service organization, opening hospitals and social service centers, as well as becoming the key representative of Jewish concerns on the national scene, especially as they concerned the status of Jews overseas.

[34] Reissner, "German-American Jews," 92–97.

[35] Michael A. Meyer, "German-Jewish Identity in Nineteenth-Century America," in Jacob Katz, ed., *Toward Modernity: The European Jewish Model* (New Brunswick: Transaction Books, 1987), 251–52.

The organization's first major effort of this kind was its campaign in 1857 against a treaty between the United States and Switzerland that would have recognized the limitations placed on Jews in the various Swiss cantons. The organization directly, and successfully, lobbied Secretary of State Daniel Webster, the chairman of the Senate Foreign Relations Committee, Henry Clay, and President James Buchanan.

This shift toward an institutional independence for the German Jewish community in the secular realm was paralleled by dramatic changes in the dominant theological orientation of German synagogues. In order to stem an acceleration of departures from the synagogue by immigrants and their children no longer attracted to Orthodox worship, and taking its cues from the Reform movement already underway in Germany proper, a new Reformed Society of Israelites, founded in Charleston in 1825, sought radical liturgical changes to include regular sermons in German or English, shorter services, the use of an organ and choirs, and mixed seating of men and women—in short, an attempt to make the Jewish service more like that of the Protestant majority.[36] American Reform crystallized as a coherent theological movement in the 1850s. The Torah and Talmud now were considered ethical documents, not imperatives to specific practices; Jewish nationality and nationalism were rejected, as was the celebration of holidays such as Purim that possessed this quality; and the yearning for a return to Zion also was abandoned.[37] As if to signify this new Judaism, shrimp was served at the opening of Hebrew Union College, founded to train Reform rabbis.[38]

Assimilation, from the vantage point of these changes, is hardly a synonym for disappearance. Rather, the term connotes a strategy for transacting with the wider society. As Olivier Zunz observes, "Assimilation is not a constant but varies according to the interplay of outside conditions."[39] The early newcomers from Germany forged this kind of association with Americans within the compass of broader German patterns. The swelling of the number of German immigrants, including Jews, after

[36] It is possible to overstate the shift from Orthodoxy to Reform both in Germany and the United States. As Carelbach has pointed out, German Orthodoxy underwent a dynamic reformulation to create a synthetic model for Jewish adaptation to emancipation by combining adherence to *halakhah* (Jewish law) and to German national culture. See Julius Carelbach, "The Foundations of German-Jewish Orthodoxy: An Interpretation," *LBY* 33 (1988).

[37] For a discussion, see Michael A. Meyer, *Response to Modernity: A History of the Reform Movement in Judaism* (Oxford: Oxford University Press, 1988).

[38] Seymour Martin Lipset, "The American Jewish Community in a Comparative Context," in Peter I. Rose, ed., *The Ghetto and Beyond: Essays in Jewish Life in America* (New York: Random House, 1969), 25.

[39] Olivier Zunz, "American History and the Changing Meaning of Assimilation," unpublished manuscript, University of Virginia, 1985. Also see Bauman's brilliant article, "Exit Visas and Entry Tickets."

1848, however, reduced the appeal and coherence of this option. The new Jewish immigrants from Germany on the whole were poorer than their forebears, more likely to work in crafts such as cigarmaking that were undergoing a painful process of proletarianization, and were more urbanized, more spatially concentrated. The wider German community distanced itself increasingly from these Jews, and, in turn, the Jews felt the slights of social exclusion. The Jewish migration networks that had located Jews within the wider German community now became more dense and self-reinforcing. As with other American ethnic groups of this period, the Jewish population came to be a more strongly bounded ethnic and religious enclave in an urbanizing society that organized its politics along ethnic and territorial lines.[40]

If the older strategy for engaging with American society could no longer work, the new mimetic one characterized by institutional independence and an imitation of larger forms successfully addressed the mix of unprecedented welcome and bounded exclusions that the Jews found in America. It also spoke to the fact that in an age of mass migration, assimilation by individuals, short of conversion, is a very limited option. As Charles Tilly observes, the very network pattern of migration makes such solutions implausible because of the collective character of the process. Individuals may strive to alter their status, but in these circumstances their success is heavily dependent on the character of the collective effort to manage relationships with the wider society.[41]

After 1848, the new institutional structure created by the Germans was made possible in part, and then sustained, by the existence of a settled, indigenous middle- and upper-class German Jewish leadership. The new Reform movement and secular institutions created in this period were funded and led by the business elite of German Jewish financiers and by leading retail merchants in the community. Interestingly, for the former group, much of the movement of economic mobility entailed a new concentration in New York City, which now emerged as the economic and organizational capital of American Jewry. The tightly knit Jewish family firms in finance were second only to a group of houses of Yankee origin in playing a key role in the development of American capital markets in the second half of the nineteenth century. The great majority of the investment banking houses were led by German Jewish families, including the Loebs, Seligmans, Kuhns, Guggenheims, Lehmans, and Strauses, who had earned their living as peddlers and retailers on arrival, and, when seeking entry into the world of finance, found themselves excluded from

[40] On the ethnic patterning of American local politics, see Ira Katznelson, *City Trenches: Urban Politics and the Patterning of Class in the United States* (New York: Pantheon Books, 1981).

[41] Tilly, "Transplanted Networks," 5.

the Yankee firms.[42] Together with the retailing elite families, including the Altman, Bloomingdale, and Gimbel families, this commercial elite furnished the lay leadership and financing for the new network of separate, but imitative, Jewish institutions.

By the early and middle 1880s, a new formula for connecting to the larger society had become well established. It is not necessary to adopt a functional causal position to recognize its functions for German Jews in the liberal setting of the United States where Jews faced virtually no legal disabilities, where politics were decentralized, where there were robust market opportunities, but where they did face social exclusion and a climate of religious suspicion. The intensification of Jewish networks together with the Americanization of Jewish institutions downplayed Jewish cultural particularity but accommodated the boundaries of American tolerance for Jews. When a nasty incident of anti-Semitism reared its head, as in the exclusion of Joseph Seligman from the Grand Union Hotel in Saratoga in 1877, the restrictions placed on Jewish entry to other resorts on the East Coast, the attempt in 1879 to keep Jews away from the new housing development in Manhattan Beach, Brooklyn, or the blackballing of Jews from social clubs and elite private schools, Jews responded by creating separate institutions modeled on those from which they had been excluded. When the Jewish elite, in short, discovered it could not enter the larger social elite, it created its own social space, and in so doing defined a Jewish civil society that was increasingly concentrated and urban.[43] Later, its institutions outfitted an infrastructure for the absorption of the unanticipated, and largely unwelcome, Russian and Polish Jewish masses after 1881.[44]

Unpleasant as some aspects of nineteenth-century interactions with America were for German Jewry, taken as a whole they represented an unprecedented success story for diaspora Jewry. Once German Jews discovered that they could no longer be inserted into the American scene as a minority strand within the larger German immigrant community, they developed an orientation to the American scene that, at once, made them

[42] "Jewish investment capital had nowhere to go except to their own banking houses since Yankee banking houses rejected Jewish representation to which the massive amount of Jewish dollars entitled them. There is no record of a Christian banking firm ever taking on a Jewish partner, although an isolated Jew might occasionally be found on the board of directors." Feingold, *Zion in America*, 79–80. The best discussion is Barry E. Supple, "A Business Elite: German-Jewish Financiers in Nineteenth-Century New York," *Business History Review* 31 (1957): 145–78.

[43] For an orientation to the complicated, conflicted, and contradictory relations between German and eastern European Jews, see Steven Ascheim, *Big Brothers and Strangers: The East European Jew in German and German Jewish Consciousness* (Madison: University of Wisconsin Press, 1982).

[44] See Higham, *Send These to Me*, 148–51.

more Jewish and more American. Institutionally, they coped with their experience of episodic and punctuated anti-Semitism by designing a separate institutional sphere that imitated and replicated larger American practices more than those of other immigrant groups. This double strategy for transacting with America concentrated Jews in specific locations, most of which were urban (one in four German Jews lived in New York City in 1880) and in specific city-based occupations of the retail trades, textile manufacturing, and finance. The definition of Jewishness and of Jewish religious identity was altered to facilitate linkages with America on terms of apartness and imitation. It was this equilibrium which German Jews seemed to have secured on largely favorable terms that was called into question by the great divide of 1881.

The immigration of Russian and eastern European Jews posed anew questions about the meaning of the American path of emancipation in all its aspects, but one of its effects, not without irony, was to reinforce the Jewish identity of German-American Jews, even the most assimilated. "Still not a part of the American establishment, but for the most part ever-more peripherally Jewish, the wealthier New York families . . . eager to separate from the newcomers . . . segregated themselves both socially and religiously on the basis of their German origins, thus braking somewhat an otherwise accelerating pace of Americanization."[45] A half-century later, the arrival of a new wave of immigrants from Nazi Germany had the effect of heightening the Jewish consciousness of second- and third-generation eastern European Jews.

From the Pale

In 1893, George Price, a Jewish doctor who had left Russia for New York in 1882, collected a series of articles he had written about the first decade of Russian Jewish immigration to New York City in the newspaper *Voshkhod* and published them in St. Petersburg as an account of *Russkie Yevrei v Amerike* ("The Russian Jews in America"). His account was remarkably unsentimental. He reported on economic exploitation (there were no Jewish unions of consequence before 1894), "the prevailing poverty," and "the helplessness and terrifying conditions of the inhabitants" of the district of ten thousand Jews in the vicinity of Stanton, Canal, and Norfolk Streets on the Lower East Side that he surveyed as a health inspector. Their situation was typical of the nearly 300,000 Jews who lived in just twenty-five blocks of the condensed neighborhood (out of a total of 700,000 Jews in the United States at that time), "which assumes the

[45] Meyer, "German-Jewish Identity," 263–64.

form of a typical Jewish city [ghetto] of the Pale." In spite of the appalling material conditions of the immigrants, the apparent absence of mobility opportunities, and the meagerness of philanthropic help in the face of the immigrants' needs, he nonetheless concluded with a section on "the moral significance of immigration," arguing that the transition to a condition of emancipation was momentous: "Anyone who saw the poor, downtrodden, frightened inhabitants of the well-known Pale, over whose head hung the Damoclean sword of cruel injustice, who trembled like a leaf at the appearance of the sheriff or policeman; anyone who saw such a Jew—who, under the struggle for existence, had become a free, independent and upright American Jew . . . anyone who saw this extraordinary metamorphosis,—cannot deny the significance of the impact of immigration."[46]

This "emancipation," however, was purchased at the apparent price of spatial and social segregation: "There is a complete isolation from the general American population, a lack of knowledge about the language of the country and its customs, distinctive clothing, distinctive language, distinctive mode of life and distinctive press—everything is different from that of the surrounding environment." Although there does not "exist a Jewish problem in the same form as it is conceived of in many countries of Eastern Europe," nonetheless the situation Jews have in common with other newcomers is compounded by native anti-Semitism; "That is why, even the American Jew, who enjoys political freedom, tries to avoid anything which might evoke enmity against him and might supply fuel to the dying flame of intolerance."[47] Over time, these circumstances eased. Jews learned English, organized unions, moved into new occupations and neighborhoods, created organizations, and participated in politics. Nonetheless, Price's stark description of the first decade of mass migration from eastern Europe did capture key aspects of the civil, political, economic, and spatial engagement of these Jews with America.

[46] George M. Price, "The Russian Jews in America," in Abraham J. Karp, ed., *The Jewish Experience in America: The Era of Immigration* (New York: Ktav Publishing House, 1969), 4: 329, 298.

[47] Ibid., 4: 329–31. With respect to the isolation of the early eastern European wave of immigrants and the remarkable degree of difference they exhibited from the German Jews, it is worth noting that of the 112,000 immigrants on the Lower East Side in 1890, Price estimated that only sixty thousand spoke English, and fewer than 7,500 had become citizens. Jewish schoolchildren likewise interacted very little with children of other backgrounds. Bernheimer's 1905 study found that fully thirty-eight of the forty-four primary schools attended by Jewish children on the Lower East Side contained populations that were over 90 percent Jewish, with most approximating 100 percent. Charles Bernheimer, ed., *The Russian Jew in the United States: Studies of Social Conditions in New York, Philadelphia, and Chicago, with a Discussion of Rural Settlements* (Philadelphia: John C. Winston, 1905), 185.

The vast majority of the new Jewish immigrants came to stay. The divide between their old world and the new was so great as to virtually preclude any going back in spite of the privations chronicled by Price. They had come from settings characterized by very rapid population growth (in the Russian empire the Jewish population increased from one million in 1800 to over five million by the end of the century), severe restrictions on residence and occupation, authoritarian politics, religious domination by the Orthodox and Catholic churches, vulnerability to conscription, and physical insecurity punctuated by outbreaks of pogroms.[48] The striking contrast between the menacing pre-emancipation situation of these Jews in Europe and the condition of Jews in the United States distinguished the Jewish population movement from those of the period's other newcomers. The Jewish rate of return migration was comparatively low. While there is some variation in estimates, the gap between Jewish and other immigrant patterns uncontestedly was very considerable. Between 1908 and 1925, when the differences between groups may have been greatest, only 5 percent of Jewish immigrants returned to Europe compared to at least 55 percent of Italians, whose rate of reemigration was the highest of the various nationality groups. Overall, the return rate for Jewish immigrants in the century's first two decades was just one-quarter of the rate for other newcomers. Jewish rates of return seemed to have varied by the state of the economy in the United States and the outbreak of pogroms in Europe. During the recession year of 1912, there was an 8 percent return rate to Russia but a nearly 20 percent return rate to Austria-Hungary, where Jews faced far less persecution.[49]

[48] See the overview in Lloyd P. Gartner, "Jewish Migrants En Route from Europe to North America," in Moses Rischin, ed., *The Jews of North America* (Detroit: Wayne State University Press, 1987). The journey to North America was fraught with obstacles, dangers, and impediments. A discussion may be found in Pamela Nadell, "The Journey to America by Steam: The Jews of Eastern Europe in Transition," *American Jewish History* 71 (December 1981).

[49] I have taken these figures from Jonathan Sarna, who treats the nonreturn of Jews as a myth. What he actually argues, in spite of his title, is that there are grounds to think that in the last two decades of the nineteenth century the Jewish return rate was approximately 20 percent, still well under the rate for other groups. Jonathan D. Sarna, "The Myth of No Return: Jewish Return Migration to Eastern Europe, 1881–1914," *American Jewish History* 71 (December 1981). The standard estimates have come from Jacob Lestschinsky, "Jewish Migrations, 1840–1956," in Louis Finkelstein, ed., *The Jews* (New York: Jewish Theological Seminary, 1960). Also see Kuznets, "Immigration of Russian Jews." Kessner's contrast between Jewish and Italian return rates is more stark than that I have cited. See Thomas Kessner, "Jobs, Ghettoes and the Urban Economy, 1880–1935," *American Jewish History* 71 (December 1981): 221–22. What does seem clear is that both the rate of immigration and the rate of return altered after the Kishinev pogrom of 1903. Between 1881 and 1889 an average of just under twenty-three thousand Jews arrived each year

Jews differed from the principally agrarian Catholic immigrants who came from the same region in other ways as well. Whereas the great majority of non-Jewish newcomers were drawn from the peasantry, servant classes, and the menial working class (three in four Italian immigrants had been common or farm laborers), just 2 percent of the Jews had worked in agriculture. Some two in three had been employed in some form of skilled manufacturing, principally in the clothing industry or in leather goods. And whereas only one in four of the non-Jewish immigrants intended to live in New York State, and principally in New York City, two in three Jewish immigrants indicated this residential preference.[50]

During this period of mass migration the situation of American Jewry was transformed utterly. The country's Jewish population increased from 250,000 in 1881 to nearly 3.5 million by 1920; or from less than 0.5 percent of the population of the United States to some 3.5 percent. The number of Jewish congregations grew from under three hundred to nearly two thousand. However impressive, data of this kind cannot capture the unevenness of the ties forged with American society by this wave of immigrants. Despite their dramatic demographic and institutional growth, they remained invisible in much of the United States. By con-

---

principally from tsarist Russia, Austria-Hungary, and Romania; just under forty-one thousand between 1890 and 1898; over fifty-three thousand between 1899 and 1902; but 123,000 between 1903 and 1907. The rate declined between 1908–14 to ninety-four thousand per year. In this period, the gross immigration of Jews numbered 2,057,000. These figures are summarized in Kuznets (39), with a table on return emigration (40). During the period of 1915–19 the average rate fell under the impact of war to thirteen thousand, but increased radically between 1920 and the closing of the open door in 1924 to fifty-seven thousand per year. At the peak of Jewish emigration from Russia, twenty-three of every one thousand residents were departing each year, constituting an exodus of stupendous scale.

The mass movement of Jews from eastern Europe to the United States was an integral part of their astounding spatial mobility. At the turn of the century, the Jewish population of eastern Europe was between six and seven million. Approximately half were involved in one of three streams of migration: from rural to urban areas within the region, from depressed to industrializing areas, and overseas migration. The more skilled, the more urban, and the more literate were the more likely to move, with the most skilled, the most urban, and the most literate likely to travel abroad. For a discussion, see Arcadius Kahan, "Economic Opportunities and Some Pilgrim's Progress: Jewish Immigrants from Eastern Europe in the United States, 1980–1914," in *Essays in Jewish Social and Economic History*, 102.

[50] Kuznets, "Immigration of Russian Jews," 102, 113. Especially illuminating is the treatment of the Jewish occupational structure and urbanization under the impact of Russian industrialization by Arcadius Kahan, "The Impact of Industrialization in Tsarist Russia on the Socioeconomic Conditions of the Jewish Population," in *Essays in Jewish Social and Economic History*. The Italian estimate is from Kessner, "Jobs, Ghettoes, and the Urban Economy," 222–23.

trast, in the leading urban centers, they became a major presence. By 1910, Jews constituted nearly 20 percent of New York City's population and 10 percent of Chicago's.[51]

The Jews further concentrated in the very dense garment district tenement areas of those cities. The Lower East Side of Manhattan swiftly transformed from a primarily German and Irish district to a Jewish area of more than seven hundred inhabitants per acre by 1900. The great majority of wage earners worked in the needle trades, where their crush of numbers had the effect in the early 1880s of cutting wages in half from fifteen dollars a week in 1883 to seven in 1885. With emancipation came pauperization and proletarianization of a sudden and brutal kind in the tightly bound-up worlds of urban slums and sweatshops.[52]

Jewish immigrants in both the German and Russian phases, as noted, arrived as integral parts of the recruitment of a vast labor supply for American industrialization that brought tens of millions of other Europeans to the New World.[53] The Russian and eastern European Jewish newcomers came during the massive new industrialization of the second industrial revolution, a period characterized by the full conquest of the continent, transformations in the scale and technology of industry, radical growth in the size of capital markets and of the role of American finance in the world economy, a rapid increase in trade, large-scale urbanization, the development of a modern state capable of at least some regulation of market capitalism, and the extension of American military might and capacity. All this they shared with other immigrants. They differed, however, in three main respects. First, the Jews had come from

[51] Baron, *Steeled by Adversity*, 271–72.

[52] Irving Howe, *World of Our Fathers: The Journey of East European Jews to America and the Life They Found and Made* (New York: Harcourt, Brace, Jovanovich, 1976), 69, 83, 115–18. A 1900 report for the United Hebrew Charities wrote, "The conditions in which the Jews of the New York Ghetto are compelled to exist are slowly but surely undermining both that moral and physical health of which we have hitherto been so proud. The unspeakable evils that the tenements and sweatshops as they still persist inevitably produce in the way of depressed vitality, sickness, consequent poverty, and death, are evils that it behooves us to endeavor to kill at the root." Lee K. Frankel, *Twenty-Sixth Annual Report of the United Hebrew Charities of the City of New York* (New York: 1900); cited in Bernheimer, *Russian Jew in the United States,* 118. Bernheimer observes that the conditions on the Lower East Side were not worse, and probably better, than the immigrant enclaves of Manhattan's Italians.

[53] Ironically, when American policy welcomed immigration because of labor shortages, Jews resisted it for fear of disrupting the *modus vivendi* they had fashioned with the wider society; later, when policy debates turned against the open door, Jews had become its staunchest supporters. See Esther L. Panitz, "The Polarity of American Jewish Attitudes toward Immigration," in Karp, *Jewish Experience in America;* and, for a treatment that includes a fine discussion of labor movement attitudes, Sheldon Morris Neuringer, *American Jewry and United States Immigration Policy, 1881–1953* (New York: Arno Press, 1980).

settings not only where the Enlightenment had yet to exert a dominant role but where they had been persecuted minorities. Second, on arrival, they were seen as different from the other newcomers by the host society, by the other immigrants, even by Jews already long established in America. Third, they experienced qualitatively distinctive exclusions of a social and economic kind. None of the period's manifestations of anti-Semitism was particularly total or, with the exception of rare incidents like the killing of Leo Frank in Atlanta, particularly brutal. Nonetheless, together with the tangible experiences of anti-Semitism first-generation newcomers brought with them, these incidents contributed to making American Jews the group of immigrants at the turn of the century most wary of the wider society.[54]

The pattern of insertion of the Russian and eastern European Jewish newcomers into American society shared many features with that of the period's far larger wave of non-Jewish immigration, but with the difference of an exaggeration of common trends. Like the others, the Jews settled in cities, but more so. They participated in politics, but with more of a tilt toward the Left. They transacted with the American economy from ethnic enclaves, but more concentrated ones. They formed labor unions, but quite segregated ones. They joined radical movements, but as special kinds of players. Adapting and modifying the institutional strategies of the German Jews, they sparred in skirmishes at the boundaries of the wider society to secure access to the open society of markets and citizens from the relatively secure locations of their spatially specific "city niches." In their quest to both defend the position of Jews from assault and to secure access to economic mobility, political participation, elite positions, and higher education, they created a densely organized civil society from which they confronted the late nineteenth- and early twentieth-century American versions of state and capitalism. Their story

[54] For an example of such a contemporary treatment of anti-Semitism, see Lee Joseph Levinger, *Anti-Semitism in the United States: Its History and Causes* (1925; reprint, Westport, Conn.: Greenwood Press, 1972). Levinger stressed limitations on Jews in the universities, the publication of anti-Semitic books and journalism, the passage of immigration legislation on a racial basis, and the rise of the Ku Klux Klan. For a consideration of the acceleration of anti-Semitism in the United States between 1870 and 1930, see Dobkowski, *Tarnished Dream.* Jews felt vulnerable in part because as the most significant non-Christian minority they were inherently separate, yet found it hard to get hold of anti-Semitism as a threat because it never was sanctioned officially. The signals Jews received thus were ambiguous and mixed. This pattern is discussed in Gerber, "Anti-Semitism and Jewish-Gentile Relations." American Jews, as I have noted, also inevitably found a reference point in their European experiences of anti-Semitism, and thus approached America with a mix of gratitude and wariness. Jewish interpretations of their plight were also informed by the main types of Jewish historiography and of popular history that stressed a historical drama in which Jews were perennial underdogs subject at all times to the traumas of exclusion.

divides in two: before 1924, when the gates to America remained open and the process of emancipation by immigration remained continuous; and, after 1924, when the potential stock of renewal from abroad was excluded, and the fates of Jews in America and Europe became radically disconnected.

City Niches

Olivier Zunz's study of ethnicity, class, and space in Detroit between 1880 and 1920 demonstrated how the residential settlements of ethnic newcomers were transformed from a situation of ethnic propinquity in spite of class to one of class propinquity in spite of ethnicity. By the end of the period, a city of semi-autonomous ethnic residential communities had given way to one whose residential organization was dictated increasingly by the class structure that had been created by the city's robust industrialization. Neighborhoods came to be dominated more by occupational than by ethnic groups, and such ethnic concentrations as existed tended to be organized rather more on specific blocks and streets than to dominate whole neighborhoods. For the first time, there emerged distinctive concentrations of factory day laborers or white-collar office workers rather than ethnic enclaves. Blue-collar and middle-class communities began to replace the ethnic neighborhood as the basic unit of social geography. "The ethnic bonds that had traditionally defined the city's spatial structures were still important, but now occupational bonds played an equal role in shaping the metropolitan territory."[55] Only the situations of African Americans and Jews differed from this dominant trend. By virtue of forced housing segregation that pressed all blacks together, they were drawn more and more into racial ghettos irrespective of class position. Jews, by contrast, had more choices but did not exercise them. Zunz writes:

> The tiny Jewish community (originally lodged in the German east side of 1900) had grown to bigger proportions; in the Jewish east side—near offices and markets—lived the white collar office worker, the peddler and street vendor, the community Talmud teacher, the factory worker, the tailor, the candy dealer, and the traveling salesman. The Jews were the only group that still displayed a real variety of jobs in their concentrated neighborhoods of 1920 Detroit. Only such a tight ethnic community resisted the impact of

[55] Olivier Zunz, *The Changing Face of Inequality: Urbanization, Industrial Development, and Immigrants in Detroit, 1880–1920* (Chicago: University of Chicago Press, 1982), 342.

social class to divide previously socially diverse, ethnically concentrated communities into more socially stratified socioethnic groups.[56]

This special concentration of Jews across class lines in big-city neighborhoods was hardly distinctive to Detroit. Outside the major urban centers of Boston, Philadelphia, Chicago, Baltimore, and especially New York, Jews displayed less dense models of spatial cohesion, but these were exceptions to the more general rule of an intensely urban existence that bound up space and ethnic identity together.[57] As Deborah Dash Moore has argued, it is Louis Wirth's spatial approach to Jewish ethnicity that best captures what was distinctive to the formation of Jewish ethnicity in the United States. As she points out, this process of group formation was immensely difficult for the Jewish immigrants who, having left the most traditional societies of eastern Europe, moved into the most modern, and modernizing, sectors of the United States. Jews managed and cushioned this radical shift, which reoriented "the locus of Jewish identity from tradition, the past and the religious community, to ethnicity, the future and the secular individual," by recreating remarkably dense shtetl-like environments as launching pads into America. The most remarkable of these settlements, of course, was the Lower East Side in New York City. At the beginning of the twentieth century, fully one-tenth

[56] Ibid., 350.

[57] See Maxwell Whiteman, "Philadelphia's Jewish Neighborhoods," in Allen F. Davis and Mark H. Haller, eds., *The Peoples of Philadelphia* (Philadelphia: Temple University Press, 1973). Deborah Dash Moore stresses that there was a further difference between the large urban centers outside of New York and that of New York. She writes: "Only Jewish immigrants who settled in New York could believe that their city *was* America. . . . Less diverse, less dense, but more integrative, the immigrant communities shaped largely by secondary migration received the particular stamp of the networks of individuals who built them. In a city like Atlanta or Milwaukee, Litvaks [Lithuanian Jews] could gain the upper hand without needing to accommodate others because there were so few of them. In Chicago or Cleveland, Zionists could capture the city's major immigrant organizations, giving an ideological identity to the ethnic community. In Baltimore or Philadelphia, an American orthodoxy could take root, and pass on its style and substance. In Cincinnati or San Francisco, the established native Jewish community could set the dominant tone and boundaries of the city's Jewish life. These possibilities existed because of the power of migration to sort out individuals. The unsuccessful ones who failed to fit in usually packed their bags again and either moved elsewhere or returned to New York City." Deborah Dash Moore, "The Construction of Community: Jewish Migration and Ethnicity in the United States," in Rischin, *Jews of North America,* 112.

The shtetl, it should be stressed, at the time of mass immigration to the United States, had already been affected by various trends of modernization and hardly constituted a hermetically sealed world. For a discussion, and example, that aims to counteract the more usual American representations see Abraham Ain, "Swixlocz: Portrait of a Shtetl," in Herbert Gutman and Gregory Kealey, eds., *Many Pasts,* vol. 2 (Englewood Cliffs, N.J.: Prentice-Hall, 1973).

of world Jewry lived on the Lower East Side, half of all American Jews, and three-quarters of New York City's.[58]

For most newcomers, the Lower East Side, as well as similar, if smaller, Jewish concentrations, provided a first, time-bound foothold in America. Between 1905 and 1915, some two in three Jews left the Lower East Side, but mainly for other Jewish neighborhoods in slightly better sections of the city, such as Harlem or, later, Washington Heights in northern Manhattan, or Crown Heights, Borough Park, and Midwood in Brooklyn. In this way, Jews began to replicate the class divisions of other ethnic groups in space, but with the key difference that they continued to live mainly with each other. Both before and after 1924, the Jews who left the Lower East Side chose "the selective paths of secondary migration, a dispersed, clustered and segregated settlement pattern."[59] In spatial terms, the Lower East Side represented the apogee of the strategy of city niches, but dense geographic concentration was characteristic for Jews well beyond that neighborhood's boundaries, and not only in New York. Wirth's dictum—"If you would know what kind of a Jew a man is, ask him where he lives"[60]—now was true both in the sense of the special importance of urban space for the great majority of American Jews and in the sense of distinguishing Jews by timing of arrival and by social class. So long as immigration proceeded unimpeded by restrictive legislation, however, those who left the Lower East Side were replaced by other arrivals, thus giving to the area the appearance of stability in spite of a great deal of fluidity.[61] Within the Lower East Side, Jews constructed a remarkably complex, cohesive, variegated civil society, constituting something of a virtually enclosed economy, polity, and welfare state.

The character of the occupational history of the eastern European immigrants between 1880 and 1920 is well known. Its most important features were its group-endogenous character and the concentration of employment in the clothing industry. During a period of rapid growth in the needle trades, the industry absorbed virtually all the Jewish newcomers who arrived with relevant skills. There was something of a mobility ladder in the industry. Many newcomers who began in the more volatile, lower-

[58] Moore, "Construction of Community," 108, 111.

[59] Ibid., 115. See also Robert A. Rockaway, "World of Their Children: Second Generation New York Jews," *Journal of Urban History* 12 (February 1986). Later, after the Second World War (which is outside the scope of this essay), Jews replicated this pattern yet again in their creation of suburban Jewish enclaves. A discussion may be found in Walter P. Zenner, "Jewishness in America: Ascription and Choice," *Ethnic and Racial Studies* 8 (January 1985).

[60] Louis Wirth, "The Ghetto," in Albert J. Reiss, ed., *On Cities and Social Life* (Chicago: University of Chicago Press, 1964), 94; cited in Moore, "Construction of Community," 107.

[61] Moore, "Construction of Community," 110–11.

paid, putting-out sweatshop sector moved after a period to employment in large-scale factory shops. Associated with clothing production as a by-product was a burgeoning clothing retail sector, linked by a process of vertical integration with manufacturing. In clothing, including the cap and millinery trades; in other sectors of the economy where Jews concentrated, notably in specific areas of the food industry such as baking and meat production where the laws of kosher food made it necessary to employ Jews at all levels; and in the building trades, in metal and machinery, and in cigar and cigarette making, the vast majority of jobs were provided by Jewish entrepreneurs. "Thus, employment of Jewish immigrants," Kahan notes, "depended upon the relative success of Jewish entrepreneurship in the clothing and related industries. This symbiosis of Jewish employees and Jewish employers created a curious interdependence which was marked by low wages, very low search costs, and low barriers of entrance into entrepreneurial activity." The continuing supply of labor by new immigration kept wages down below those in other industries. Nevertheless, Jews did not leave the garment trades. So long as their relative wages did not fall, as they did not, "there was no marked exodus of Jewish immigrant workers from this industry." Indeed, within its embrace, a mobility ladder was established. "As long as the industry was absorbing new immigrants, with older cohorts moving from the home industry sector, from the sweatshops into the factories, into clerical positions, management, and entrepreneurship, there existed a special dynamic pattern of economic adjustment for this group, the largest single occupational group in the Jewish immigration."[62] Thus, the economic concentration and isolation of the eastern European Jews interlaced their spatial separation, as most of the clothing industry was located at or very near their places of residence, a pattern that grew increasingly atypical during the period of the second industrial revolution.[63]

Within ten to fifteen years of their arrival, each cohort of Jewish immigrants caught up with the earnings of native American workers within similar occupations, a feat that quickly put them at the top of immigrant economic performance. Most of the children of garment workers found

[62] Kahan, "Economic Opportunities," in *Essays in Jewish Social and Economic History*, 105–6. A fine overview history is provided in Jan Lin, "The Social Geography of Garment Production in Lower Manhattan," Working Paper Series, Research about Lower Manhattan (New York: New School for Social Research, March 1989). Bernheimer's 1905 overview also took note of the economic enclosure of the Jewish community: "Almost every newly arrived Russian Jewish laborer comes into contact with a Russian Jewish employer, almost every Jewish tenement dweller must pay his exorbitant rent to a Russian Jewish landlord. . . . It is extremely probable that at present the majority of Russian Jewish workers work for Russian Jewish employers." Bernheimer, *Russian Jew in the United States*, 104.

[63] See Zunz, *Changing Face*, and Katznelson, *City Trenches*.

employment outside this launching-pad industry. And, after 1900, increasing numbers of Jews found work as professionals—doctors, dentists, lawyers, teachers, and rabbis—or as municipal civil service employees.[64]

Stanley Lieberson's account of the relative economic success of white immigrants as compared to native-born blacks provides important clues to this success story. He argues that ethnic group mobility niches, those concentrations in certain jobs that reflect either cultural characteristics, special skills initially held by some members, or the opportunity structure at the time of arrival provided advantageous jumping-off points into the larger economy. The stereotypes of the Irish cop, the Swedish carpenter, the Japanese truck farmer, and the Jewish tailor are rooted in empirical reality. The special niches occupied by blacks, he shows, were from the start both less desirable and more vulnerable.[65] The Jewish experience was further differentiated from that of the other white ethnics by virtue of the degree of their economic insularity, the availability of internal mobility ladders, the advantageous location of Jews in an industry that was rapidly growing for which they brought relevant skills, and the unusual overlap of segregated workplaces and homes. A great paradox was at work: the long initial stage of segmented economic incubation for Jews provided them with the most successful platform of any group of immigrants for achievement within the larger American economy.

Their insertion into the economic mainstream remained highly partial and segmented well after the cessation of new immigration. Indeed, as Nathan Glazer observed in his retrospective look in the 1950s on the attainment of middle-class rank by the majority of Jews, and with it the erosion of the boundary that earlier had distinguished the attainments of German and East European Jews, this shift entailed a *reconcentration* of Jews in specifically urban economic niches: in the legal and medical professions (whose numbers were held down until well after the Second World War by discrimination—Jews composed half the applicants to medical schools in 1935, but only 17 percent of the entering class), and in such other intellectual professions as engineering, journalism, and teaching at all levels (where, too, segmentation could be found, with a much higher proportion of Jews with advanced degrees teaching in secondary

[64] "The skills embodied in the labor force, the further investments in their human capital, and their consumption and savings patterns enabled the wage-earners among them to reach, within an approximate fifteen year period after arrival in this country, an income level and life-style equal to that of the native-born wage earners." Arcadius Kahan, "Jewish Life in the United States: Perspectives from Economics," in *Essays in Jewish Social and Economic History,* 129.

[65] Stanley Lieberson, *A Piece of the Pie: Black and White Immigrants since 1800* (Berkeley: University of California Press, 1981).

than in higher education). With the lowering of barriers to government employment during the mobilization of the First World War, with new opportunities created during the war for self-employment and entrepreneurship by the liberal extension of credit, and, later, as a result of the new professional opportunities created by the New Deal bureaucracies and the decline in the opportunity costs of education during the Great Depression, Jews began to cast their proletarian status aside. By the end of the 1930s, only about half of first-generation Jews were still workers, and the majority of the second generation had at least secured positions as office workers, clerks, salesmen, and the like.[66]

These positions, as well as the places Jews obtained as owners and managers in business and commerce, continued to be distinguished by their nichelike qualities. Most Jewish economic activity was urban (only eighty thousand out of thirty million American farmers in the mid-1930s were Jewish) which was the reason, *Fortune* observed, why Jews seemed to be more important to the American economy than they in fact were. Indeed, what is so striking about the magazine's definitive account of the economic place of the Jews in America in the mid-1930s is the number of key areas from which Jews were absent:

> First of all and very definitely, they do not run banking. They play little or no role in the great commercial houses. Of the 420 listed directors of the nineteen members of the New York Clearing House in 1933 only thirty were Jews and about half of these were in the Commercial National Bank & Trust Co. and the Public National Bank and Trust. There were none in the Bank of New York & Trust Co., National City, Guaranty Trust, Central Hanover, Bankers Trust or New York Trust. Indeed, there are practically no Jewish employees of any kind in the largest commercial banks—and this in spite of the fact that many of their customers are Jews. In the investment field although there are of course Jewish houses, of which Kuhn, Loeb, & Co., Speyer & Co., J. & W. Seligman, and Co., Ladenburg, Thalman, & Co., and Lehman Bros. are the best known, they do not compare in power with the great houses owned by non-Jews.[67]

Likewise, Jews had a limited role on the stock exchanges and were nearly wholly absent from the large insurance companies. Their role in heavy industry was even less significant than in finance (which they were thought to control). With the exception of Inland, the steel industry was entirely non-Jewish, as was the case with automobiles. The managements of the great coal, rubber, and chemicals corporations likewise were almost en-

[66] Nathan Glazer, "The American Jew and the Attainment of Middle Class Rank: Some Trends and Explanations," in Marshall Sklare, ed., *The Jews: Social Patterns of an American Group* (Glencoe, Ill.: Free Press, 1958).

[67] "Jews in America," 130, 133.

tirely non-Jewish. Equally, with a handful of exceptions, there were no Jews of consequence in transportation. In all, "a vast continent of heavy industry and finance may therefore be staked out in which Jewish participation is incidental or nonexistent. To this may be annexed other important areas into which Jews have rarely penetrated such as light and power and telephone and telegraph and engineering in general and heavy machinery and lumber and dairy products. In brief, Jews are so far from controlling the most characteristic of present day activities that they are hardly represented in them at all."[68]

In the unusual instances where Jews controlled parts of heavy industry they were found in highly specific peripheral niches, such as scrap metal, a half-billion-dollar business in 1929 that was 90 percent Jewish owned, an outgrowth of the junk business that Jews had run in cities since the late nineteenth century, and in the waste-products industry that disposed of paper, cotton rag, wool rag, and rubber. Other areas of Jewish industrial concentration were kosher meat packing, upholstered furniture, tobacco manufacturing, and, above all, the clothing business, over 90 percent of which remained in Jewish hands in the 1930s. These sectors, of course, were precisely the niches entered by Jewish proletarians a half century earlier, and they were characterized by their location at the intersection of manufacturing and merchandising. There was a substantial presence of German Jews in the ownership of large department stores, and Jews dominated the apparel trade. By this period, Jews had also begun to establish publishing houses (such as Knopf, Simon and Schuster, Random House, and Viking, which did not yet rival the non-Jewish houses); they dominated the new media of radio and movies; and they had taken on a growing share of the theater, located as it was in New York. In each of these instances, the training ground and model for Jewish activity was the Yiddish theater and Jewish entertainment zones of the big cities, especially New York.

The distinctive profile of Jews within the higher reaches of American capitalism was the product of three main factors, whose relative significance is not easy to ascertain. These are exclusionary discrimination, the extension of the economic niches, particularly in the needle trades that Jews had fashioned and occupied for some time, and their urban location.

New York, distinctive in so many ways from other world cities such as Paris, Rome, London, and Tokyo, is unique in the extent to which its population has been so different from that of the rest of the country. As a result of the patterns of settlement of the Jewish immigrants and their concentration in residential as well as occupational niches, New York has

[68] Ibid., 133. The subsequent discussion is mainly drawn from this source.

been the only significantly Jewish city in the country; its Jewish population since 1915 has never fallen below one in five. In the popular imagination, New York has been thought of as a Jewish city. It is impossible to conceive of the special role of Jews in such areas as the clothing business, entertainment, and the more avant-garde areas of publishing without taking the specific concentration of New York's Jews into account. Jews on the Lower East Side, and later in concentrated sections primarily in Manhattan, Brooklyn, and the Bronx, utilized their propinquity and networks to fashion opportunities otherwise not available to them.[69]

At the elite levels, the other main loci of Jewish employment were in law and medicine, where barriers to Jewish penetration of the American mainstream were felt acutely. Much as Jews had dealt with exclusion from industry and commerce by establishing parallel institutions as in the Jewish publishing houses or by dominating the sectors that grew most organically from the main centers of Jewish working class employment, so too in these fields Jews created separate entry points for themselves. In New York, where one-third of the population was Jewish, so too were one-third of the city's doctors and lawyers, but this in spite of the much higher levels of educational attainment of the period's Jews. Between 1900 and 1909, the same proportion of Jews as non-Jews in the relevant age cohort attended college, 17 percent. Thereafter, there was a widening gap. In the teens, 29 percent of Jews attended, compared to 18 percent of non-Jews; in the twenties the proportions were 42 and 18 percent, respectively; and in the 1930s, 47 and 23 percent.[70] Moreover, these numbers were artificially compressed for the Jews by virtue of self-conscious quotas on admission of Jews to elite universities at the undergraduate and professional school levels. Only because of availability of state-funded alternatives were Jews able to secure this share of higher education.[71]

Throughout the period, the legal profession remained segmented, with

[69] This discussion is informed by Nathan Glazer, "The National Influence of Jewish New York," in Martin Shefter, ed., *Capital of the American Century: The National and International Influence of New York City* (New York: Russell Sage Foundation, 1993).

[70] Andrew Greely, *Ethnicity, Discrimination, and Inequality* (Beverly Hills, Calif.: Sage Publications, 1976), 32.

[71] The story of Jewish quotas is very well told in Oliver P. Pollak, "Anti-Semitism, the Harvard Plan, and the Roots of Reverse Discrimination," *Jewish Social Studies* 45 (Spring 1983); Dan Oren, *Joining the Club: A History of Jews and Yale* (New Haven: Yale University Press, 1985); Harold Wechsler, *The Qualified Student: A History of Selective College Admissions in America* (New York: John Wiley and Sons, 1977); Jerome Karabel, "Status-Group Struggle, Organizational Interests, and the Limits of Institutional Autonomy: The Transformation of Harvard, Yale, and Princeton, 1918–40," *Theory and Society* 13, no. 1 (1984); and Sherry Gorelick, *City College and the Jewish Poor: Education in New York, 1880–1924* (New Brunswick, N.J.: Rutgers University Press, 1981). Also see Leonard Dinnerstein, "Education and the Advancement of American Jews," in Dinnerstein, *Uneasy at Home.*

Jews coping with exclusion from the leading firms by founding their own. The most prestigious and lucrative corporate law practices excluded Jews; the non-Jewish firms almost without exception had no Jewish partners in the mid-1930s even though they had many Jewish clients. Jewish specialities, by contrast, were found in bankruptcy proceedings, real estate law, and litigation of all kinds. Likewise in medicine, Jews were far more likely to be found in general practice than in leading hospital positions, with the exceptions of the hospitals run by Jewish philanthropic organizations.

Most Jews remained in the working class during the time assayed in this volume. They were likely to be employed by other Jews, and they remained heavily rooted in the garment trades. Excluded from many of the crafts organized by the American Federation of Labor (AFL), and not found in the heavy industries organized by the Congress of Industrial Organizations (CIO) in the 1930s, it is not surprising that the main efforts of Jews to organize as labor was in the clothing industry. As in the other arenas of the economy, in this regard too they crafted a special niche.

I do not wish here to recapitulate the familiar history of the organization of Jews in this industry, except to stress that Jewish labor relations were far more intracommunal in the character of their class struggle than exemplary of the wider labor movement (this in spite of the fact that Samuel Gompers, the leader of the AFL, was an English Jew, an aspect of his life that found little resonance in his politics or personal identification). Jewish labor was bound up tightly with various left-wing movements led by a politicized intelligentsia that did not choose between its Jewish and socialist identities. In this way it connected up to movement and electoral politics of a highly unusual kind. Near the end of our period these impulses transmuted into support for the New Deal and in this way joined the American mainstream, but the roots of this political liberalism were distinctive to the Jewish community, and the character of this liberalism with a socialist heritage has proved more durable than the more situational liberalism of Catholic ethnic groups. Moreover, by the end of the New Deal Jewish liberalism proved to have something of an inverse relationship to the prototypical American pattern in which the working class organized as labor at the workplace but as ethnics off work. Jews, whose proletarian status lasted in most cases but one generation, produced a unionism that was unusually intertwined with their place of residence and with their local, frequently socialist politics. With the decline of the socialist alternative to the New Deal, Catholic ethnics built powerful, labor conscious CIO unions and connected to the Democratic Party, off work, mainly through the instrumentalities of Irish-dominated political machines. Again by contrast, the Jews played only a minor role in the

CIO (mainly as labor organizers, often as Communist cadres) and developed a relatively distant and agnostic relationship with the political machines. Instead, their commitments were more to the ideological and normative aspects of the New Deal.

Although most Jews on the Lower East Side and in comparable places of settlement voted principally for the Democratic party, their relationship to the Irish-dominated party machines was not characterized by much rapport. What is most striking about the place of Jews in early twentieth-century electoral politics at the municipal level—and it was this level in the federal system that was critical to the patterning of political participation by new immigrants, since only at the local level was mass participation organized in the absence of a strong state or national party system—is how half-hearted it was; this realm belonged to the "other." Jews never secured the political representation that their numbers seemed to entail. Turnout was low, as Jews shunned regular municipal politics in larger numbers than other groups. There was no district in the city with a lower voter turnout than the overwhelmingly Jewish Eighth Assembly District in 1912. In New York City as a whole, just six of the thirty-six district leaders of the Democratic party were Jews in 1923 (and not until 1973 was a Jew elected Mayor). To be sure, some important offices were filled by Jews; in 1901, Jacob Cantor was elected borough president of Manhattan and Aaron Levy became the Democratic leader in the State Assembly. But the dominant pattern was one of relative disinterest and abstention, the product for the eastern Europeans, as compared to the Germans, of an utter lack of experience with parliamentary institutions as well as the absence of a common discourse and political culture with the Irish leadership of Tammany Hall.

The emergence of dense concentrations of Jews with the capacity to elect Jewish candidates was a source of concern to German Jews, who feared the public display of the overt and overwhelming Jewishness of their eastern European brethren. The influential New York lawyer Louis Marshall, an "uptown" communal leader, for example, reacted with horror to the idea of the formation of Jewish clubs in support of the candidacy of President Taft in 1912: "While I am strongly in favor of the renomination and re-election of President Taft, I am utterly opposed to any plan whereby the Jewish people shall segregate themselves from the remainder of the citizens of this country for political reasons. We have no political interests which are different from those of our fellow-citizens. We would subject ourselves to just criticism if we organized political clubs on our own."[72]

Caught between the indifference of the eastern Europeans and the hos-

[72] Cited in Baron, *Steeled by Adversity,* 317–18.

tility to Jewish self-identification in politics of the Germans, Jewish politicians were unable to routinely mobilize sufficient support to make them leading political players in the federal system. In fact, the most successful Jewish politicians were elected to high office from regions without substantial Jewish populations. Between 1879 and 1912, three Jews from Louisiana, Maryland, and Oregon served for single terms in the United States Senate. Idaho, Utah, and the Washington territory had Jewish governors in the first two decades of the twentieth century. In 1920, eleven Jews were elected to the House of Representatives. With the exception of one Socialist from New York and two urban Democrats, from Chicago and New York, all the others were Republicans from mainly non-Jewish districts. The promise of Enlightenment liberality was redeemed most fully on an individual basis in areas where Jews as a collectivity largely were invisible. In the executive branch of the federal government, the highest appointive Jewish official was Secretary of Commerce Oscar Straus (the first president of the American Jewish Historical Society) in the cabinet of Theodore Roosevelt (1906–9). Most dramatic of all, of course, were the appointments of two Jewish justices of the Supreme Court, Louis Brandeis and Felix Frankfurter.[73]

The political situation of Jewish socialists (virtually the only socialists of consequence in the United States) was quite different. Deeply embedded within the immigrant Jewish community, the socialists contended to become the dominant political voice within the eastern European Jewish community, especially in areas of first settlement. In this they had a good deal of success. Their story begins with the garment unions.

In the needle trades, eastern European Jewish employees squared off against both German and eastern European Jewish employers. At first, as John Commons argued in his 1901 testimony to the U.S. Industrial Commission, Jewish workers in the garment industry, with little by way of a trade union tradition to guide them, were prepared to use the strike

[73] For a provocative consideration of these two figures, see Robert A. Burt, *Two Jewish Justices: Outcasts in the Promised Land* (Berkeley: University of California Press, 1988). Burt treats Frankfurter and Brandeis as emblematic of the choices elite Jews had to make. Each found a distinctive path to a partial integration into the top levels of American politics and society; each felt a continuing partial homelessness. Brandeis is treated as a figure at the margins of capital and labor; Frankfurter as a person at the "racial margin."

Jews also entered the state through access to the military. During the Spanish American War, the five thousand Jews who enlisted did so at a rate disproportionately high for their population, especially when it is considered that virtually all were German Jews. There was a handful of West Point officers and more than a hundred noncommissioned officers. Fifteen Jews went down with the *Maine.* One hero of the war, Edward Taussig, achieved the rank of Rear Admiral in 1909; Joseph Strauss achieved that rank during the First World War. He later became commander-in-chief of the Asian fleet in 1921. See Baron, *Steeled by Adversity,* 319.

weapon but not to form durable unions. In the terms of E. P. Thompson, they rebelled within the framework of the moral economy of the Jewish community rather than within the framework of a transcommunal class struggle. This pattern, Commons averred, contrasted with the way German workers had oriented themselves to their unions. "If, perchance, a local branch has a steady thousand members from year to year, and they are indeed paying members, it is likely that they are not the same members as during the year before. A German union, on the contrary, will have the same members year after year, well or ill, with little change. The Jew joins the union when it offers a bargain and drops it when he gets, or fails to get, the bargain."[74]

With the arrival of immigrants with organizing experience in the *Bund* in the late 1890s, there was an acceleration of class rhetoric, union persistence, and militant activity. The United Hebrew Trades, a federation of Jewish unions that had suffered from left-wing factional socialist disputes in the 1890s, achieved some degree of durability and effectiveness in the first decade of the twentieth century. By 1910, it embraced eighty-nine unions with some 100,000 members. During the First World War its member unions grew to a total of 250,000. In this heyday, the UHT was deeply entwined with the radical, nationalist, nonreligious, anti-Zionist, Yiddishist strands of the Jewish community.[75]

However distinctive from the local Jewish bourgeoisie, this organized working class was prepared to have its conflicts with the bosses mediated by and within a Jewish communal framework. The most significant instance occurred during the strike wave of 1909–10, when the stoppage of work by some twenty thousand members of the International Ladies Garment Workers Union (which had been founded in 1900) was followed by the strike of some sixty thousand cloakmakers who later affiliated with the Amalgamated Clothing Workers of America. These strikes were settled under the auspices of the organized Jewish community by the mediation of Louis Brandeis. The "Protocol of Peace" of July 1910 that he negotiated was notable for its establishment of an intracommunal Board of Arbitration, a Board of Grievance, and a Joint Board of Sanitary Control to provide a framework for the prevention of future labor strife. Further, this agreement initiated and regulated an industry-specific mini-welfare state, administered within the confines of Jewish employer-employee relations.[76]

[74] Cited in Selig Perlman, "Jewish-American Unionism, Its Birth Pangs and Contribution to the General American Labor Movement," in Karp, *Jewish Experience in America,* 5:215.

[75] Handlin, *Adventure in Freedom,* 136.

[76] See the discussion in Baron, *Steeled by Adversity,* 302–3. Selig Perlman saw the results of this conflict to have provided an important learning experience for the later CIO labor movement and for the New Deal. I am skeptical.

The Jewish labor movement was tied by people and by ideology to the various socialist currents in the community. Unlike the situation that prevailed in most immigrant areas, where the spatial separation of work and home reinforced a pattern of class formation that divided the labor impulse at work from the ethnic impulse off work, in the Jewish city neighborhoods the close intertwining of work and home, the intracommunal character of industrial relations, and the existence of first-generation immigrants with substantial socialist experience promoted an unusually robust socialist politics spanning work and home. Indeed, it is no exaggeration to say that with the principal exception of German socialism in Milwaukee, American socialism and the socialism of the Lower East Side were synonymous. Jewish electoral socialism was the core of the national movement; or, more to the point, Jewish socialism was exemplary of a niche politics that found little resonance outside its bounds.

The heart of the Lower East Side fell within the Ninth Congressional District. The Socialist candidate, Morris Hillquit, a union organizer, secured 21 percent of the vote in 1904, 26 percent in 1906, and just 21 percent again in 1908; in each case he ran ahead of the Republican alternative to the Tammany Hall congressman, Henry Goldfogle. By the end of the decade, a new wave of Jewish immigrant voters influenced by the rise of socialism in their home countries augmented the vote potential of Socialist candidates. The Socialist vote grew to 31 percent in 1910 and 1912. In 1914, Meyer London, the party's candidate, was elected to the first of three terms in the House of Representatives by securing 48 percent of the vote in a three-candidate race.[77] The next year a Socialist state assemblyman was elected from the area. The organizational basis for these electoral efforts was provided by the garment unions, which, for all practical purposes, were synonymous with the Socialist party. The combination of the demise of the short-lived Progressive party and, more important, the rise of coherent, durable garment unions provided the Socialists with the chance to become both the party of reform against the predations of machine politics, which were associated mainly with Irish patronage and corruption in which Jews shared only on the margins, and the organic representative of the Jewish proletariat as a whole at work and off work. The culmination of Socialist strength came in 1917 when the party's candidate secured an absolute majority in the Lower East Side. That year, the Socialists elected ten assemblymen, seven city councilmen, and one municipal court judge. Never able to build support among the Catholic immigrants, however, the Socialist party fell victim to internal factionalization (including the founding of a Communist

[77] There is a descriptive account in Arthur Goren, "A Portrait of Ethnic Politics: The Socialists and the 1908 and 1910 Congressional Elections on the East Side," in Karp, *The Jewish Experience in America*, vol. 5.

party after the Bolshevik Revolution), to occupational and neighborhood mobility as many of its supporters moved away, and to a concerted attempt by Tammany to give more recognition and patronage to the Jews. By 1922, Democrats were securing well over 60 percent of Jewish votes on the Lower East Side, as they inherited political support from the Socialists.[78] Later, the New Deal built on this record. It decisively preempted the political space of the Socialists and fused a broad coalition of ethnic voters for the Democratic party.[79] As Martin Shefter has observed, the Democratic machine worked successfully to extrude left-wing challenges. To the extent Jews entered fully into this electoral coalition, the organizational underpinnings as well as the organic links of the Jewish community to radicalism were undercut.[80]

The experience of the eastern European socialists in America contrasts rather starkly with the role Jews played as Social Democrats in Germany. There, socialism represented one path to assimilation and to the achievement of a universal role. In the United States, by contrast, Jewish socialism was a substitute for assimilation, just as it provided an alternative to Orthodox Judaism. "It was the choice of the Jewish poor," Bauman observes, "who had every reason to consider their plight the result of class as well as national oppression. The exploiters, whom they all knew directly and who caused them the most suffering, were all Jews. They inscribed their grievances and their hopes alike within the framework of the Jewish community." Socialism, from this perspective, was the effect of emancipation on the lower reaches of the class structure. The larger host society seemed too remote and too inaccessible. Jewish socialism, as compared to universal socialism, did not promise such access. "On the contrary, it was bent on redeeming the Jewish tradition by liberating it from dominant class enemies."[81] Drawing on Sorin's research, which shows just how devoted to their Jewish roots America's Jewish socialists

[78] A carefully crafted electoral analysis is provided by Thomas M. Henderson, "Tammany Hall and the New Immigrants" (Ph.D. diss., Catholic University, 1976).

[79] See Melvyn Dubofsky, "Success and Failure of Socialism in New York City, 1900–1918: A Case Study," *Labor History* 9 (Fall 1968); and Zosza Szajkowski, "The Jews and New York City's Mayoralty Election of 1917," *Jewish Social Studies* 32 (October 1970). On the ethnic politics of the New Deal, see Joseph A. Pike, "Interest Groups and the White House under Roosevelt and Truman," *Political Science Quarterly* 102 (Winter 1987–88).

[80] Martin Shefter, "Political Incorporation and Political Extrusion: Party Politics and Social Forces in Postwar New York," in Shefter, *Political Parties and the State: The American Historical Experience* (Princeton: Princeton University Press, 1994). Also see Deborah Dash Moore, "The Rise of the Jewish Democrat" in Moore, *At Home in America,* chap. 8.

[81] Bauman, "Exit Visas," 72–75; Gerald Sorin, *The Prophetic Minority: American Jewish Immigrant Radicals, 1880–1920* (Bloomington: Indiana University Press, 1985). Sorin's meticulous and very interesting work is based on 170 case histories. For a treatment of the relationship of American Jews to Communism, see Paul Buhle, "Jews and American Communism," *Radical History Review* 23 (Spring 1980).

were, Bauman stresses that Jewish socialists were authentically Jewish, seeing no contradiction between their socialist values and their Jewishness. In Germany, Jews had joined the socialist movement; in the United States, they were the movement.[82]

Uncertain Margins

The First World War followed the high point of Jewish immigration, population growth, and urban concentration, as well as occupational and political distinctiveness. During the war, when American Jews numbered just over three million, or some 3 percent of the population, they also composed 3 percent of the armed forces. Of the nearly ten thousand commissioned Jewish officers, 101 attained the rank of lieutenant colonel or higher, including Marine Brigadier General Charles Laucheimer and Rear Admiral Joseph Strauss, who commanded the laying of mines in the North Sea.[83] This entry into institutionalized patriotism appeared to signal that Jews, however distinctive, at last were at home in America.

For Deborah Dash Moore, it is just this appellation that best describes the circumstances of the second generation eastern European New York Jews in the period following the war. They moved to salubrious neighborhoods in Brooklyn and the Bronx, gained access to middle-class occupations, successfully inserted their children within high-quality public schools, and developed new networks of secondary associations, including "Center" synagogues that served social and educational functions, and a citywide coordination of Jewish social services. By the Second World War, these Jews had virtually caught up with their German forebears, so much so that the old distinctions between the two sets of Jews had lost most of their practical force to become rather matters of sentiment. This is the story that can be told confidently in the terms chosen by Lucy Dawidowicz, of Jews in America coming of age "On Equal Terms."[84]

[82] In the politics of the main centers of Jewish settlement—New York, Boston, Philadelphia, and Chicago—and in state and national elections, most Jews voted not for Socialists, but for Republicans and Democrats. "Of these," Lawrence Fuchs writes, "more probably chose Republican than Democratic candidates in every Presidential election from 1900 to 1928 with the exception of 1916." Republican pluralities before the New Deal realignment, he argues, were the results of three factors: the tilt toward the Republican party by long-settled German Jews, immigrant gratitude to the administration in power, and animosity between Jews and the Irish at the local level. See Lawrence H. Fuchs, *The Political Behavior of American Jews* (Glencoe, Ill.: Free Press, 1956). The subject of Jewish political behavior remains vastly understudied.

[83] For military participation rates, I draw on Gumpertz, *Jewish Legion of Valor*, 189–90.

[84] Moore, *At Home in America;* Lucy S. Dawidowicz, *On Equal Terms: Jews in America, 1881–1981* (New York: Holt, Rinehart, Winston, 1982).

But equal terms with uncertain margins: some inherent in the deepest roots of the Enlightenment, some the product of particularities and exclusions spawned under the banner of universality, some the result of the marriage of an open economy and polity with social and economic anti-Semitism. Even as they became more American, American Jews became more Jewish; even as they achieved mobility, they remained partially segregated in their places of residence, types of work, and social bonds. Even after leaving their neighborhoods of first settlement, they recreated tight ties between their residential location and ethnic dispositions. New York's Lower East Side, Chicago's West Side, and Philadelphia's South Side now became reference points for the identity of those who had moved on, both in memory and as places to visit and to shop. But even as Jews dispersed, they constructed modern neighborhoods in the concentrated style of the old, with living space near synagogues, ethnic shopping, and a dense array of communal institutions. What was different in these neighborhoods was their distance from places of work. Nonetheless, the residential areas as well as the continuing occupational concentration of mobile Jews persisted as "city niches" from which they could relate to an uncertain and unpredictable wider society. In the period between the two world wars, Jewish ethnicity did transmute into something more cultural and symbolic, the basis of an interest group politics. But it also remained spatially and institutionally specific, guarded about politics, concerned about potential assaults, even afraid that under some conditions the special gift of the American experience would be withdrawn. If, no doubt, America was different, it also was precariously so. Jews sought to preserve their distinctiveness not only as an end in itself but as a strategic resource capable of forwarding their engagement with America on terms as favorable and as secure as possible. Writing in 1934, one of the country's leading rabbis observed that American Jews had left one world in which they could no longer live only to go to another they could not fully enter: "Only a people of acrobats could preserve a semblence of poise on a footing so unstable." It was not Father Coughlin but *The Christian Century*, the leading organ of liberal Protestantism, that asked in 1937, "Can democracy suffer a hereditary minority to perpetuate itself as a permanent minority, with its own distinctive culture, sanctioned by its own distinctive cult form?" It was not just Hitler's rise to power that confirmed for Jews the cherished qualities of their American home, while reminding them how much they remained strangers at home, at the margins of American liberalism.[85]

[85] Milton Steinberg, "First Principles for American Jews," *Contemporary Jewish Record* (December 1941); "Jewry and Democracy," *The Christian Century*, 9 June 1937, 734–35. Both are cited in Arnold M. Eisen, *The Chosen People in America* (Bloomington: Indiana University Press, 1983).

SEVEN

THE EMANCIPATION OF JEWS IN ITALY

Dan V. Segre

FOR MANY JEWS and non-Jews, the history, indeed the very existence of Italian Jewry, has been discovered in this century. Contributing to this discovery, especially on the other side of the Atlantic, were the writings of Primo Levi, H. Stuart Hughes, Susan Zuccotti, Giorgio Bassani, and Italo Svevo, the "Proust" of Trieste, whose work had to wait half a century before achieving worldwide recognition.[1]

To the new popularity of this literary contribution one must add other factors of notoriety, such as the growing Italian involvement in Mediterranean politics; the growth of a vociferous, even if probably a superficial current of anti-Semitism in a country believed immune from it; the spectacular visit by Pope John Paul II to the Great Synagogue of Rome; and, last but not least, the inclusion in fashionable tourism of Jewish historical sites that has revealed unique and unknown treasures of art to European and American visitors.

Such a boom of interest in Italian Jewry raises, or rather raises again, old questions concerning the evolution of this little community, especially from the time of Napoleon's first invasion of the peninsula in 1798 to the almost total destruction of Italian Jewry by Nazism and Fascism during the Second World War.

The question this article tries to answer concerns the uniqueness of this very ancient Jewish tribe, and whether its emancipation has followed a different course from that of other Jewish communities in Europe. To search for the answer means to ask many additional questions: for example, why has their number—between thirty-five and forty thousand—remained unchanged in spite of the great migratory movements that took place in Europe during the last century? To what degree and in what

[1] Primo Levi, *If This Is a Man* (New York, 1959); idem, *The Reawakening* (New York, 1965); idem, *The Periodic Table* (New York, 1984); idem, *The Drowned and the Saved* (New York, 1988); H. Stuart Hughes, *Prisoners of Hope: The Silver Age of the Italian Jews, 1924–1974* (Cambridge, Mass., 1982); Susan Zuccotti, *The Italians and the Holocaust: Persecution, Rescue, Survival* (New York, 1987); Giorgio Bassani, *Il Giardino dei Finzi-Contini* (Milan, 1965); Italo Svevo, *A Man Grows Older* (London, 1983); and idem, *A Colquhon* (London, 1991).

period is it legitimate to speak of the transformation of the Jews of Italy into Italians of the Jewish faith? Why has their political and economic role in the making of a unified Italy been so great? Why have they reacted in such a singular way to the great internal conflicts of modern Judaism—orthodoxy and reform, tradition and assimilation, Italian nationalism and Zionism? To what extent has their Italian identity influenced the Jewish identity of larger Jewish communities of the Mediterranean, from Tunis to Rhodes, from Libya to Greece, not to mention the prominent role of Italian Jews in the development of Italian colonialism and Fascism?

These last questions go beyond the specific theme of this article—the emancipation of Jews in Italy. They must, however, be raised because of the growing interest they elicit among contemporary Jewish and non-Jewish historians.[2]

The accepted view, popular among the Italian Jews to this day, but also shared by people such as Chaim Weizmann, the first president of Israel, and Antonio Gramsci, the Marxist thinker and founder of the Italian Communist party, is that the emancipation of the Italian Jews followed an unusual course. Weizmann, in his Memoirs, defines Italian Jewry as a community made of "sujets d'élite." It had for him "the fascination of mystery" insofar as "none of the motivations which justify the development of Zionism in other countries apply to the Italian case," so different from that of "those people of the Mosaic persuasion" whom Weizmann was accustomed to meeting in France and Germany. What baffled him was the fact that the Italian Jews were at one and the same time completely assimilated and so proud of their Judaism.[3]

Such particularism was due to a mixture of Jewish pride and Italian loftiness that ceased to manifest itself through an attachment to biblical tradition and to Hebrew culture, which had been flourishing in Italy for centuries.[4] To quote Eugenio Artom, a prominent cultural and political

[2] Renzo de Felice, *Gli Ebrei nella Libia contemporanea tra colonialismo, nazionalismo arabo e sionismo (1935–1970)* (Bologna, 1978). Also idem, *Il fascismo e l'oriente, Arabi, Ebrei e Indiani nella politica di Mussolini* (Bologna, 1988), esp. part 2, 125–86; idem, "Arabi e medio oriente nella strategia politica di guerra di Mussolini, 1940–43," in Renzo de Felice, ed., *Storia Contemporanea* 17, no. 6 (December 1986): 1255–1359; Simonetta della Seta, "Gli Ebrei del Mediterraneo nella strategia politica fascista sino al 1938: Il caso di Rodi," in Renzo de Felice, ed., *Storia Contemporanea* 17, no. 6 (December 1986): 997–1032; Attilio Milano, *Storia degli Ebrei italiani nel' Levante* (Florence, 1949); and Sergio Minerbi, *Angelo Levi Bianchini e la sua opera nel Levante, 1918–1920* (Milan, 1967), extracted from *Rivista di Studi Politici Internazionali* (Florence) 34, no. 1 (January-March 1967).

[3] Chaim Weizmann, *Trial and Error* (London, 1954), 286.

[4] Attilio Milano, *Storia degli Ebrei in Italia* (Turin, 1953); Arnaldo Momigliano, "Jews of Italy," *New York Review of Books* (October 1985); and L. Allegra, "La comunitá di Torino attraverso gli archivi di famiglia," in *Ebrei a Torino: Ricerche per il centenario della sinagoga 1884–1984* (Turin, 1984), 31–36.

Jewish personality in Italy, the Italian Jews were "a conglomeration of people characterized at least up to the First World War, by a certain nobility."[5] As for Gramsci, we shall see later why he thought the Italian Jews had become different from their coreligionists in Europe.

A quite different view is held by Andrew Canepa, an American scholar who dwelt extensively on the subject of Jewish emancipation in Italy. His claim is that there is nothing special in the Italian Jewish emancipatory experience. For him, the apparent singularity of the case is due to the fact that the Italian Jews were few, less concentrated than in large communities elsewhere in Europe; that anti-Semitism always existed in Italy but took a less apparent form because of the liberal lay regime of the Piedmontese state that conquered the rest of the peninsula.[6]

My contention is that all these claims do not pay sufficient attention to the different stages of Jewish emancipation in Italy that changed dramatically from the eighteenth to the twentieth century. Generally speaking, it is true that the emancipation of the Italian Jews has been in many respects similar to that of Jews elsewhere in Europe: economic development, rapid assimilation to the Gentile society, renunciation of Jewish tradition through conversion and mixed marriages, adhesion to liberal and Marxist movements. Yet it is equally true—and this is the point this article tries to make—that in the period between 1830 and 1870, corresponding with that of the Risorgimento (the Italian national revival), the emancipation process assumed political, psychological, economic, and cultural characteristics unique in the contemporary history of European Jewry. As a result, the Italian Jewish community, despite its small size, developed a group consciousness, a feeling of security and an (incorrect) image of itself that later had important consequences. It prevented, for instance, the Italian Jews from realizing the seriousness of Fascist anti-Semitism but it allowed them to react to it with surprising ideological and military vigor through Zionism and armed resistance to the German occupation.

If Artom's claim, that the Jewish case in Italy "goes beyond the frontiers of Italian and Jewish historiography and represents a world experience," seems exaggerated, it certainly expresses the (unfounded) feeling of elitism that at least three generations of Italian Jews felt because of the

[5] Eugenio Artom, "Per una Storia degli Ebrei nel Risorgimento," *Rassegna Storica Toscana* 24 (1978): 137–44.

[6] Andrew M. Canepa, "L'immagine dell'Ebreo nel folclore e nella letteratura del post-Risorgimento," *Rivista Mensile Israel* (hereafter *RMI*) nos. 5–6 (1978): 383–99; idem, "Emancipazione, integrazione e antisemitismo in Italia, Il Caso Pasqualino," *Communitá* (Milan) 29, no. 174 (June 1975): 165–203; and idem, "Cattollici ed Ebrei nell'Italia liberale (1870–1915)," *Comunitá* 32, no. 179 (April 1978).

share Italian Jewry took in the drastic changes brought about by the Risorgimento to the different societies of the Italian peninsula.

The Demographic and Historical Background

The Jewish presence in Italy is ancient and precedes the destruction of the Second Temple in Jerusalem by Titus in the year 70. Throughout many centuries, the Jewish communities concentrated themselves in the south of the peninsula, in Sicily and Sardinia. To this latter island, the Romans directed many thousands of Jewish war prisoners to work as slaves in agriculture and in the mines.

The prosperity of the Jewish communities in these areas, and especially in the south of Italy, must have been considerable if a paraphrase of Isaiah (2:3) and Micah (4:2) boasts that "from Bari shall come forth the Law and from Taranto the word of the Lord." The city of Oria was one of the celebrated centers of Jewish learning in the Middle Ages. Although we do not have precise data, the Jewish population in this period must have been considerable. An eighteenth-century historian puts the Jewish population of Sicily as high as 10 percent of the population, with fifty-seven organized communities.[7] In 1494 there were 150,000 Jews in southern Italy, dispersed among 161 localities. In the Papal States there were, according to the same source, 115 communities by 1564, a very high percentage of the population. A leading modern Italian demographer, Roberto Bachi, believes that after a period of decadence during the Middle Ages, the Jewish population in Italy reached its peak in the fifteenth century.[8]

The year 1492 represents—in southern Italy as well as in Spain—the end of the Golden Age of the Jewish communities. The edict of expulsion by Ferdinand and Isabella caused large-scale demographic movement among the Jews within the peninsula and outside, and affected a population that probably numbered not less than 150,000 people.[9] Furthermore, the expulsion of the Jews from the Spanish possessions coincided with a series of political and natural catastrophes that decimated the Jew-

[7] Giovanni di Giovanni, *L'Ebraismo in Sicilia* (Palermo, 1748), 21. The figure of 150,000 Jews reappears in subsequent statistical studies. In any case, taking into account the fact that the total population of the "Meridione" (the south) was much smaller at the time, the percentage of Jews must certainly have been high.

[8] Roberto Bachi, "La Demografia del Ebraismo Italiano prima del Emancipazione," *Essays in Honor of Dante Lattes* 16 (Tel Aviv, 1938): 257–320.

[9] Nicola Fedarelli, *Gli Ebrei nell'Italia meridionale al secolo XVIII,* edited by *Il Vessillo Israelitico* (Turin, 1915).

ish as well as the Italian population. In 1638 the Jews are believed to have been no more than twenty-five thousand, namely 2 percent of the total population. Their numbers grew to thirty-one thousand in 1770, to forty-eight thousand in 1918, including six thousand "permanent resident foreigners" but excluding some three thousand "transitory" foreign Jews. Bachi thus believes that the Jewish population of Italy during 160 years was never less than thirty thousand souls, and never more than fifty thousand.

The geographical distribution of this population was such that there were practically no Jews in southern Italy and the islands after the end of the fifteenth century. In the Papal States the Jews were grouped in three main locations: Rome, Ancona, and Ferrara. Some twenty-five thousand Jews lived in the Po Valley and in Tuscany. This geographical distribution was the result of the persecution to which the Jews were subjected in the sixteenth and seventeenth century. For instance, the Jews were expelled from Sicily in 1492 and in 1639; from Genoa in 1550 and 1737; from Naples in 1510, in 1541, and in 1702;[10] from Piedmont (which will be dealt with at greater length below) in 1452, 1454, 1560, and 1561, following expulsion orders that—at least in Piedmont—were usually never applied. In Rome, after the brief reign of Clement XIV (1769–74), Pius VI acceded to the papacy (1775–99); although as a cardinal he was considered by the Jews to be very friendly, as soon as he became pope he turned out to be one of the severest with regard to Jews. In the middle of the Enlightenment he prohibited Talmud study, burial processions, relations between Jews and their Christian neighbors, the opening of shops outside the ghetto area, the sale of meat, bread, and milk by Jews to non-Jews, the employment of Christian servants, and the overnight stay of Jews outside the ghetto. He also forced the Jews to wear a yellow sign and made rabbis personally responsible for the attendance of their community's members at conversion sessions.[11]

According to generally accepted estimates, since the middle of the nineteenth century the Jews in Italy have represented one-thousandth of the total population. One-third lived in thirty-eight communities in the areas of Mantua, Veneto, Emilia, and Romagna. On the west of the peninsula, in Piedmont, 16.7 percent of the Jews lived in nineteen small communities. In the east, in Venezia-Giulia, 9 percent lived in five communities, of which Trieste was the largest. Another 19.7 percent lived in Tuscany, with Leghorn as the main community. Finally, some three thousand Jews lived in Rome. Since a third of all these Jews lived in cities of over 100,000 inhabitants, and the rest in smaller centers, one can say that

[10] On the strange circumstances of the recalling of the Jews to Naples and their almost immediate reexpulsion, see Mario Stock, *RMI,* nos. 1–2 (1977): 32–35.

[11] Attilio Milano, *RMI,* no. 1 (1953): 118–25.

starting from the eighteenth century, the Jewish population of Italy was an urbanized population, residing in small towns or large villages; that it was not very mobile nor suffered serious persecution; that it exported a considerable number of its members all over the Mediterranean; that it remained outside the great migratory Jewish currents from eastern Europe toward western Europe and the Americas. This last fact is rather surprising considering that up to 1918 Trieste was an important port in the Austrian Empire and an embarkation point for tens of thousands of eastern European Jews. Some of the possible reasons why eastern European Jews did not enter Italy in spite of the existence of flourishing Jewish communities and relatively few legal obstacles, are the Italian language, which was as unfamiliar to the Ostjuden as Yiddish was to the Italian Jews; the late industrialization of Italy; the decadence of Jewish culture in Italy; and perhaps the strong anti-Italian propaganda within the Austro-Hungarian Empire.[12] On the other hand, for the Italian Jews, their long residence in small urban centers, the favorable climatic conditions, and the similitude of the dialects and cultures of the various Italian states did help to reinforce their peculiar character, as well as facilitate their movement from one state to another.

Economic Problems

The legal emancipation of Italian Jews was the result of the events of the Risorgimento, which in turn was politically and militarily led by the House of Savoy.

Following the fall of Napoleon, the House of Savoy regained possession of its kingdom and received the territory of the by-then defunct Republic of Genoa. This state, called the Kingdom of Sardinia, was geographically and economically divided into four areas. There was, first of all, the large island of Sardinia, backward and "beyond the sea," in which serfdom continued almost to the middle of the nineteenth century, and which politically and economically played little role in the Risorgimento. There were no Jews in Sardinia since their expulsion by the Spaniards in 1492. The second area was Savoy, the cradle of the monarchy but in fact cut off from Piedmont by the Alps, which did not permit much contact between the two, and eventually became French territory follow-

[12] Alfonso Pacifici, in his "Considerazioni sulle communitá separate, L'Unita' d'Israele e le communitá ebraiche d'Italia, Saggi sull'ebraismo italiano," *Essays in Memory of Sally Mayer (1875–1953)*, Sally Mayer Foundation (Jerusalem, 1956), 302–3, attributes to the growing divergence of standards of Jewish culture between Italian and eastern European Jews the fact that so few entered the peninsula during this period of great Jewish migration from the east.

ing a plebiscite in 1860. The Jewish presence in Savoy was minimal. Thirdly, there was Liguria, namely the territory of the former Republic of Genoa, which was also cut off from Piedmont by the Apennine Mountains, lower than the Alps but which constituted—given the means of communication of the time—a serious barrier. Because of these geographical, historical, and cultural differences, the Sardinian kingdom was, even in the agriculturally rich Piedmont region, an underdeveloped state. It did not have important commercial connections and suffered from aggressive economic competition from Lombardy, the nearby eastern region, more developed and better administered by the Austrians. Savoy, on the other side of the Alps, had more natural links with France than with Piedmont. Finally, the government of the House of Savoy lacked commercial maritime experience, which prevented it from making full use of Liguria.

This situation had a direct and indirect impact on the situation of the Jews in the kingdom. All the documents dealing with them at the end of the eighteenth century, whether favorable or not to their emancipation, show the obsession that the rulers, as well as simple people, had with "the immense riches amassed by them." There exist no records of such riches, which probably were far inferior to what people believed, yet there is no doubt that, as a group, the six thousand Jews of the kingdom were in a far better position than the rest of the population and, what is more important, possessed relatively large liquid capital. Whatever the real amount of this capital, it was regularly exploited by the Piedmontese king—as by other rulers of the Italian states—as a permanent source of income in exchange for individual or collective protection of Jews.

In Italy, the wealth of the Jews was unevenly distributed among the members of the community and among the communities themselves. In Turin, for instance, official documents dated 1832 classify 1,131 Jews as "poor" out of a total Jewish population of 1,368. In Rome, in 1860, half of the population was officially described as "poor." It is not, however, clear, what this "poverty" meant. Because of an efficient and established system of communal social assistance, the poor of the ghettos were certainly less poor than those outside. In Florence, for instance, in 1810, 31.7 percent of the Jewish population was officially listed as well-off against 11 percent of the non-Jewish population. In Leghorn, in 1841, Jews classified as "poor" represented only 10 percent of the community, while in Rome, where conditions in the ghetto were certainly worse than in the rest of Italy, 25 percent of the Jews were officially listed as "rich."

The ability of the Jewish communities to mobilize substantial capital in case of necessity can be seen in the documents concerning the war taxes imposed by the French, the Austro-Hungarians, and by the papal troops, who followed one another in their extortions of money from the small community of Ancona in the years 1797–99. The contribution of the 312

Jews of which the community was composed—out of which only 130 were taxable—was eight hundred scudi per head of family, equivalent to eighty thousand bajocci. At the time a kilo of bread cost six bajocci and a "new, three-story house overlooking the harbor" could be bought for five hundred scudi.[13]

Furthermore, communities had at their disposal considerable investment capital, both for the beautification of their synagogues (even in very small centers like Cherasco, in Piedmont, or Coneliano Veneto, not to speak of the splendid synagogues of Venice and Leghorn) as well as for collective financial operations. For instance, in 1664, the "Nazione ebraica" of Leghorn made an agreement with the government of the Grand Duke to put at the disposal of the Customs 100,000 ducats at 6 percent interest per year.[14]

The central argument of the most important book on the emancipation of the Italian Jews, Carlo Cattaneo's *Ricerche economiche sulle interdizioni imposte dalla legge civile agli Israeliti* is that the granting of civil rights to the Jews was necessary in order to put into circulation the "immense riches" accumulated by them, for their benefit and that of the state.[15] In any case, whatever the economic condition of Italian Jews may have been at the end of the eighteenth century, it is quite clear that they improved dramatically following the French occupation and the

[13] From the reports of the French prefects, one can draw a different impression. In 1801, in the District of the Po, which included 1,710 Jews, the prefect's report states that in Turin there "are no beggars or prostitutes" among the Jews. See Giorgina Levi, *L'Evoluzione Sociale Politica degli Ebrei in Piemonte dalla Rivoluzione Franceze alla Emancipazione, 1789–1848* (Ph.D. diss., University of Turin, 1932–34), 82. A similar situation existed also in other parts of Italy. At Ancona, a region less developed than Piedmont, out of 1,603 Jews listed in the 1807 census (among whom thirty-six foreign Jews were also included) the merchants were 250, the "industrialists" or employees in manufacturing 495, shop owners 178, porters 183, and the poor 451. This distinction was made for the purpose of fixing taxation, only the first two categories being liable to assessment. Giuseppe Lara, "Un Censimento degli Ebrei di Ancona dell'1807," *Rivista Italiana di Studi Napoleonici* (special issue on Italian Jews under Napoleon) (Pisa, 1980). Raoul Elia, "Contribuzione di guerra imposte agli Ebrei di Ancona dal 1797 al 1799," *Essays in Memory of Sally Mayer,* 82–88.

[14] Alfredo S. Toaff, "Cenni storici sulla Comunitá ebraica e sulla Sinagoga di Livorno," *RMI* 21, no. 9 (September 1955), 364.

[15] Carlo Cattaneo, *Ricerche economiche sulle interdizioni imposte dalla legge civile agli Israeliti* (Rome, 1932). Quite different is the opuscule published by the Marquis Massimo d'Azeglio, *Sulla emancipazione civile degli Israeliti* (Florence, 1848), to support the efforts of his brother Roberto in favor of the emancipation of the religious minorities in Piedmont. Massimo d'Azeglio, great patriot and future prime minister of Victor Emanuel II, attributes the accumulation of wealth by the Jews to the restrictions imposed on them by the regimes of the states in which they resided, but justifies the emancipation mainly as a moral and religious Christian duty. No less important were the efforts of Vincenzo Gioberti, philosopher, clergyman, and for a brief period also prime minister of Piedmont, who defended the granting of equal rights to all religious minorities in numerous publications, such as *Primato morale e civile degli Italiani* (Brussels, 1843), 1: 378–80; *Introduzione allo studio della Philosophia* (Brussels, 1844), 3:230–349.

granting of equal rights to Jews for fifteen years, even if this first emancipation was accompanied by heavy taxation for military purposes. Cattaneo, incidentally, only elaborated in a more scientific way the arguments of the functionaries of the Kingdom of Sardinia, upheld in their reports to the king, to show that a strict application of the severe post-Napoleonic restrictions imposed on the Jews were harmful to the economy.

In the light of these claims, it is important to try to evaluate the economic situation of the Jews in the period at the end of the eighteenth and the beginning of the nineteenth century.

The two most enlightening and scholarly studies on the economic role of the Jews in the Risorgimento are, strangely enough, ignored by the historians of that period.[16] They consist of the many historical monographs of Salvatore Foa, which, however, deal mainly with the pre-Risorgimento period,[17] and of Giorgina Levi.[18]

According to Foa, the Jews in the territories of the Duke of Savoy in Piedmont numbered no more than four hundred in the sixteenth century. Slightly fewer lived in the Marquisate of Monterrato and about one hundred in the Marquisate of Saluzzo, two fiefdoms that later on came under the control of the House of Savoy through marriage. At that time there were probably no more than one hundred Jews in Nice. After the Battle of Saint Quentin (1557), won by Duke Emanuel Filibert of Savoy on behalf of Emperor Charles V, the Jews, whose presence in Piedmont dated from the thirteenth century, were invited to immigrate into the duke's possessions in order to contribute to their economic development. This invitation (which, by the way, was accepted with enthusiasm by both my father's and my mother's families living in southern France) created a prolonged conflict between the duke and Emperor Philip II of Spain,[19] a conflict that also helped to institutionalize a formal relationship between the Jews and the House of Savoy that lasted, with various fluctuations, for the next three centuries.

[16] For example, the definitive biography of Cavour by Rosario Romeo, *Vita di Cavour* (Bari, 1984), ignores the Jewish financial contribution to the Risorgimento.

[17] The work of Salvatore Foa, a secondary school teacher, historian, and probably the last of the Jewish Orthodox "scholars" of Turin, is still, to a large extent, unpublished. It has a great value insofar as many of the archives on which he worked were destroyed during World War II. In particular, there is no trace of his notes to the article he prepared for the *Dizionario del'Risorgimento Italiano,* written in 1922–23 but published only in 1931, under the heading "Israeliti" (cols. 523–35). This article was republished by Carocci in 1978. With regard to important aspects of Jewish Piedmontese economy, see his articles in *Israel* 21 (1955), "Banchi e Banchieri Ebrei nel'Piemonte dei Secoli Scorsi."

[18] Giorgina Levi, "Sulle premesse social-economiche dell'emancipazione degli Ebrei nel Regno di Sardegna" (on the basis of documents dating from 1814–40), *RMI,* no. 10 (1952); and idem, "Gli Ebrei in Piemonte nell'ultimo decennio del secolo XVIII," *RMI,* nos. 10–12 (1952).

[19] Chaim Beinart, "Jewish Settlement in the Duchy of Savoy" (Hebrew), *Essays in Memory of Daniele Carpi,* Sally Mayer Foundation (Jerusalem, 1967), 72–118.

It consisted of a treaty called "Condotta," renewed every ten years by the duke, which allowed the Jews to open lending banks, to inhabit and carry out commercial operations in various areas of the state, and to enjoy the protection of the sovereign in exchange for the payment of rather high sums that were collected communally. In March 1574, they amounted to twenty thousand scudi, out of which four thousand were paid immediately and in cash.[20]

The importance of such agreements, which the Piedmontese administration always carefully registered, were used by the functionaries of the kingdom after the Restoration to prove how it was impossible, without causing serious damage to the state, to abolish the ancient prerogatives of the Jews that, they claimed, Napoleon had only enlarged.

From the point of view of the Jews, these ancient privileges and the Condotta system helped—up to the Emancipation—to maintain the authority of the rabbis over their congregations. In fact, it was the rabbis and the notables of each community who were responsible not only for the collection of contributions to the sovereign, but also for discipline within the ghettos, the education of Jewish children, the strict observance of religious tradition, and assistance to the poor.

The communities in the State of Sardinia, called "Universitá," thus became for centuries—as rightly pointed out by Giorgina Levi—strong corporations with direct access to the prince, of whom the Jews became "preferential subjects."[21]

Socially marginalized from the rest of the population and subjected, at various times, to more or less severe restrictions, the Jews often found themselves in a privileged situation compared with other subjects of the House of Savoy, and in any case better protected from the arbitrariness of the feudal lords. As a result, we find that in Piedmont a tradition of communal Jewish autonomy developed and with it, a strong feeling of collective responsibility and religious pride.

The arrival of French troops in Italy in 1797, the extension of civil rights to the Jews of the peninsula, the confiscation of ecclesiastical property and the possibility of the Jews purchasing them because of their liquid assets, access to public posts, and relatively high ranks in Napoleon's army—combined with their familial international relations and their higher level of education—permitted many among them to enrich themselves at an extraordinary speed and allowed the entire community to improve their lot. The point, therefore, that must be borne in mind when dealing with the emancipation of the Italian Jews, and more particularly with that of the Piedmontese Jews, is that in the course of fifteen years

[20] Foa, "Banchi e Banchieri," 96.

[21] Giorgina Levi, "Sulle premesse," 4ff.

they were propelled to the center of a tiny Piedmontese bourgeoisie that, like them, was interested in maintaining the freedoms it had begun to enjoy under French rule.

Because the Piedmontese middle class was sandwiched between the aristocrats, who were living on large *latifundia* (landed estates), and those who were kept in a situation of quasi-serfdom, the lack of international commerce, institutions of commercial credit, and basic industry made the development of an entrepreneurial bourgeoisie extremely difficult. The Jews of Piedmont were not, therefore, merely a fringe of this emerging bourgeois class but an integral part of it, numerically of relative importance but economically decisive. Furthermore, this emerging Jewish Piedmontese bourgeoisie shared with the rest of their class financial interests and political ideals that coincided with those of the ruling House of Savoy, less interested to reestablish its past absolute right than to contain the popular republican forces unleashed by the French Revolution.

The result was twofold. New political ideas, projects for agrarian reform, social assistance, and popular education became expressions of the rise of the bourgeois class, while the laws, the written opinions formulated by the bureaucrats, and in general the whole attitude of the Sardinian government toward the religious minorities in the realm—Jews and Protestants—became a mirror of the uncertainty provoked by the conflict between the forces of reaction and the new liberal ones.

It is therefore impossible to explain the exceptional military role of the Jews in the Risorgimento without taking into consideration their equally preeminent commercial, industrial, and economic role in the Sardinian kingdom before emancipation. This role is clearly reflected in the difficulties the Turin government encountered in the application to the Jews of the legislation predating the French conquest.

This legislation of the *ancien régime* was reestablished for all the subjects of the kingdom by the edict of King Victor Emanuel I, dated 21 January 1814, which restored the royal constitutions of 1770 without any change. In this first edict, there was no specific mention of the Jews. Until March 1816 they therefore hoped to be allowed to retain the goods and rights obtained under the French, and above all to avoid being forced back into their ghettos. They developed intensive efforts about which we have no direct documentary proof, but there are very convincing echoes in the official documents and in the individual petitions dealing with the question of their retention of real estate possessions. We also hear of an offer of one million lire to the government, about which we unfortunately have no documentary confirmation. To understand what a million lire meant at that time and in the disastrous economic conditions of the Sardinian kingdom, one has to remember that such a sum would have represented about one-third of the government income from the extraordinary taxation on real estate imposed on 29 March 1815, and that the Turin government hoped would bring in seven to eight million lire.[22]

The offer—if it was ever made—was not accepted, but an idea of the economic resources of the Piedmontese Jews can be obtained from the fact that the "Universitá," the communities of the kingdom, amounting to six thousand souls—women, children, old people, and paupers included—underwrote the government's forced loan with 300,000 lire as against the two million paid by the rest of the population, three million strong.[23] The Regie Patenti dated 1815, which were supposed to regulate once and for all the status of the Jews, paid full attention to their new entrepreneurial role. They also granted many of the Jewish requests: they abolished the obligation to wear the infamous yellow sign on their clothing, allowed the Jews to be active in every type of trade or artisan work, and authorized them to stay outside their ghettos overnight for reasons of work. Finally—and this is the most significant point concerning the Jewish entrepreneurial role and their penetration into the bourgeois class—the *Patenti* allowed a period of five years to the Jews to get rid of the real estate acquired under the French, and one year for the properties obtained against credit.[24] This provision was never applied and in many cases we find that the king himself intervened to authorize the richest Piedmontese Jews not only to keep their goods but also to enlarge their possessions outside the ghetto. The only point on which the Jews did not obtain satisfaction was the right to reside outside the ghetto, a situation that very rapidly proved itself to be of great discomfort to the authorities

[22] Ibid., 20, which quotes Antonio Fossati, *Documenti di storia economica piemontese: Origini e sviluppi della carestia del 1816–17 negli Stati sardi di terrafera* (Turin, 1929), 34. It is unclear whether the loan mentioned by Fossati is the same one mentioned by Levi. In any case, the Jewish contribution remains not only important but totally disproportionate to their numbers, especially if one remembers that at least half of these Jews were considered "paupers."

[23] Giorgina Levi, "Sulle premesse," 12.

[24] The principal historical sources concerning the Regie Patenti are contained in the State Archives of Turin, ecclesiastical matters section, category 37, "Jews," bundles 3–12. These sources have been carefully studied by Giorgina Levi and Salvatore Foa, and they have also been used as a base for another important study on the situation of the Piedmontese Jews during the Restoration: Arturo Carlo Jemolo, "Gli Ebrei Piemontese ed il Getto Intorno al 1835–40," *Memorie della Academia delle Scienze di Torino,* serial 3, vol. 1, published as a separate extract in 1952, following a memoir previously presented to the Academy by Jemolo on 17 December 1951. He gives a detailed account of the housing problems of the Jews, especially in Turin, where the overcrowding of the ghetto had become an economic and health hazard for the inhabitants and the authorities in the city. Furthermore, Jemolo, in his capacity as well-known historian and lawyer, as well as a member of the bourgeois elite in Piedmont, is able—better than Jewish historians—to focus on the ambivalence of behavior of the Piedmontese bureaucracy and nobility toward the Jews, including that of personalities well known for their philo-Semitic feelings.

because of the unhealthy conditions these overcrowded urban areas created, usually at the very heart of the towns.

From a perusal of the documents for and against the forced sale of Jewish real estate outside the ghettos, it is possible to have an idea of the economic weight of the Jewish communities in the economy and finances of the Piedmontese state, although they were certainly not the richest in the peninsula. In fact, in none of the states bordering Piedmont—France, Austria, the Duchies of Parma and Modena, the Grand Duchy of Tuscany—was their situation so bad. Only in the Papal States was it worse.[25]

The Piedmontese nobility, newly returned from a long exile, and a large part of the kingdom's bureaucracy, were ferociously attached to the absolutist principles of the *ancien régime.* They were, at least in the first years after the Restoration, totally opposed to any change, and as far as the Jews were concerned, noblemen, bureaucrats, clergy, artisans, and farmers seem to have been constantly preoccupied by possible competition from the Jews. Such a policy was—as we shall see later—the very opposite of that which the House of Savoy and a large part of the nobility were to follow three decades later, when Piedmont became the standard bearer of liberation in the peninsula. Yet Piedmont was the only state where the departure of the French did not cause acts of violence against the Jews.[26] This was probably due to their dispersion among small centers where they lived in a long-standing symbiosis with the local population and to the fact that during the Napoleonic period, the Piedmontese Jews who held public office opposed the radical expressions of anticlericalism—a behavior, by the way, that characterized the Jews also after the emancipation.[27]

It is, however, important to remember the situation of economic underdevelopment of the Piedmontese kingdom, the lack of ideological and humanitarian feelings of the nobility and of the clergy toward the Jews, the permanent prejudice of the administration and of the population against innovation, in order to appreciate the meteoric ascent of a small community that with few exceptions did not possess personalities of international stature or great wealth. This ascent was favored by the disastrous economic situation of Piedmont, the drought and famine that afflicted the country in the first years of the Restoration, the lack of investment capital, the lack of a system of credit, the flight of capital

[25] Jemolo, "Gli Ebrei Piemontese," 32.

[26] In 1799 the ghettos of Pitigliano, Lugo, and Arezzo were sacked. At Sinigaglia, thirteen Jews were murdered. In Arezzo another thirteen Jews were burned at the stake. In Verona, the Austrian army intervened to put an end to anti-Jewish riots. In Acqui, on the other hand, the Jews were saved from farmers' attacks by the Bishop. The same happened in Ivrea. In Savigliano, in 1796, Jews were saved by the intervention of French troops.

[27] Canepa, "Emancipazione," 117.

abroad, the backwardness of the commercial regulations, the total misunderstanding of the needs of the few industries by the royal administration, and the need of the government to find some remedy for the growing unemployment and the dangerous phenomena of vagabondage and begging.

The king and the rising bourgeoisie believed that the few hundred Jewish families who, under the French, had accumulated "great wealth," had achieved—in spite of the large number of poor people within the ghettos—a very great importance. Thus we find that their social and economic problems were closely linked with those of the ruling class.

The Jewish economic influence in Piedmont before emancipation manifested itself in four fields: maritime trade and harbor commerce; investment in agriculture; textile industry; and real estate.

The Congress of Vienna had transferred, as already mentioned, the territories of the Republic of Genoa to the House of Savoy. These territories included the ports of Genoa, Savona and Nice. From 1815 on, the crisis in port activity that had already begun in the last years of the Genoese republic increased considerably. The Genoese asked the government in Turin to put an end to the protectionist regulations imposed by the Piedmontese government. The latter was interested in attracting Jews to Liguria, hoping that they would develop its ports as they had done with great success in Tuscany with the port of Leghorn. Furthermore, in Nice lived a rich and powerful Jewish family, the Avigdors.[28] They were the commercial representatives of the king of Prussia and of the grand duke of Tuscany. According to the intendente generale (the top official responsible for trade and economy) of Piedmont, one of the Avigdor brothers gave "a livelihood to 450, and at certain moments to over 500 persons."[29] He objected, therefore, to any attempt to force the Avigdors to sell the properties acquired during the Napoleonic period and underlined the fact that important international relations of these Genoese Jews, particularly with the House of Rothschild in Paris, could intervene in favor of all the Jews of Nice with the Piedmontese ambassador in France.

As for real estate, it is difficult to know how well-founded was the fear of Piedmontese functionaries that the massive sale of Jewish property would disrupt the market. In the petitions submitted by private persons or institutions, interested to see the restrictive laws against the Jews fully applied, we always find the claim that the sale of properties of a few hundred Jews could not have a dramatic effect on the prices of the market. This was probably true, but the Piedmontese functionaries responsi-

[28] On the Avigdor family in Nice, see *Dizionario del Risorgimento Nazionale* (Milan, 1930), 2: 131–32.

[29] Giorgina Levi, *Sulle premesse*, 20–21.

ble for the economy of the state objected to the forced sale of these properties for another reason: they realized that the majority of these buildings owned by the Jews outside the ghetto walls were not used for private but for industrial purposes. In fact, in most cases they consisted of large buildings, often former convents like those bought by the Levi family at Chieri, which because of their size could be converted into textile plants. The problem of real estate thus combined with that of Jewish industrial investment in a country where industry was still almost nonexistent. The most important industrial activity was that of silk, which provided work in normal times to between sixty-five and eighty-five thousand people.[30] But at the time of the Restoration, these industries went through a very serious crisis because of an antiquated system of production, strong competition from Lombardy and Tuscany, and the anti-economic import policy of the government. In 1816 the number of looms in Piedmont was half that existing before the French Revolution. Many weavers had moved to Lyons. In 1822, out of 2,182 looms, 1,426 were idle. From a calculation of the number of looms and of the "fornelletti" (the vats in which the silkworms cocoons were boiled, and on the basis of which production taxes were fixed), one-third of the Piedmontese textile production was in the hands of the Jews. They were also among the few industrialists of the time who possessed the cash needed for the creation of new industries and the modernization of machinery.

In the field of agriculture, the activities of the Jews aroused a lot of hostility. In a typical petition to the ministry of the interior dated 28 February 1881, a certain Carlo Antonio Gamba explains how the Jews have been able to create what he calls a monopoly of agricultural loans within the limitations imposed by the law on levying interest.[31] The system used by the Jews, and against which Gamba protests, consisted of their employment by Christian agents who approached the farmers at fairs or at the church doors on religious holidays. These agents offered the farmers loans at 6 percent interest (a far lower rate than those asked by non-Jewish moneylenders), but they paid only half of the loan in cash. The other half was provided in goods that Jews had accumulated and on which—according to Gamba—they realized enormous profits, since these goods were bought by them much more cheaply. Gamba, like other traders, priests, artisans, and landowners, asked the government to prohibit the Jews from being present at the fairs, to close down their shops outside the ghettos, and forbid their agents from operating in the church porches. These petitions were regularly rejected by the authorities, who on many occasions used them to express favorable opinions of the Jews and of their lending activities, because of the very low rate of interest they charged.

[30] Carlo Giulio, *Notizie sulla Patria Industria* (Turin, 1944), 225–51, quoted by Giorgina Levi, *Sulle premesse,* 29.

[31] Giorgina Levi, *Sulle premesse,* 23.

In an interesting book of memoirs, *Ausonia,* a member of the Levi family of Chieri writes that the breaking of the ban on non-Catholics in Piedmont possessing real estate was one of the reasons for the revolution in the real estate market, and became "a seed of moral and economic strength in Piedmont." The noblemen returning from exile, incapable of engaging in productive work, did not care for their immense latifundia, with the result that non-Catholic families (Protestants and Jews) joined Catholic and bourgeois families in purchasing these vast properties in order to resell them in sections and on long-term payments to the farmers. These small agricultural properties, writes Levi, "improved by the sweat of their new proprietors," increased their value and led to the creation of a new class of small landowners who became the backbone of Piedmont.[32] It was, as Levi points out, a typically capitalistic system, which, incidentally, was to be practiced by the Jews all over Italy long after emancipation.[33] It is clear in any case that the close collaboration of the Jews with the emerging Piedmontese bourgeoisie preceded the emancipation by at least twenty years. This convergence of economic and social interests gave the Jewish communities of Piedmont a position of influence unrelated to their numerical strength. It created a strong basis of common economic and financial interests that were later to be crowned by an appropriate ideological superstructure. "The Jews of the Kingdom of Sardinia," writes Levi, "are the allies of the liberals . . . not only because of a constant and inborn thirst for freedom . . . but because the small group of Piedmontese Jews (six thousand people) turns into an active part of the rising bourgeoisie. It inserts itself into the relations of bourgeois productivity, it controls and knows how to use capital, creates and guides manufactories of great importance to the country."[34]

The Restoration did not stop this process; in fact it accentuated it by the weaknesses and contradictions of the government and by the ancient custom of the prince negotiating with the Jewish communities, the sense of the Jews' arrogance, security, and aggressiveness—economic, political, and social—unparalleled by Jewish behavior in other countries of Europe.[35] The study of documents relating to the Jews during the period

[32] David Levi, *Ausonia: Vita d'Azione (dal 1848 al 1890)* (Turin, 1882), 40–41.

[33] As exemplified by my family from 1880 onward: Dan V. Segre, *Memoirs of a Fortunate Jew* (London, 1987).

[34] Giorgina Levi, *Sulle premesse,* 4.

[35] At Vercelli, Jews adopted the habit of visiting cafes, provoking the local patrons by their "arrogant behavior and by their refusal to remove their hats." Although scorned, they obtained tickets for the local theater and used to attend performances. In 1827 at Venaria Reale, an important cavalry garrison, Jews were forbidden to enter the town because a Jew from Savigliano did not pay his gambling debts to local officers amounting to two thousand lire. Giorgina Levi, "Gli Ebreiin Piemonte," 115. On the other hand and in spite of all social and legal obstacles, it is clear that there existed considerable mingling between Jews and non-Jews, as shown by the case of a collapse of the floor of a Jewish house in Alessandria in

1814–48 shows how, under an absolutist government not particularly friendly to the Jews, in spite of the presence of a clergy, of corporations that were weaker than before but deeply anti-Semitic, it was possible to create a large movement of interest and sympathy toward the Jews among the intellectuals, the military, the high officials of the government, and even among the nobility and some members of the clergy; and how this liberal ferment that preceded emancipation was determined essentially by the close community of economic interests between the Jews and the new, young bourgeoisie.[36]

These elements, which characterized the emancipation of the Piedmontese Jews, operated, as already mentioned, in a very favorable environment due to the radical change of political course that took place in Piedmont from 1848 onward. The ambition of the House of Savoy to unite Italy, or at least as a first stage to bring under its control the northern part of the peninsula, transformed the Piedmontese kingdom from an autocratic, Catholic, aristocratic state into a liberal, secular, and democratic one. It was this change and the opportunities opened to the Piedmontese bourgeoisie by the successful wars of independence that transformed the Jews of Piedmont into an "exemplary" group to be imitated by the rest of the Jews of the peninsula, and gave them that particular character which would distinguish them from the other Jews of Europe.

The Political Aspect of Jewish Emancipation

Two general observations should be made about the political emancipation of Italian Jews. The first is chronological, insofar as there is a profound difference between the first emancipation following the arrival of French troops in Italy in 1797, and the second, following the proclamation by King Carlo Alberto of a new Constitution in 1848, is sociocultural. Up to the middle of the nineteenth century, the Jews of Italy, especially in Piedmont, acted as a homogeneous, compact group, submitting to a still-recognized communal-religious authority. This homogeneity and compactness broke down with surprising speed after the closing of the ghetto and was accompanied by a dramatic lowering of the Jewish cultural level and communal consciousness.[37]

The first emancipation found Italian Jews still fully immersed in the

1835. It was caused by the weight of people attending a Jewish wedding, and among the victims were seventeen Catholics, including a colonel, three captains, two lieutenants, and friends of the bride's family, who died together with the Jews.

[36] Giorgina Levi, *Sulle premesse,* 6.

[37] Marco Momigliano, *Antologia di un Rabbino Italiano* (Palermo, 1986), with a preface by historian Alberto Cavaglion.

traditional Jewish system of life in the ghettos, which were established in many Italian cities beginning in the sixteenth century.

The Jews welcomed the French as liberators, erected "trees of liberty" in every ghetto square, participated with enthusiasm in every public manifestation in favor of the French Revolution, although the arrival of the French meant heavier taxation and, sometimes, unexpected violence. Such was the case in the town of Acqui in November 1799, where General Miollis ordered his troops to attack the ghetto in order to obtain immediate cash payment of the sixteen thousand lire he had requested from the Jews of this tiny community.

The situation of the Jews became precarious with the first withdrawal of the French army two years later. They left behind a critical economic situation and strong, popular anti-French feelings instigated by the clergy and the local aristocratic regimes. The Jews were obviously identified as partisans of France and suffered accordingly. However, after Napoleon's conquest of the entire peninsula, and the creation, first, of the Cisalpine Republic in the north of Italy, and later of the Kingdoms of Italy and of Naples, Jews were reconfirmed in their full rights as citizens.

Some of the rich Jewish families, like the Levis of Chieri and the Ottolenghis of Acqui, supplied senior administrative personnel to the new administration. In relatively large numbers Jews joined the National Guard and advanced rapidly in rank because of their loyalty to the French regime and their higher standard of education. In smaller numbers they also joined the French regular army. Their communities were heavily taxed. Those of Piedmont, for instance, were required to cover two forced loans, of a quarter million and twenty-five thousand lire, respectively. The documents of the time show that the Jews also voluntarily contributed large sums to the French and did so with an enthusiasm proportional to the economic and social advantages the new regime offered them.

Italian Jews were asked by Napoleon to send their representatives to the Sanhedrin in Paris. The importance attached by the French administration to those of Piedmont is shown by the fact that Rabbi Salvatore Benedetto Segre (1757–1809) was appointed vice president of the Paris rabbinical assembly. He was a faithful representative of those momentous times of transition from one culture to another. A lawyer, a municipal councilor in the city of Vercelli, a poet, and an emphatic preacher, his rabbinical role was quite equivocal: he did not, for instance, oppose the French request that the Paris Sanhedrin should declare itself in favor of mixed marriages. He was also an unabashed flatterer. In a speech dated 25 August 1807, he stated that Napoleon was superior to every biblical figure. He was accused by his Italian colleagues of political intrigue,[38]

[38] I. Carmi, "All'Assemblea ed al Sinedrio di Parigi, 1806–1807" (Reggio, 1905), quoted by G. Levi, "Gli Ebrei in Piemonte," 158.

but his behavior shows the close cooperation existing between the Jewish Piedmontese establishment and the French administration. The latter considered the Italian Jews on the whole, and those of Piedmont in particular, as faithful subjects of the Empire, so much so that it exempted them from the "infamous decree" promulgated at the conclusion of the Sanhedrin, which aimed to limit the economic activities of the Jews in France and in other parts of the empire.

The very rapid process of economic development of Italian Jews under the French does not, however, coincide with a general process of socialization and acculturation. The Jews, in the first two decades of the century, still lived according to their ancestral traditions, were preoccupied by problems of Jewish education of their sons, and continued to submit to rabbinical authority. The impact they felt from the Revolution and the first emancipation remained, however, dramatic. Thus, when the Italian Jews, after the fall of Napoleon, were forced to go back into their ghettos (with the exception of the Duchy of Parma, governed by Napoleon's wife), they were individually and collectively transformed. They had tasted freedom and equality of rights; in some cases they had filled important posts in public administration; they had learned the use of weapons; they had established new and strong business relationships and political links with Christian liberals. Some of them, like Rubino Ventura, born in Finale Ligure near Genoa, chose adventure: a soldier in Napoleon's army at the age of seventeen, he became the commander of a small army of Sikhs in India. He conquered "Little Tibet" on behalf of the Sultan of Lahore and died in 1859 after having married off his daughter to a Belgian Marquis.[39]

It was, however, the resentment Jews felt at the loss of their civil rights that pushed them to adhere, in much greater proportions than the local population, to the secret revolutionary societies—the "Carbonari." These societies struggled, if not yet for the unification of Italy, certainly for the end of the aristocratic, absolutist regimes reestablished in the various states of the peninsula.

At least until the middle of the nineteenth century, the Carbonari and other groups favoring Italian nationalism were limited to a small, elite group divided into two main ideological currents: the Republicans inspired by Mazzini and the monarchists loyal to the House of Savoy. Both trends were favorable to the emancipation of the Jews because they realized the great advantages that could be gained from collaboration with a compact group of people, economically and culturally strong, who shared their political and economic interests, and who did not represent political competitors. Once the second emancipation was granted to the

[39] Guido Bedarida, *Gli Ebrei d'Italia* (Leghorn, 1950), 235–36 n. 2.

Jews of Piedmont in 1848, this collaboration explains the very rapid rise of Piedmontese Jews in the economic, military, political, and social fields of the kingdom.

Contrary to what was happening in France (where the Jews turned themselves in many cases into theoreticians of the secular republican state) or in England (where the Jews as a collective remained politically passive), in Italy, and especially in Piedmont, the Jews operated as a politically conscious community.[40] After 1848 this communal action broke down for lack of clear Jewish aims. It is thus possible to divide the story of their emancipation into three periods during which Italian Jews developed those characteristics of Jewish-Italian "aristocracy" mentioned by Artom and Weizmann: 1820–48; 1849–70, and 1870–1914.

To support this chronological division we have fortunately much comparative statistical material.[41] It has been widely used by Jewish authors to prove the contribution of Italian Jews to the Risorgimento, and to justify the socioeconomic rise of the Jews in the peninsula. In general, their works, compiled in the post-Risorgimento period or—as in the case of the study of Bedarida—after World War II, lack critical content and overlook the reasons that completely transformed the early character of Italian nationalism. Franca Fubini, in an interesting study on the evolution of the Jewish mentality throughout this period, shows the rapid erosion of—but not the main reasons for—the unique position of the Italian Jews, and their return to the fate of their coreligionists in the rest of Europe.[42]

Going back to the statistics, the main works are those carried out by

[40] The importance of Italian Jews as a subversive group appears from all the police documents of the time, which portray the Piedmontese Jews in particular as "truest and most fiery Jacobins," "enraged democrats and haughtily contemptuous of respectable persons," "servile and revolutionary instruments," "weak, seduced, impious, fanatic revolutionaries," "wearers of the red beret, promoters of Jacobin clubs," or just "open partisans of democracy." Fiorini-Lemmi, "Periodo Napoleonico dal 1799–1814," *Storia Politica d'Italia* (Milan, 1881), 451. It was not just the opinion of local policemen. Prince Metternich believed that the Jews of Leghorn, who since 1593 enjoyed special privileges under the special constitution granted to them by the Medicis, *La Livornina,* were "a shipyard for the Revolution." Guido Bedarida, "Gli Ebrei e il Risorgimento Italiano," *Israel* 27, nos. 7–8 (July–August 1961): 108–299. The spirit of independence of Leghorn Jews has been well known since the eighteenth century, if one can believe a French tourist guide, *Dictionnaire Geographique Portatif* (Paris, 1759), 247, which warned Christian travellers to Tuscany that it was "safer to hit the Grand Duke than a Jew."

[41] Flaminio Servi, *Gli Israeliti d'Europa nella Civiltá: Memorie storiche biografiche e statistiche dal 1789 al 1870* (Florence, 1817); *Statistica comparativa della popolazione israelita d'Italia negli anni 1839, –61, –69* (Florence, 1872); Giorgina Levi, *Gli Ebrei alla luce della statistica* (Florence, 1919–20); Bedarida, *Gli Ebrei d'Italia;* and Foa, *Gli Israeliti nel Risorgimento.*

[42] Franca Fubini, *Il Vessillo Israelitico: 1900–1914: Laurea in Lettere e Filosofia* (University of Turin, 1975–76).

Livi and Servi on the archives of most Italian Jewish communities, and on the data preserved by the Italian national census of 1861 and 1869. Also important are the statistical researches of Count Sertori in the period before 1840[43] and more recently by Roberto Bachi, as already mentioned. They confirm the fact that for more than a century the relationship between the Jewish and non-Jewish population oscillated between 0.7 and 1 per thousand, with only two sectors in which these percentages remained constant: prostitution and prison populations.[44] Otherwise the one-per-thousand proportion is nonexistent. Infant mortality was twice as high for non-Jews as for Jews; in the field of education, we find 645 illiterate non-Jews per thousand as against fifty-eight for the Jews. Suicides are of particular interest. The yearly average for the Jews was one per 6,250 people, seven times higher than for the non-Jews, and three times higher than the average for the Jewish population in Europe. This may indicate a situation of particular psychological stress due to the need for an extremely rapid adaptation of the Jews to new styles of life and the abandonment of a deeply rooted tradition. Many suicides are caused by the family tensions created by the growth of mixed marriages. Another interesting fact underlined by Servi, on the basis of a study by the famous Jewish criminologist Cesare Lombroso,[45] is the higher recorded rate of insanity: among the Jews, one per 391 patients in mental hospitals as against one per 11,047 for the non-Jews. But this figure may be due to the fact that, especially among Italian peasants, until recently madmen were kept in the family and not sent to asylums.

The fact that the number of Jewish beggars at the end of the 1860s was twenty times lower than for the Italian population should not be surprising in view of the higher economic positions prevailing among the Jews. What is, however, surprising, is the ratio between Jews and non-Jews in the military and political fields.

In the military domain it is important to distinguish between volunteers and conscripted soldiers. The former joined the Piedmontese army and the Garibaldi militias—from all parts of Italy—under the spur of strong ideological and romantic motivation, and with the aim of fighting for the unity of the peninsula and against the aristocratic regime of the Italian states. They were typical representatives of that small Italian liberal bourgeoisie that would in time become the major political-economic force in the peninsula, and on which the House of Savoy relied in its fight against the antiliberal regimes of the other Italian states. The proportion of Jewish volunteers in this group—a faithful sample of the newly emerging class—is significant: on the basis of actual population figures, there

[43] L. Sertori, *Statistica d'Italia* (Florence, 1842).

[44] Servi, *Gli Israeliti,* 289.

[45] Ibid., 290.

should have been one Jewish volunteer to every thousand non-Jews. Instead, in the two first wars of independence (1848 and 1849) there were fifty-five Jewish volunteers per thousand; in the war of 1859, one hundred fifteen; in the war of 1860–61, one hundred ten; and in the war of 1866, seventy-four. In the regular army also, the ratio between Jewish and non-Jewish conscripts was inconsistent with their respective demographic size: one hundred thirty-nine instead of one for every thousand officers, and two and a half for every thousand simple soldiers, a discrepancy due far more to education than to ideology.

Since the unification of Italy was achieved through the military conquest of the various states by the Piedmontese army and the Garibaldi militias,[46] it was natural that Jewish political and bureaucratic representation should reflect their disproportionate role on the battlefield. Thus, it is not by chance that Italy had the first Jewish minister of war in modern Europe, General Count Ottolenghi, a former member of Garibaldi's militias. In 1869 the sixteen and a half million Italians eligible to cast a vote elected one deputy for every fifteen thousand citizens. On a basis of one to a thousand, the ratio of Jewish deputies was seven times higher than the non-Jewish: in 1871 there were eleven Jews in the Rome Parliament as against five in Vienna, six in Paris, and eight in London, countries in which the Jewish populations were much larger than in Italy. Italy was the first European country to have a Jew, Luigi Luzzati, serving twice as prime minister. At the time of the arrival of Fascism, Italy had twenty-four Jewish deputies and eleven senators.

In the political field during the Risorgimento we find Jews in charge of many ministries in the Provisional Revolutionary Governments of Venice and Rome, as well as in high places in the secret service and the diplomatic corps of the Piedmontese government. Mazzini used to disguise himself as a rabbi when traveling illegally in Italy to escape the police and died in the house of the Jewish mayor of Rome. The Jewish Bank of the Tordros's family financed his unsuccessful *coup d'état* against the House of Savoy, in Savoy in 1822, and many Jews were arrested in this unsuccessful revolt. During the 1848 revolution against the Austrians, a Jew from Lombardy, Finzi, was sentenced to death but later reprieved. The Fascist regime gave his name to a U-boat, a unique case in the history of European navies. Some thirty Jews were ennobled, as elsewhere in Europe, for their political and financial services. However, only in Piedmont were these new noblemen mentioned in the official Gotha as coming from Palestine.[47]

Finally, Bedarida has compiled a list of 770 "famous" Italian Jews from

[46] Bedarida, *Gli Ebrei d'Italia,* 295.

[47] R. Prefettura di Torino, *Elenco ufficiale e definitivo delle famiglie nobili e titolate del Piemonte* (Turin, 1886).

1848 to 1948. When broken down into categories, the largest group of personalities is doctors, physiologists, and anthropologists (eighty-four), and the smallest archaeologists (four). The politicians and top civil servants number sixty-five, famous musicians forty-four, physicists nineteen, military and naval experts eleven, and explorers nine. Today, of the six recent Italian Nobel prize-winners, three are Jews (namely Levi-Montalcini, Modigliani, and Loria).

What do all these figures mean? Bedarida points out that the large Jewish participation in secret societies and revolutionary nationalist movements never had, "contrary to what anyone might think, a specific political, social program." From the Jewish point of view it was, according to him, an identification "with that small minority which by itself created the unity of Italy rather than leading up to it."[48]

It is from this activism, rather than from ideological ambitions, that was born the Italian Jews' illusion that their fate differed from that of Jews in the rest of the world, and that they were unique in Jewish history. This was a feeling that could be justified during the Risorgimento, namely between 1830 and 1870, a period during which the Jews, newly out of their ghettos and actively engaged in the liberal struggle against the aristocratic regimes of the Italian states, witnessed the realization of the "miracle" of Italian unity. Until 1860, this unity still looked illusory to the majority of Italians as well as to the majority of Europeans, in the light of the strong political and military opposition it had to face (Austria) and the absence of a rooted common national consciousness among the peoples of the peninsula. It was a dream of a small number of liberal, bourgeois patriots, who, to make things more difficult, were deeply divided among themselves about ways of achieving this unity, namely, whether to create a republican state (as Mazzini wanted) or a federation of states presided over by the pope, or a monarchy under the House of Savoy.

For the majority of the population—composed of illiterate farmers—such unity meant nothing. As for the ruling classes in the various states, they remained linked to the regional political institutions, even though it was clear that a small duchy like Parma had no further *raison d'être*. If ancient naval republics such as Genoa and Venice were politically, militarily, and economically exhausted, the Kingdom of the Two Sicilies in the south and the Papal States and the Grand Duchy of Tuscany in the center of the peninsula still had strong state structures, international influence, and an experience of government equal to that of the Piedmontese state.

[48] Bedarida, "Gli Ebrei e il Risorgimento Italiano," 289.

The idea of "Italianita" was, and to a certain extent still remains, more a cultural and geographical concept than a political one. Therefore in the first half of the nineteenth century the number of "Italians" was small, although politically and ideologically very active. Among these "Italians," the Jews represented a relatively high percentage, being a psychologically, ideologically, and economically compact group. They could boast, as Bedarida says, that there did not exist in Italy "one city, or a population of thirty-five to forty thousand . . . which contributed in every field—arts, politics, economics, military—to the fatherland, like the thirty-five to forty thousand Jews."[49]

In other words, during the Risorgimento, the Italian Jews had the feeling that they had not been admitted to a preexisting economic, social, and political system but had created it, that they were cofounders together with the other Italian patriots of something totally new. To be a Jew in Italy meant, like for many Jews in America, to feel or believe oneself to be fully integrated in the non-Jewish society, whereas for the other Jews in Europe and the Islamic world, being a Jew meant never being 100 percent German, French, or Arab, because they could not claim to be part of the host nation from its origin.

The Italian Jews, contrary to the majority of the peninsula's inhabitants, had no identity or emotional roots with the regional states, because these states, including Piedmont until 1848, were ruled by Catholic, aristocratic, basically anti-Semitic regimes. The Risorgimento, on the other hand, both in its republican and monarchical trends, drew its legitimacy from its secular, bourgeois, liberal ideology. The Jews, as non-Christians and as potential bourgeois entrepreneurs, had every interest in supporting the Risorgimento and fighting within its framework for the destruction of states that for centuries had marginalized them from civic society. The identity of interests and ideas between Jews and Italian nationalists up to the conquest of Rome in 1870 was so complete that it is not surprising to find that they idealized their new and transitory situation, even when they realized that the Risorgimento, as a secular, emancipatory, and assimilatory movement, was bound to destroy their own particularism —a trend the Italian rabbis understood and sometimes denounced but against which they did not know how to fight. Antonio Gramsci, the main Italian Marxist thinker, well understood this situation of the Italian Jews, which was similar to that of other non-Jewish groups in the peninsula as far as the new Italian national identity was concerned. He wrote: "The formation of the national consciousness of the Jews of Italy developed parallel with the formation of the Italian national consciousness of

[49] Ibid.

the Piedmontese, Venetians, Neapolitans, and therefore it did not insert itself into an already existing national consciousness."[50] This could indeed be seen as a unique situation for Jews in Europe.

To this self-image of the Italian Jews there was no corresponding image on the Italian side.

In Piedmont, as in the rest of Italy, broad sectors of the population remained hostile to the Jews. It was not only a religious hostility but one linked to their identification with the Jacobins, the French conquerors, the Liberals, and usurers. These feelings could not reveal themselves openly under a regime that was becoming progressively secular, liberal, and democratic, in which the Jews fulfilled an important economic role. Paradoxically, on the thorny question of the relations between the Italian kingdom and the church, the position of the Jews, and particularly of the Jewish members of parliament, was so moderate that the pope himself regretted that there were not more Jews in the new Italian administration.

In the Italian mentality there existed, however, a considerable hiatus between the image people had of the Jews in general and the image they held of the Italian Jews, between the mythical and the real Jew. The former was conceived and usually described in the literature as a kind of gypsy, or as an uneducated miser. Although there were no attempts to demonize him, there were in Italy, as in other places in Europe, anti-Jewish writings, mainly inspired by Catholic, antiliberal, antisocialist, and later nationalist groups. Yet only after World War I did Jews begin to be denounced as members of "a state within a state," foreign elements within the Italian nation, incapable of assimilating. Before this time, one can find traces of anti-Semitism even in the works of great writers such as Pastonchi (*Dreyfus e Gesú,* 1899), Antonio Fogazzaro (*Il Santo,* 1906), Giosué Carducci (*In Una Chiesa Gotica,* 1902), and Gabriele d'Annunzio (*Il Piacere,* 1889, and *Piú che l'Amore,* 1905).[51] They describe the Jews as vulgar persons, materialistic, cowardly, but not as a racial, corrupting danger as in the rest of Europe at that time. Against this negative, stereotypical image, there was that of the Jew whom Italians met in everyday life. For a population ignorant of Judaism he was a completely different person. How wide this gap was can be measured at the time of the publication of the racial laws in 1938, when the ministry of the interior in Rome received requests from many provinces to send them "samples" of Jews to help them know how and against whom to apply the new regulations.

[50] Antonio Gramsci, *Quaderni dal carcere,* vol. 3, *Il Risorgimento* (Turin, 1966), 166ff.

[51] Canepa, "L'immagine dell'Ebreo nel folclore e nella letteratura del post-Risorgimento," *RMI,* nos. 5–6 (1978), 383–94.

At the level of the Italian elite, however, there never was that perception of a "primogeniture of Italianness" that the Jews believed themselves to possess, but rather a benevolent attitude of condescension on the part of the aristocracy toward the Jews throughout the Risorgimento, and an interest in their services. Arturo Carlo Jemolo was correct when he wrote that "the position of the Piedmontese aristocracy, indulgent or favorable toward the Jews, was similar in 1840 to the position of the northern American of 1865, who was prepared to fight a civil war to put an end to the horror of slavery but burst out laughing when a pro-Negro European suggested that the best way to defend the rights of the blacks was to elect one of them to Congress."[52]

The transfer abroad of the archives of the House of Savoy following the fall of the dynasty in 1946 makes it impossible to verify the feelings of Victor Emanuel II, the king who achieved Italian unity, toward the Jews. In public, he never expressed any hostility, and after his wife's death, he maintained close relationships with women bearing typical Jewish names.[53]

In sum, the attitude of the Piedmontese aristocracy toward the Jews during the Risorgimento was not very different to that which they had toward their servants, perhaps of the rank of chief butler, a relationship that sometimes transformed itself into a social or matrimonial relationship, but was always accompanied by a certain condescension.

The behavior of the Piedmontese policy-making elite toward the Jews was totally different. For the revolutionaries, the conspirators, the Carbonari, the partisans of Mazzini, and the officers of Garibaldi, the Jews, before emancipation, were indispensable allies. They looked upon them as people always ready to finance risky political operations and make large financial contributions to idealistic causes. Contrary to the provincial Italian bourgeoisie, the Jews possessed useful international contacts, spoke in a dialect and wrote in a language that the police of the various Italian states did not understand, and thus could be used for secret correspondence by the conspirators.

Ideologically and because of personal interest, the Jews had espoused with enthusiasm the secular liberal cause. This transformed them in Piedmont and elsewhere in Italy into a major instrument in the hands of Count Cavour, the prime minister of the Kingdom of Sardinia, for the realization of his policies. In the military field, as already mentioned, the Jews became an example of courage and devotion to the cause of the House of Savoy; in the diplomatic field, their dispersion all over the Ital-

[52] Jemolo, *Gli Ebrei Piemontese,* 35.

[53] I possess a gold watch bearing the effigy of the king, which Victor Emanuel II gave to my great-uncle in gratitude for a "love debt" he never repaid and for which my great-uncle never asked.

ian provinces was exploited to foment intrigues and support Cavour's foreign policy; in the field of finance, the Jews of Piedmont were openly used to develop the personal relationships of the prime minister with the great Jewish financial establishment in Europe and especially in France. In the field of propaganda, Giacomo Dina, the editor of *l'Opinione,* Cavour's mouthpiece, was probably his most authoritative spokesman. Scores of Jews founded or directed important newspapers to support Piedmontese politics and to diffuse the knowledge of the Italian language all over the peninsula.[54] Last but not least, the residents of the Turin ghetto, who found themselves included in Cavour's constituency, became one of his electoral assets, with their chief rabbi, Lelio Cantoni, as his active electoral agent. To him Cavour owed part of his success in the very important elections of 1852 that returned him to the Turin parliament.

For Count Cavour, Piedmontese Jews were efficient collaborators, often confidants and friends, totally acculturated and socialized into the liberal Piedmontese society. A typical example of these close personal relations of the Count with the Jews is his long-standing friendship with Enrico Avigdor, which terminated in a duel between the two because of opposing political ideas, an event that could not have taken place if the two protagonists had not been regarded as belonging to the same social rank.

The emancipation of the Jews in Italy followed the march of the Piedmontese army southward. The last Jews to be emancipated were those living in Rome. They were freed in a quite symbolic way: the famous "breach of Porta Pia," in the walls of Rome, was opened by the guns of a Jewish captain, Segre (paradoxically the guns were set in the gardens of the nearby Villa Torlonia, future residence of Mussolini, where in 1938 he signed the order to expel the Jews from Italian society); the commanding officer of the shock troops who were first to enter Rome was another Jewish officer, named Mortara. He was the brother of that Monsignor Mortara who had been kidnapped as a baby, baptized, and never returned to his family, in spite of the emotion that the "Mortara affair" aroused all over Europe in the 1840s. No less significant was the letter the Roman Jews sent to General La Marmora, commander-in-chief of the Italian troops. In it, they wrote that "as from this day" (namely, the fall of Rome), they would be "only and solely Italians."

This unsolicited testimonial of loyalty consecrated the process of assimilation of one of the most ancient Jewish communities. At the same time, it coincided with the end of the Piedmontese phase of Italian nationalism and with the birth of a new collective Italian consciousness, in

[54] Ermanno Loewinson, "Camillo Cavour e gli Israeliti," *La Nuova Antologia* (Rome, 1910), 253–64.

which the Jews could not have a major part. The conquest of Rome, in fact, gave Italians the choice between two forms of collective national identity: Catholic universalism and pagan Roman universalism, two traditions with which the Jews—and indeed also the Piedmontese—could not fully identify themselves, since these traditions had developed throughout the centuries outside Piedmont, and, in the case of the Jews, against Judaism.

The realization of the political unity of the peninsula also greatly diminished the military, administrative, diplomatic, and financial role of the Jews, which Cavour, Mazzini, and King Victor Emanuel had so clearly appreciated. The new Italian nationalism could not but be indifferent to the Jewish role in the Risorgimento, revealing itself, in unison with other European nationalisms, as hostile to the Jews, in its exaltation of the community of origin, of blood, of history, and of religion of the new Italian state. The development of anti-Semitism within fascism was thus an inevitable phenomenon, in spite of Mussolini's repeated declarations on the nonexistence of anti-Semitism in Italy and his open support of Zionism.[55]

The Political-Cultural Aspect of Jewish Emancipation

The Italian Jews, like other Jews in the nineteenth century, had to face the great internal problems of their time, including assimilation, reform, anti-Semitism, Zionism, Marxism, and secularism. Some of these problems never deeply influenced the Italian communities. The distinction between Sephardim and Ashkenazim did not arouse in Italy even a folkloristic interest.[56] The same can be said of hasidism. The Reform movement, so important in Germany and Anglo-Saxon countries, struck no

[55] Renzo de Felice, *Storia degli Ebrei italiani sotto il Fascismo* (Turin, 1961), 116; Meir Michaelis, *Mussolini and the Jews: German-Italian Relations and the Jewish Question in Italy, 1922–1945* (Oxford, 1978). See also the very important article by Mario Toscano, "Gli Ebrei in Italia dall'emancipazione alle persecuzioni," *Storia Contemporanea* 17, no. 5 (October 1980), 905–55—one of the best and most concise summaries of the evolution of the Italian Jewish community from the time of the Risorgimento to the Fascist persecution.

The recently published biography of Margherita Sarfatti will probably remain a classic on both Mussolini and the Jewish "uncrowned queen" of Italy under Fascism. See Philip Cannistraro and Brian Sullivan, *Il Duce's Other Woman: The Never-Before-Told Story of Benito Mussolini's Jewish Mistress and How She Helped Him Come to Power* (New York, 1993).

[56] Rather than Sephardic or Ashkenazic, it is the Apam liturgy that has been followed in the little communities of Asti, Fossano, Alessandria, and Moncalvo, the initials of which form the word "Apam" in Hebrew. All these communities have meanwhile disappeared, with the exception of a tiny one in Allesandria.

roots in Italy, although it aroused debates in the Jewish press. Its major victory was the introduction of the organ in Italian synagogues, played on the High Holidays by non-Jews.

The Italian Jews and their rabbis remained faithful to the Orthodox trend in the same manner that many Italians clung to Catholicism: they did not fight against tradition but neither did they respect it much. Assimilation produced its effect, but most of the nonobservant, traditional Italian Jews expressed their Judaism, up to World War II, through family attachment that was often more a demonstration of elitism than of religious particularism.

Of all these problems, the Jewish press throughout this period collects echoes and debates. But it is a press, with the exception of the *Corriere Israelitico* of Trieste (and later the Zionist periodical *Israel*) that remained anemic, conformist, and defensive, fighting a lost battle against assimilation and without any true cultural, religious influence on the Italian Jews. Most attempts to remedy this situation failed with the birth and almost immediate death of new and more serious publications.[57]

The process of decline of Italian Jewry was reflected in the only periodical that survived, *Il Vessillo Israelitico*. Founded in 1853 by Giuseppe Levi in Vercelli, under the title *L'Educatore Israelitico,* it changed its name in 1874, when, upon the death of Levi, it came under the editorship of Rabbi Flaminio Servi, who directed it from the little Piedmontese town of Casale until 1922.

The fifty volumes of this publication, called "Monthly Journal for the History and Spirit of Judaism," is a faithful mirror of the rapid disintegration of Italian Jewry. It was "a banner [vessillo] to all winds," without any clear ideological direction.[58] Its interest was focused on the debate concerning the organization of Italian Jewish communities that remained in a chaotic state until 1929, when the Fascist government defined the relations between the state and all religious communities in the

[57] For a detailed study of the Jewish press in Italy, see Attilio Milano, ed., *Essays in Honor of Dante Lattes* (Tel Aviv, 1938), 86–93. The first Zionist publication, *L'Idea Sionista,* appeared in Modena in 1901 and continued publication until 1910. Under the same heading, another Zionist publication appeared in 1930 in favor of the Zionist Revisionist trend. A unique Jewish publication is the *Nostra Bandiera,* official spokesman of "Italians of Jewish Religion," founded in 1934 by Ettore Ovazza, openly nationalist and Fascist but at the same time strongly favorable to the creation of a spiritual Jewish center in Palestine. It is interesting to note that before the Italian conquest of Libya in 1911, *Eco di Tripoli,* founded by Gustavo Arbid in 1909, supported the idea of Italian colonization. During the Italian colonial period, four Jewish periodicals were intermittently published in Libya, while from 1928 to 1936 the Jewish community of Rhodes published an interesting bulletin in Ladino, called *El Bulletin.*

[58] Fubini, *Vessillo Israelitico.*

kingdom. The Jewish institutions were then reunited under a central roof, the Unione delle Communitá Israelitiche, a decision that put an end to the confusion created by the Rattazzi law in 1857.[59]

Other themes of permanent interest for *Il Vessillo Israelitico* were naturally those of mixed marriage, the decadence of Jewish culture, and the growing lack of attachment to Jewish tradition. When Zionism first appeared on the Italian Jewish scene, *Il Vessillo* took a hostile position; but from 1902, following the favorable reception by many Italian notables of Herzl, the sympathy shown by King Victor Emanuel III to this new national movement, and the open support that the most influential rabbis on the peninsula gave to it, the journal changed its attitude. On the whole, *Il Vessillo* remained to the very end the true spokesman of an affluent, bourgeois group, fearful of any excess, faithful to the government in power, flattering its notables, and chiefly preoccupied with avoiding polemics, particularly political ones.

The position taken up by *Il Corriere Israelitico,* published from 1862 to 1914 in Trieste, was quite different. From 1896, when Dante Lattes, one of the greatest revivers of Jewish culture in Italy, was invited to edit it, *Il Corriere* became an organ of political and religious leadership for the Italian-speaking Jews, even if its circulation was limited by the fact that it was published in Austrian territory. The heritage of *Il Corriere*—which was forced to cease publication in 1914 at the outbreak of war—was passed on to *Israel.* This publication, founded in 1916, remains to this day the most influential spokesman of Italian Jewry, together with its monthly supplement, *La Rassegna Mensile d'Israele.*[60]

[59] The Rattazzi law, promulgated in 1857, was never applied to all the Jewish communities in the newly formed Kingdom of Italy. It stated that the communities in the north could be public corporations like the municipalities. All Jews were obliged to register after one year of residence in a given locality. These communities depended directly upon the ministry of the interior. On the other hand, in other regions of the peninsula, communities were left free to organize themselves in associations according to statutes approved by their own members, who were obliged to pay a minimum contribution and prove themselves to be taxpayers. These communities had the right to elect and discharge their own rabbis. The Rattazzi law immediately aroused strong criticism from converted or nonreligious Jews, who did not want to be forced to register as Jews. Their protest led, in 1872, to a "historic" decision by the Supreme Court of Turin, according to which a Jew was not allowed to avoid the payment of the communal taxes by virtue of his declaration that he had abandoned the Jewish religion, without proving that he had joined another faith, a sentence that remained for a long time the object of violent debate in the Jewish press.

[60] See for example the position taken by E. Benamozeg, rabbi of Leghorn and an influential philosopher and moralist with a large audience also outside the Jewish community, in a special publication on 20 March 1898 in honor of the fiftieth anniversary of the emancipation of the Jews. In an article entitled "Intimo Accordo del Messianismo con la Patria Attuale" ("Intimate Agreement of Messianism with Our Present Fatherland"), Benamozeg wrote: "In conclusion, the more the Jew will be a Jew, the more he will be an Italian, a

It is around *Israel* that there developed the new elite of Italian Jewry under the guidance of rabbinical personalities, such as Margulis, Artom—father and son—Cassuto, Dante Lattes, Prato, as well as of Orthodox romantics like Alfonso Pacifici. And it is around this publication that a new, young, cultural Jewish intelligentsia was created and coalesced under the Fascist regime, which turned into the main leadership for the rest of the Jewish community when the anti-Semitic Fascist law burst upon them in 1938.

The price paid by Italian Jewry during World War II is high, even if numerically small when compared with victims of the Holocaust: seven thousand deported, twelve thousand emigrants and converts. Over one thousand Italian Jews went to Palestine, while the Jewish share in the resistance against the Germans and the Republican Fascists from 1943 to 1945 was as high as the participation of the Jews in the wars of the Risorgimento.

In these conditions, one might think that a century after emancipation Italian Jewry was doomed to disappear. However, it continues to show considerable vitality, expressed in the revival of religious and cultural activities, the maintenance of a previously nonexistent, broad school system, a lively communal press, and a new generation of young rabbis, better trained than in the past in both Italian and Jewish cultures.

Half a century after the trauma of the racial laws, the Italian Jewish community, reinforced by the arrival of Jews from Libya, Egypt, and Iran, does not seem to bear out the pessimistic forecast made by Enrico Castelnuovo (1839–1915) in his novel *I Moncalvo*: "Everywhere there was a debasement of character, a wreck of convictions, a cynical disparagement of Jewish qualities, a renunciation of all sacrifice, a frenetic rush to obtain ephemeral honors and quick profits."[61] The Jewish destiny, wrote Castelnuovo, was "a destiny envied by the world but leading to the falling apart of Italian Jewry."

Of this disaster, the great empty synagogues of Italy, true architectural horrors of a time of arrogant illusions, continue to bear witness. They do not explain, even less justify, the reborn interest in Italy in every aspect of Jewish culture and Jewish problems.[62]

The explanations for this phenomenon of Italian Jewish revival are

---

Frenchman, an Englishman. The more he will love Palestine, the more he will love Italy, France, England, and vice versa, because this is the new message: particularism and universalism grow up in Judaism in direct relationship one with the other."

61 Quoted in Alessandro Levi, *RMI*, no. 10 (1949), 476.

62 The publishers' statistics are evidence of this upsurge: from 1848 to 1948, 2,948 books on Jewish subjects were published in Italy; from 1948–88, there were over 3,000, and their number has been rising continuously since then. Giorgio Romano, *Bibliografia Italo-Ebraica (1848–1977)* (Florence, 1979).

numerous and the creation of the State of Israel, together with the polemics on the Palestine question, are certainly two of the major factors. Yet there are deeper reasons that could profitably be investigated.

After World War II, the Republic of Italy tried to decentralize the strong, unitarian structures it inherited from the Italian kingdom. It has also tried to solve many social and economic problems by enthusiastically supporting European unity. In this context it is understandable that Italians feel the need to think again about their history and to return to the roots of their multiple regional cultures. In this search for the past, which is also a search for an identity, the Italians discover that one of the most ancient tribes of the peninsula, and probably one of the few that has been able to survive culturally, is the Jews.

Thus it is possible that, in the search for their own identity, many modern Italians perceive that in their own culture there is an ancient genuine element of Judaism.

EIGHT

FROM *MILLET* TO MINORITY: TURKISH JEWRY*

Aron Rodrigue

THE DEVELOPMENTS that led to the transformation of Turkish Jewry in the nineteenth and twentieth centuries can be understood properly only within a comparative perspective. The history of Sephardi Jewry in the modern period, just as the history of the Middle East in general, has too often been treated as an exotic specialty, as a study of rare and quaint communities far from the mainstream of central developments that all took place elsewhere. I will attempt here to place the history of Turkish Jewry within the contexts of both modern Jewish and Middle Eastern history by concentrating upon the twin processes of the emergence of the modern Turkish state and the emancipation of the Jewish communities under its rule.

The focus will be the Ladino (Judeo-Spanish) *Kulturbereich* of the Ottoman Empire with the communities in Macedonia, Thrace, and the Aegean at its core. Most of these, with the exception of Salonica, were to become part of the Turkish Republic that was to emerge in 1923, and it is their fate during the process of transition from empire to republic that is my central concern here.

A distinct Judeo-Spanish culture area came into being in the Ottoman Balkans and the Aegean littoral with the mass arrival of the Iberian exiles of the late fifteenth and the sixteenth centuries. Eventually four major urban centers, Istanbul, Izmir, Salonica, and Edirne, emerged where most of the Judeo-Spanish populations lived. Many satellite communities also came into existence in the various hinterlands of these cities, such as Sarajevo in Bosnia and Monastir (Bitola) and Uskup (Skopje) in Macedonia on the overland trade route from the Adriatic to Salonica; Sofia, Plovdiv, Ruse, and Widdin in Bulgaria on the trade route from Edirne to the Danube and then further north and west; and the numerous communities of Asia Minor, such as Bursa, Aydin, Manisa, and Bergama around the trade routes between Istanbul and Izmir.

For more than three centuries, the Judeo-Spanish community lived as a

* A part of this article appeared previously in my book *French Jews, Turkish Jews: The Alliance Israélite Universelle and the Politics of Jewish Schooling in Turkey, 1860–1925* (Bloomington, Ind., 1990).

distinct unit with its particular religion, culture, and language in the mosaic of different religious and ethnic groups that together comprised the Ottoman Levant. Tolerated and protected by the state but socially and juridically inferior to the Muslims, enjoying considerable relative autonomy, the Jewish community constituted a recognized non-Muslim group in the Ottoman realm, a *millet,* to use the appellation that gained formal currency in the nineteenth century. The boundaries of Judeo-Spanish ethnicity underwent considerable change and reconstruction over time marked by the constant give-and-take with the surrounding groups and cultures in the areas of foodways, dress, music, popular beliefs, economic activity, and social interaction. This dialectic, which is characteristic of all ethnicity, played itself out in the Judeo-Spanish case in an articulation that led to the domestication and co-optation of the "other" through its Judaization by normative rabbinical Judaism, and its Hispanicization through the medium of the Judeo-Spanish language. The separate Judeo-Spanish identity, legitimated both by the Jewish tradition and the ruling authority, remained paramount and all-encompassing.

In the middle of the nineteenth century, it is estimated that there were 150,000 Jews in the empire,[1] with the Judeo-Spanish communities of the Balkans and western Asia Minor constituting about half this population. Their numbers had increased by another 100,000 on the eve of the Balkan wars of 1912–13 when Salonica was annexed by Greece. In 1911, there were close to 140,000 Jews in an area within the borders of present-day Turkey.[2]

Some of the most important developments of modern Jewish history are closely intertwined with the unfolding of modern state-building practices in Europe, and their gradual extension to the non-European world. Jewish corporate autonomy was slowly eroded as the absolutist state evolved in western and central Europe. The French Revolution, bringing about the elimination of all corporate groups, abolished the juridically accepted Jewish "nation" when it emancipated the Jews in 1790 and 1791. The concepts of citizenship and equality also entailed the divesting

[1] [Jean Henri] A[bdolonyme] Ubicini, *Letters on Turkey,* trans. Lady Easthope (London, 1859; reprint, New York, 1973), 18–19, 22. This is the only source that reports the results of the census of 1844, which is otherwise not available. See Kemal H. Karpat, *Ottoman Population 1830–1914: Demographic and Social Characteristics* (Madison, Wis., 1985), 116.

[2] *Bulletin semestriel de l'Alliance Israélite Universelle,* 36 (1911): 86–115. For Ottoman censuses, see the discussions in Stanford J. Shaw, "The Ottoman Census System and Population, 1831–1919," *International Journal of Middle Eastern Studies* 9 (1978): 325–36, and Karpat, *Ottoman Population.* For the figures reported in Ottoman censuses in the first decade of the twentieth century, see Justin McCarthy, *The Arab World, Turkey and the Balkans (1878–1914): A Handbook of Historical Statistics* (Boston, 1982), 64, 101, and Karpat, *Ottoman Population,* 161–90.

by hitherto distinctive groups of all that had made them legally and culturally separate. The emergence of the modern nation-state brought with it a concerted effort to "nationalize" all groups under its rule, to forge and often create from scratch a nation, one and indivisible.

This process was also to be relevant to the history of Turkish Jewry. However, its evolution was to be marked by some of the particular features of its Ottoman setting, especially by the nature of the Ottoman state.

The Ottoman social formation did not develop feudalism. Instead, it was deeply marked by a strong patrimonial state that received its legitimation both from Islam and from the pre-Muslim Middle Eastern and Asian empire traditions. There was no division of religion and state, with the Sultan Caliph being responsible for the implementation of the *sharia,* the Muslim religious law, in the pursuit of justice. He was also technically the owner of all the land and of his subjects. The strong centralized bureaucracy, the military with a slave army, the janissaries, at its core, and the religious clergy, constituted the three pillars of the ruling elite. These were the groups exempted from paying taxes. The rest of the population, the taxpaying subjects, known as the *reaya* (the flock), were strictly separate from the ruling class. However, access to the latter was not through hereditary succession, but through education and military achievement.[3]

Ottoman society was marked by the lack of a large scale landowning class. The social base was constituted by a free peasantry tilling the soil on relatively small plots over which it had the usufruct. The ruling elite, whose economic existence was dependent upon the reproduction of the system, and upon the extraction of surplus in the form of essentially tributary taxes from the *reaya,* systematically eliminated all concentrations of power, whether economic or social, that could challenge its authority. Hence, no horizontal ties could be developed that could eventually evolve autonomous forms of authority and legitimation. All power and status was dependent upon a vertical linkage to the center. The result was a weak civil society in the face of a strongly bureaucratized ruling apparatus.[4]

[3] For the classical period of the Ottoman Empire, see Halil Inalcik, *The Ottoman Empire: The Classical Age* (London, 1973).

[4] Some of the best studies of the Ottoman social formation and state are Serif Mardin, "Power, Civil Society and Culture in the Ottoman Empire," *Comparative Studies in Society and History* 11 (1969): 258–81; Metin Heper, "Center and Periphery in the Ottoman Empire," *International Political Science Review* 1 (1980): 81–105; idem, *The State Tradition in Turkey* (North Humberside, Eng.: 1985); Ali Kazancigil, "The Ottoman Turkish State and Kemalism," in Ali Kazancigil and Ergun Özbudun, eds., *Atatürk, Founder of a Modern State* (Hamden, Conn., 1981), 37–56; and Çaglar Keyder, *State and Class in Turkey: A Study in Capitalist Development* (London, 1987). For a discussion of state traditions in an Islamic context see Brian Turner, *Weber and Islam* (London, 1974), and

Non-Muslims, who were by definition outside the ruling elite open only to Muslims, were an important part of the *reaya* class. Nevertheless, the fact that they were outside the dominant systemic paradigm of society, and were allowed a degree of autonomy in their internal affairs, meant that they were in some respects better off than their Muslim counterparts. They were the only groups that could function with their alternative power and legitimation systems and develop their own institutions. In many ways, they were the only legitimate corporate groups within the empire. This would prove to be pregnant with consequences for the development of nationalism among the Christian populations under different conditions that evolved in the nineteenth century.

Economic, political, and military factors all converged from the end of the sixteenth century onward to bring about the decline of the empire. Growing incorporation into the capitalist world system proved to be corrosive for the Ottoman economy, aligning certain areas of the empire toward export-oriented agriculture and away from the control of the bureaucracy. Inept leadership and defeat in war precipitated a crisis in the body politic that was to last centuries. The control by the center began to slip considerably in the period of decline. Tax farming, a favorite means of raising revenue in the empire, proved to have disastrous consequences in a period of weakening supervision and leadership, with a large amount of wealth siphoned off from the coffers of the state into private hands. Peripheral landed elites, the *ayan,* began to emerge, challenging the authority of the bureaucracy and demonstrating hitherto unseen independence from the center.[5]

By the end of the eighteenth century, segments of the bureaucratic section of the ruling elite began increasingly to look upon the West for blueprints to put the tottering Ottoman house in order. The westernizing reforms that were to be adopted as the panacea for all the ills facing Ottoman society were, hence, not merely acts of mimesis, of blind emulation of a victorious West, but measures designed to reassert control by the center over the periphery, of destroying the emergent alternative loci of power. The rationalizing and streamlining of the ruling apparatus by the borrowing of the centralizing measures of European states, especially of the strong French nation-state, were all designed with this aim in sight.

Bertrand Badie, *Les deux Etats: pouvoir et société en Occident et en terre d'Islam* (Paris, 1986). For an analysis of the western state, see Bertrand Badie and Pierre Birnbaum, *The Sociology of the State* (Chicago, 1983).

[5] The major studies of the process of incorporation of the empire into the capitalist world economy have been conveniently collected in Huri Islamoglu-Inan, ed., *The Ottoman Empire and the World Economy* (Cambridge and Paris, 1987). See also Resat Kasaba, *The Ottoman Empire and the World Economy* (Albany, N.Y., 1988), and Keyder, *State and Class.*

The new policies of centralization were to have consequences for the non-Muslims also. Not only were the new measures designed to reassert control by the center, but the growing familiarity with contemporary European political systems made the maintenance of the status quo with respect to the non-Muslim communities undesirable.

The age of reforms, referred to collectively as the *Tanzimat,* inaugurated the period of change in the legal status of the non-Muslims. The *Hatti Serif* of Gülhane (the Noble Rescript of the Rose Chamber) of 1839 introduced the new principles with the announcement by the Sultan of a series of reforms guaranteeing the life, honor, and property of all the subjects, those who belonged to "the people of Islam and other nations."[6] The latter clause, implying a certain equality between "believer" and "unbeliever," and clearly designed to please European powers concerned with the welfare of the Christians of the empire, represented a potentially radical development. This innovation, implicit in the rescript of 1839, became explicit with the reform decree of 1856 that granted equality to all non-Muslims. This constituted a dramatic change in their status and was perceived in the West as heralding the emancipation of the Christians and the Jews. In the following decades, Christians and Jews began to participate in local municipal and regional councils.[7] In 1869, a new citizenship law formulated explicitly the new conception of Ottoman citizenship, which included all the subjects of the Sultan irrespective of their religion, with rights and obligations now in theory flowing mutually between the state and the individual without any mediating bodies, such as religious organizations, in between.[8]

The Ottoman reformers were concerned, at least ostensibly, to create a unified patriotic citizenry and to downplay the importance of ethnic and religious divisions. In this respect, the 1856 decree and the citizenship law of 1869 can be interpreted as having legally emancipated the non-Muslims, and among them, the Jews of the Ottoman Empire.

The moves toward equality were slowly accompanied by legislation seriously eroding the communal autonomy of the *millets.* New conceptions of citizenship were incompatible with old *millet* privileges. According to the provisions of the Reform Decree, criminal, civil, and commercial

[6] "Ahal-i Islam ve milel-i saire." The original text can be found in facsimile in Maarif Vekâleti, *Tanzimat* (Istanbul, 1940–), 1:48–49. For an English translation, see Jacob C. Hurewitz, ed., *The Middle East and North Africa in World Politics* (New Haven, 1975–79), 1:269–71.

[7] The changes in local government have been discussed by Ilber Ortayli, *Tanzimat'tan sonra Mahalli Idareler* (Ankara, 1974).

[8] For a discussion, see Kemal H. Karpat, "*Millets* and Nationality: The Roots of the Incongruity of Nation and State in the Post-Ottoman Era," in Benjamin Braude and Bernard Lewis, eds., *Christians and Jews in the Ottoman Empire* (New York, 1982), 1:162–63.

cases were to be tried by mixed tribunals of Muslims and non-Muslims established in the 1840s.[9] In 1850 the French commercial code and in 1858 the French penal code were adopted and were made to apply to all subjects of the empire.[10] Indeed, for all intents and purposes, the autonomy of the *millets* in matters concerning civil, criminal, and commercial cases had come formally to an end in 1856. The decree gave the non-Muslims the option of continuing to use their own courts in cases involving family, inheritance, and divorce litigation. Matters concerning personal status were all that remained of the juridical autonomy of the *millets.*[11]

The decree of 1856 also called upon the non-Muslims to institute "reforms required by the progress of civilization and the age."[12] New regulations reorganizing communal bodies prepared by the Greeks, Armenians, and the Jews came into effect in the decade following the decree. The new administrations were now explicitly hierarchical organizations with the laity having a major say in the running of communal affairs.[13] The religious leaders of the *millets*—in the case of the Jews, the chief rabbi—were now formally the juridically recognized leaders of the communities and acted as their representatives in affairs that were of concern to them. The new organs appear to have been mainly confessional bodies, with most matters outside the religious realm falling outside their purview.

The serious erosion of the autonomy of the non-Muslim *millets,* did not, however, take place in a context of a total rationalization of the Ottoman legal system. The reformers, introducing the changes from

[9] See Clause 12 in Hurewitz, *The Middle East,* 1:317.

[10] Bülent Tahiroglu, "Tanzimat'tan sonra Kanunlastirma Hareketleri," *Tanzimat'tan Cumhuriyet'e Türkiye Ansiklopedisi* 3 (1985): 588–96.

[11] In the case of the Jews, some commercial litigation still found its way to the Jewish religious courts. But in the light of the clauses of the 1856 decree, the ruling of these courts in this area did not have the force of the law. The erosion in the juridical autonomy of the *millets* has been discussed in passing in several works dealing with the Christian communities under Ottoman rule. For example, see Télémaque Tutundjian, *Du pacte politique entre l'Etat ottoman et les nations non-musulmans de la Turquie* (Lausanne, 1904), 56–58; F. van den Staen de Jehan, *De la situation légale des sujets ottomans non-musulmans* (Brussels, 1906), 95–108; Constantine G. Papadopoulos, *Les privilèges du Patriarcat oecuménique dans l'Empire ottoman* (Paris, 1924), 103–13; and Vartan Artinian, "A Study of the Historical Development of the Armenian Constitutional System in the Ottoman Empire" (Ph.D. diss., Brandeis University, 1970), 51. None of these works, however, provides a thorough study of this problem in the nineteenth century. It is to be hoped that, eventually, Ottoman archives will be more accessible, and that scholars will undertake in depth studies of this question.

[12] "Asar-i medeniyet ve malümat-i müktesibenin icap ettirdigi islahat," from the text of the decree to be found in Enver Ziya Karal, *Nizam-i Cedid ve Tanzimat Devirleri, 1789–1856,* 2d ed. (Ankara, 1956), 259.

[13] For the Judeo-Spanish translation of the statutes concerning the Jews see *Konstitusion para la nasion israelita de Turkia* (Istanbul, 1865).

above, did not replace already existing legal systems but simply added to them. Hence, until the end of the empire, there continued to exist at least four different and often competing legal systems: the new secular courts, the Islamic courts, the *millet* courts, and the consular courts with jurisdiction over non-Ottoman citizens.

The dualism between the western and eastern that was to mark the last century of the empire reflected to some extent the balance of forces. The westernizing Ottoman state, while acquiring the trappings of the European state, remained at the same time firmly anchored in its more traditional moorings; the Islamic character of its legitimation system could not be challenged under the Sultan Caliph. The tradition of bureaucratic action from above precluded any real understanding of societal developments. The role of the economy in the reforms was neglected by a bureaucracy long accustomed to an essentially tributary financial relationship with the subjects. Military and bureaucratic reforms in the age of capitalist industrialization in the West was not enough to "save the state," the major concern of the reformers. By 1875, the empire was bankrupt, and large sections of its economy had entered under the control of foreigners.

In fact, the multiple competencies in the legal arena point to the essentially hybrid nature of the reforming state in the nineteenth century. The weight of conservative forces on the Muslim side, and the protection by western powers of the Christian groups of the empire, hampered seriously the implementation of the Ottomanist agenda of the reformers. Old and new coexisted uneasily side by side, diluting the impact of the reforms on the practical level.

This is further evidence of the failure of the state to forge a common Ottoman identity for all its citizens. Indeed, the state was relatively late in attempting to reform the system of education, the primary element in the making of nations in the West. The cultural realm proved particularly intractable to centralization because of the multicultural composition of the empire, growing nationalism among several ethnic bodies, and resistance from the devout Muslim population to the notion of a common educational system that would have had to divorce itself from Islam to have any appeal to non-Muslims.

The *Tanzimat* announcements of 1839 did not even mention education. The reforms introduced slowly in this field in the following decades concerned only the Muslim schools, and even in this area concerned themselves exclusively with secondary education, neglecting elementary education that until the 1870s remained a monopoly of the Muslim clergy. The autonomy of Christian schools was jealously guarded by western powers that reduced considerably the freedom of action of the

Ottoman reformers. The schools established by the state to create a modern army such as the naval school founded in 1773, the artillery school founded in 1796, and the medical school created in 1827, were all theoretically open to non-Muslims, and indeed a few did attend these schools in the course of the nineteenth century.

Following the Reform decree, the *rüsdiyes* (lower secondary schools), which had begun to be established by the state, became open to all non-Muslims in 1861, while the principle of separate elementary education for each religious group remained intact.[14] This was changed in the 1870s when secular primary schools, the *iptidais,* were created following a reorganization of the educational system by the Public Education Law of 1869, and non-Muslims could now attend these newly founded institutions (Clauses 33 and 42).[15] The law contained provisions for the registration and control of non-Muslim schools (Clause 129), but these do not appear to have been acted upon until 1886 when an inspectorate of non-Muslims schools was created.[16]

It was only in 1876 that the short-lived first constitutional regime adopted Turkish as the official language of the state.[17] In the 1890s, teachers were sent by the education ministry to all non-Muslim schools to teach Turkish. However, the language of instruction in these schools remained the language chosen by the directors. Most taught Turkish in a fairly rudimentary manner. The attempt by the state to impose closer control over non-Muslim schools in a proposed 1909 education law was postponed when faced with stiff opposition from the Christian *millets.*[18] Though the law of 1913 reasserted the principle of inspection,[19] the fact remains that the separate educational system of the non-Muslims, although under attack by the early twentieth century, remained intact until World War I. The Turkish state schools were too few and weak to have any appreciable impact on the non-Muslim masses who continued to attend their own school systems. In 1895, two decades after state ele-

[14] Osman Ergin, *Türkiye Maarif Tarihi* (Istanbul, 1939–43; reprint, Istanbul, 1977), 2:606–7; Nevzad Ayas, *Türkiye Cumhuriyeti Milli Egitimi* (Ankara, 1948), 688; Faik Resit Unat, *Türkiye Egitim Sisteminin Gelismesine Tarihi Bir Bakis* (Ankara, 1964), 22; Bayram Kodaman, *Abdülhamid Devri Egitim Sistemi* (Istanbul, 1980), 43; Ilhan Tekeli, "Tanzimat'tan Cumhuriyet'e Egitim Sistemindeki Degismeler," *Tanzimat'tan Cumhuriyet'e Türkiye Ansiklopedisi* 2 (1985): 468.

[15] Kodaman, *Abdülhamid Devri,* 100–101.

[16] Ibid., 66–67; Unat, *Türk Egitim,* 25, 28.

[17] Enver Ziya Karal, "Tanzimat'tan sonra Türk Dil Sorunu," *Tanzimat'tan Cumhuriyet'e Türkiye Ansiklopedisi* 2 (1985): 317.

[18] Ayas, *Türkiye Cumhuriyeti,* 690; Cemil Koçak, "Tanzimat'tan sonra özel ve Yabanci Okullar," *Tanzimat'tan Cumhuriyet'e Türkiye Ansiklopedisi* 2 (1985): 488.

[19] Ayas, *Türkiye Cumhuriyeti,* 690; Koçak, "Tanzimat'tan Sonra," 488.

mentary education had become open to non-Muslims, only eighty non-Muslims were attending these schools in all of the empire.[20] Both the order of priorities of the reformist bureaucracy, unused to the mass mobilization policies of activist social engineering, and the constant pressure from European powers to safeguard the privileges of foreign and non-Muslim schools prevented the implementation of an "Ottomanist" educational policy.

The belatedness in the creation of an education system that would also accommodate and integrate the non-Muslims into a united citizenry was part of the general problems faced by the Ottoman state in the course of its westernization attempts. Non-Muslims were given equality in 1856, and yet the poll tax remained, hidden as the exemption tax, separating the Muslim from the non-Muslim. The juridical system was reformed, but no unitary system emerged. Overlapping competencies in all areas of life together with the impossibility of finding a unifying ideology that would cement the various groups together and provide a centripetal force meant that in spite of its centralizing impulse, the impact of the reforming Ottoman state on civil society remained highly uneven.

This had important consequences for the Jews. In Europe, one of the major factors in the "modernization" of the Jewish communities was the crucial and decisive impetus given by the state, which, from the period of the Enlightenment onward, steadily dismantled corporate bodies and intervened in the life of the Jewish community by sponsoring a policy of "nationalization" with education as its mainstay. Even in states such as Russia or the Habsburg Empire where, unlike in France, the erosion or dissolution of the Jewish corporate body was not accompanied by the granting of civic equality, the governments had embarked upon a policy of creating schools for the Jews with the ultimate aim of hastening their assimilation. This European model applies only partially in the case of the history of Turkish Jewry in the last century of the Ottoman Empire. A mobilized civic culture did not emerge, and the Jews, together with other non-Muslims, continued to remain dissociated from and non-integrated into a poorly developed public sphere.

An astute observer pointed to this fact in a letter written in 1893:

> What strikes a Bulgarian Jew when he enters Turkey is, before everything else, the air of freedom that one breathes. Under a theoretically despotic government, one definitely enjoys more freedom than in a constitutional state. . . . One almost does not feel that there is a government. . . . The absence of an irksome police, of crushing taxation, of very heavy civic duties, here is what the non-Muslim subjects of the Sultan should appreciate;

[20] Stanford J. Shaw and Ezel Kural Shaw, *History of the Ottoman Empire and Modern Turkey* (Cambridge, 1977), 2:113.

> the Jews in particular, can, quite justifiably, consider themselves in this country as the happiest among all their coreligionists in the world: enjoying all the rights, they have almost no duties.[21]

The relatively weak impact of the westernizing Ottoman state on civil society is very aptly rendered in this letter.

The main impetus for cultural change for Turkish Jews would come from a different source, from western Jewry. The nineteenth century saw a growing intervention by western Jews in the affairs of their eastern coreligionists. European Jewry, in the space of the century from 1750 to 1850, had changed dramatically. The *Haskalah,* the whittling away and the abolition of Jewish corporate autonomy, the granting of emancipation, and the demands and attractions of the European nation-state had eroded Jewish traditional society and culture in western Europe. Leading sections of western Jewry were now socially, politically, and ideologically quite different from their brethren elsewhere. The western Jew had begun to perceive the eastern Jew (whether eastern European or Middle Eastern) as somehow inferior, and with this had come the desire to transform, to "civilize," to "regenerate" this less fortunate coreligionist, to remake him or her in the image of the emancipated, acculturated European Jew.[22] The reports published in western Jewish newspapers such as the *Jewish Chronicle,* the *Archives Israélites,* the *Univers Israélite,* and the *Allgemeine Zeitung des Judenthums* in the 1840s and 1850s, highlighting the fallen state of Middle Eastern Jewry, its economic misery, and its "ignorance" and "superstition," created the contours of a "Jewish Eastern Question."[23] For western Jews, it was imperative to solve the Jewish Eastern Question by instituting the appropriate reforms, most notably in the domain of education. This was seen both as an act of solidarity and charity, and as a political necessity. The eastern Jew was an embarrassment to the emancipated western Jew.

The Alliance Israélite Universelle, an organization founded in Paris in 1860 by French Jews, was the very incarnation of the reforming impulse of western Jewry vis-à-vis the Jews of the East. It was active in defending the rights of the Jews throughout the world. But its real work was to be in the field of education. Starting in 1862 in Tetuan in Morocco, it opened

[21] Archives de l'Alliance Israélite Universelle, Turquie 74. E., Arié, 17 November 1893.

[22] Rodrigue, *French Jews, Turkish Jews,* 8–17. See also Michel Abitbol, "The Encounter between French Jewry and the Jews of North Africa: Analysis of a Discourse (1830–1914)," in Frances Malino and Bernard Wasserstein, eds., *The Jews in Modern France* (Hanover, N.H., 1985), 31–53, and Esther Benbassa, "Israël face à lui-même: Judaïsme occidental et judaïsme ottoman (19e–20e siècles)," *Pardès* 7 (1988): 105–29.

[23] See the series of articles by Ludwig Philippson in *Allgemeine Zeitung des Judenthums* 18 (1854): 152–54, 189.

elementary and eventually secondary schools for Jewish boys and girls throughout North Africa and the Middle East. By 1913, it had established a network of 183 schools with 43,700 students in an area ranging from Morocco in the West to Iran in the East. Generations of Sephardim were educated in Alliance institutions that provided an essentially French instruction with Jewish subjects such as history, religion, and Hebrew added to the curriculum. The Alliance played an important role in the westernization process of Sephardi Jewry.[24]

The first school in Turkey was established in Edirne in 1867. This was followed by schools for boys and girls in Istanbul and Izmir in the 1870s. In 1911, there were 9,764 students in Alliance institutions within the borders of present-day Turkey.[25] By 1914, each Turkish Jewish community had an Alliance school.

After often rocky beginnings, the schools slowly became accepted by the local communities. At first, they began as private establishments, with very few students. Eventually they gained in popularity. For the first time in the history of Sephardi Jewry, girls also began to attend schools. Indeed, this was perhaps the most revolutionary development that followed the establishment of western education in the Judeo-Spanish communities. It became normal and desirable for girls to receive an education, and this eventually opened new paths for Jewish women, not only in the professional realm, but also in contributing to the social advancement of women within the family and within society at large.

It would be a mistake to assume that the Alliance came just as a missionary body. There were local forces at work in Turkish Jewry that favored its activities, and indeed often invited it to establish schools long before the Alliance had any plans to do so in a particular locality. One important elite that supported the work of the Alliance very actively was made up of foreign Jews, called Francos, most of them Italian Jews long present in the Levant for the purposes of trade.[26] Their links with the West had never ceased. Local notables, who, together with the Francos, were aware of the need for the Jews to acquire new skills to compete

[24] For general studies of the Alliance, see Narcisse Leven, *Cinquante ans d'histoire: L'Alliance Israélite Universelle (1860–1910)*, 2 vols. (Paris, 1911–20); André Chouraqui, *Cent ans d'histoire: L'Alliance Israélite Universelle et la renaissance juive contemporaine (1860–1960)* (Paris, 1965); Aron Rodrigue, *De l'instruction à l'émancipation: Les enseignants de l'Alliance israélite universelle et les Juifs d'Orient, 1860–1939* (Paris, 1989).

[25] Rodrigue, *French Jews, Turkish Jews*, 92.

[26] The "protection" enjoyed by the Francos under the capitulations, and the relations of the Francos of Salonica with the French in the late seventeenth and early eighteenth centuries, has been discussed in Simon Schwarzfuchs, "Sulam Saloniki," *Sefunot* 15 (1971–81): 79–102. The status of the Jews is discussed in Minna Rozen, "Strangers in a Strange Land: The Extraterritorial Status of Jews in Italy and the Ottoman Empire in the Sixteenth to the Eighteenth Centuries," in Aron Rodrigue, ed., *Ottoman and Turkish Jewry: Community and Leadership* (Bloomington, Ind., 1992), 123–66.

better with the Greeks and the Armenians, were also active supporters. There were a few local *maskilim* in touch, through the Hebrew press, with developments in the wider Jewish world, who were also active in the creation of these institutions. Slowly but steadily, these elements influenced the local rabbinate, which became less hostile toward the activities of the Alliance. The deep economic misery of the communities lowered the resistance from the more traditional quarters who could not put up a strong fight against an institution that also had begun to spend substantial sums of money. Many of the schools began to be integrated in communal life, often receiving small subsidies from the communal bodies.

The Alliance institutions expanded particularly rapidly at the turn of the century. Large centers such as Istanbul, Izmir, and Salonica had more than one school for boys and girls each. In many cases, what began as elementary establishments slowly became secondary ones. Accountancy classes were added. Vocational training schemes were established to teach new trades to boys and girls. Many youth clubs, alumni organizations, mutual help groups, and libraries were set up around the schools. The language used in all these centers was of course French; Hebrew was not ignored, though it was taught mainly for the purpose of enabling the students to read and understand the Bible and the prayer book.[27]

It is quite clear that not all Jewish children of school age went to the Alliance institutions. The traditional *Talmudei Torah* survived for a long time. Nevertheless, here too the action of the Alliance made itself felt. The Alliance directors were highly critical of traditional education, which consisted essentially of the learning of Hebrew and the translation of the holy texts into Judeo-Spanish. Report after report from the directors paint the darkest possible picture of these institutions, which were seen as centers of ignorance and obscurantism. The language of the directors is strongly resonant with the motifs of the diatribes of European *maskilim* against the traditional *heders*. The clash of the two different educational systems, indeed of two worlds, is crystal clear in their discourse.

Once the Alliance schools were secure, the attention of the organization turned to these *Talmudei Torah*. The Alliance in the end succeeded either in the outright fusion of these institutions with its schools, or in introducing substantial reforms, such as the introduction of the teaching of French through the appointment of an Alliance teacher as the director of the *Talmud Torah*. Hence its influence extended far beyond its own establishments.[28] By 1914, it can be said that in the Judeo-Spanish-

[27] For an analysis of the Alliance's activities in Turkey, see Rodrigue, *French Jews, Turkish Jews.*

[28] See Aron Rodrigue, "The Alliance Israélite Universelle and the Attempt to Reform Rabbinical and Religious Instruction in Turkey," in Simon Schwarzfuchs, ed., *L'"Alliance" dans les communautés du bassin méditerranéen à la fin du 19ème siècle et son influence sur la situation sociale et culturelle* (Jerusalem, 1987), 53–70.

speaking communities of the Ottoman Empire, the Alliance was the force with the greatest influence on all the Jewish educational establishments and came close to establishing a monopoly on Jewish education.

But the real importance of the schools should be interpreted in the context of the rivalry between the non-Muslim groups of the empire. The nineteenth century saw the final incorporation of the Levant into the capitalist world economy. The Anglo-Ottoman trade convention of 1838 heralded the beginning of free trade with the West, with the lowering of taxes on trade and the abolition of state monopolies.[29] Accompanied with the introduction of the steamboat to the Mediterranean, commerce with the West increased dramatically by the middle of the century. The Greek and Armenian commercial classes, by now the traditional intermediaries with the West, benefited tremendously from this development.

It was French that had emerged as the lingua franca of all trade and commerce in the Levant, and its acquisition was essential for success in the international and indeed local marketplace now dominated by western economic interests. The popularity of the Alliance schools in Turkey was the result of this larger development. A western orientation in general, and knowledge of western ways and languages in particular, were considered crucial for Turkish Jewry by its commercial elite (mostly of Franco origin) to compete effectively with the Greeks and Armenians, and to improve the lot of the desperately poor masses. With Jews flocking to Alliance schools, and eventually, in much lesser numbers, even to other establishments such as Catholic and Protestant schools set up by missionaries, a major cultural opening to the West took place in the decades that preceded World War I. In the context of the larger westernization of the empire and the domination of its economy by Europe, western education came to constitute for the Jews a major tool for the reestablishment of economic links with the West that had been lost in the previous two centuries.

In one city, Salonica, the Jews clearly gained the upper hand in the economy. They made up more than half the population of this major port city on the Aegean—an important entrepôt for all the commerce between the eastern Mediterranean, the Balkans, and Europe, a boom town in the second half of the nineteenth century—and emerged as the masters of its economic life.[30] By the 1880s, most of the Salonica economy was in their hands.[31] They were particularly active in banking and finance, in the

[29] Sevket Pamuk, *Osmanli Ekonomisi ve Dünya Kapitalizmi (1820–1913)* (Ankara, 1984), 18–19; Charles Issawi, *The Economic History of Modern Turkey* (Chicago, 1980), 74–82.

[30] On the Jewish community of Salonica, see Paul Dumont, "La structure sociale de la communauté juive de Salonique à la fin du dix-neuvième siècle," *Revue Historique* 263 (April-June 1980): 351–93.

[31] David (Daout) Levi, "Peilut ha-yehudim be hayei ha-mishar," in David Recanati, ed., *Zikhron Saloniki* (Tel Aviv, 1971–86), 2:198–201.

grain trade with the West, in the textile and tobacco industries, and in wine and beer production.[32] The firms of Burla, Botton, and Gattegno were the most important local representatives of European firms doing business with the Levant. The Allatini and Modiano banks, as well as the Bank of Salonica, all established by Jews with Jewish capital, were the major financial forces behind the Jews' rise to preeminence in the economy of the city.[33]

Interestingly, Salonica, which was a leading nodal point of the incorporation of the empire into the capitalist world economy, also saw the emergence of the first and only Jewish socialist movement among the Sephardim of the eastern Mediterranean. The Labor Federation of Salonica, led by Avraham Benaroya, was a mostly Jewish organization, with its support coming from the large Jewish working class of Salonica. The movement flourished briefly after the Young Turk revolution of 1908 and was dissolved by the Greeks after the annexation of the city by Greece in 1912.[34]

The other Judeo-Spanish communities did not see the same economic rise as in Salonica. The Greeks and Armenians were much more numerous in the cities of Istanbul and Izmir, much more entrenched in the leadership positions of the economy. For example, in Istanbul in 1885, the Jews constituted 5.49 percent of the working population, and 5.24 percent of the total engaged in commerce, trade, and industry.[35] In contrast, the Greeks and Armenians, making up respectively 22.52 and 20.58 percent of the working population, constituted 25.41 and 26.99 percent respectively of the total involved with industry, trade, and commerce.[36] The Muslims were underrepresented, comprising 49.4 percent of the total in the workforce and 38.32 percent of the total in trade and industry.[37]

The position occupied by the Jews relative to the other non-Muslims had not changed much by 1900. In that year, the Jews made up 17 percent of the total non-Muslim population of the city, but 13 percent of those engaged in trade and commerce, 6 percent of those in the liberal professions, and only 3 percent of those active in industry.[38]

Even though no community was to reach the economic heights achieved

[32] Centre de recherche sur le Judaïsme de Salonique, ed., *Salonique, Ville-mère en Israël* (Hebrew) (Jerusalem, Tel Aviv, 1967), 235ff.

[33] Itshac Emmanuel, "Los jidios de Salonique," in Recanati, *Zikhron Saloniki,* 1:19–26.

[34] See Georges Haupt and Paul Dumont, *Osmanli Imparatorlugunda Sosyalist Hareketler* (Istanbul, 1977).

[35] Stanford J. Shaw, "The Population of Istanbul in the nineteenth century," *Tarih Dergisi* 32 (1979): 412.

[36] Ibid.

[37] Ibid.

[38] Archives de l'Alliance Israélite Universelle, Turquie 2. C. 8, A. H. Navon, 15 January 1900.

by that of Salonica, there is no doubt that the opening to the West as a result of western education and growing involvement with European economic interests did lead to increased upward social mobility among the Jews of Turkey in general. The widespread acquisition of French by the Jewish community was a significant step in elevating the hitherto relatively undeveloped Turkish Jewish bourgeoisie into the ranks of the predominantly non-Muslim mercantile classes that served as intermediaries between the world and local markets.

Trade and commerce were much more lucrative than state service. The numbers of Jews who mastered the Turkish language sufficiently well to aspire to positions within the civil bureaucracy and who succeeded in occupying such positions remained statistically insignificant. In 1885, there were ninety-nine Jews in state service in Istanbul, a mere 0.41 percent of the total of those employed by the bureaucracy. Other non-Muslims also remained underrepresented, with the Greeks and Armenians constituting 1.44 percent and 2.05 percent respectively of those in state service. In contrast, Muslims made up 95.34 percent of the total.[39]

These figures illustrate two principal factors that affected the history of the non-Muslims in the last decades of Ottoman rule. Non-Muslims had entered the economic orbit of the commercial interests of Europe and had remained dissociated from the Ottoman body politic in direct continuity with the situation that had prevailed in the previous centuries. At the same time, in spite of a relative opening of the state toward all its subjects irrespective of their religious background, there remained considerable blockages to the insertion of non-Muslims into the state apparatus. Old attitudes, alliances based on networks of interest, and in many cases outright prejudice based on religion created barriers to the advancement of non-Muslims in bureaucratic ranks. In spite of several individual non-Muslims reaching important positions in the administration, their marginality in the state service persisted till the end of the empire.[40]

The impact of western schooling on the cultural orientation of Turkish Jewry was considerable. French became almost a second mother language for the elite and even began to encroach on the Judeo-Spanish spoken by the masses. The opening up to Europe of Turkish Jewry led to new avenues, to new contacts with western culture. The rise of a secular Judeo-Spanish literature, the rise of the novel and drama in this medium, the efflorescence of the Judeo-Spanish press that also acted as a major transmitter of western news and ideas and worked in close collaboration with the Alliance schools, all were some of the results of westernization.

[39] Shaw, "Population of Istanbul," 412.

[40] Carter V. Findlay, "The Acid Test of Ottomanism: The Acceptance of Non-Muslims in the Late Ottoman Bureaucracy," in Braude and Lewis, *Christians and Jews,* 1:365.

By eroding and then totally supplanting the traditional education system, and hence destroying the main channel of the reproduction of traditional Jewish culture from generation to generation, the Alliance schools as well as other institutions dispensing a European education contributed to a growing trend of secularization. Religion lost its centrality in Jewish ethnic identity.

But this was not accompanied by a growing integration of the Jews into Ottoman society. European schooling contributed to an alienation of the community from its surrounding. Just at the time that the Ottoman state had embarked upon the policy of centralization and greater control over the groups that lived under its rule, the Turkish Jewish community assumed an increased non-Turkish orientation. The changes in the cultural make-up of the Jewish *millet* did not move in a parallel fashion to the changes instituted by the Ottoman state. Unlike western Europe, "modernization" for Turkish Jewry was not accompanied by integration into the culture of the surrounding society, or into the culture officially sponsored by the state.

In fact, the acquisition of French, far from weakening Judeo-Spanish ethnicity, simply marked it even more. French became domesticated, Judaized, Hispanicized. Speaking French on a daily basis became yet another ethnic marker in the local context. Ethnic boundaries shifted and accommodated French and western ways, and emerged strengthened. A strong Jewish identity and ethnicity, though now secularizing, remained paramount in the self-definition of the group.

The underlying cause of this development was the stalemate in which the westernizing elite at the helm of the state found itself. The reforms it adopted to "save the state" and bolster its own position introduced a degree of centralization and rationalization hitherto unseen in the annals of the empire. However, the development that had prompted it to initiate the reforms in the first place, the growing military, political, and economic domination of the Middle East by European powers, also prevented it from taking the reforms to their logical conclusions. The western powers were interested in reforming of the Ottoman Empire only in so far as this would increase the efficiency of the infrastructure of trade and commerce that was beneficial to them, would protect their economic and often political allies, the non-Muslims, and would prop up the empire against the growing expansion of Russian influence toward the Mediterranean. Otherwise, they were not interested in the creation of a strong Ottoman state that could hamper their freedom of action in the Middle East.

This stalemate resulted in the eventual bankruptcy of the Ottomanist agenda. The state could not bring about a united cohesive citizenry sharing common assumptions and orientations and it could not conjure up new loyalties. New economic and political links with Europe had disrupted old networks of power in the various areas of the empire, leading to the rise of new elites. At the same time, the *millets* had lost much of their autonomy without being integrated into the larger polity. The centralizing impulse of the state, even though uneven, was sufficiently corrosive to contribute, in reaction, to the constitution of new identities. In this context, the ascriptive religious affiliation that had been at the core of traditional group identity in the empire began in the course of the nineteenth century to be slowly accompanied by a nationalist one.

This process, particularly significant in the emergence of Balkan, Greek, and Armenian nationalisms, was also to mark the Judeo-Spanish communities of the empire. The removal of censorship after the 1908 Young Turk revolution saw the advent of Zionist activity in the major cities, with Istanbul and Salonica taking the lead. Newspapers, youth clubs, and Hebrew language associations sprung up. Major struggles of power within the communal administrations emerged between the Zionists and their opponents.[41] In Istanbul the 1910–11 communal elections saw the victory of the Zionists, to be repeated in the immediate aftermath of World War I. The same development took place also in Salonica, with the Zionists coming to power after the annexation of the city by the Greeks.

Zionism in the local context was less a movement of mass emigration to Palestine than an ideology of nationalism that reinterpreted the old religiously sanctioned sense of Jewish peoplehood in the language of modern nationalism. Ottomanism had opened few practical avenues of social integration for the Jews. Growing familiarity with the West had furthermore put Turkish Jewry into increased contact with the rest of world Jewry and with developments that affected it as a whole. With *millet* identity surviving intact the uneven centralizing policies of the reforming Ottoman state, an ideology of Jewish nationalism did not need belaboring to appeal to large sections of Turkish Jewry. Political infighting within the elite as well as class frictions also favored the utilization of Zionism as a tool in the power struggles within the community.

At the same time, and unlike other nationalist movements of the non-Muslims, Jewish nationalism in Turkey does not appear to have favored a break-up of the empire. Rarely was there talk among Turkish Zionists of an independent Jewish state in Palestine. The interests of the Jews were well served by the continuation of the empire as a multi-ethnic entity. Like their Hapsburg counterparts, the Jews were one of the few *staat-*

[41] On Zionism in Turkey, see Esther Benbassa, "Haim Nahum Effendi, dernier Grand Rabbin de l'Empire ottoman (1908–1920), son rôle politique et diplomatique" (Ph.D. diss., University of Paris, 1987). See also idem, "Le sionisme dans l'Empire ottoman à l'aube du 20e siècle," *Vingtieme Siècle* 24 (1989): 69–80.

serhaltende groups in Turkey at a time when separatist nationalisms had made deep inroads into the non-Muslim populations, and the ruling Turks themselves had begun to abandon Ottomanism for a more exclusive Turkish nationalism. Jewish nationalism in Turkey, though using Zionism as its political discourse, appears in fact much closer to the diaspora nationalism of Dubnov. It constituted a modernized reformulation of the traditional Ottoman paradigm within which the Jewish *millet,* restored to its corporate autonomy, would coexist with other groups within a multi-ethnic and multireligious empire.

In contradistinction to Zionism, the weak integration of the Jews precluded the emergence of an "assimilationist" movement. There were indeed individuals such as David Fresko, Abraham Galanté, and later on Moise Kohen Tekinalp, who would call for such a move.[42] But they remained isolated voices. The "patriotism" of such figures was met by a lukewarm response from the Jewish masses when it came to putting it in practice by serving in the army, as is attested by the considerable increase in Jewish emigration following the conscription law of 1909. In the first decade of the twentieth century, many Jews from the Ottoman Empire emigrated to France, the United States, and Latin America, the rate of emigration increasing considerably after 1909.[43] The Judeo-Spanish newspaper of New York, *La Amerika,* estimated that in 1911 there were twenty thousand "Levantine" Jews in the United States.[44]

Jewish participation in Turkish politics also remained low. There appears to have been a brief flurry of activity at the time of the Young Turk movement. There was considerable support for the Young Turks among the Jews in the years 1908–9.[45] Individual Jews such as Albert Fua, Emmanuel Carasso, and Nissim Mazliach were active in Young Turk politics. But there was no real mass involvement by the Jews in the public arena. This low level of extracommunal political activity by the Jews was a direct outcome of their continued marginality within the Ottoman body politic. The emergence of Zionism, and indeed of socialism in Salonica, was an expression of this continued marginality deeply rooted in the Ottoman past, a marginality enduring, indeed strengthening as a result of the complex reverberations of the process of westernization in the Ottoman Empire.

42 On Galanté see Albert Kalderon, *Abraham Galanté: A Biography* (New York, 1983). On Tekinalp see Jacob Landau, *Tekinalp: Turkish Patriot, 1883–1961* (Leiden, 1984). No studies exist on David Fresko.

43 David de Sola Pool, "The Levantine Jews in the United States," *American Jewish Yearbook* 15 (1913): 209.

44 Ibid.

45 See Feroz Ahmad, "Unionist Relations with the Greek, Armenian, and Jewish Communities of the Ottoman Empire, 1908–1914," in Braude and Lewis, *Christians and Jews,* 1:425–28.

The emergence of the Republican state out of the ashes of the Ottoman Empire after close to a decade of crisis and military combat with the Balkan wars of 1912–13, World War I, and the Turkish war of independence of 1920–22 altered radically the contours of non-Muslim existence in Turkey. Most of the Armenian community perished, and the Greeks, with the exception of the Istanbul community, were transferred to Greece in return for the transfer of most Turks to Turkey. This meant in effect that the large Christian non-Muslim bourgeoisie of the prewar years was no longer present on most of Turkish soil. Many members of this bourgeoisie remained in Istanbul, but did not constitute a significant force. The Jews did not necessarily benefit from this development, as the triumphant Turkish nationalist state was determined to foster the growth of a "national," i.e., Turkish Muslim middle class, with the full weight of the economic policies of the government geared toward this agenda.[46]

The modern Turkish nation-state, now divested of its multi-ethnic ballast, could act much more decisively than the ramshackle Ottoman Empire. The bureaucratic military elite, continuing in its ruling role into the republic, could now take the reforms of the Ottoman period to their logical conclusion, unhampered by foreign intervention. The republican state, like the western one on which it modeled itself, hence went much further than the Ottoman one. Under its western-oriented bureaucratic leadership, not only was it concerned with controlling civil society, but it now also wanted to reform it, to "civilize" it, to bring it up to the level of western European societies. The model for the republic was the French Jacobin state, highly centralized, with no intermediary bodies between the citizenry and the state. The republic drew upon this western tradition as well as the specifically Ottoman one that stressed the omnipotence of the rulers. Under Ataturk, Turkey would see the separation of religion and politics through the effective disestablishment of Islam, the adoption of western institutions in all areas of life, the creation of a universal secular education system, and the putting in place of a republican ideology and populist nationalism designed to act as an agent of integration.

The new political system had a major impact on the Jewish community. It now found itself not in a multi-ethnic, multireligious setting, but in a relatively homogeneous nation-state. It was no longer part of a plural society but rather of a more monolithic unitary system. The *millet* as a juridical entity had become totally nonoperational, and any legal autonomy that had remained was abolished.

The Lausanne peace treaty of 1923 signed between Turkey and the Entente powers had stipulated that the rights of the non-Muslims would be protected. They would be free to use their languages, even in the court

[46] Keyder, *State and Class,* 71–90.

system, and could continue to operate their schools and charitable organizations as well as to regulate matters of personal and family status according to their religious laws.[47] However, these clauses of the treaty were renounced by the non-Muslims themselves in 1925, following the abolition of the caliphate and of Muslim religious courts in 1924 and the public disclosure of plans to adopt a new legal system modeled on the Swiss, Italian, and German codes.[48] There is considerable circumstantial evidence to suggest that the non-Muslims were in fact pressured to renounce these clauses of the treaty and were not acting on their own free will, although this is impossible to prove without access to the Turkish archives, which remain closed. The argument put forth by the official announcements on the part of the non-Muslim communities was that since the legal system of the state was no longer to be based on Muslim religious law but was to adopt secular western legal codes, the need had disappeared for non-Muslims to apply their own separate laws in matters concerning personal and family status.

With these developments, the last vestiges of the old *millet* privileges came to an end. No legal distinctions whatsoever remained in the statute books separating Muslim from non-Muslim. Finally, Islam ceased to be the religion of the state in 1928. The Jewish as well as the other non-Muslim communities became strictly voluntary confessional organizations.

The republican state also embarked upon a policy of "Turkicization" for the whole country, which also had major consequences for the Jews. The Young Turk governments had already tried to implement the beginnings of such a policy in the educational sphere. In 1915, the new regulations for private schools called for the teaching of the Turkish language, history, and geography in these schools by Turks (meaning Muslim Turks only) in Turkish.[49] This regulation was passed again by the Republican state in 1923.[50]

In the all-pervasive ultranationalist first years of the Republic, it was inevitable that the schools of the non-Muslims could not function as before. In 1924, the Alliance schools were banned from maintaining any links with "a foreign organization" and were from then on called communal schools.[51] Later on in the same year, the state curriculum was imposed on all Jewish schools, and the numbers devoted to French were severely curtailed. The Jews were presented with the option of either

[47] See the texts of the Lausanne treaty, Clauses 38 to 44 in Hurewitz, *Middle East,* 2:330–31.

[48] *Stamboul,* 20 October 1925.

[49] Cemil Koçak, "Tanzimat'tan sonra özel ve Yabanci Okullar," *Tanzimat'tan Cumhuriyet'e Türkiye Ansiklopedisi* 2 (1985): 489.

[50] Archives de l'Alliance Israélite Universelle, Turquie II. C. 8, Nathan, 14 May 1935.

[51] Ibid.

teaching in Turkish or "in their mother tongue," which the Ministry of Public Instruction declared to be Hebrew. This was a clever move, as very few Turkish Jews were familiar with Hebrew as a living language, and almost all spoke Judeo-Spanish, not recognized by the state as their mother tongue.[52] All the schools ended up by having to choose Turkish as their language of instruction. The teaching of French was relegated to a few hours a week. The last relatively autonomous pocket of action available to the Jews, that of education, hence was closed in 1924.

The Jews of Turkey, for the first time in their history, faced a full-fledged attack on their distinctiveness during these first decades of the republic. Communal autonomy had disappeared completely. Freedom of action in the field of education was lost. The usage of Judeo-Spanish was frowned upon and many organizations were founded to encourage the Jews to speak Turkish. The dominant secular ethos of the republic, which had launched a fierce attack on Islam, also accelerated the process of secularization that had been well under way for Turkish Jewry since the introduction of western education half a century ago. Religious and communal institutions atrophied further and lost their hold on most of the community. The new republican generation, now trained in Turkish schools, especially elementary ones, became really fluent in Turkish for the first time.

Nevertheless, one can speak of only a gradual integration of the community into its new "national" Turkish setting. The Jewish *millet* as an institutional structure had disappeared. But openings in society for the social integration of the Jews did not materialize. In fact, in many ways, the opposite happened. Non-Muslim bureaucrats were all dismissed from their posts in 1923–24.[53] Legal equality did not guarantee equality in the public or social spheres. The Jews remained overwhelmingly concentrated in commercial occupations in spite of the fact that the intermediary role that their elite had occupied between the world and local markets was no longer as significant in the new conditions that obtained in republican Turkey, where a national "Turkish" bourgeoisie was slowly coming into being.

On the whole, in direct continuation with Ottoman times, Jews did not participate in the political process of the country. Zionism went underground but remained significant and contributed to the mass departures to the state of Israel after 1948. Several anti-Semitic incidents in the 1930s and 1940s, together with the continued nonintegration of the Jewish masses, facilitated the receptivity to Zionism.

The recent cultural ideals oriented toward the West that the commu-

[52] Ibid.

[53] *El Tiempo*, 23 October, 7 November, 16 November 1923; *Paix et Droit* 3 (October 1923): 11.

nity had adopted in the previous fifty years also proved resistant to change. This was paradoxically strengthened by the official state policy of radical rupture with the Islamic East and realignment with the West. If the West was to be the model, then the Turkish Jewish community, now relatively more westernized than the bulk of surrounding society, could consider itself as already well advanced on the path of progress. Hence the community continued to maintain a distinct polyglot cultural profile that set it apart from the rest of Turkish society. It was still customary for the Turkish Jewish bourgeoisie to send its children to foreign schools that taught European languages after the compulsory Turkish elementary education.

In many ways, within the perspective of modern Jewish history, one would be tempted to argue that Turkish Jewry had become "normalized" under the Republic. The episode of westernization through the action of the Alliance, inextricably linked to the conditions prevailing in the Ottoman Empire, had left a decisive imprint, but had come to an end. The creation of the modern Turkish nation-state, the logical conclusion of the centralizing reforms begun in the previous century, had brought about total legal emancipation and state policies to "nationalize" the Jews, policies broadly similar to the ones adopted by many western and central European states in the age of emancipation. The Jews had ceased to be a distinct *millet* and had become a minority with a few special particularities.

Nevertheless, the survival of the Ottoman state tradition well into the republic added a few twists to this model. Ataturk's revolution was a revolution from above, with weak participation by the masses. The radical westernizing reforms of the 1920s and 1930s were all imposed from above onto an often recalcitrant population deeply attached to its old Islamic belief system. The old chasm between the ruling elite, now reduced with the elimination of the religious clergy to two constituent groups—the higher bureaucrats and the military, and the subjects—remained as wide as ever. Nationalism acted both as a factor of integration of the subjects and as a tool for radical Westernization. Nevertheless, political participation by the citizenry outside the shadow of the state did not begin to emerge until the 1950s when a "national" bourgeoisie, itself created and fostered by the state, for the first time challenged the old elites for the political leadership of the Republic.

The continuing weakness of civil society in Turkey, as well as an exclusivist nationalism adopted by the state, which, in contradiction to its professed ideals, still discriminated on the basis of religious and ethnic origin, both contributed to the weak social integration of the Jews. As in many parts of the world, the state had to fabricate the "nation" and in the process fabricated "minorities" that were excluded from the "national." More important still, the traditional allies of Jewish emancipation in the West, the bourgeoisie, had been composed in Turkey of non-Muslim groups with separatist agendas and no real commitment to the independence of the state. They were slowly replaced by a "national" bourgeoisie during the republic that, while trying to emerge from under the shadow of an all-powerful state, adopted at the same time many of its modes of action and did not create a liberal culture. The Turkish Jewish path of emancipation, state-guided and imposed, was an emancipation without liberalism, and as such left the Jewish community without its own institutions and at the same time without integration into the public and social spheres.

How can the story of the Judeo-Spanish community, indeed, of Sephardi and eastern Jewry as a whole in the nineteenth and twentieth centuries, be placed within the continuum of modern Jewish history? An understanding of how the impact of the West unfolded is crucial for this task. Here I take this process to denote the spread, either through force or emulation, of a distinct configuration of state, society, and culture—based first in the western Europe of the Enlightenment and then subsequently underpinned by the rise of triumphant industrial capitalism and imperialism—that eventually came to affect most areas of the world. The response of various populations, their engagement with the West, whether in emulation, adoption, adaptation, or rejection, provides one of the central leitmotifs of modern history.

This process came to affect all of world Jewry, though in an uneven way. One can discern three different routes undertaken by the Jews—all ideal types, of course. The first one is that of the relatively small Jewish communities of the core, of western Europe—the quintessential and archetypical "other" of western society since the Middle Ages—which were the communities affected most radically, bearing the full brunt of the modern state and the Enlightenment and post-Enlightenment demands for the transformation and the reform of all nonmetropolitan traditional societies and cultures. These communities, largely benefiting from the spread of industrial capitalism and undergoing an important process of embourgeoisement, divested most of their particularisms, integrating and acculturating into the surrounding societies and polities, though eventually constructing the vocabulary and articulation of a new modern Jewish ethnicity deeply marked by an ongoing dialectic with non-Jewish society.

The second route can be described as the eastern European/Russian one, that of an uneven westernization, with strong conflicting and ambiguous pressures from the Russian state with no liberalization, and with a weakly developed capitalism. The lack of a developed liberal bourgeoisie and a closed hostile state meant that the voice of the westernizers within the Jewish community, the *maskilim,* eventually became transmuted into more radical contestatory calls for solutions that eventually were supplied by socialism and Zionism, which became the central carriers of westernization, albeit surrounded by large numbers of rejectionist traditionalist Jews. Blocked integration fueled activist politics of exit and of radical social transformation.

The third route, closer to the Russian case than the western European one, is, of course, the Sephardi route. However, three factors marked the Sephardi Jews' engagement with the West and made it distinctive. First, weakened local state and social formations, even though embarked upon westernizing reforms, exerted an inconsequential impetus for change, either in a positive or negative way. There was neither a call for liberal assimilation nor for anti-Semitic exclusion. Second, in this context, colonialism in North Africa, or semicolonialism in the Ottoman Empire, set the contours of Sephardi Jewry's encounter with the West. Modern western economic and political imperialism confirmed and deepened the role of the Jews as intermediaries between local and international markets, between the locality and the colonial power. Third, the action of western Jews, engaged on their own *mission civilisatrice* of universalizing their own route of reform and regeneration, of making it normative and prescriptive for world Jewry, played a crucial role in the reshaping of the cultural profile of Sephardi Jewry, leading to the cultural reorientation of large sectors of the Jewish populations toward the West.

As illustrated by the Ottoman case, but also demonstrated in North Africa and elsewhere in the Middle East, these developments led to the drift of Sephardi Jewry away from its traditional moorings in Middle Eastern society, to its entry into the orbit of European interests, and to a growing perception by local non-Jews of the Jews as allies of the triumphant and triumphalist West. The Sephardi route of westernization, unlike that of the Jews of western Europe, led to the radical dissociation of the Jews from the surrounding societies. And in the local context, to use Ottoman vocabulary, even though the juridical *millet* disappeared, the Jews' *millet* identity remained intact.

NINE

RUSSIAN JEWRY, THE RUSSIAN STATE, AND THE DYNAMICS OF JEWISH EMANCIPATION

Michael Stanislawski

ANY ATTEMPT to systematize our understanding of the dynamics of Jewish emancipation must begin with an obvious, though oft-forgotten or misapprehended point: that through the course of the nineteenth century, the vast majority of world Jewry remained unemancipated. By 1871, the end of the four-year period that witnessed the most dramatic concurrence of emancipatory decrees, the Jews of western and central Europe as well as the British Isles and America were indeed emancipated—equal and free citizens of confident new states. But in that same eventful year, of the approximately seven and a half million Jews in the world, at least five million, and probably closer to six million Jews, were not emancipated, and would remain unemancipated until the twentieth century. This does not, of course, mean that the unemancipated Jewries were not affected by the process, the goals, the culture, of Jewish emancipation. But the point is worth making and reiterating: at the height of the greatest period of Jewish emancipation in the nineteenth century, emancipated Jews comprised at best one-quarter of the total Jewish population of the world.

The extent to which the other 75 percent were affected by the process of Jewish emancipation is a terribly difficult question to answer, not least of all since we do not yet have a clear enough understanding of many, if not most, aspects of Jewish life and culture in the major unemancipated communities—those in the vast Russian and Ottoman Empires. And even those questions that have been studied extensively—the political and legal history of these communities, or the extent of their modernization or westernization—desperately require careful reevaluation and systematization.

As a result, the goal of this paper cannot be to attempt an exhaustive reconsideration of the effect of the process of emancipation on Russian Jewry. That cannot be done until our collective understanding of Russian Jewish history is far more complete than at present, based in part on an examination of crucial archival materials in the former Soviet Union that have only very recently become accessible to scholars. The goal of this paper, then, is merely to point to some of the most pertinent and compelling facets of the problem, and to some of the possible building blocks of an eventual reevaluation.

The first and in some respects most formidable question to address is the external context of Jewish emancipation, the nature of the Russian political and legal system and the place of the Jews in that system. The classic historians of Russian Jewry viewed this question with clarity and unanimity: the Russian state, motivated by an unrelenting, theologically based anti-Semitism compounded by economic competition and the whims of evil rulers, consistently and continuously viewed the Jews as foreigners and subjected them to unique and unparalleled persecution. Alone among the ethnic and religious minorities of tsarist Russia, the Jews were singled out for discriminatory treatment, ghettoized in the Pale of Settlement, denied their innate individual and group rights, tortured physically and economically, and ultimately subjected to vicious pogroms and forced emigration.[1] This view has recently been challenged by a new generation of Russian-Jewish historians, influenced at once by trends in the contemporary historiography of western European Jewries and perhaps most especially by the attempt, in the last several decades, by western historians of Russia—and, most recently, historians in Russia as well—to reconstruct Russian political and legal history in the last centuries by rejecting the categories and modes of analyses that have dominated the standard accounts both in the West and in the Soviet Union.

Most relevant to our concerns here are the current debates over the extent to which the term feudalism can be used meaningfully to describe imperial Russian society; the nature and meaning of the peculiar Russian estate or corporate structure—the so-called *soslovie* system; and the nature and meaning of legality—or even of law itself—in both imperial and Soviet Russia.[2] For if Russia never experienced feudalism in the western sense; if until the last years of the nineteenth century the very idea of estates or corporate social and political entities was not developed in Russia; and if the Russian legal system—and hence, the Russian state—never adhered to the same basic premises as those that obtained in the West, then, it is obvious, the entire question of the relations between the

[1] For the classic statement on Russian-Jewish history see Simon Dubnov, *History of the Jews in Russia and Poland,* 3 vols. (Philadelphia, 1916).

[2] For a cogent statement on this problem and citation of the relevant literature see Gregory L. Freeze, "The *Soslovie* (Estate) Paradigm and Russian Social History," *American Historical Review* 91 (1986): 11–36. For a substantially different view see Richard Pipes, *Russia under the Old Regime* (New York, 1974).

Russian state and the Jews must be reconsidered from an entirely different vantage point from that of the classic histories of Russian Jewry.

While there is, to be sure, no consensus yet on these questions among Russian historians in the West or the East, the following observations and tentative conclusions can be posited. In sharp contrast to the Polish-Lithuanian Commonwealth, the Russian Empire was an autocratic monarchy that did not share in the feudal heritage of western Europe. Here, all laws issued directly from the sovereign, and more: in the eyes of the Russian rulers, their subjects enjoyed no innate or inviolable rights that did not issue from the crown. Indeed, for most of the imperial period, the Russian autocracy refused to cede its monopoly on political power to the nobility or the clergy, to say nothing of the peasantry or what passed in Russia for the urban classes. Nobles, though theoretically freed from compulsory service, continued to remain almost entirely beholden to the autocracy and its stranglehold on bureaucratic and military service. Priests could be forced to surrender to the state not only the real property of the churches and monasteries but also the secrets of the confessional booth. Merchants could be transferred from one end of the empire to the next at the whim of the emperor and had no control over their goods or trade. And the vast majority of the population was harnessed, until 1861, in a system of enserfment that was at once the most longevous in European history and the least based on what is now increasingly recognized as the defining principle of western feudalism, the recognition of reciprocal rights between lord and vassal.

At the same time, it would be equally misleading to depict the Russian state as an efficient totalitarian monolith based on a coherent ideology or even *raison d'état.* On the contrary, even under its most successful and intelligent rulers the tsarist state was enormously inefficient, unruly, and uncoordinated; oftentimes, the most critical issues facing the country were handled casually and spontaneously, with no clear forethought or direction. To impute a rational or coherent motive to every policy or act of the Russian government, state, or tsar is to risk misunderstanding and misrepresentation.

In this political universe, the Jews of Russia were but a minor and marginal constellation, and they would remain so for most of the imperial and a good part of the Soviet periods—contrary to the impression one gets from the standard accounts of Russian Jewish history. Put crudely, the tsars—and later the commissars—had far more pressing and important problems facing them than the Jews, and only rarely, if ever, did the "Jewish problem" become one of the most central concerns of the Old Regime—except insofar as it impinged on the question of the revolutionary threat to the state. In consequence, policy on the Jews—and thus the legal and political status of the Jews—was never addressed rationally or coherently by the Russian state; sporadic measures were taken to confront individual and isolated problems, with no articulation of a clear goal or end to these policies. As a result, contradictory impulses and even contradictory actions continued to define the state's actions in regard to the Jews, until the tsarist state itself collapsed under the weight of far more urgent matters.

What is clear, then, is that a legal emancipation on the order of either the French or central European examples could never have been promulgated in regard to the Russian Jews before 1905. For, as Salo Baron long ago explained, Jewish emancipation in the West was, in essence, a contract between the modern nation-state and the Jews, in which the Jews' recognized rights as one of the corporate estates of the post-feudal order were exchanged for a new type of right: that of the citizen.[3] Until 1905, neither the quid nor the quo of that contract was in effect in the Russian realm: there did not exist a citizenry into which the Jews could be merged as equals, and there was no clear and consistent recognition of the inherent rights of corporate bodies on the western model—not to speak of the Jews as one of these corporate bodies. To understand the relationship between the Jews and the Russian state one must, therefore, engage in a careful parsing of the legal and social status of the Jews from 1772 to 1905, before large-scale generalizations and comparisons can be hazarded.

Until the Polish Partitions of 1772, 1793, and 1795 there were virtually no Jews in the Russian realm, and no formal recognition of any legal Jewish presence whatsoever in the land of the tsars. As Catherine the Great herself explained, the Russian state pretended not to notice the few Jews who were indeed living and trading in Russia, given the long-standing prohibition of Jews residing on the soil of Holy Russia. With the acquisition of the Belorussian, Lithuanian, and Ukrainian lands—among the culminating acts in Russia's emergence as one of the great colonial powers in the world—the Russian state inherited approximately one million Jews, by far the largest Jewish community in the world.[4]

Faced with the task of absorbing the huge and diverse population recently conquered on fronts from the Baltic to the Black Sea and well into

[3] Salo Wittmayer Baron, "Ghetto and Emancipation," *Menorah Journal* 14, no. 6 (1928): 515–26, and idem, *Social and Religious History of the Jews*, 2d ed., vol. 1 (New York, 1952).

[4] The following discussion of Jews in Russia under Catherine II follows in its broad strokes and assumptions, if not in all details, Richard Pipes, "Catherine II and the Jews: The Origins of the Pale of Settlement," *Soviet Jewish Affairs* 5 (1975): 3–20. For a different point of view, see Shmuel Ettinger, "Ha-yesodot ve-ha-megamot be-'izuv midiniyuto shel ha-shilton ha-rusi kelapei ha-yehudim 'im halukat polin," *He-'Avar* 19 (1972): 22–29.

the Asiatic steppe, the Russian government at first did all it could simply to keep a grip on what and whom it now controlled. Its first reflex was to grant all the national, religious, and ethnic minorities under its sway the right to run their lives in accordance with the rules that had obtained before the Russian conquest. Only slowly, haphazardly, and often unselfconsciously did the authorities in St. Petersburg attempt to impose unity on the patchwork of provinces and provincials they now controlled. The result for the Jews was a slow, insistent, and largely incoherent projection of Russian governmental control over the Jews that lasted for the rest of the tsarist era, matched by an even more fitful, hesitant, and ultimately unsuccessful attempt to integrate the Jews into the social categories of the Russian Empire.

From the start and until the end, the basic question confronting and confounding these efforts was the fundamental dilemma of how to define the Jews legally both as individuals and as a collectivity. On the one hand, the Russian state recognized and insisted on the fact that the Jews were obviously a distinguishable entity in and of themselves, organized in autonomous communities run by executive agencies ratified—until 1844—by Russian law. In many official documents, therefore, the Jews were referred to and treated as a discrete estate—known in Russian as a *soslovie*. On the other hand, beginning with Catherine the Great, the Russian state attempted to reorganize the estate structure of the empire to conform with the general outline of western Europe, including the restructuring of the urban and commercial population into an entity that embraced all those who were neither nobles, peasants, nor clergy. Either the Jews were to be left entirely out of the new social and political structure of the empire, or they had to be subsumed under its new categories. This quandary presaged the essential dilemma that would arise throughout Europe in the next several decades: inclusion of Jews in the overall body politic seemed to require the elimination of the traditional autonomy the Jews had enjoyed for centuries.

The solution was a remarkable taxonomic muddle: Russian law recognized the Jews simultaneously as members of two separate social and legal groupings: the legally recognized autonomous Jewish community and the *soslovie* in which they were enrolled individually, on the basis of their residence and capital holdings. In fact, then, the Jews did not constitute a recognized corporate estate in tsarist Russia—as they had, *mutatis mutandis,* in the Polish-Lithuanian Commonwealth, not to speak of pre-Revolutionary France.

For the vast majority of the Jews in Russia this did not create an insuperable problem, for they were registered in the urban dwellers' estate (*meshchantsvo*) that was itself structured as a loose conglomeration of local urban communities. However, from the start, a significant number of Russian Jews availed themselves of the option of enrolling in the merchant or agriculturist estates, a move that resulted in the acquisition of various privileges, including exemption from the rolls of the Jewish community proper, for crucial purposes such as taxation and military service. Similarly, a smaller but still important number of Jews were granted the designation Honorary Citizen, a title that also removed its holders from enrollment in any Jewish community and vouchsafed them residence and commercial privileges. Finally, a tiny but vastly influential group of Jews were recognized as nobles by the tsarist government in the nineteenth century, even if their patents of aristocracy were not issued directly from the Romanov dynasty, but instead by one of its sister clans in the West.

Thus, even had the legal integrity of both the *soslovie* system and the autonomous Jewish community been maintained by the Russian authorities, Russian Jewry would have been plagued by a built-in centrifugal force that encouraged those at both the top and the bottom of the Jewish social fabric to divorce themselves from the community as a whole in the name of legal and social betterment. In the event, of course, the tsarist state subverted both its own estate structure and Jewish communal autonomy, with results that were unforeseen and, unfortunately, largely impervious to systematic evaluation.

Most dramatically, as is well known, in 1844 the Russian government abolished the *kahal.*[5] This act has been fundamentally misapprehended and misrepresented in the historical literature, partially as a result of a well-grounded terminological confusion: the Jews in Russia as elsewhere often used the terms *kahal* and *kehillah* interchangeably to refer to the autonomous Jewish community as a whole. However, in Russian administrative parlance a crucial distinction was drawn between the autonomous community, known in Russian as the *evreiskoe obshchestvo* and in Hebrew and Yiddish as the *kehillah,* and the executive agency of the Jewish community—the *kahal* (*kagal* in Russian). The ukase of 1844 abolished only the latter; the legal integrity and autonomy of the Jewish community itself remained unassailed in Russian law, as was its ability to adjudicate matters of "religious" concern among the Jews on the basis of Jewish law, *halakhah.* What the Russian state insisted upon was that in place of the *kahal,* a new group of communal leaders were to be elected, carrying out the same functions as their predecessors but lacking their previous legal status and subjected to closer scrutiny by the non-Jewish local and provincial authorities.

Exactly what this meant in reality we simply do not know; several historians have posited that this was just a paper reform with no practical

[5] See the discussion in my *Tsar Nicholas I and the Jews: The Transformation of Jewish Society in Russia, 1825–1855* (Philadelphia, 1983), 123–33; for a more detailed treatment, see Isaac Levitats, *The Jewish Community in Russia, 1772–1844* (New York, 1943).

consequences, and that after 1844 the Jewish communities were run in exactly the same fashion, and very often by the same people, as before 1844.[6] But the fact of the matter is that the documentation for this claim is completely compromised by a crucial aspect of Russian-Jewish life in the latter half of the nineteenth century: the putative existence of an organized Jewish communal agency resembling the *kahal* became an extremely controversial object of anti-Semitic diatribe in Russia, due in large measure to the tireless efforts of a famous Jewish convert to Russian Orthodoxy to assert that the *kahal* continued to exist after 1844 as part of a worldwide Jewish conspiracy to control all governments in the name of talmudic theocracy. As a result, for the bulk of the period from 1844 to 1917, the Jewish communities in Russia strove mightily to hide or disguise their internal organizations and deliberations, lest they be accused of perpetuating the *kahal*. Exactly how the Jewish communities in Russia were run in the half-century preceding the Revolution remains an unanswerable question, pending the discovery of pertinent archival data.

What can be asserted with certainty is that the vast majority of Jews continued to be enrolled in and recognized as members of their local Jewish communities, while a growing number formally separated themselves from their communities by means of registration in the merchant or agriculturist estates—or by taking advantage of the variety of legal escapes from the urban classes that were made available to the Jews during the reign of Alexander II, such as registration in artisan guilds or as students in institutions of higher learning. Even those Jews who were thus exempted from the laws and restrictions incumbent on the vast majority of their coreligionists were, however, still subjected to many restrictions and prohibitions on account of their Jewishness, and most, if not all, were not in the least integrated into their *soslovie* in any real terms.

Perhaps the clearest and most important illustration of the contradictory impulses and dynamics of Jewish legal classification in tsarist Russia is the question of residence rights—a matter that merits careful explication.

As noted above, by far the majority of Russian Jews were registered in the urban dwellers estate, a designation that accorded both with their actual socioeconomic status and with their desire to remain recognized as members of the autonomous Jewish community. However, there was one substantial problem associated with the Jews' enrollment in this estate: *meshchane* were not permitted to reside outside urban areas—in villages and rural settlements—where a large proportion, and sometimes the majority of Jews, happened to live.

The government first attempted to address this problem in 1782, when

[6] See Azriel Shochat, "Ha-hanhagah be-kehillot rusyah 'im bitul ha-kahal," *Zion* 44 (1979): 143–223.

orders were issued and measures taken to forbid all urban dwellers, Christian or Jewish, from living in the countryside (and, not incidentally, from engaging in the liquor trade—a mainstay of the Jewish economy in eastern Europe).[7] Tsarist administrators had to decide whether these rules applied to the Jews. Not surprisingly, the answer was positive, and substantial numbers of Jews were driven from their breweries and distilleries and from their villages into cities and towns. Though most of the Jews were not ejected from the liquor trade or from rural settlements, an important point had been made: a measure directed at the broad sweep of urban inhabitants throughout the Russian Empire could have a particularly negative effect on the Jews; being treated "equally" with other urban dwellers could have distinct, if not disastrous, disadvantages for the Jews.

The expulsion of the Jews from the countryside, however, also had disastrous consequences on the areas in which they lived—a fact recognized by many local administrators and St. Petersburg officials already in the late eighteenth century, who argued that such measures deprived the local economy of their most important commercial leaven. Therefore, a fascinating compromise was gradually worked out: although merchants and townfolk were, indeed, forbidden from living permanently outside of towns and cities, they were permitted to reside there on a temporary basis, especially if their relocation to urban centers was deemed impractical. Thus, it was decided, Jews could legally reside in the countryside, run taverns, or engage in any occupation deemed suitable by the authorities, while being registered as urban residents—ostensibly on a temporary basis, though all knew that this was, in fact, a permanent arrangement. That this decision contravened all the legal precedents as well as the regime's stated desire to develop a middle class in the cities was simply one of the more obvious expressions of the chaotic self-contradictions of Russian legislative practice. Indeed, for more than the next hundred years, the presence of Jews in villages and rural settlements and their dominance in the liquor trade—again, both privileges denied to *meshchane* as a whole but anomalously extended to the Jews—would continue to be a most controversial and thorny issue. Every few decades a new tsar would heed the advice of advisers recommending the expulsion of the Jews from the countryside, and a new series of cruel evacuations and expulsions would ensue. Soon, the impossibility of carrying out a full-scale resettlement of the Jews in cities would assert itself, as would the damage to the non-Jewish economy—and the state treasury—by the removal of the Jews from the rural areas and the liquor trade, and the expulsions would cease, awaiting the next cycle.

[7] See Dubnov, *History of the Jews,* 1:310.

Even in Catherine's time, the question of Jewish residence outside of towns and cities invariably raised the broader question of Jewish residence rights as a whole. Thus, in 1790, a group of Jewish entrepreneurs, buoyed by the legal compromise that allowed the Jews to live in areas forbidden in theory to them, applied to move to Moscow. The government denied their request, but at the same time extended the right of urban residence of the Jews beyond the former Polish terrain to the Crimean peninsula and New Russian territories—the two most recent conquests in the south, which Catherine the Great was eager to settle and develop. Many historians have viewed this law as the beginning of the Pale of Settlement. The great historian Simon Dubnov, for example, dubbed this ordinance "the first step in robbing the Jews of their freedom of movement" and the creation of the "first territorial ghetto" for the Jews of Russia.[8] This interpretation, however, hangs on the assumption that the Jews—or for that matter, any non-nobles in the Russian Empire—enjoyed "freedom of movement." That was not the point of view of the Russian authorities, who believed that rights were simply privileges handed out at the discretion of the sovereign, usually in exchange for service. What westerners would decry as limitations on residence rights—or for that matter, on economic activity, intellectual pursuits, or any other facets of life—were in the Russian legal system not the result of deliberate restriction, but rather of the lack of positive legislative permission. In this view, Catherine was not rescinding or restricting the Jews' rights of mobility, since they never enjoyed any such thing; on the contrary, she was extending their privilege of residing in Russia to new terrain.[9]

That terrain, of course, was to grow dramatically very soon thereafter, for in January 1793 Russia and Prussia once more carved up large chunks of Poland. Soon thereafter, in June 1794, the Empress extended the right of Jewish settlements to the newly annexed regions, as well as to bordering territories in the Ukraine that had not previously been open to Jewish settlement. This edict, too, has been seen as creating the Pale of Settlement—a term that did not exist at the time.[10] After the Third Partition of Poland in 1795, the remainder of Lithuania, Belorussia, and the eastern Ukraine were added to the Russian realm, and Jewish residence was permitted in these new territories.

From this date on, however, a steadily mounting number of distinctions were introduced between Jewish and non-Jewish residents of the

[8] Ibid., 316–17. For another early and influential analysis, see Iulii Gessen, *Istoriia evreiskogo naroda v Rossii* (Leningrad, 1925), 1:50.

[9] See Pipes, "Catherine II and the Jews."

[10] For the clearest exposition of the term "Pale of Settlement" and its regulations through the tsarist period, see Gr. Vol'tke, "Zhitel'stvo i peredvizhenie po russkomu zakonodatel'stvu," *Evreiskaia entsiklopediia* (hereafter *EE*) (St. Petersburg, n.d.,) 7:590–94.

cities and towns of the empire. Historians have adduced various explanations for this shift in Catherine's policy on the Jews, focusing on her shocked reaction to the French Revolution: in the wake of the excesses of regicide and terror, Catherine, like other monarchs, realized the errors of her previous ways and became far more conservative and even xenophobic. But equally plausible is a simpler explanation: Catherine's previous policy of equal treatment of Jewish and Gentile urban residents was adopted when the empire contained only the relatively modest Jewish population of Belorussia—some sixty thousand souls. Like many other states before and since, Catherine's Russia shifted its treatment of Jews when their numbers increased dramatically.

But the new, blatantly discriminatory, policy did not always work to the detriment of the Jews, as has usually been assumed. Beyond the theoretical question of the difficulty, if not the impossibility, of comparing the status of different groups in a multinational society lacking the concepts of individual liberty or corporate autonomy, the discrepancies in law were frequently not unpalatable to the Jews. Most importantly, despite continued attempts to induce or impel the Jews to move to cities, they were still permitted to live in villages—a privilege, to repeat, not extended to non-Jewish urban dwellers; while they remained subject to the courts of the estates in which they were enrolled, the *kahal* was still granted competence over all matters regulated by Jewish law. And perhaps most dramatically, a crucial differentiation between Jews and other *meshchane* was drawn in another realm of life: in September 1794, the government established a new policy on military recruitment, requiring *meshchane* and peasants to present conscripts for the armed services of the realm, while merchants would be exempted from personal service upon payment of a five hundred ruble fee. All Jews, however, regardless of estate classification, were for the purposes of recruitment regarded as merchants and permitted to pay the exemption tax rather than serve in person in the Russian army or navy. This extension of a privilege generally reserved for but a small part of the population to all Jews undoubtedly did not result from a benevolent concern for their welfare; rather the Jews were exempted from military service because the government viewed them as morally and biologically incapable of being soldiers. But once more, had a policy of equal treatment of all townfolk been enforced, the Jews would have been conscripted in 1794.

The contradictions and unintended consequences of Catherine the Great's policies in regard to the Jews persisted long after her rule, and through the reign of Nicholas I, who ruled from 1825 to 1855.[11] Under Nicholas, the Jews' legal status remained basically unchanged, though along with

[11] This discussion follows my *Tsar Nicholas I and the Jews.*

the formalization of the Russian legal system itself, the rules governing Jewish life, however capricious and contradictory, were at least codified and accessible to jurists, bureaucrats, and the Jews themselves. Most important—and contrary, once more, to oft-repeated statements in the historical literature—the Jews were formally recognized as native subjects of the Russian Empire, liable to the general laws of the state in all cases for which there was no special legislation in their regard. Throughout this period, the marginality of the Jewish question remained intact, although, in line with its policy of intruding itself more and more into the inner workings of all the groups and territories incorporated into the Russian state in the previous century, Nicholas's government did begin to pay more attention to the way in which the national, religious, and ethnic minorities governed themselves. But this attention was still fundamentally quixotic, sporadic, and based on an overarching ignorance of and lack of interest in the cultures and traditions of the subjugated groups.

The most fundamental acts in regard to the Jews in this period betrayed the uncoordinated, largely reflexive policy of the government in their regard. On the one hand, the Jews began to be conscripted into the Russian army in 1827—meaning that their previous privilege of being considered as merchants in regard to conscription, regardless of actual social class, was rescinded. But this had little, and perhaps nothing, to do with Nicholas I's specific views on the Jews. Rather, the tsar believed that the only way to solve any problem in his realm was to conscript the parties involved, be they Jews, orphans, déclassé nobles, even recalcitrant clergymen. Although, as is well known and as I have described in great detail elsewhere,[12] the conscription of the Jews under Nicholas I had a profound effect on Russian Jewry, the decision had no bearing on the Jews' essential legal status, and it did not betoken any major shift in the government's perception of them. Indeed, the essential thrust of Nicholas's Jewish policy—inasmuch as there was a coherent policy—was precisely the same as his grandmother's: to attempt to break down the traditional divides between the Jews and their non-Jewish neighbors without in the least restructuring the fundamental contours of the overall social fabric. Indeed, Nicholas's efforts in this regard were far more successful than Catherine's—a truth often obscured by the intense cruelty and horror of his actions: the conscription ordeal, for example, resulted not only in a substantial demographic disaster for the Jews, but also in an unprecedented ideational and sociological revolution in Jewish society. The perception began to grow among the broad masses of Russian Jewry that their suffering was not shared equally by all members of their community. The rich and the powerful, the learned and the well-connected

[12] Ibid.

were perceived as having saved their own sons, evading the horrors, and frequently even dissociating themselves from the community that suffered.

Although impossible to gauge with any precision, the dislocation that resulted from this perception was of crucial import. The binding strength of Jewish society in eastern Europe had always been its sense of solidarity, its essential unity—despite grievous social, economic, and sectarian divisions—in the face of adversity from without. But the antagonisms that resulted from the conscription debacle were never truly assuaged and led to the intensification of centrifugal pressures that tore at the seams of Jewish communality. Riots and attacks were launched against the *kahal* leaders and their depraved posses who had rounded up Jewish children for service in the army; cases of informing to the government incidents of malfeasance and corruption within the Jewish community increased; several groups even took the radical step of applying for legal separation from the Jewish community. These requests for juridical independence now took on increasing importance and resonance, as the Jewish communal structure was reorganized in the wake of the decree of 1844 abolishing the *kahal,* and as the already frail Jewish economy was ravaged by other governmental actions, which promoted the emergence of a Jewish upper bourgeoisie at the expense of the economic livelihood of the masses. The government claimed—and perhaps even truly intended—to rationalize the economic order of the Jews; all it accomplished was to spawn more poverty, as well as competition, among the ever-growing Jewish population.

The resultant differentiation between rich and poor only deepened the erosion of cohesiveness and solidarity that resulted from other policies of the administration. Most important—and relevant to our concerns here—was the cultural and educational policy of Nicholas's regime, its conscious and deliberate support of Jewish Enlightenment in Russia. This story is, to be sure, too long and complicated to be rehearsed here; suffice it to say that from the 1840s on, the Russian government effected an allegiance with the modernist wing of Russian Jewry—the *maskilim*—that led to strengthening the Jewish Enlightenment movement in size and prestige and ultimately, to the emergence of a self-conscious and self-confident secular intelligentsia among Russian Jews, dedicated to creating a new life and a new culture for its community.

The accession to the throne of Alexander II in 1855, though usually viewed as a revolutionary event that stood tsarist policy on the Jews on its head, actually resulted in a continuation and intensification of the processes set in motion during the reigns of Catherine II and Nicholas I. In consonance with his desire to reform Russia from above and within, the new tsar issued many decrees that mitigated the horrors of his predecessors' acts regarding the Jews—forbidding the conscription of child-recruits; allowing Jewish professionals and officially recognized students to reside outside the Pale of Settlement; and liberalizing the censorship rules. But even Alexander II, who in 1861 emancipated the serfs and three years later introduced a western-style judicial system into Russia, did not believe in the least in transforming Russia into a state based on a western notion of the rule of law, the recognition of individual rights, or the transformation of the estates into truly autonomous corporate bodies, or in fashioning legislative institutions that would even partially compromise the autocrat's monopoly on political sovereignty. As a result, although the lives of the Jews in Russia under Alexander II were far more pleasant than under his predecessors, and although many Jews believed that his ameliorative acts would eventually lead to their emancipation, such a result was inconceivable given the overall postulates and structures of his state.[13]

While Alexander II's reign did not transform the essential legal and political contours of Jewish life in Russia, his reforms did intensify and promote the related processes of Russification and embourgeoisement that had begun fitfully among Russian Jews during the previous reign. Most visibly, from the late 1850s on, Jews began flocking to the Russian-speaking state-sponsored schools established for them in the previous reign, and perhaps more importantly, to the gymnasia and universities that had not officially been closed to them under Nicholas I but were now much more attractive to them, in part due to the new possibility of gaining residence and commercial rights outside the Pale of Settlement both for study and upon graduation. While, to be sure, the number of Jews attending Russian institutions of higher learning was still a minuscule proportion of the Jewish population at large, and was by far outweighed by the number of students in traditional *hadarim* and *yeshivot,* the entry of Jews into Russian gymnasia and universities was impressive, and seemingly inexorable—and continued through the latter part of Alexander II's reign that was marked by an inchoate but nonetheless perceptible political retrenchment.[14]

By 1865, 990 Russian-Jewish students were enrolled in gymnasia—

[13] For the most recent exposition of Alexander II's policy of reform from above, see Richard Wortman, "Rule by Sentiment: Alexander II's Journeys through the Russian Empire," *American Historical Review* 95 (1990): 745–71. For a summary of Alexander's policies regarding the Jews, see my *Psalms for the Tsar: A Psalms-Society in the Russian Army, 1864–1867* (New York, 1988), 25–27.

[14] For the best survey of Jewish education under Alexander II, see Gr. Vol'tke, "Prosveshchenie," *EE,* 13:49–58. For the overall context, see Ben Eklof, *Russian Peasant Schools: Officialdom, Village Culture, and Popular Pedagogy, 1861–1914* (Berkeley, 1986).

some 3 percent of the total student body; that number grew to 2,045 in 1870 (5.6 percent of the total) and 7,004 in 1880 (12 percent). At the same time, several thousand additional students attended gymnasia for girls and Realschulen, and the number of Jewish students in non-Jewish elementary schools rose dramatically (to 15,619 in 1886). Even the number of Jewish students at Russian universities was substantial, rising from 129 in 1865 (3 percent of the total student body) to 1,856 two decades later—approximately 14.5 percent of Russian university students. (In some faculties, such as medicine and law, the proportion of Jews rose to as much as 40 percent already by the end of Alexander II's reign.) These students were, moreover, supplemented by an ever-growing number of students at government-sponsored Jewish elementary schools and by an undoubtedly even larger but undocumented number of Russian Jewish youths who studied with private tutors or on their own, in preparation for a gymnasium or university career that may or may not have materialized.

This pathbreaking entry of Jews into the Russian educational system was, of course, only a small refraction of the larger phenomenon of an ever increasing Russification among Jews. Despite the stereotypical presentation of eastern European Jewry in the nineteenth and even twentieth century as virtually an exclusively Yiddish-speaking community, the fact is that from the 1840s on, and increasingly through the remaining decades of the nineteenth century, a significant proportion of Russian Jews were learning and speaking and even thinking in Russian.[15] By the end of the century, census figures maintained that while only 3 percent of Russian Jews claimed Russian as their mother tongue, 32 percent of Russian Jewish males and 17.5 percent of Russian Jewish females could read Russian; if one subtracts from this number children under the age of ten, the figures rise to 45 percent of the males and 25 percent of the females; among urban Russian Jews the rate rises even higher—to 51 percent of the males and 31 percent of the females.

While the exactitude of these statistics and the depth of Russian knowledge they reveal can be questioned, there is no doubt that they betoken a radical shift not only in the cultural life of Russian Jewry—a subject beyond the limits of this study—but also the economic profile of that community. For the dramatic Russification of the Jews paralleled and made possible their entry into new professions and mercantile realms, themselves now open to the Jews as a result of liberal governmental policies. All this was typical, to be sure, of the process of Jewish embourgeoisement throughout Europe and the New World. Similar forces were at play not only in America, England, France, Germany, and Austro-Hungary, but in Congress Poland, Romania, and parts of the Ottoman

[15] Ia. Shabad, "Gramotnost' evreev v Rossii," *EE,* 6:756–59.

Empire. Like their middle-class counterparts elsewhere, the Jews of increasingly affluent and mobile families in Russia rushed headlong into the liberal professions and into cultural and commercial roles at which they were particularly adept. Thus, Jews in the major cities of the Russian Empire from the 1860s on became lawyers, physicians, bankers, pharmacists, engineers, international traders, journalists, and publishers in numbers far out of proportion to the size of their community. In Russia even under Alexander II, even more than in Germany, Jews could not aspire to the higher ranks of the military or civil service or the academe, and therefore the many Jews who set their sights on such positions converted to Christianity to attain them. But by far most Jews hesitated before such a step and remained in the middle rung of their professions and eschewed the lowest rungs of the military and civil service theoretically open to them.[16]

This twin process of Russification and embourgeoisement continued, as we have already seen, after Alexander II's assassination in 1881 and the assumption of power by his son, Alexander III. But in Alexander III's reign, a dramatic change did take place in regard to the legal status of the Jews, tied to and aimed at stemming the integration of Jews into Russian society, and especially the increasing access of Jews into the educational and professional upper stratum of Russian society. This largely unstudied facet of Jewish life under Alexander III was at least as crucial to the fate of Russian Jewry as the better-known eruption of acts of physical violence against Jews in the form of pogroms, the acceleration of Jewish mass migration from Russia, and the overall retrenchment of politics that led many, if not most believers in the possibility of Jewish emancipation in Russia to abandon hope in such a goal, in favor either of autoemancipation, revolution, or abandonment of Russia itself.[17]

Virtually from the start of the new reign, a fundamental transformation occurred in regard to the essential relationship between the Jews and the Russian state. The new tsar promulgated a series of decrees that betokened a structural shift in Jewish legal status beyond their toll of misery,

[16] Unfortunately, there are no reliable statistics—or even estimates—of the number of Russian Jews in the civil or military service. For the most reliable information on the rules and regulations regarding Jewish service in the Russian state service, see Gr. Vol'tke, "Sluzhba gosudarstvennaia," *EE,* 14:390–91, and idem, "Nizhnie chiny," *EE,* 11:697–701. See, too, my *Psalms for the Tsar,* for a detailed description of one group of Jews serving in the tsarist forces and general comments about the problem. On the conversion of Jews in Russia, both for reasons of professional advancement and otherwise, see my "Jewish Apostasy in Russia: A Tentative Typology," in Todd Endelman, ed., *Jewish Apostasy in the Modern World* (New York, 1987), 189–205.

[17] See Jonathan Frankel, *Prophecy and Politics: Socialism, Nationalism, and the Russian Jews* (Cambridge, 1981), and my *For Whom Do I Toil: Judah Leib Gordon and the Crisis of Russian Jewry* (New York, 1988).

suffering, and disillusionment. Before briefly examining some of these laws, however, it is important to return for a moment to the question of the uniqueness of Russian policy on the Jews over the course of the imperial period. As I have attempted to explain, until the reign of Alexander III the Jews in Russia were treated in a unique, but not anomalous fashion—anomalous, that is, vis-à-vis the overall legal and political system of the empire and the rules governing the other minorities. There is no question that in eighteenth- and nineteenth-century Russia, the life and fate of the Jews was conditioned inexorably by anti-Jewish prejudices that infected virtually all strata of non-Jewish society, if at times unself-consciously. But the assumption that this theologically motivated bias translated neatly and universally into anomalous treatment cannot be accepted with any degree of confidence. For in a state such as imperial Russia in which no innate individual rights were recognized; where even the rights of the nobility and clergy were highly restricted; and where a substantial and growing number of nationalities and religious minorities held separate and unique sets of privileges and duties, it is virtually impossible to posit an objective evaluation of comparative status that is not based on ethnocentric special pleading. In other words, an assessment of Jewish legal status in tsarist Russia must proceed from a suspension of the axiomatic notions of Jewish anomalousness that have informed scholarship until recently.

After 1881 and continuing to the end of the tsarist rule, however, the Jews of Russia were indeed subjected to a series of laws, ordinances, and administrative practices that both departed significantly from the overall contours of governmental policy and were aimed quite self-consciously at the Jews. This shift was but part and parcel of an overarching transformation of Russian governance that has led several influential Russian historians to claim that from 1881 Russia ceased to be an autocratic monarchy in any but the formal sense, becoming a proto–police state.[18] Be that as it may, it is clear that Alexander III's Counter Reforms included a number of measures aimed specifically at reversing the integration of Jews into Russian society.

This policy was most overt and effective in regard to the educational and professional advance of the Jews. In 1882, the first Jewish quota was introduced in a Russian educational institution: 5 percent of the students in the Military Medical Academy.[19] In the following year, Jews were limited to the same proportion in the College of Mines; in 1885, a 10 percent quota was set for Jews in the newly established Kharkov Technological Institute; and in 1886 the Kharkov Veterinary Institute was closed com-

[18] See Pipes, *Russia under the Old Regime*, 297–318.

[19] Vol'tke, "Prosveshchenie," 51–52.

pletely to further Jewish admissions. Finally, in 1887 the Russian Ministry of Education established a formal *numerus clausus* for Jews at all educational establishments under its control: 10 percent within the Pale of Settlement, 5 percent outside the Pale, and 3 percent in Moscow and St. Petersburg.[20] Although these norms were not, in fact, instituted uniformly and efficiently across the board and across the Empire, they did result in a substantial diminution of Jewish attendance at gymnasia and institutions of higher learning and heralded the introduction of other limits on Jewish professional advance. Thus, in 1889 the Ministry of Justice issued an order stipulating that henceforth all "non-Christians" would be admitted to the bar only upon special permission of the minister of justice himself; the term "non-Christians" was then defined to pertain only to Jews. For the next fifteen years, no Jews were recognized as barristers in Russian courts, and the small number of Jewish graduates of Russian legal faculties were permitted to function only as assistant attorneys.[21] This clearly anomalous practice had deeply symbolic resonances, beyond the actual harm inflicted on a sizeable portion of Russian-Jewish intellectuals: for the judicial reform introduced by Alexander II in 1864 was the most effective embodiment of western norms in the tsarist government, by common consent the most successful of the Great Reforms and the only one, in fact, to survive to the end of the Old Regime. The introduction of a court system and a bar modeled on the Anglo-Saxon experience gave great hope to those who struggled to transform Russia into a *Rechtsstaat*. There could be no clearer indication of the place of the Jews in the state that actually ensued than the closing of the bar to Jews.

Similarly, the one area of Russian governmental service that had been truly open to Jews, the medical corps, was gradually subjected to quotas and norms that restricted the number of Jews serving as "city-physicians," as physicians in state hospitals, and as army doctors. Although the stated quota of 5 percent was never fully implemented, the access of Jews to the medical profession was severely limited.[22]

Alexander III's Counter Reforms dramatically affected the Russian Jews at the other end of the economic spectrum—the vast majority of the community who earned their keep through crafts, petty trade, and local commerce. One of the most striking lacunae in our knowledge of this period is the precise effect of the so-called May Laws of 1882 on the Jews, which did not, as is often claimed, forbid all Jewish settlement in villages and rural settlements, but only all new Jewish settlement outside

[20] Ibid.

[21] M. Krol', "Advokatura v Rossii," *EE*, 1:469–72.

[22] Gr. Vol'tke, "Meditsinskiia professii po deistvuiushchemu russkomu zakonodatel'stvu," *EE*, 10:780–82.

of cities and towns. Nevertheless, whatever future research will demonstrate about the number and nature of forced Jewish expulsion from rural habitations in the last decades of tsardom, it is certain that the pace of Jewish urbanization in the Russian empire—already noticeable and important from the 1820s—was inexorably quickened and accelerated from the 1880s until the First World War, at the same time as several million Russian Jews took to the seas as emigrants—a move not discouraged by the Russian authorities, despite the fact that emigration was formally illegal in Russia.[23] As the most recent work on internal migration within Russian Jewry has established, the number of Jews migrating from one place to another within the Russian Empire between 1881 and 1914 was well beyond what had previously been imagined, and probably as high as 1.2 million. This internal migration was virtually entirely synonymous with an ever-increasing urbanization of Russian Jews—another demographic phenomenon at play in Russian Jewry (as in every other modern Jewish community) since the beginning of the nineteenth century, but intensified in the last decades of tsarist rule.

Clearly, the remarkable flight to the cities on the part of Russian Jews was the result not only, or even especially, of their legal and political decline, but was a largely unconscious response on the part of masses of Jews to the overarching economic transformation of the Russian empire as a whole, especially the government-inspired and -directed industrialization program. Though we are very far from having as yet a full picture of the impact of industrialization on the Jews of Russia, the work of the late economic historian Arcadius Kahan has called into question the hitherto accepted notions that the Russian government's economic and industrial policies, coupled with the move of newly emancipated peasants into the cities and into areas of economic competition with the Jews, narrowed the opportunities of Jewish entrepreneurs, on the one hand, and resulted in a drastic diminution of the number of Jewish artisans and craftsmen, on the other, leading invariably to the growth and radicalization of the Jewish proletariat. Rather, Kahan asserted, the available evidence indicates that the industrialization process in Russia actually widened the area of choice for Jewish entrepreneurs, and resulted in a steady rise in the number of Jews working as craftsmen and artisans, both employers and employees, in the late tsarist years. Indeed this growth of the Jewish artisanate was linked to the processes of internal migration and urbanization, in that the move to larger and larger urban settlements made possible the acquisition of new skills and the development of

[23] For the best survey of this problem, see Hans Rogger, "Government Policy on Jewish Emigration," in Rogger, *Jewish Policies and Right-Wing Politics in Imperial Russia* (Berkeley, 1986), 176–87.

new forms of employment on the part of a large segment of Russian Jews.[24]

These conclusions do not, of course, deny the problem of increasing pauperization and proletarianization of Russian Jews in the last decades of the Old Regime. But they do demonstrate the need for far more careful and objective research on the economic and social history of the Jews of Russia under Alexander III and Nicholas II before large-scale generalizations can be made.

With the enactment of a quasi-constitutional monarchy in 1905, the Jews in the Russian Empire entered into an entirely new legal and political universe—and one that has also not yet been subjected to independent and thorough research. As a result, only the broadest outlines of the new juridical and political context can be sketched here: in the last twelve years of tsarism the Jews were indeed what many had claimed they were earlier—formally second-class citizens of the Russian state, permitted to exercise the electoral franchise and to organize political parties in line with the general rules, but restricted in law and in fact—as were, not incidentally, other minorities—from enjoying many of the rights and freedoms vouchsafed to the majority of the population. It is in this period that a struggle for legal emancipation could and did proceed on a front analogous to that which obtained in western European lands—a struggle for public opinion, a heated discussion in the press, parliamentary debates. The rather peculiar feature of the Russian debate over Jewish emancipation was the fact not only that Jews were elected to the parliament deliberating over this issue—that is, that Jews were granted political rights in many ways before they attained civil rights (the reverse of the western norm), and thus Jewish members of parliament joined non-Jewish representatives in the Duma to demand Jewish equality. Perhaps even more anomalous was the participation in this debate of legally recognized and fully organized Jewish political parties—liberal, Zionist, socialist. (The dramatic decision of the Russian Zionist Organization in 1906 to recognize the legitimacy of *Gegenwartsarbeit*—to fight for Jewish emancipation in Russia while maintaining in theory a rejection of the efficacy of emancipation as a solution to the plight of the Jews—is but the most famous manifestation of the multiple new dilemmas and opportunities afforded by this remarkable situation.)

In the end, of course, the tepid constitutionalism engendered by the 1905 Revolution was subverted by both the monarchy and its allies and

[24] Arcadius Kahan, *Essays in Jewish Social and Economic History* (Chicago, 1986), 1–100.

by those on the Left who rejected the very idea of constitutional compromise. Hence the Duma as a whole—not to speak of the emperor himself—never accepted the goal of Jewish emancipation.

That emancipation would come only after the dissolution of the tsarist state itself. One of the first acts of the Provisional Government was the promulgation, on 2 April 1917, of the "Decree Abolishing Religious and National Restrictions," which began with the following words:

> Whereas it is our unshakable conviction that in a free country all citizens should be equal before the law, and that the conscience of the people cannot acquiesce in legal restrictions against particular citizens on account of their religion and race:
>
> The Provisional Government has decreed: All restrictions on the rights of Russian citizens which had been enacted by existing laws on account of their belonging to any creed, confession, or nationality, shall be abolished.[25]

Thus, in a process reminiscent of the drama that took place in Paris 128 years earlier, the creation of a new Russian state, a democratic republic founded on the notion of citizens free and equal before the law, necessitated and resulted in the emancipation of the Jews.

The fate of Jewish emancipation after the Bolshevik Revolution is, of course, another equally complicated and compelling story.[26] Here we can only provide a short summary of that history, in the form of an intriguing epilogue to the dynamics of Jewish emancipation in tsarist Russia.

After the collapse of the Provisional Government and the seizure of power by the Bolsheviks, Jewish emancipation was not only maintained in law, but was reinforced by Lenin's decision to traduce his own ideology and recognize the Jews as a nationality—a national entity with distinct cultural and political rights. This recognition was manifested, for example, in an act that later became symbolic of anti-Jewish animus in the Soviet Union, but was originally precisely the opposite: the inclusion of Jewishness as a recognized nationality in Soviet law and hence in the Soviet passport. Based on this recognition of the nationality of the Jews, the regime sponsored the creation of a so-called proletarian Jewish culture in the Yiddish language. And perhaps most glaringly indicative of the recognition of Jewish national rights, the Soviet government in the 1920s and 1930s even designated part of its far eastern territory, the

[25] See the translation of this decree in Paul Mendes-Flohr and Jehuda Reinharz, eds., *The Jew in the Modern World* (New York, 1980), 349.

[26] For the best summaries of Soviet-Jewish history, see Lionel Kochan, ed., *The Jews in Soviet Russia since 1917* (Oxford, 1978), and more recently, Benjamin Pinkus, *The Jews of the Soviet Union: The History of a National Minority* (Cambridge, 1988).

regime known as Birobidzhan, as the Jewish Autonomous Region of the Soviet Union: a mini-Jewish state within the fabric of Soviet socialism.

At the same time, and perhaps most significantly, the revolutionary recasting of Soviet society that accompanied the brutal collectivization of agriculture and the massive industrialization of the economy, opened up countless opportunities for Jews to be employed in new white-collar, managerial, and bureaucratic positions. Through the devastating years of the 1930s, Jewish scientists, economists, writers, musicians, party functionaries, soldiers, and laborers played a fundamental role in the construction of the new Soviet society, and rose to unprecedented and unparalleled positions of eminence, fame, and even power. The most reliable estimates hold that Jews constituted some 6 percent of the Soviet ruling elite in the 1920s and 10 percent of its economic elite.[27] Indeed, at the same time as millions of peasants starved to death, the social and economic status of the Jews continued to climb, establishing them as perhaps the most educated, the most professionally successful, the most economically secure minority in the country.

In sharp contrast to this social advance, however, there was now increasing cultural devastation: the original contradictions in the Leninist-Stalinist nationality policy came to the fore. All attempts at creating a Soviet Yiddish culture worthy of the name, a Jewish Autonomous Region, or a Leninist Jewish scholarship succumbed to the overall obliteration of artistic and intellectual creativity and autonomy. This was not the result, it must be stressed, of anti-Semitism, but of the overall dynamics of Stalinism—and post-Stalinism. The vast majority of the Jews, however, still remained well-integrated and successful members of Soviet society.

Viewed through the lenses of comparative Jewish history, we see in this idiosyncratic case a paradox at work that recalls in a strange and entirely unpredicted way the famous summation of the contract of Jewish emancipation enunciated by one of the chief proponents of Jewish emancipation in the French National Assembly in 1789–91, Count Clermont-Tonnerre: "To the Jews as individuals, everything; to the Jews as a nation, nothing." For Jews as individuals, Soviet society provided unparalleled opportunities for social, economic, and even political integration; for the Jews as a collective national, religious, and cultural entity, however, the policies and practices of the Soviet Union were disastrous.

In time, moreover, the devastations of the public realm were transferred to the private realm: the integration of Jews as individuals was reversed, they were excluded more and more from positions of power, influence, and prestige, and ultimately from any possibility even of social

[27] Pinkus, *Jews of the Soviet Union,* 83.

and economic success as well. And at the same time they were unable to escape their collective fate by simply disappearing, melting into the Soviet citizenry or other nationalities, obliterating their formal identity as Jews.

To the Jewish historian, the ironies abound even further: in the course of the great debate over Jewish emancipation in the nineteenth century, one of the principle strategic debates among Jewish proponents of emancipation was whether to pursue what became known in Germany as *privatbürgliche Gleichberechtigung*—equality in economic and civic rights or *Bürgliche Gleichberechtigung,* which included and insisted upon full equality in political rights. This divide was primarily between German Jews of different political, and perhaps religious, orientations, for the more traditional Jews cared little for political franchise and public office, as opposed to increased economic and residential rights. What the Soviet case provided was, however ironically, the most extensive example of *privatbürgliche Gleichberechtigung,* and more: The Soviet case demonstrated, in the long-run, the tragic impossibility and self-destructiveness of such an economic and social, as opposed to political, emancipation of the Jews. One need not succumb either to a lachrymose or to a determinist view of history to see that this could not but happen, for the Soviet emancipation of the Jews was not in fact premised on a true recognition of the Enlightenment's first principle, the inviolable integrity of the individual, just as the Soviet recognition of Jewish nationality was not based on an honest appraisal and recognition of Jewish group rights.

In the end, the dismal story of the fate of Jewish emancipation in tsarist Russia and the Soviet Union can yield a crucial lesson about the possibilities for Jewish emancipation in any society. What Clermont-Tonnerre or the other drafters of the contract of Jewish emancipation could not foretell, and what we are now able to see only with the enormous luxury of hindsight, is that legal guarantees of the equality of individual Jews, or even commitments to Jewish group rights, were insufficient to ensure a successful emancipation of the Jews. Equally insufficient, it turned out, was a social integration in which their right to choose how to define themselves, how to live their lives as Jews, was effaced. Emancipation could only succeed in societies based not only on a firm commitment to the inviolable integrity of the individual but, equally important, to its corollary as well: the right of individuals to exercise whatever group ties, loyalties, and characteristics they choose.

In short, only in the presence of both democracy and pluralism would Jews experience the full fruits of emancipation—a fate not yet granted to the Jews of Russia.

CONTRIBUTORS

Geoffrey Alderman, formerly Professor of Politics and Contemporary History at Royal Holloway College, University of London, is Head of the Academic Development and Quality Assurance Unit at Middlesex University. He has researched and written extensively on the history of Anglo-Jewry. His many publications in this field include *The Jewish Community in British Politics* (1983) and *Modern British Jewry* (1992).

Pierre Birnbaum is Professor at the University of Paris I and presently a member of the Institut Universitaire de France. His publications include *The Heights of Power* (with Bertrand Badie, 1982); *Sociology of the State* (1983); *States and Collective Action: The European Experience* (1988); and *Individualism* (edited with Jean Leca, 1992). He has written extensively on Jewish themes, including *Anti-Semitism in France: A Political History from Léon Blum to the Present* (1992); *Les Fous de la République: Histoire des Juifs d'Etat de Gambetta à Vichy* (1992); and *"La France aux Français": Histoire des haines nationalistes* (1993). He has also edited *La France de l'Affaire Dreyfus* (1994).

Hans Daalder was Professor of Political Science at Leiden University from 1963 to 1993. One of the founders of the European Consortium for Political Research, he was the first Head of the Department of Political and Social Sciences at the European University Institute in Florence, from 1976 to 1979. He has published widely on Dutch and European comparative politics, on university governance, and on Marxism and nationality. A selection of his major Dutch and English essays and a complete bibliography were published as *Politiek en Historie: Opstellen over Nederlandse politiek en vergelijkende politieke westenchap* (1990).

Ira Katznelson, who has taught at the University of Chicago and the New School for Social Research, is Ruggles Professor of Political Science and History at Columbia University. His books on American political development, cities, and the comparative analysis of race, class, and ethnicity include *City Trenches: Urban Politics and the Patterning of Class in the United States* (1981); *Schooling for All: Class, Race, and the Decline of the Democratic Ideal* (with Margaret Weir; 1985); *Working Class Formation: Nineteenth Century Patterns in Western Europe and the United States* (edited with Aristide Zolberg; 1986); and *Marxism and the City* (1992).

Werner E. Mosse was Professor of History at the University of East Anglia from 1964–1983, and is Chairman of London's Leo Baeck Institute.

He has also been a Fellow of Corpus Christi College, Oxford, and a member of the teaching staff at the Universities of London and Glasgow. His vast stock of publications in German and English include *Deutsches Judentum in Krieg und Revolution* (1971); *Juden im Wilherlminischen Deutschland, 1890–1914* (1976); *Jews in the German Economy: The German-Jewish Economic Elite, 1820–1935* (1987); *The German-Jewish Economic Elite, 1820–1935: A Socio-Cultural Profile* (1989); and *Second Chance: Two Centuries of German-Speaking Jews in the United Kingdom* (co-ordinating editor, 1991).

Aron Rodrigue is Associate Professor of Jewish History at Stanford University. Some of his recent publications are *French Jews, Turkish Jews: The Alliance Israelite Universelle and the Politics of Jewish Schooling in Turkey, 1860–1925* (1990); *Images of Sepharadi and Eastern Jewries in Transition, 1860–1939* (with Esther Benbassa, 1993); and *The Sepharadi Jews of the Balkans: The Judeo-Spanish Community, 15th to the 20th Centuries* (1995).

Dan V. Segre is Professor Emeritus of Political Science at the University of Haifa, where he held the Ruben Hecht Chair of Zionism. He also has been Senior Research Fellow at St. Antony's College, Oxford, and Visiting Professor at Stanford University. His publications include *Memoirs of a Fortunate Jew* (1984); *The Private War of Lt. Guillet: A History of Italian Resistance in Ethiopia, 1941–1942* (1991); and *End of the Israeli-Arab Conflict?* (1994).

Michael Stanislawski is Nathan J. Miller Professor of Jewish History and Associate Chair of the Department of History at Columbia University. He is the author of *Tsar Nicholas I and the Jews: The Transformation of Jewish Society in Russia, 1825–1855* (1983); *For Whom Do I Toil? Judah Leib Gordon and the Crisis of Russian Jewry* (1988); and *Psalms for the Tsar* (1988), as well as numerous articles on the culture and intellectual history of Russian Jewry.

INDEX